INTELLIGENCE WORK

Film and Culture

The Land (Robert Flaherty, 1941). Production still. Courtesy of The Robert and Frances Flaherty Study Center, Claremont School of Theology.

Intelligence Work

The Politics of American Documentary

JONATHAN KAHANA

Columbia University Press   *New York*

Columbia University Press
Publishers Since 1893
New York   Chichester, West Sussex
Copyright © 2008 Columbia University Press
All rights reserved

Library of Congress Cataloging-in-Publication Data
Kahana, Jonathan, 1966–
The Politics of American documentary / Jonathan Kahana.
p. cm. — (Film and culture)
Includes bibliographical references and index.
ISBN 978-0-231-14206-9 (cloth : alk. paper)—ISBN 978-0-231-14207-6
(pbk. : alk. paper) — ISBN 978-0-231-51212-1 (e-book)
1. Documentary films—United States—History and criticism. 2. Documentary
films–Social aspects—United States. I. Title. II. Series.

PN1995.9.D6K25 2008
070.1'8—dc22
2007050034

⊗

References to Internet Web sites (URLs) were accurate at the time of writing.
Neither the author nor Columbia University Press is responsible for URLs that may
have expired or changed since the manuscript was prepared.

For J.H.

CONTENTS

ILLUSTRATIONS

ACKNOWLEDGMENTS

Material support for different stages of the work that went into this book came from a variety of sources. The Social Sciences and Humanities Research Council of Canada and the Woodrow Wilson National Fellowship Foundation made possible preliminary research and writing. A Junior Faculty Research Leave from Bryn Mawr College and a Goddard Junior Faculty Fellowship from New York University gave me time away from teaching to substantially complete the manuscript in its current form. Grants from the University Research Challenge Fund at NYU and the Dean's Discretionary Fund at Tisch School of the Arts helped me produce the illustrations.

At Columbia University Press, I benefited from Juree Sondker's firm and encouraging conviction that this would make a good publication. Juree and other editors arranged for the manuscript to be evaluated by anonymous readers whose suggestions both focused and broadened the writing in important ways; I thank those readers for their criticism, care, and time. Jennifer Crewe, Michael Haskell, and Milenda Lee were a pleasure to work with and helped smooth the transition to print. Any errors that survived the expert proofreading of Paul Fileri and Al Horne were just meant to be there.

In early stages of this project, John Mowitt, Bruce Robbins, Joan Scott, and Michael Warner shaped it by their generous engagement with my ideas and prose and by the model of their own work, which continues to challenge me. Paula Rabinowitz has encountered the project in its earliest and latest forms; her astute assessments of its problems and its value have been a consistent source of inspiration, as has her own writing on documentary. That John Belton chose to work with me on various incarnations of this book is a great honor. His tireless scrutiny of my writing and my thinking made it a better book than it would otherwise have been, but that it is a book at all is due in no small part to his support for it at every turn. Roger Hallas, Michelle Lekas, Bethany Schneider, Gus Stadler, Tess Takahashi, Michael Tratner, and Jennifer Zwarich each read individual chapters, which improved with their incisive criticism. Dana Polan very kindly offered to read the entire manuscript when he had deadlines of his own. On more than one occasion, Tim Corrigan read the whole thing; I cannot thank him enough. Joseph Chaves has long been my ideal of a reader, a role I asked him to perform a number of times with this book.

In other ways, Bryn Mawr and NYU have provided important audiences for parts of this work. My sense of how to frame its arguments and examples pedagogically has been shaped by the classes on documentary that I have had the good fortune to teach at both schools. I was assisted with research by students from both, including Nora Gully, Jihoon Felix Kim, and Sangjoon Lee; I am especially grateful to Molly Finnegan and Cynthia Lugo, whose own engagement with questions of documentary, combined with their hard work and skill as researchers, made them valuable interlocutors.

Many people helped me locate and gain access to materials and films that would otherwise have remained obscure. Arleen Zimmerle, media librarian extraordinaire at Bryn Mawr, divined many sources of print and video for me. Dan Streible connected me with people and materials that changed my understanding of documentary history in crucial ways. Debra Zimmerman unearthed historical resources from the Woman Make Movies archives, as did Susan Williams at the Highlander Research and Education Center, Greg Yates and Carol Roberts of the Tennessee State Library and Archives, Maxine Fleckner Ducey at the Wisconsin Center for Film and Theatre Research, and Jack Coogan and his staff at the Robert and Frances Flaherty Study Center. I thank Margarita De la Vega-Hurtado and Mary Kerr, Executive Directors of the Robert Flaherty Film Seminar, for connecting me to Jack, and for letting me listen to archival recordings of the seminar. At Anthology Film Archives, Andrew Lampert gave up an afternoon to help me reproduce frames from Emile de Antonio's personal print of *Underground*; Bill Brand did the same on a later occasion. I am grateful also to Alfred

Leslie and Nancy de Antonio for arranging my access to this print. At Colorlab Corp., Thomas Aschenbach and the legendary Russ Suniewick gave me a priceless education in film preservation and reproduction techniques while creating most of the images from *Attica* that appear in this book. The staff of the Digital Studio at NYU, including Richard Malenitza, Jennifer Vinopal, and Marcos Sanchez, came up with ingenious solutions to the problem of moving images from one medium to another. Chris Pavsek pretended to begrudge me help with my endless technical questions, but nonetheless patiently explained the intricacies of digital imaging.

Many filmmakers, including Jon Alpert, Paul Chan, Mike Gray, Liza Johnson, Julia Meltzer, Robb Moss, Brian Springer, David Thorne and Travis Wilkerson, have been kind enough to provide me with copies of their work, answers to my inquiries, or both. Jill Godmilow has done so many times over the course of several years. Cinda Firestone Fox granted me a long interview during a visit to New York City; she and her husband, Manny Fox, went out of their way to help me gain access to a new print of *Attica*, as did Terry Lawler of New York Women in Film and Television and Anne Hofmann and Elizabeth MacMahon at the Donnell Media Center of the New York Public Library.

"Without my mother's encouragement, I would never have been able to write this book." This is what my mother, Jackie Kahana, told me to write here. Because it is true, I have done so. The same goes for my father, Leo Kahana, who would never have let me forget his contribution, as if I had a choice. I wish that he had lived to see this in print.

"All of the above" doesn't begin to capture the role that Jennifer Horne has played in this work. Her good sense and critical acumen have sharpened nearly every thought and page. Any idea worth sharing with others was usually tested on and refined by her first. And she has supported this book in countless other ways, invisible to the reader but invaluable to its conception and completion. It is dedicated to her, with love.

INTELLIGENCE WORK

INTRODUCTION
THE INTELLIGENCE WORK OF DOCUMENTARY
Publics, Politics, Intellectuals

Since the late 1920s and early 1930s, when filmmakers and critics in the United States, England, and other Western industrial nations began regularly to use the term "documentary" to refer to a discrete practice of filmmaking, it has been understood as a form of democratic and social pedagogy. Retooling producer and critic John Grierson's 1929 definition of documentary as the "creative treatment of actuality," Paul Rotha insists that the essence of the documentary method is its "intellectual ability" to draw out the "meaning *behind* the thing and the significance *underlying* the person." Indeed, Rotha writes in 1935, because social contradiction and the technical means of cinema conspire to obscure the truth, documentary is used to "express a meaning within a meaning."[1] It is impossible even now to separate the critical potential of documentary from this analytical function. The flexibility and endurance of the documentary apparatus, its simultaneous appeal to both state and capitalist institutions *and* their critics, owes much to this capacity for intellection and its varieties: ideology, theory, imagination, and belief.

Documentary has always leveled distinctions, challenging traditional oppositions between official and vernacular speech, between high art and mass culture, and between academic knowledge, folk traditions, and popular belief. It is one articulation of what the philosopher Charles Taylor calls a "social imaginary." It makes the lofty principles and institutions of the public and political domains seem real, and it helps us envision the collective consequences of our thoughts and actions, no matter how ordinary or idiosyncratic. Suspended between the remote domain of theory and the collective realm of experience, the social imaginary can be a "common understanding that makes possible common practices and a widely shared sense of legitimacy." And as Taylor points out, the function of a social imaginary is not limited to the creation of consensus but may also animate criticism and change. At the same time that it can provide people with a vision of the "normative notions and images" that underlie daily life, a social imaginary can express the unmet expectations we hold and our ideas for bridging those gaps.[2] Thought of along these lines, documentary—or, more precisely, social documentary, the variant that is the focus of this book, although I often use the broader term for the sake of brevity—is not merely an instrument of common sense. If social documentary is a way of grappling with the systems of knowledge, production, and power that alienate modern individuals, it is a form of abstraction in its own right, one that does its cultural and political work with metaphor, analogy, allegory, and generalization.

It may seem counterintuitive to describe documentary as an abstract form, since, among all genres of film and culture, documentary is the one we associate with the local, the particular, and experience. But the political force of documentary, whether in the service of reform, repression, or revolution, depends upon its ability to make an experience available for interpretation by an array of institutions and organizations, from government agencies and corporations to political movements and community groups. To put this another way, documentary is an essentially transitional medium: it carries fragments of social reality from one place or one group or one time to another, and in transporting them, translates them from a local dialect to a lingua franca. It collects the evidence of experience in the most far-flung precincts, in coal mines, cornfields, cell blocks, convention halls, corporate boardrooms, and city slums. Then it delivers these social facts to a broader public, where they can be used for a variety of ideological ends.

All forms of cinema, including the various modalities of the electronic moving image that now supplement the public projection of film, can be described as public by virtue of their capacity for dissemination and collective reception, which extends to the discourse communities of criticism and fandom they generate. Audio-visual forms may also be perceived as serving the public interest by providing an account or record of collective experience when they incorporate and represent the social world, which they do almost reflexively, an effect of the indexical relationship of photography, film, and video- and audio-recording media to their physical environment. And to the extent that they depend on governmental or noncommercial sources of funding and support, they may be public in another way, the products of a people's shared investment in its culture. But none engages the concept of publicness on all levels—conditions of production, textual structures, spaces and practices of circulation, contexts of reception—so thoroughly, or in such fraught and complex ways, as the documentary.

In the simplest sense, documentaries are public by virtue of the collective effort that goes into their making and their use. Although documentary production and exhibition are by no means exclusively noncommercial enterprises, the history of social documentary is impossible to imagine without the financial support of state, civic, and nonprofit agencies, foundations, and societies, including unions, civil rights organizations, religious groups, political action committees, clubs, and so on. Such entities usually expect to generate cultural, political, or ideological, rather than financial, returns on their investment. Likewise, the circuits and venues of documentary exhibition, while often (and increasingly) sharing the marketplaces of commercial entertainment, have as often opted or been forced to bypass these venues for irregular itineraries and audiences outside of the commercial mainstream: the newsreel and specialty theaters of documentary's theatrical heyday, the proverbial church basements, union halls, classrooms, student unions, co-ops, pubs, barracks, and living rooms of nontheatrical film and video distribution, as well as the off-prime hours of broadcast schedules and the news, history, arts, and public-access channels of cable television. Cutting across this economic and social definition of documentary's public character is the question of how this publicness is borne out in its discourse. How do documentary works address their audiences? How does this address anticipate a response and, in doing so, make possible the articulation of social and political desire in forms of collective identification and association?

Producers and critics of documentary have made the case for documentary as a public form since the earliest years of its consolidation as a mode of cinema. Introducing Paul Rotha's *Documentary Film* (1936), one of the first book-length English-language studies of documentary,

John Grierson writes that "documentary has a public importance beyond itself," an idea that is echoed in Rotha's definition of documentary as a message destined for "a community. Its purpose is not only
to persuade and interest imaginations to-day"—as does any evening's
entertainment—"but several years hence." [3] This obligation to the life
of a community beyond its present form makes it clear that Rotha is
thinking of documentary as something more than a kind of filmmaking
and more than the experience of watching particular films, something
closer to an idea, a form of social intellection.[4] Rotha begins a section
of *Documentary Film* on the making of documentaries by demurring
that the form is "so closely related to current thought and activities"
that it requires a "frequent re-orientation of theory." Something happens to people in their engagement with the film. Organized into one
kind of social group—an audience—they can be made to strengthen or
loosen their identification with another sort of group: a nation, a class,
an ethnicity, a religion, and so on. Rotha calls this process a "disturbing" one for filmmakers, but it is no less disturbing for the audience.
Because "impartial discussion of the economic, political, and social
systems which control our citizenship" is not easy to hear, "anyone
who throws doubt on respected beliefs is subject to attack." [5] Creating
such disturbances is the vocation of the social documentarist. "Public
discourse circulates," observes Michael Warner, "but it does so in struggle with its own conditions." [6] That struggle—its place in documentary,
and the place of documentary within it, under the particular conditions of the rise and decline of the welfare state in the United States—is
the subject of this book.

DOCUMENTARY AND ALLEGORY

In an oft-cited 1926 review of Robert Flaherty's Polynesian film *Moana:
A Romance of the Golden Age* that he wrote for the *New York Sun,* John
Grierson established "documentary" as a term to be applied to a category
of cinema, adapting the French term *"documentaire"* to account for certain reality effects, similar to those of the well-established genre of the
travelogue, in Flaherty's film. That Grierson did not mean to institute
the category at the time is evident from the offhand and dismissive

tone that attends the appearance of the term: "Of course *Moana,* being a visual account of events in the daily life of a Polynesian youth and his family, has documentary value."[7] What Grierson calls the *documentary* in *Moana,* its quotidian rhetoric, is less a property of Flaherty's film than an effect of the uses to which it, or some of its images, might be put, a "value" that might accrue to it by its insertion in some future act of analysis or study. In fact, Grierson emphasizes that the instrumental elements of Flaherty's film do not inhibit what is truly admirable about the film: its capacity to link us to the timeless values of nature, human and otherwise. Just as Moana, the young hero of the film, transcends the physical suffering he undergoes during a painful tattooing ritual in order to develop "a bravery that is healthful for the race," Flaherty converts the particular, documentary character of the film to the universal values of the beautiful and the true: "time and again," Grierson writes, *Moana* "induces a philosophic attitude on the part of the spectator. It is real, that is why."[8] In other words, what is significant about the world depicted or imagined by the film and its audiences lies beyond its merely evidentiary function, some inducement to a dream of times and places far removed from the "grime of modern civilization."[9] This supplementary relationship between what Grierson calls the "documentary" and what he refers to as the "real" is what gives the documentary mode in film and literature after Flaherty its ideological force. The process of documentary representation must maintain a tension between the particular and the general. The appearance (or irruption) of moments of authenticity, reality, and truth in this process is the guarantee that the film operates on democratic lines, responsible at once to the individual instance and the totality.

But what "real" turns out to mean, in this context, is that the film creates the dynamic that the sociologist Luc Boltanski calls "distant suffering": it induces emotional effects in its viewers—sadness, pain— that correspond to the physical pain depicted in (and, in this case, partially caused by) the film.[10] "Moana, whom we begin to like during the first reel," observes Grierson, "is really tortured and it affects us as no acting could"[11] (see figure i). Grierson's attention to the situation of the spectator recalls an older mode of nonfiction film that Tom Gunning has called "views," a category that describes films in which the emphasis is at once on the object or scene represented and the position

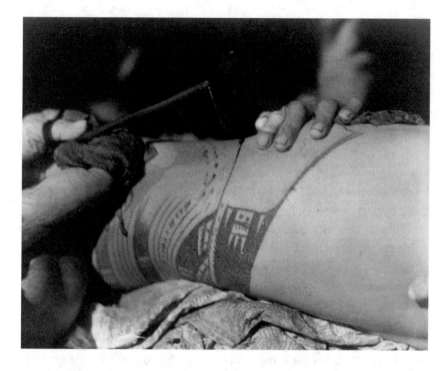

Figure i. *Moana: A Romance of the Golden Age* (Robert Flaherty, 1926). Production still taken by Frances Flaherty. Courtesy of The Robert and Frances Flaherty Study Center, Claremont School of Theology.

from which it is filmed or seen. In early films of science, travel, nature, industrial processes, military activities, and news of the day, the discursive principles of argument and narration, characteristic of mature documentary, are merely two among many modes of organization and presentation, and they are subordinated to the broader motives of attracting viewers' attention and of working out a language and a syntax for the visual description of the social and physical world. Some of these films amount to little more than "a drama staged between camera and subject, the observer and the observed, and ultimately, the 'view' and the audience," according to Gunning.[12] Their "view aesthetic" lays bare the dynamics of power and desire inherent in cinematic looking. Grierson's later writing on documentary has been characterized by Gunning and other historians as a polemic against this earlier period, a tendentious rereading of film history meant to advance the cause of what Grierson and other Anglo-American writers of the 1930s called documentary, a cinematic social pedagogy addressed by an individual or corporate author to the citizen of the modern industrial nation-state. But the persistence of the view aesthetic into Grierson's totemic 1926 review, in his attention to what he imagines is his fellow viewers' suffering, reminds us that this allegorical structure is fundamental to documentary and that the knowledge produced by documentary—the "philosophic attitude"—is always its audiences' knowledge of their own situation. Documentary is always about something more or other than what it depicts.

Put simply, allegory is a story that explains one thing by being a story about something else. My use of this term throughout this book is meant to describe a type of narration and cultural analysis in documentary and to bring the operations of inscription and transposition that the allegorist performs into the foreground. My usage is closest to that of James Clifford, who defines allegory as a "continuous double structure" of writing that allows the local or particular to retain its specificity and authenticity while serving as the medium for a lesson of general significance for others.[13] What Clifford calls ethnographic allegory presumes that "a difference is posited and transcended" *at the same time,* by the same discursive operation. To call documentary allegorical is to highlight its capacity to mediate. Documentary mediation is not only, as Grierson and Gunning observe, between the documentary subject and the observer with the camera, or the screen and the audience, but also between the realms of theory and practice. Tracing an intellectual path from questions of resemblance and representation (what does this film say about its subject, and does it say it accurately?) to questions of meaning and mediation (why was this filmed? for whom? why am I moved by it?), Grierson's review of *Moana* establishes a central and primary role for interpretation in documentary.

In fact, we might say that Grierson's review of *Moana* functions as a moment of origin for documentary precisely because it is ambivalent, or simply uncertain, about what the term "documentary" stands for, and about whether its value is in what it shows or how it shows it. As will be demonstrated by the historical case studies of American documentaries that the following chapters undertake, this confusion between two senses in which documentaries "stand for"—as sign, and as act on behalf of principle or people—is crucial to their political effects. There is, as Gunning and others have argued, good reason to be skeptical about the historical originality of Grierson's use of the term "documentary." But we can still suppose that this usage founds an allegorical tendency that becomes central to the form. In this sense, more important than Grierson's nomination of one kind of film rather than another as a documentary—which, as we see, is incidental to his appreciation of *Moana*—is the process of writing that links the act of making a film and the act of watching one. Documentary interpretation is thus both a technique to be applied during documentary production and a product of viewing, a subject position that viewing can instantiate. As we shall see, this ambivalence is crucial to the political and ethical claims made by and for documentary.

Moments of authenticity can be said to function as guarantees that documentary operates liberally, responsible at once to the individual instance and the totality. In this respect, the allegorical meanings of documentary mimic a governmental institution, insofar as the process of documentary representation both depends upon and displaces the particular value of the individual case, affirming its value in the name of an abstract principle.[14] Insofar as particularity and its many variants—authenticity, actuality, the ordinary, the untold, the individual—are the documentary's stock in trade, every encounter with documentary produces a similar connection, or tension, between the singular and the universal. Its claim to serve the public interest in a capacity I am calling "intelligence work," a phrase I take from Walter Lippmann, is based on the maintenance of this tension.

In *Public Opinion* (1922), his study of the problems facing the United States and other democratic nations after the First World War, Lippmann described a cadre of expert intellectuals who mediated between the highly visible agents of political power—the state and its officials—and ordinary Americans, mired in ignorance about their government and the rest of organized society. These intellectuals convert the false images of the state that Americans carry around with them, a result of mass communication and the spread of public relations into politics, into "a National Will, a Group Mind, a Social Purpose."[15] The forms of documentary I examine, ranging from capital-intensive, widely circulated works of state propaganda and mainstream film and television to the ephemeral, handmade productions of radicals, artists, and amateurs, all can be said to perform, in one way or another, a similar intelligence work, by making visible the invisible or "phantom" realities that shape the experience of the ordinary Americans in whose name power is exercised and contested.

The concept of intelligence work was part of a far-reaching critique of democratic processes, institutions, and theory undertaken by Lippmann and other American social and political scientists in the 1920s. The formative force of this critique in the early development of the social documentary idea cannot be underestimated, even if it has sometimes been assumed, especially in American writing on the subject, that the relationship between documentary and democracy is an obvious and uncomplicated one.[16] Thus, it is worth exploring the prehistory of this problem before taking up the problematic of the public sphere.

INTELLIGENCE WORK

In a series of lectures given in 1929 at Swarthmore College, the political philosopher A. D. Lindsay addressed the idea, then commonplace among academics and pundits, that modern people no longer cared for democracy. "Men feel disillusionment about political democracy," Lindsay said, not only when they compared their present political life to a time when direct participation in government was possible, but also when they considered their experience of politics against that of other contemporary settings for self-government, the "innumerable smaller societies" like union locals, church groups, and other self-contained congregations in which individuals serving a common purpose meet to discuss their views, air their differences, and to learn how to get along.[17] Lindsay, who was a formative intellectual influence on John Grierson,[18] was responding in particular to a critique of the theory and practice of democracy being advanced in the 1920s by American social scientists. This critique found different spokesmen, including John Dewey, whom Grierson had read as a student at Glasgow University, and the political scientists Charles Merriam and Harold Lasswell, both of whom Grierson encountered at the University of Chicago, which he visited on a three-year Rockefeller Foundation fellowship, beginning in 1924, to study the effects of the mass media on popular attitudes and feelings.[19]

But the critic that all felt obliged to respond to in the period was Lippmann. In *Public Opinion,* his analysis of the role played by communications media and mass society more generally on the institutions and practices of politics, Lippmann concluded that the inevitable result of mass mediation was misinformation and distraction: symbols, stereotypes, fantasies, and other "pictures in our heads" that stand in for social realities too complicated for the ordinary person to comprehend and on the basis of which she or he forms the vague notions of the social world—a world whose national or international scope ordinary people could scarcely comprehend—which Lippmann termed "public opinions."[20] Managed and manipulated by state and nonstate agents, this process gave modern citizens an inflated sense of the importance of their judgments and feelings, while weakening the democracy of institutions whose legitimacy was based on an appeal to groups of such citizens. Lippmann observed that this appeal had been reduced to an invitation to say "yes" or "no" to initiatives crafted at the top levels of industries, social groups, and governments. The problem was especially acute in politics: "The present fundamentally invisible system of government is so intricate," Lippmann wrote, "that most people have given up trying to follow it, and because they do not try, they are tempted to think it comparatively simple. It is, on the contrary, elusive, concealed, opaque."[21] When government officials or their advisors responded to this political imaginary, rather than to facts or reason, they tended to make bad decisions. This situation could be overcome, Lippmann argued, by the development of an agency he called "intelligence work," an office of knowledge and analysis that would provide sound, nonpartisan expertise to the "man of action" in every kind of social institution.[22] Unlike some of his intellectual contemporaries, Lippmann did not long nostalgically for immediate, subnational forms of democracy, nor did he imagine that it was possible to do away with the "unseen reality" of modernity.[23] Rather, he called for an instrument of expert social knowledge to represent what he liked to call the "environments" of late-modern democracy. By making visible the operations of groups and institutions to themselves and their publics, to political leaders, and to scholars, intelligence workers would make possible more hospitable environments for social and political action.

The conception of social documentary cinema that John Grierson developed during his research in the United States was shaped by *Public Opinion* and the intellectual debates it generated. Grierson goes so far as to claim, in a retrospective lecture from 1943, that the "idea of documentary in its present form came originally not from the film people at all, but from the Political Science school" at the University of Chicago, where Lippmann's critique had taken root. Grierson even credits Lippmann with turning his attention away from the medium of the newspaper, which had been his primary object of analysis, and toward film.[24] And in his foreword to Rotha's *Documentary Film* (1935), Grierson seems to have this "school" in mind when he speaks of documentary as a "social power" that constitutes a "first concrete reply to the unnecessary pessimisms of democratic theory."[25]

Grierson's idea of documentary as a corrective social agency is, in this way, aligned with John Dewey's pragmatic response in *The Public and Its Problems* (1927) to Lippmann's blend of idealism and pessimism. To Lippmann's conception of intelligence bureaus in every social and political institution, streamlining the production of public intelligence, Dewey objects that such a "class of experts," separated from "common interests," would constitute "a class with private interests and private knowledge, which in social matters is not knowledge at all."[26] Dewey's folksy analogy for the effective limits of expertise—"The man who wears the shoe knows best that it pinches, and where it pinches, even if the expert shoemaker is the best judge of how the trouble is to be remedied"[27]—described a gap between official knowledge and the domain of experience. But unlike some of the Chicago theorists, Dewey's acknowledgment of the experiential dimensions of social knowledge did not mean that mass democracy or the mass publics on which it depended were irrational and impossible. As A. D. Lindsay observed when he took up the shoe-pinching argument in *The Modern Democratic State* (1943), administrative democracy presumed this discrepancy and required institutions that were flexible and responsive to the complaints of ordinary people. Citizens' feelings, he suggested, might even be incorporated into the mechanisms of government: "If government needs for its task an understanding of the common life it exists to serve, it must have access to all aspects of that common life."[28] Grierson echoed his former professor when, in his 1943 lecture to the Winnipeg Canadian Club, he defined documentary as a movement that sought to "'bring alive' to the citizen the world in which his citizenship lay, to 'bridge the gap' between the citizen and his community."[29]

But like Lippmann's extension of the term intelligence work to any kind of expert knowledge production that performs a socially mediating role, the shoe-pinching metaphor is meant to be taken loosely. After all, democracy is more abstract and less tangible than a pair of shoes, and how it should feel when it fits is a difficult question to answer. It is one thing to claim that the problems and complaints of individuals or specific groups of individuals can be represented, aired, studied, and disseminated in documentary film. It is another to suggest, as Grierson does, that the social technology of documentary might *solve* these problems or, indeed, that it might avoid the problems of abstraction that are inherent in technological media production. Grierson inscribes an analogy between documentary and democracy, one that ties the cinematic impression of reality to a collective activity of perception—literally, a common sensing. Although Grierson is usually associated with a specifically British framework of governmental and liberal-capitalist institutions, his programmatic statements from the 1920s through the 1940s presume a broadly Anglo-American philosophical and political field of discourse. Writing from and about Canada (which he called "a good country in which to study the terms of democracy"), Grierson insisted that democracy "must perfect its system of communication so that individuals and localities may draw from the deepest source of inspiration [and] challenge authoritarian standards," and he placed his work to date in documentary film within this scope of this governing idea.[30] This formulation expands upon the famous passages in one of his early essays on Robert Flaherty, where he claims that the medium of cinema "itself insists upon the actual," and is thus the instrument with which modern industrial subjects can be made to "accept the environment in which they live," a first step to inspiring them to "create and find well-being" as a national group.[31]

Lippmann was being figurative or ironic in using a term usually understood to mean military espionage in describing the work of intellectuals for public and civil institutions. Likewise, my use of the term is not meant to designate only those kinds of documentary films in which information is collected in clandestine ways, or with the aim of gaining knowledge of a political enemy. There is, of course, a long history of governments using documentary film, video, and other moving-image media for the purposes of reconnaissance, spying, or surveillance, and the connection between this intelligence work and civil documentary is well known: obvious examples include the work of British documentarists such as Humphrey Jennings with the Mass-Observation movement of the 1930s and their subsequent service in the Ministry of Information during the Second World War; their North American counterparts, who served similar functions inside and outside of the state, reporting on domestic populations; or the abundance of propaganda documentary made by nationalized film units during every major war of the twentieth century, often the product of filmmakers who worked independently of the state in peacetime. John Grierson was himself accused of spying for the Soviet Union in Canada during the infamous "Gouzenko Affair" that resulted in his departure from the National Film Board and the country, and the purging of staff administrators and filmmakers at the NFB.[32] It is equally well known that the 16mm technological innovations used in *cinéma vérité* in the 1960s and 1970s—a technique that constitutes a kind of domestic spying—were the direct result of the military use of such equipment in the Second World War.[33] Oppositional filmmakers have occasionally refashioned the technology and material of this history in their own work. *Attica* (Cinda Firestone, 1973), a film I discuss at length in chapter 4, relies on the startling reframing of surveillance footage shot by the state during its suppression of a prison rebellion, a technique used in nearly every American film about prison made in recent years. Recent films, including *It's Not My Memory of It: Three Recollected Documents* (The Speculative Archive, 2003), make a similar use of documentary materials fabricated by the U.S. government for propaganda, counterinsurgency, and disinformation campaigns.[34] More broadly, American social documentary has frequently operated in a mode somewhat closer to Lippmann's idea of a check on government and corporate monopolies on knowledge production, from the counterterrorist newsreel work of the Workers Film and Photo League, capturing and distributing the images of striking Ford workers gunned down by antiunion thugs (*Detroit*

Workers News Special 1932: Ford Massacre [Detroit and New York Workers Film and Photo League, 1932]), which commercial newsreels refused to show, to Peter Davis's controversial film for "CBS Reports," *The Selling of the Pentagon* (1971), which criticized public-relations efforts by the U.S. military and brought its producers under congressional scrutiny. While making *The Energy War* (D.A. Pennebaker, Chris Hegedus, and Pat Powell, 1978), a film for PBS about energy legislation in the Carter administration, one of the film's main subjects called the filmmakers "snoops," and American liberal and left documentarists have embraced this job description.[35] The most famous invocation of this metaphor is James Agee's description, at the beginning of *Let Us Now Praise Famous Men: Three Tenant Families* (1941), a project initially undertaken for *Fortune* magazine, of himself and the photographer Walker Evans as "spies" who "counted their employers and that Government likewise to which one of them [Evans] was bonded, among their most dangerous enemies."[36] Many of the Popular Front writers and filmmakers I discuss in chapters 1 and 2 felt placed in the position of double agency by their work on behalf of the welfare nation-state and the ideological project of the New Deal. American documentary filmmakers have often occupied this duplicitous position, whether they employ a relatively invisible observational style (Robert Drew, Frederick Wiseman, Barbara Kopple), the noisy interventionism of Michael Moore, or the listening devices of Errol Morris to expose the inner workings of state and capitalist institutions. One of my goals in this book is to demonstrate, however, that the faculty of social intellection I am describing as intelligence work is not only embodied in individuals who perform a specialized labor function—thinking—and therefore should not be thought of as a capacity of only certain people, but can be enacted intersubjectively, through a cultural technology like cinema.

This is an important difference between my use of the term "intelligence work" to apply to documentary film and the way that Lippmann, who believed ever more strongly that ordinary people formed an inert, unredeemable mass, intended it. Like the bureaus of experts Lippmann recommended for every political, social, and industrial organization, documentary cinema mediates between power and the social, but with one significant, paradoxical difference: it takes up the very instruments said to be responsible for mass ignorance and distraction, adapting

them to socially and culturally productive ends. Its aesthetic of truth—
of objectivity, authenticity, accuracy, spontaneity, exposure, and free
speech—has made documentary an important crucible of responses to
this perceived crisis of democracy, and a crucible, as well, of the role of
the intellectual in mediating between dominant and oppressed groups,
between state and people.

THE PROBLEM OF THE PUBLIC

If the problem of the public was a catalyst for the early theory and practice of social documentary cinema, it has received relatively scant attention in recent criticism.[37] This can be explained in part by a resistance
in scholarship on North American documentary film of the past two
decades, which comes as often from the perspectives of ethnic studies,
feminist and gender studies, and queer studies as from film and media
studies, to the concept of totality entailed by the previous generation
of American scholarship on documentary. Books like William Stott's
Documentary Expression and Thirties America (1973) and William Alexander's *Film on the Left: American Documentary Film From 1931 to 1942*
(1981), along with articles and interviews in journals like *Cineaste,
Cinema Journal,* and *Film Quarterly,* helped to canonize documentary
work in which a collective figure of the working class—white, mascu-
line, and poor—was used by a largely middle-class white left, either in
line with or in opposition to the state, depending on the personnel and
period of production, in a struggle to redefine the nation. The nation
was presumed as the object and addressee of this documentary work,
whether its audiences were in practice local or genuinely widespread.
In my book, chapters 1 and 2 explore the variations on this theme
across the period of the New Deal, within the American cultural left
and in the public relations offices of the nascent welfare state. Chapters 3, 4, and 5 take up revisions of the statist conception of national
documentary work by later progressives, while the avant-garde and
amateur projects considered in chapter 6 test in a different way the national premise of both leftist and governmental traditions of American
documentary, and of what the linguistic theory of enunciation calls
the "roles" assigned to subjects in discourse: the conventional political

positions of patriot, conservative, liberal, and radical. These corporate agents of documentary, the state and the left—treated, in the historical work of the 1970s, as relatively coherent entities—were taken to represent what Thomas Waugh calls a "common fund" of social realism, a "consensus of audience with practitioners" about what constitutes the real.[38]

This presumption was convincingly and decisively challenged, as Waugh notes, by the introduction of semiotics to the study of documentary, first by British film scholars and later by their North American counterparts. A different, equally trenchant critique of this "common fund" was produced somewhat later by cultural historians such as Thomas Cripps, Michael Denning, and Paula Rabinowitz, whose studies of specific cultural and institutional configurations of American documentary in the New Deal period reinserted race, gender, sexuality, and a more nuanced conception of class into this history.[39] In his introduction to *"Show us Life": Toward a History and Aesthetics of the Committed Documentary* (1984), one of the last and best studies of documentary to take the workerist-international left of the 1920s and 1930s as its point of reference, Waugh, poised between an earlier, affirmative conception of documentary realism and the skepticism of semiotics and cultural studies, uses the concept of the public to express what he calls the ideological "teetering" between one critical platform and another. Documentary, he writes, "continues to be a privileged medium—indeed, *the* privileged medium—for committed artists and their public."[40] *"Show Us Life"* marked a shift in focus, one that can be glimpsed in the table of contents, toward the study of discrete, socially and politically specific cultures and subcultures of documentary, more local, partial, and tactical than the national-public model associated with Grierson and his partisans. But as is indicated by verb tense ("continues") and the subtle downscaling from "the" to "their" public, new studies of documentary did not necessarily abandon the public as its horizon of social effect, even if the term appears almost nowhere in this criticism.

Uses of the term "public" have tended, over the last decade or so, to be tentative and sometimes confused, an effect of the ongoing rethinking of the concept of publicness spurred by the English-language translation and critique of Jürgen Habermas, on the one hand, and the progressively bleak outlook for public infrastructures of noncommercial media production and distribution in the United States, on the other. (Frequently invoked signs of the latter include congressional death threats to the Corporation for Public Broadcasting and to its associated network, PBS; the withering of state funding agencies; and the continuing failure of the American cable industry and major city governments to protect the infrastructure of public-access cable, as mandated in federal legislation.) "Public" can index contradictory meanings and desires, especially when applied to activist video producers working within or on behalf of un- or underrepresented economic, racial, ethnic, or sexual minorities. In this context, it can mean both a "volatile and necessary"[41] movement of independent and experimental culture and the oppressive conditions that call for such radical activity. In her study of AIDS-activist video of the 1980s and 1990s, for example, Alexandra Juhasz asserts that despite having "brought 'new' ideas about AIDS to the 'general public' . . . the construction of an apolitical, amorphous, but very moral 'general public' still organizes the voice and intended reception of mainstream AIDS reportage";[42] here, "general public" is opposed to the term that appears frequently in this study and elsewhere in critical work of the period, "community." Community is self-organized and active; public is normative, passive, and established and enforced by laws and conservative mores. And yet Juhasz's ironizing of "general public" signals a suspicion or a hope that the term can mean something else. Thus, a few pages later, the term is inverted to describe the efforts of Juhasz's own video collective to reach beyond itself, "working together as a group against a cause [sic] and making our ideas and demands public."[43] Going public clearly still holds an appeal that the address to a community cannot satisfy, despite—or because of—the contradictions of this act.[44]

This problem dates at least to what is still the major published study of American government documentary, Richard Dyer MacCann's *The People's Films: A Political History of U.S. Government Motion Pictures* (1973). MacCann's book began as his 1951 doctoral dissertation, and it reflects Cold War concerns about state publicity as a form of didactic national culture. Seeking to define American documentary in ways that distinguished it from educational or informational film and, on the other hand, from government propaganda, MacCann put the problem in terms that invoked, somewhat perversely, the name for the U.S. military strategy in Vietnam. Documentary appealed, MacCann maintained, "not only to the mind but to the heart," and was "well suited to an age which needs the heart of its public problems made meaningful to the public."[45] But MacCann's study is essentially a production and exhibition history of government filmmaking from the New Deal to the Johnson administration, and much of the book is spent recounting the bureaucratic and political processes of making and showing films under the auspices of agencies like the Department of Agriculture, the United States Film Service, the War Department, and the United States Information Agency. MacCann's analysis of documentary's public is therefore limited to citations of the number of prints in circulation, secondhand references to a given film's popularity (or lack thereof) among critics, eyewitness accounts by bureaucrats and diplomats present at screenings, and MacCann's own judgment of the films' interest: "audience response to *The River* was extraordinary," as evidenced by the "deafening applause" that it reportedly received, while the "primitive appeals" of informational films made by various government agencies around the same time, which MacCann considers "hardly . . . motion picture[s]," merely addressed "the darkness of projection rooms." And because a Treasury Department film that used Donald Duck to explain the value of paying taxes and saving money (*The New Spirit* [1942]) played in 11,785 theaters in six weeks, MacCann concludes that "the people liked it."[46]

But what exactly is the nature of this appeal, when its goal is collective attention and enjoyment? And what is a public when it can be formed by such an appeal? These are not easy questions to answer. Complicating them is the idea, derived from the work of Lippmann and Dewey, that the public of a democracy in the age of communication knows itself through its uptake of publicity. A merely speculative public of this sort is quite different from the built-in, internally coherent publics of the films cited by Waugh and other historians of the new social movements in documentary, which presume a completed act of communication. In these historians' descriptions, a scene of conversation in a documentary film or a face-to-face audience discussion afterward is often held up as the ideal manifestation of a public discourse.[47] But the democratic citizen addressed by publicity has the right, as MacCann puts it, "to pay no attention."[48] What kind of discourse community can be defined by its participants' inattention to a message? Because Lippmann's *Public Opinion* is MacCann's theoretical touchstone, however, he presumes, as is conventional in American media theory, that the individual is free to choose what ideas to take interest in and that democratic states do not force ideology on their subjects. Thus, there is little room in his analyses for the interesting theoretical questions raised by the circulation of public address in documentary form.

MacCann's venerable history was written and rewritten in the period of a significant transformation of liberal arguments about communication and the public realm. *The People's Films* and other classic texts of American media history do not, by and large, reflect this transformation, an oversight that has produced certain liberal commonplaces about documentary, its audiences, and the relation between them. The political and theoretical genealogy of American documentary that is reconstructed in the following chapters deviates from that tradition, while returning to some of its key works. In establishing this genealogy, it is worth observing that Hannah Arendt's important revision of the concept of publicity occurs in the period between MacCann's doctoral research and his revision of his thesis as a book. Her documentary account of the 1961 trial of Adolph Eichmann, first written for the *New Yorker* magazine and then republished in book form as *Eichmann in Jerusalem: A Report on the Banality of Evil* (1963), essentially reverses the terms of MacCann's premise and undoes his ideological opposition between propaganda and democratic publicity, exploring how it is possible for citizens of a totalitarian state to choose not to pay attention and for a liberal state to enforce the conditions of spectacle and propaganda in and through its public institutions. In *The Human Condition* (1958), Arendt reconnects publicness to classical ideas of the polis as a "common world" that "can survive the coming and going of the generations only to the extent that it appears in public."[49] The meaning of public in *The Human Condition* modifies the American liberal tradition of social theory in a number of significant ways, including Arendt's emphasis on the intersubjective character of public experience and her insistence that this experience, which she calls "appearance," is at once aesthetic and social, the product of a collective process, not only an individual perspective. Arendt employs the concept of appearance, anathema to Progressive Era social theorists (with its suggestion of mass illusion or self-deception), without presuming that the sources of this phenomenon are undemocratic or irrational, even though it transcends the private individual:

> It [public] means, first, that everything that appears in public can be seen and heard by everybody and has the widest possible publicity. For us, appearance—something that is being seen and heard by others as well as by ourselves—constitutes reality. . . . Each time we talk about things that can be experienced only in privacy or intimacy, we bring them out into a sphere where they will assume a kind of reality which, their intensity notwithstanding, they never could have had before.[50]

And as if to make explicit a thought that remains implicit in the Progressive notion of public intelligence, where reason is idealized as a self-instantiating and asocial category, Arendt emphasizes that public things do not *just* appear, in some quasi-natural event, but are the result and the legacy of human fabrication, of work:

> The term "public" signifies the world itself, in so far as it is common to all of us and distinguished from our privately owned place in it. This world, however, is not identical with the earth or with nature, as the limited space for the movement of men and the general condition of organic life. It is related, rather, to the human artifact, the fabrication of human hands, as well as to affairs which go on among those who inhabit the man-made world together. To live together in the world means essentially that a world of things is between those who have it in common, as a table is located between those who sit around it; the world, like every in-between, relates and separates men at the same time.[51]

Since it brings together the themes of reality as a social construction, of human labor as an art form from which a life-world is shaped, and of the agency of collective thought and perception, it is interesting, to say the least, that Arendt's discussion of the public appears rarely in the analysis of documentary film. This omission is all the more surprising since Arendt herself authored an important work of documentary and modeled the figure of the engaged intellectual that documentary makers and critics frequently hold up as an ideal.

It is no less surprising that, until quite recently, little use has been made by North American scholars of documentary of the concept of publicness developed at the same time as Arendt's, and in dialogue with it, in the early work of Jürgen Habermas. Rather than contrasting the modern notion of publicity to the classical ideal, Habermas adopts the Frankfurt School perspective of Marxist sociology and traces the public sphere to its origins in the class-specific cultural formation of bourgeois print culture. In *The Structural Transformation of the Public Sphere* (1962; 1989), his paradigmatic study of print culture and its political effects, Habermas pointed out that the activist character of readerships during and after the rise of the American and Western European bourgeoisie depended no less upon their members' awareness that the works they consumed were objects that circulated in a marketplace of ideas and commodities than upon the criticism of social and political institutions these works contained as content.[52] The accessibility and impersonality of their address, which offered a theoretically infinite expansion of this reading public, was an immanent challenge to externally imposed configurations of society: membership in this public was potentially available to anyone with the means to read, not granted by preexisting markers of class and status. Publics are thus seen as "scenes of self-activity," as Michael Warner puts it, "of historical rather than timeless belonging, and of active participation rather than ascriptive belonging."[53] One of the most thoughtful readers of Habermas, Warner has demonstrated the obvious limitations of Habermas's paradigm while arguing for the extension of this paradigm into new contexts: anywhere the dynamic of address and attention is produced between strangers and a text—an extremely capacious term—a public is in effect. As both Habermas and Warner make clear, this sense of "public" is quite different from the usual sense of the term, where it is taken to mean a group of people at once fixed in its constituency and *merely* virtual—in other words, "everyone," and, specifically, the everyone reached by or sending en masse a message: the voting public, the viewing public, and so on.[54] But in the public spheres described by Habermas and Warner, the publics that form recognize themselves as temporary and partial representatives of a larger entity whose extent is both material and not yet known. This inchoate and flexible character allowed early modern publics to challenge the totalizing power of the state and the church.

Their memory inspires cultural producers and critics alike to extend the public sphere ideal past the limits of its classic situation.

The obvious historical and ideological limitations of Habermas's model do not preclude its value for describing different kinds of modern and late-modern public experience. The appeal of this model for cultural theorists such as Warner, Miriam Hansen, and Benjamin Lee is that in it, as Lee writes, public "communication is seen not as a face-to-face relation between men"—a common misreading of Habermas—"but rather as mediated by a potentially limitless discourse."[55] Nevertheless, the dim view Habermas takes in *Structural Transformation* of the public potential of radio, film, and television, beyond the most monolithic commercial-industrial examples, radically limited the appeal of his analysis for film and media studies, where one might have expected it to have had the impact it had in literary studies, gender studies, history, sociology, political theory, and a host of other disciplines. As Hansen and others have noted, the disciplinary dominance of paradigms of spectatorship that were idealist in their own way made Habermas's historical account of an emergent medium, where the conditions of textuality and subjectivity reflexively determine each other, incompatible with the state of the discipline.[56] At the same time, rapid and disorienting technological changes to the media and environments of film presentation seemed to portend the decline of cinema as a public activity, and many film theorists and historians turned their attention to revisions of the classical paradigms of spectatorship and consumption to suit these new economic and technological realities. Although such shifting terrain might have made the "critical norm" of the historical public sphere an even more useful tool, anxieties about the disappearing specificity of the medium on which the discipline's professional and institutional status hinged meant that thinking of film in an analogy with emergent print culture was simply not an option for most film studies scholars.[57]

The case was somewhat different for scholars of documentary film, which had never enjoyed the kind of stature as a scholarly object that the fiction film or even the experimental film had. Important as it was to the fortunes of documentary film studies as a subfield of film studies more generally, the turn in earnest toward semiotic and psychoanalytic models of spectatorship by North American documentary film scholars at about the same time that *Structural Transformation* appeared in English meant a lost opportunity to theorize documentary as an important difference *within* cinema and within film studies, one that has the potential to change the way that film studies is conceived and conducted. Instead, scholars of documentary settled for a taxonomic compromise, according to which, as William Rothman succinctly puts it, "although documentaries are not inherently more truthful than fiction films, there are important differences between them."[58]

Although it draws certain principles from this latter phase of accommodation with structuralist film theory, my book maintains a slightly different view of documentary truth. Documentary is a process by which certain traits of cinema as such—the indexical character of its auditory and visual signs; the capacity to separate the audio track from the visual track, and to recombine them in different ways; its ability to incorporate other performance, textual, and recording media; its portability; and its ability to be viewed by one or many—are brought to bear on a social topic. Insofar as it traffics in special kinds of stories, using techniques of representation and structures of meaning that remain fairly constant from work to work and that are, in certain ways, distinct from other modes of narrative realism, historical explanation, and social analysis, it is accurate to refer to documentary as a genre. But one of the defining features of this genre is its insistence on authenticity, in its subjects and its own form. By definition, each work of documentary is, in a way, unique, the record of its producers' attempt to raise specific historical, social, or ethical questions by grappling with the subjects it speaks of, to, or for. Documentary is a kind of metagenre, constantly raising the question of how the social context of cultural representation becomes its content, that is, how the outside of a work of art becomes its inside.

And this process also works in reverse. When documentary compels our attention or addresses us in certain ways, when it makes us think about the world outside the sphere of media consumption or reflect on the meanings of it and other forms of publicity and information, and when it invites us to speak with others about these reactions, whether we actually do or not, it evokes forms of public subjectivity and civil interaction that transport viewers beyond the immediate context of viewing. This process is by no means specific to cinema. Early publics of print were already based upon textual metaphors of speech and dialogue, ones that intersected with political metaphors like "the people" and "the voice of the people."[59] It was this textual power that allowed American state constitutions, written and printed, to bring into being a "people" that did not otherwise exist. This is the power by which a medium and its politics determine each other.[60] A documentary film can be said to reanimate these metaphors when it presumes to let the social speak for itself through audio-visual representation or when it addresses its audiences as if they were present before a speaker, as much as when it becomes, as it does on rare occasions, a topic of discussion by the so-called general public. But it is a mistake to think that these reality effects are an illusion, as some have argued, meant in the sense of a perceptual error or unconscious delusion, or that the films are understood in a purely mimetic way by viewers.[61] An audience comes to understand itself as an agent of change when it figures out how to generalize from the case on screen to other situations or cases. This dynamic of interpretation allows viewers to understand their own situation as no less a representation than what they perceive on screen.

The room I give in this book to examples and their interpretation is intended, in part, to emphasize the hermeneutic agency of documentary and to foreground its relation to the process I earlier described as institution, the intellectual activity by which singularity (a new idea, a unique individual) and social structure are reconciled, or, rather, the process by which the former is reconducted or reproduced in the latter. The powers of documentary depend upon this dialectic, which takes the rhetorical form of a tension between argument and example. Indeed, it might be said that social documentary does not only argue by example but often argues *for* the example and its special qualities.

My arrangement of examples within and across chapters follows this logic. The argument that accompanies them maintains that the self-evidence of social reality is itself ideological and, at the same time, that this abstraction always articulates, as John Tagg writes, "challengeable political perspectives which have to be constructed and are not given."[62] The documentaries examined in the first part of the book, which covers the period of the Depression and the New Deal, stress operations of typification and generalization; the varieties of national documentary discussed in chapters 1 and 2 make Americans separated from the rest of society by time and tradition, geography, or economic circumstance into problems to be solved by formal or informal institutions of movement, front, or state. In the course of describing these Americans, mired in particularity, a model or allegory of the nation is formed. Chapters 3 and 4 deal with a tipping of the balance in documentary practices of the 1960s and 1970s from paradigmatic to idiomatic speech and expression. In documenting two kinds of outlaw, the protester and the prisoner, documentaries of the Vietnam era used idiomatic techniques to test the very conditions of representability of the particular case. Chapter 5, a study of the documentary preoccupation with the intimate and personal aspects of the American presidency, brings the two sides of the problem together. Chapter 6 reflects on the discourse of crisis both studied and occasioned by recent critical work in and on documentary, a discourse in which problems of national and international scale are met not with the indifference presumed by so many casual commentators on the postmodern condition but by hyperparticular forms of the public sphere. This concluding chapter considers some recent guises of American documentary, each offering a different ironic strategy of authenticity to counter the disbelief—or the widespread idea of disbelief—that attaches to both documentary and the state today.[63]

Some of the examples I deal with at length—films by D. A. Pennebaker, Frederick Wiseman, and Michael Moore, for instance—are well known to many contemporary readers, who will have encountered them in commercial theaters, on television, or at home on video or DVD. Others, like the New Deal documentaries produced by Pare Lorentz or the CBS television documentary *A Tour of the White House with Mrs. John F. Kennedy* (1962), were seen by large audiences in their day, are still widely discussed in certain academic settings, but are rarely screened today. In some cases, readers may know only by name or reputation some of the films I deal with in detail, especially those produced by groups like Frontier Films and Top Value Television, which had modest resources for advertising and distribution and little, if any, institutional affiliation. And a few of the films I deal with, like Robert Flaherty's film *The Land* (1941), had only a brief nontheatrical distribution, or, like the Film Group's *Cicero March* (1966), none at all. These films are known only to a small coterie of researchers and archivists lucky enough to view them at libraries and archives, at seminars and festivals, or through the underground economy of bootleg copies that has sustained the study and appreciation of alternative and independent cinema in the United States for decades. This range is part of the book's point: as a method and a principle of representation, documentary has claimed as its constituency the entire social spectrum.

The next section deals with an example that will be familiar to many, even the nonspecialist reader, which makes it at once common and—given that it is a work of documentary film, and one on abstruse scientific problems—extraordinary. I present it for two reasons: because it elucidates another important aspect of documentary intelligence, its association with intellectuals and intellectual labor; and because it demonstrates the importance of the example *as such* in social documentary. The power of social documentary comes, as I have already suggested, from its allegorical displacement of particular details onto the plane of general significance. This power is enhanced by the impression that individual works can contain both the ordinary and the exemplary and can effect the transformation from one to the other.

DISSEMINATING INTELLIGENCE: THE EXEMPLARY AL GORE

In her influential essay "Political Mimesis," Jane Gaines asks how feelings are connected to action in the political documentary. Gaines means not only to pose a question about viewer psychology but also to challenge the premise of rationality that underlies the conventional history of social documentary in the era of the welfare state. Her example is an analysis Brian Winston offers in *Claiming the Real: The Griersonian Documentary and its Legitimations* (1995) of films by American liberal feminists in the 1970s, films like *Union Maids* (Julia Reichert and Jim Klein, 1976) and *The Life and Times of Rosie the Riveter* (Connie Field, 1980). Winston places these films in the Griersonian tradition of humanist advocacy, in which the victims of an unfair social system are presented as the reason that others, at a safe distance from the site of suffering, should be moved to act. Because the film programs guided by Grierson were connected to the state and to major capitalist institutions, no "Griersonian" filmmaking practice, argues Gaines, can produce actions that lead directly to social change (rather than, say, operating at the level of opinion formation and public policy). In the face of this legacy, a genuinely effective politics of documentary will move beyond the pursuit of "a combative form," which Gaines, echoing Walter Benjamin in "The Author as Producer," defines as one that "poses the right questions in the intellectual struggle against capitalism." Rather than being preoccupied with the discursive level of politics, a politics of documentary will attend to the question of how a film compels its viewers to feeling and thus to action, by which she means, quite literally, "what it is that the body is *made to do* by the political film."[64] Gaines is quick to point out that such direct correspondence between massed or struggling bodies on screen and similar movements in the world of the audience is largely a radical fantasy; the single example she points to, of a college audience destroying an ROTC office after a 1969 screening of antiwar films, seems meant as an exception that proves the rule. Thus, one could take her apparently naïve defense of a concept of realism as, in fact, its canny opposite, a perverse but effective case for thinking of documentary as a series of copies whose "authors" include the audience itself. By this logic, the audience is not conceived in empirical terms, as the point where perception confirms the indexical effect, but rather as an entity constituted by a public act of imagination.

Gaines's opposition of the documentary mind and its heart (or fist) is a dialectical one: it is not meant to diminish the importance of the "intellectual struggle" so much as to place it in a "realm of the unactualized."[65] By opening the question of when and how a political effect can be said to occur, Gaines establishes what Foucault calls a problematic. As opposed to the idea, which can be grasped through its representation, a problematic is a reflection on thought, or a context for thinking. More precisely, it is a way of thinking about how thought and experience are related: "for a domain of action, a behavior, to enter the field of thought," says Foucault, "it is necessary for a certain number of factors to have made it uncertain, to have made it lose its familiarity, or to have provoked a certain number of difficulties around it."[66] This temporary suspension of received wisdom "pose[s] problems for politics," since politics in the usual senses implies a well-defined terrain, population, or institution on which action can be taken now.

Commenting on this passage, Michael Warner writes that problematization "must have a public scene, not just a reflexive relation to one," and a distinct temporality as well.[67] Social documentary, I am suggesting, is one manifestation of this other public scene.

When former U.S. congressional representative, senator, vice president, and presidential candidate Al Gore remarks, near the beginning of his illustrated lecture about global warming, *An Inconvenient Truth* (Davis Guggenheim, 2006), that "I've been trying to tell this story for a long time, and I feel as if I've failed to get the message across," he indicates this eccentric staging of the political in documentary. Following a montage of archival images from Gore's political campaigns, and spoken in what Charles Wolfe calls the "elsewhere" of voice-off,[68] the remark is at once a personal reflection and an appeal to the film's audience to constitute itself as a field of possibility. Where other media of social change, including that of formal politics, failed to deliver Gore's warning, the medium of documentary may yet do so. This utopian projection is reinforced by the visual logic of the sequence. As he muses aloud, we see Gore, who is riding in the back of a limousine, look into the screen of an Apple laptop computer on which he is presumably composing the presentation we are about to witness. Then Gore looks out the window, and a false eyeline match shows us the object of his gaze: the very ice floes he will ask us to help him save (see figures ii and iii). This spatio-temporal sleight-of-hand establishes an allegorical setting in which the film will attempt to perform its public service. This space is counterposed to the temporality of politics, which, in an earlier moment from the presentation, Gore marks (as impossible) with the laugh line, "I am Al Gore. I used to be the next president of the United States of America." It is in the guise of the so-called public intellectual that Gore will transcend his previous failures (to be heard, to become president), a transformation that depends upon the film's own capacity to restage the lecture, an address bound to a particular time and place, on a scale even more significant than the large numbers of its theatrical release (a twenty-three week run, during which the film grossed over twenty-three million dollars in nearly six hundred theaters in the United States and Canada alone, extremely high numbers for a feature documentary) and its subsequent DVD and digital distribution.[69]

Figures ii–iii. *An Inconvenient Truth* (Davis Guggenheim, 2006). Still captures from DVD.

Apart from Gore's self-deprecating joke—a reference to the drama of the 2000 presidential election, as well as to his failed presidential campaigns of 1988 and 1992—relatively little mention is made of politics during the lecture portion of the film, where Gore recounts his education in the science of climate change and, with the aid of lavish visual aids, presents various scientific arguments about causes, proofs, and solutions. In publicity for the film, Gore speaks of himself as a conduit between the community of professional scientists and the general public. In an interview with the PBS talk-show host Charlie Rose, Gore said:

> For the last thirty years, one of the roles that I've tried to play on this, Charlie, is to immerse myself deeply in the science, to the point where they are willing, they the scientists, to take the time to explain to me in simple terms that I can understand as a lay person, and I've always believed that if they can get it to the point where I can understand it, then I can communicate it to anybody.[70]

His identification as a scientist is important to the film's strategy of a parapolitical intelligence work. More precisely, this identification is *with* science, a language that even a layperson can speak and can communicate more effectively to other laypeople *as* a nonprofessional. Although his remark to Rose would seem to obviate the need for the film and contradict the statement he makes *in* the film about his failure to get his message across, we can understand these two statements as driving at the same point: documentary film and science help each other speak to those who have been baffled by politics, including politicians themselves.[71]

Gore's embodiment of the values of science through these multimedia presentations is the antidote to his appearance in the tragicomic opening sequence of *Fahrenheit 9/11* (Michael Moore, 2004). There, in video footage, he is seen accepting the Supreme Court's decision about the Florida vote count in the 2000 election and refusing, while presiding over a joint session of Congress, to admit formal objections to the results by African American and Asian American congressional representatives whose petitions were not signed by a senator. These actions—or, more accurately, failures to act—cast him as the film's first villain. (To California representative Maxine Waters's tart riposte that "I don't care that it is not signed by a member of the Senate," Gore quips, "the rules do care," which gets a big laugh.) These scenes of Gore in his political role present a very different valence of disinterestedness than his scientific persona. Where the latter reads as an objective and benevolent devotion to truth, the former appears as the robotic capitulation to system and callous indifference to injustice, a contempt for "the people" that the masses expect of their politicians today.

Gore's role in and around *An Inconvenient Truth* exemplifies John Michael's contention in *Anxious Intellects* that scientists who become public intellectuals, by speaking accessibly in the popular media about difficult ideas, represent "the last, forlorn hope that something like a universal intellectual or a philosopher king might be found to save us from our political disputes."[72] That someone with Gore's years of experience in politics at the highest national levels can appear in this guise testifies to the remarkable versatility of this figure. But it also indicates the power of documentary for both creating and drawing on the "universalized specificity" of the public intellectual, which has historically required the mediation of mechanical devices, starting with those in the laboratory. Michael's example is the portrait of Stephen Hawking in Errol Morris's film *A Brief History of Time* (1992), where Hawking's reduction to a mechanically assisted talking brain turns him from the unparalleled genius that his family and colleagues, interviewed in the film, claim he is into the most typical modern intellectual because of a dependence on technological mediation that incorporates him into the medium of the film itself.[73] Assisted by the close-up, reflective voice-off, and other filmic devices for creating character and interiority, Gore's performance in *An Inconvenient Truth* is a version of this idea. The backstory of Gore's rural childhood; the entirely prosthetic theatrical setting, which recalls other settings (the classroom, the precinematic illustrated lecture, and the mythical town hall of primitive democracy); the moments when Gore performs discomfort with a piece of stage technology, in the manner of a professor fumbling with the video remote in front of the class (as when he says to the audience before climbing on an electric platform next to the huge screen backdrop, "Now if you'll bear with me, I want to really emphasize this point, the crew here has tried to teach me how to use this contraption here, so if I don't kill myself . . ."): these populist and nostalgic touches go beyond what Miriam Hansen has called the "syncretistic and contradictory public character" of late-modern public spheres, like the vaunted electronic town hall, an ideological device favored by the Clinton administration.[74]

An important intertext for *An Inconvenient Truth* is the spate of recent documentary portraits of well-known progressive intellectuals, such as Noam Chomsky, Jacques Derrida, Edward Said, Howard Zinn, and the monotonous parade of talking heads marshaled by producer-director Robert Greenwald for his video broadsides against the Bush administration and multinational corporations. These are people, one might say, who serve the professional function of thinking and thus save the rest of us from having to do so, and the films about them seem, in Richard Dyer MacCann's terms, hardly like films at all. Even when the subject is as animated as the iconoclastic Slovenian theorist Slavoj Žižek, a quasi pop star of a certain intellectual milieu, such films are usually content to observe the great man reflect on big ideas in public or private, and a more boring premise for a film can hardly be imagined. In this respect, the startling commercial success of *An Inconvenient Truth,* as well as its impact amongst columnists and pundits, could be attributed to the family resemblance between Gore's character in the film and the strategic stupidity of the protagonists played by Michael Moore, Morgan Spurlock (in *Super Size Me* [2004]), and Sacha Baron Cohen, whose Ali G and Borat Sagdiyev characters represent the outsourcing to Europe and Central Asia of the village idiot character played by Moore, and whose potential for social and political disruption Moore has begun to exhaust.[75] The bumbling, all-too-human interventions these characters make into various kinds of social and public space, though no more authentic than the performances of any other documentary character, reveal the limits of the rationalist ideal that public intellectuals and their stages—the university, the newspaper, talk radio and television—are called upon to represent. To the extent that Gore's narrative and physical mobility in *An Inconvenient Truth* can be placed with these performances in a tradition of physical and verbal performance, including those of film, television, and theatrical comedy, the film demonstrates how the public sphere of documentary cannot survive only on the analogy with the classroom or the town hall. These concessions to spectacle acknowledge what hardly needs admitting: that documentary cinema is often boring and that its viewers submit to its address with the same reluctance and distraction that they do any formal obligation of citizenship, like jury duty and voting. No analysis of what Bill Nichols has called the "discourses of sobriety" of documentary will accurately gauge the power of this analogy without taking into account the imperfect and inconstant nature of this attention. Thus, the anti-intellectual (and, one might say, typically American) shading of Gore in *An Inconvenient Truth* is the site of its properly cinematic and agitational impulse: if an ordinary guy like Al Gore can get the hang of the mechanical devices that surround him, never mind the more abstract problem of global warming, so can you.

One might in fact say that *An Inconvenient Truth* is a most typical documentary, since its main character embodies the simultaneously universal and specific nature of the documentary film as an apparatus of knowledge. Gore's figure condenses Antonio Gramsci's two types of intellectual: the "traditional" intellectual, the elite knowledge professional whose functions include announcing crises that require the state's intervention in the social to solve; and the "organic" intellectual, who reflects the principle that "all men are intellectuals . . . but not all men have in society the function of intellectuals."[76] Along these lines, we are compelled to ask: does not every documentary aim to give its audience a knowledge at once specialized and generalized, and are these not the very condition of its (specializing) genre and its (generalizing) medium? Indeed, the poverty of the term "public intellectual" becomes clear when we recognize that the goals of social documentary include: (1) making anyone who encounters it a critical thinker temporarily engaged with issues of universal significance; and (2) disseminating intelligence, so that it need not be the burden of individuals.

Each chapter of this book explores a specific instance and location of the state, as this concept is engaged by a set of social agents whose identities—government; the left; radicals; intellectuals—are consistent from chapter to chapter in name only. The same is true of the people or nation or public or others in whose name the struggle is waged. In an emancipatory gesture that readers will find repeated over and over in the works I deal with, each style of documentary claims in its way to liberate its viewers from ignorance, prejudice, false consciousness, or illusion. The journey to this enlightened place retraces a path already undertaken by the subjects or the makers of the work. Although it is frequently maintained that the work of consciousness, insight, or inspiration performed by documentary goes beyond politics or ideology and gets at truths public (of information and history) and private (of memory and experience), the desire to think, feel, and live outside of ideology is itself a trademark of liberal ideology.[77] Behind the traditional documentary gestures of unmasking or uncovering the truth is the wish for an apolitical unconscious, diagnosed by Fredric Jameson as "the neo-Freudian nostalgia for some ultimate moment of *cure*," a moment in which we see clearly what determines our actions and our desires.[78] Not that I propose any method for liberating documentary from this dilemma: the goal of my method in this book, in fact, is to demonstrate how a politics of truth depends upon symbolic discourse. Only in this way we will come to some understanding of the remarkable pliability of documentary's function for popular intelligence.

Revisionism of this type also implies the value of defining politics in elastic (not to say loose) terms. I aim at detail and precision in the interpretations that follow, but precisely in order to be attentive to the ways that the power-knowledge relation plays out in particular cultural and historical situations. If the examples I deal with often refer to the narrower sense of the political, those venues where a struggle ensues between the state and its various partners and competitors for sovereignty, that is because I want to underscore the function of the political *as* a social imaginary, or an ideology, one that is constructed and contested in specific ways through the discourse of documentary. One template for this approach is the Gramscian concept of hegemony, wherein, as Stuart Hall writes, "the concept of the state is not so much an entity, or a particular complex of institutions, so much as it is a particular site or level of the social formation."[79] This ambiguity is a necessary characteristic of "the political" itself. As Ernesto Laclau and Chantal Mouffe write in their study of hegemony, "it is impossible *to fix the literal sense* of each struggle, because each struggle overflows its own literality."[80]

One reason for the invention of American social documentary was the imputed failure of democratic institutions, including both state and nonstate agencies of government. By promising to restore directness and transparency to these agencies, documentarians established a parallel between the immediacy of the visual (and, later, audio-visual) apparatus of cinema and the democratic processes. In this respect, it could be argued that American documentary constitutes a kind of late public sphere, an aesthetic and ideological response to the obsolescence of an earlier model of the public sphere, as it encounters the mass publics of the twentieth century. Political differences among users of the same documentary forms within a single period are one indication of this dialectical impulse. Another is the periodic remaking of documentary form to renew its capacity for truth telling, once this capacity seems to have lost its potential to convince, shock or amaze. To highlight these genealogical contrasts, I concentrate on certain periods of heightened documentary activity around the problem of the state, a focus I maintain at the expense of a more comprehensive account of American documentary history. I have left out certain periods in this history not because no public or political work of documentary was conducted then but because other moments better demonstrate how the emancipatory energies of social documentary inspire formal and technological innovation, or vice versa.

From this perspective, the book tracks a simple historical shift between two structures of feeling, from trust to suspicion. While the chapters focus on documentary production during roughly ten-year periods, this historical orientation is not meant as an exhaustive catalogue of all the work produced at a certain time. Rather, each chapter illustrates a paradigmatic position in the formation of American documentary culture. These positions do not necessarily plot a strictly historical progression, although the three parts of the book correspond to three iterations of the new as an instance of the political imaginary: the New Deal, the New Left, and what Jürgen Habermas calls the New Obscurity, one way of describing the condition of diminished expectations otherwise known as postmodernity.[81] The first part of the book, "The Sentiment of Trust: The Documentary Front and the New Deal," explores the function of documentary in a regime of patriotism in which both the state and its critics took part during the 1930s. Hegel described patriotism as a "political sentiment" and claimed that its highest expression was trust.[82] Accordingly, the modes of documentary perfected in this period emphasize a certain directness of address and pursue the ideal of diffusing social knowledge among the widest possible audience. In the periods after 1960 that are covered by the second and third parts of the book—"Lyrical Tirades: New Documentary and the New Left" and "The Public Sphere of Suspicion: Documentary in the New Obscurity"—this faith in an overarching idea, one held by both the managers of state power and their challengers, begins to fray. The chapters that compose these two parts explore documentary manifestations of a discourse of doubt and criticism, one that emerges amid historical conditions—widespread cynicism about politics; the gradual death of the welfare state; the occlusion of public channels of information by noise and spectacle—that should make documentary impossible but that end up revitalizing it.

Treating Depression-era documentary realism as one version of what Michael Denning calls the "cultural front," chapter 1 describes the function of documentary prose, poetry, photography, and film in the creation of imagined communities of Americans, in the early years of the welfare state. I explain how this national vocation provides a solution to the crisis of legitimacy experienced by liberal and left intellectuals, faced with the demand to align themselves with movements for popular sovereignty. In my readings of nonfiction works of prose and poetry by such authors as James Agee, Erskine Caldwell, Meridel Le-Seuer, and Muriel Rukeyser, I describe the transformation of literary vocation, from author to observer, among writers on the American left in the 1930s. Crossing social and generic borders, these texts collect firsthand accounts of the Depression, in the process turning authorship into a form of indirect discourse through which abstract social entities like the state or the people may metaphorically speak. Remaking the literary device of voice along audiovisual lines, these authors offer an alternative to Enlightenment conceptions of a literary public sphere of solitary readers. The chapter culminates in an examination of a collective work of filmmaking that brings together the various strands of the documentary front in the Frontier Films project *People of the Cumberland* (1938).

For the authors of the work I deal with in the first chapter, documentary methods were a way to rehabilitate the professional and social status of authorship as an occupation. Transforming writing into a mechanical or scientific form of representation on the order of photography or cartography would allow literature to express the material particularity of social distinctions like class and region and thus to better serve the unifying (and, in the period of the Popular Front, explicitly American and patriotic) cause of socialism. In the second chapter, I define a competing apparatus of totality, the epic documentary cinema of the New Deal. Although the authentic representation of immediate suffering was the starting point of this cinematic enterprise, the filmmakers' objective was to turn documentary methods to the ends of social and political fantasy, depicting a future projected by state policy and planning, from the agricultural reform called for in *The New Frontier* (1934), *The Plow That Broke the Plains* (1936), and *The River* (1937) to the rural electrification projects promoted by *Power and the Land* (1940), the highway systems and greenbelts visualized in *The City* (1939) or the welfare and health care networks that *The Fight for Life* (1940) advocates for enclaves of urban poverty and ethnicity. If documentaries were going to transform the spectator from passive consumer into citizen, the relation between spectators, the screen, and the public spheres of cinema would also have to change. This ambitious experiment in state cinema ended quickly, besieged by all manner of political adversaries, from the Hollywood studios to congressional Republicans and critics to the left of the New Deal, and displaced in studios and theaters by the onset of war. The formal complexity of these modernist works is an attempt, I suggest, to figure the resolution of these political differences.

Whatever its political orientation, classical documentary aimed to model coherent forms of identity within a unified social field. Not only in its message but in its visual and rhetorical forms, as well, documentary was a tool for teaching its audiences that others' experiences of privation could produce identification with such unities as nation, class, or popular movement. The audio-visual composition of the classic documentary text worked to sublimate the material particularity of its discrete elements and the traces of individual experience for which they stood. In chapters 3 and 4, I focus on producers and works that adopt a quite different strategy. While documentary became a fixture in American commercial television of the 1950s and 1960s, methods were being invented for representing and interpreting the ordinary plight of new classes of Americans, some of whom had not previously featured in left-liberal documentary. Where the documentary forms of the New Deal and Second World War emphasized hierarchy, planning, and abstraction, new forms of documentary began to spring up—funded and distributed, to an increasing degree, outside of the highly centralized infrastructures of the state and the mainstream communications industry—that looked and sounded uncontrolled and local. This blossoming of forms and methods in documentary is matched, however, by increasing suspicion of the concept of the public, and the public sphere, in American culture; indeed, publicness began to be constituted, I argue, by a discourse of suspicion.

In chapter 3, I show how the insecurity that was said by the American government to pervade domestic and foreign relations during the Cold War is turned against the state by liberal left and radical filmmakers in their manipulation of sound-image relations. I focus in this chapter on the work of filmmakers explicitly identified with political and cultural movements on the left, paying special attention to the use of nonsynchronous sound in the films made by the radical Newsreel collective, filmmakers aligned with Vietnam Veterans Against the War, and the independent Marxist filmmaker Emile de Antonio in support of the counterculture and revolutionary groups in the United States and in the Third World. Their aesthetic of dissonance was meant to challenge the arbitrary, secretive, and silent power of the state. In contrast to the ethic of free speech that inspired much of liberal documentary of the period, the radical aesthetics of noise were meant to challenge the ideology of independent thought and rational debate, the premises upon which producers of mainstream documentary claimed their films contributed to the international spread of democracy. Chapter 4 is devoted to one specific allegory of this counterpublic activity, the documentary investigation of American prisons. Setting such films as *Titicut Follies* (Frederick Wiseman, 1967), *Teach Our Children* (Christine Choy and Susan Robeson, 1972), and *Attica* (Cinda Firestone, 1973) in a context of popular cultural and literary accounts of prison radicalism and unrest, I show how the space of the prison became, in the discourse that these works generated, a vexed form of public sphere. Breaching the state's authority over public institutions, these films and tapes constitute, in their production and circulation, an alternative public sphere, raising questions about how and where the public takes place. And by focusing on the technical and formal problems filmmakers faced in representing the guarded, obscure interior of these institutions, I demonstrate that this aesthetic of liberation straddled a contradiction. While it brought prisoners' voices into public spaces to which they were denied legal and physical access, it also revealed the function of the prisoner for a public economy of repression in which both the state and its critics were invested.

In chapter 5, I present a short history of attempts to revitalize the democratic process with new documentary technologies, from 1960 to the present. The films, television programs, and videotapes I deal with in this chapter represent a wide variety of experiments with mobile recording and broadcast technologies: lightweight synch-sound cinematography, video Portapaks, satellites, and digital video. Each, in its own way, increases the tension between the local and global dimensions of the public sphere of American politics, in both its dominant and oppositional varieties. In the works I examine this tension is borne by the presidential body, which is observed in states of pleasure, suffering, and distraction, dispositions it shares with the viewer him- or herself.

At the heart of the chapter is a discussion of the relationship between Richard Nixon and John F. Kennedy as icons of high politics and the egocratic personality. Their intimate images set the tone, I argue, for subsequent works of film and video about presidential elections and campaigns, from the pioneering tapes made by the Top Value Television video collective at the 1972 Democratic and Republican National Conventions to recent efforts like *Feed* (Kevin Rafferty and James Ridgeway, 1992), *The War Room* (Chris Hegedus and D. A. Pennebaker, 1993), and *Journeys with George* (Alexandra Pelosi and Aaron Lubarsky, 2002). In their emphasis on the time and space that viewers share with their representatives, such films can be read as a sign of confusion about how to deal with the rise of political spectacle. On the one hand, these forms of representation are meant to humanize both the political process and the technologies that represent it to the viewer, bringing the viewer closer to the human and ordinary interactions out of which campaigns and candidates are made. On the other hand, these eyewitness depictions can be said to reify the very spectacles of charisma their users set out to critique.

From scrutiny of the political body, the concluding chapter returns to the abiding documentary issue of the body politic. Taking stock of contemporary political documentary—a genre whose recent mainstream success belies the conventional wisdom that politics and reality have become immaterial to a media-saturated American public—this chapter examines a variety of responses to the American state of crisis that defines the present experience of national subjectivity, both in the United States and abroad. Noting the interest among theorists and producers of documentary alike in problems of reference and performance, this chapter explores the relation between ethics and politics in documentary, a tension that is expressed as a dilemma of acting, in various senses of the term. This chapter maps a new documentary front, one that reaches from major media corporations to the ateliers of high art and higher education, and from bona fide documentary auteurs to amateur and student filmmakers. The concept of the front recalls the 1930s, and much of this work calls implicitly or explicitly upon the endlessly regenerative resources of documentary film history. But to the extent that the past and the new are presented as problems in these recent films, they also provide the opportunity to emphasize the critical instability of the documentary present.

PART I

The Sentiment of Trust

The Documentary Front and the New Deal

1 / NATIONAL FABRIC

Authorship, Textuality, and the Documentary Front

Established in 1935 by George Gallup, the American Institute of Public Opinion (later the Gallup Organization) was one of the means created in the 1930s for giving form to what, according to historian Warren Susman, was until then a vague abstraction to most Americans: an American culture. In fact, Susman suggests, the concept of "most Americans" would have been relatively meaningless to most Americans before the 1930s, when new intellectual, technological, and cultural forms allowed the consolidation of a felt sense of national identity.[1] Polling was one of a number of cultural technologies refined in the period to give the authority of large numbers, technology, and scientific expertise to aspects of experience that otherwise remained "in solution," as Raymond Williams says, as feelings within and about social and national life.[2] What came in the period to be called the documentary drew social and political authority from its manipulation of this tension between particularity and generalization, between the subjective and the social, between what Williams calls "practical" and "official" forms of consciousness.[3] In Susman's apt phrasing, the "whole idea of the documentary . . . ma[de] it possible to see, know, and feel the details of life, its styles in different places, to feel oneself part of some other's experience."[4] But the empirical economy in which "oneself" is both a unique entity and mere evidence of a larger social phenomenon, outside of which one's individual experience is meaningless, presents a paradox that social documentary has never been able to resolve. In a survey conducted a month after the theatrical release of Michael Moore's blockbuster documentary *Fahrenheit 9/11* (2004), the Gallup Organization predicted that a majority of American adults would see the film: in addition to the 8 percent of poll respondents who had already seen the film, 18 percent claimed they intended to see the film in the theater, and another 30 percent said they would see it when it was released on video.[5] Moore's proud claim about Gallup's *Fahrenheit 9/11* poll—that "no one could remember when a film posted those kinds of numbers"[6]—embodies this paradox.

The commercial success of Moore's muckraking first-person films, from *Roger & Me* (1989) onward, might seem something of a contradiction, especially since the remarkable popular appeal of these films, indicated by domestic box-office grosses of $6.7 million for *Roger & Me,* $21.6 million for *Bowling for Columbine* (2002), nearly $120 million for *Fahrenheit 9/11* (2004), and more than $22 million in the first month of release for *Sicko* (2007), has been leveraged by equally remarkable budgets for production and promotion. Some of Moore's detractors seize upon the apparent discrepancy between these numbers and the character he plays in his films, the earnest rube from the Michigan working class, to call into question his integrity and the authenticity of his films and his politics.[7] As evidence of Moore's duplicity, these critics point to the fact that Moore did not grow up in the General Motors company town of Flint but in a middle-class suburb nearby and that he maintains homes in New York City and a wealthy resort area of northern Michigan. Such literal readings of the character Moore creates in *Roger & Me, Bowling for Columbine,* and, to a lesser extent, *Fahrenheit 9/11* are tendentious and shortsighted. Nevertheless, they are faithful to the empirical logic of Moore's style, which holds that the value of first-person testimony is that it comes from a speaker who can be held accountable, unlike the empty institutional speech of corporations and the state, and whose accountability is manifest most strongly in the speaker's apparently naïve response to the recording apparatus. Thus, in *Michael Moore Hates America* (2004), one of several conservative films made to answer *Bowling for Columbine* and *Fahrenheit 9/11,* the director, Michael Wilson, takes Moore's pursuit of General Motors chairman Roger Smith as a model for his own attempt to conduct an interview with Moore, with the aim of forcing Moore to apologize for his unaccountably gloomy view of America. Although he fails to meet with Moore, Wilson encounters along the way Americans from different walks of life—some of whom appear in *Bowling for Columbine* and

Fahrenheit 9/11—who reflect Wilson's Horatio Alger vision of the United States as a place where adversity (losing a job or a limb) only makes the inevitable rewards of citizenship sweeter.[8] Although its shrill interviews with conservative celebrities and pundits do little to convince viewers not already opposed to Moore, by engaging Moore's subjects and methods Wilson's film raises the important question of how documentary can make credible claims to speak for a collectivity. This question is not entirely answered by Moore's facile claims that the popularity of his films is a measure of their fidelity to public opinion, and that buying a ticket is a form of political speech for those otherwise disengaged from the political process.

A more sympathetic, and far more interesting dialogue on the problems of Moore's empirical populism is opened by Morgan Spurlock's clever *Super Size Me* (2004), a film that combines the crusading anticorporatism of Moore's films with the pranksterism of conceptual art and reality television. Taking the empirical premise to extremes, Spurlock makes himself into the experimental subject of his film, which tests the proposition that too much fast food is bad for your health.[9] Restricting himself to a month-long diet of food purchased at McDonald's restaurants across the country, taking no more exercise per day than the "average" American, Spurlock quickly gains weight and eventually becomes seriously ill. But despite the film's welter of professional experts, attesting to the dangers of overconsumption and the role of corporations in promoting it, it remains unclear precisely why Spurlock undertakes and persists in his experiment. When his doctors warn him that he risks irreversible organ failure by continuing, his commitment to finishing the experiment seems merely pathological. The apparent impetus for the film is a line quoted early in the film from a legal ruling in a lawsuit against McDonald's, asserting that the claimants may have a valid case if it can be demonstrated that McDonald's encourages daily consumption of McDonald's products. But Spurlock's remark about this possibility—that "people were suing the 'Golden Arches' for selling them food that most of us know isn't good for you to begin with. Yet each day one in four Americans visits a fast food restaurant"—suggests that he is undecided about whether the corporation or its clients are at fault. The film's obsessive visual attention to grossly overweight bodies makes clear that it bears as much contempt for ordinary people as for corporate capitalism. In the end, his demonstration seems inspired as much by a terror of the statistical person Spurlock risks his health to become as by any political or ethical principle.[10] If it retains any of the oppositional sense of demonstration, it is a petulant anger directed at large numbers—the profits of multinational corporations, the masses who consume their products, and the weight of individual bodies larger than Spurlock's "own"—as well as at the professionals and activists who seem incapable of stemming this flow of statistics. Parodying both the passive "everyman" and the activist's commitment, *Super Size Me* appears to invert Moore's approach: where Moore attempts to fashion a position between particular individuals and the abstract systems that oppress them, Spurlock attempts to inhabit both sides of the opposition at once, with disastrous results.[11]

As is clear from the degree to which Moore, Spurlock, and other first-person filmmakers share themes, styles, narrative structures, and rhetorical devices with one another and with previous generations of American documentary, the place of the critical intellectual in the social fabric, relative to the common people and their antagonists, is a problem both generic and enduring. Their films are only the latest manifestation of a longstanding question in American progressive culture about how to give problems like commitment, character, and collectivity effective form. Experimenting with social recording and reporting in the 1930s, progressive writers, intellectuals, and artists treated documentary as a crucible of their cultural authority. Documentary offered a means for grounding political abstractions like state, party, movement, and nation in the apparently natural formation of the American people. At the same time, documentary practice also tested the categories by which intellectual production had been justified and valued as an individual craft: as authorship and signature, as subjectivity, as calling, as career. Pursuing "living history," progressive documentary attempted to express the sense of change that Williams calls a structure of feeling, "a social experience which is still *in process*," and not yet frozen in an established idea, position or institution.[12] Various protocols of leftist documentary work, including the hybridization of forms and media, the "proletarianization" of author or artist, and the artist's itinerant movement between classes and locations, suited this fluid sense of experience. Documentary film, the medium with which the chapter concludes, was one among many in which these themes could be explored, as well as a privileged case of this experiment, because film presented the most dramatic contradiction between fixed forms of representation and knowledge and the capacity for resubmitting those forms to popular subjectivity, opening social and political thought to the "undeniable experience of the present."[13]

THE VOCATION OF DOCUMENTARY

What William Stott later termed the "imaginative tendency" of American documentary in the 1930s began to appear, by the end of that decade, a coherent cultural practice. In works of literary and journalistic prose, poetry, photography, film, theater, radio, audio recording, painting, and dance, artists and critics began to discern the regular features of a style of representation to which the term documentary could be applied in a programmatic way.[14] Typical of these efforts was the statement produced by one of the avatars of Depression-era documentary, Dorothea Lange, for a show of photographs at the San Francisco Golden Gate Exposition in 1940. "Documentary photography records the social scene of our time," Lange wrote. "It mirrors the present and documents for the future. ... It is pre-eminently suited to build a record of change."[15] Among many cultural forms capable of registering the effects of social and technological progress on the "facades" and deep structures of human beings—from "customs" to academic disciplines—documentary, Lange asserts, "stands on its own merits and has validity by itself."[16]

But in the formulation that follows this confident announcement, Lange seems to immediately change her mind about what, if anything, constitutes the essence of the documentary:

A single photographic print may be "news," a "portrait," "art," or "documentary"—any of these, all of them, or none. Among the tools of social science—graphs, statistics, maps, and text—documentation by photograph now is assuming place. Documentary photography invites and needs participation by amateurs as well as by professionals. Only through the interested work of amateurs who choose themes and follow

them can documentation by the camera of our age and our complex
society be intimate, pervasive, and adequate.[17]

Sentence by sentence, this statement expresses some of the fundamental
ambivalence of the documentary mode. Is documentary characterized
by a material inscription—the document—or its use in a discourse? Is
it a textual practice, or an intertextual one? Lange's grappling with the
ontological question of documentary form seems to predicate an institutional crisis. No sooner can it be said that documentary is established
as a legitimate practice of social knowledge than one must worry about
its vitality, as if the incipient professionalization that marks its matu-
rity as a form of knowledge is, at the same time, a threat to its social
relevance. Lange thus reiterates a dynamic central to the conception
of documentary in the 1930s and after, a formal instability that mirrors, or allegorizes, its mobility between different levels of the social.
She suggests that to define the documentary, one must look beyond
the camera and what it produces: authenticity, the source of its social
power, comes not merely from some technical capacity but is realized
in the diffusion of documentary into a number of different, even antithetical, practices. It would thus be a mistake to see the motility of
documentary, in Lange's definition, as imprecise thinking, or even to
see it as the product of an individual consciousness. This material and
conceptual itinerancy (which, as we shall see, could even take physical form for artists who made the documentary commitment) was one
of the distinguishing features of documentary discourse. Within this
discourse, "everyman" was at once the content, audience, and idealized
author of the documentary.

   The idea of a cultural technology whose public was also its product
does not, of course, originate with the documentary mode, nor must it
be grounded in the nineteenth- and twentieth-century media of mass
mechanical reproduction associated with documentary. As historians
and theorists of print culture have argued, the eighteenth-century concept of the public sphere rested on just such a notion of printed texts as
the instrument of social mediation.[18] Print was more than a technological medium for civic discourse in the formative years of the American
republic. It was also a social metaphor, a way of imagining relationships among people and imputing to those relationships a solidity and

stability (or, by contrast, a dispersion and heterogeneity) they did not yet have—indeed, never could have—in practice.[19] What was revolutionary about constitutional discourse in the early American republic, as Michael Warner points out, was less its claim that the people were sovereign than the grounding of this claim in the performative nature of its medium: "By constituting the government," Warner remarks, "the people's text literally constitutes the people. ... The text itself becomes not only the supreme law, but the only original embodiment of the people" (102). Because print had come to signify publication, in the sense of circulation among an indefinite and unidentified social body, the very printedness of federal and state constitutions could be understood as the vehicle, if not the engine, of democracy. Within such a historical context, the writing and printing of constitutions made possible, Warner argues, the "abstract and definitionally nonempirical character of the people." The "opacity of signification," as Warner observes, became "a political fact" (103).

How, then, to make sense of the contradiction between that "fact" and the claims by, and on behalf of, American social documentary in the 1930s to achieve the same ends through an empirical and transparent representation of the ordinary lives of ordinary people? Within the state, outside it, or somewhere in between, partisans of documentary claimed it would extend the polity through a style that would overcome, in its transparency and empiricism, the alienation of the people from representation, in both the figural and political senses. Documentarists could claim to do so by combining textual and social features of literary print culture with those of the mass media, even as both were decried by cultural liberals and leftists as forces contributing to popular alienation.

The artists struggling with this contradiction were by no means unaware of its paradoxes and debated them endlessly, even in their art, where the very form of the work might be used to display contradiction. Hence the apparent confusion governing James Agee's contribution to one of the period's exemplary texts, his prose-photo collaboration with Walker Evans, *Let Us Now Praise Famous Men: Three Tenant Families* (1941). On one page, Agee might sound like Benjamin or Georg Lukács of the same period, "reflect[ing] deeply on the conditions of present-day production," as Benjamin urges in "The Author as Producer," and thus creating literary works which are "always, at the same time, on the means of production,"[20] as when Agee agonizes over

'the whole subsequent course and fate of the work: the causes for its non-publication, the details of its later acceptance elsewhere, and of its design; the problems which confronted the maker of the photographs; and those which confront me as I try to write of it: the question, Who are you who will read these words and study these photographs, and through what cause, by what chance, and for what purpose, and by what right do you qualify to, and what will you do about it; and the question, Why we make this book, and set it at large, and by what right, and for what purpose, and to what good end or none.'[21]

Only a couple of pages later, Agee appears to simply wish away the material opacity of the form:

'But to a person of my uncertainty, undertaking a task of this sort, that plane and manner are not within reach, and could only falsify what by this manner of effort may at least less hopelessly approach clarity and truth.'

'For in the immediate world, everything is to be discerned, for him who can discern it, and centrally and simply, without either dissection into science or digestion into art, but with the whole of consciousness, seeking to perceive it as a stands: so that the aspect of a street in sunlight can roar in the heart of itself as a symphony, perhaps as no symphony can: and all of consciousness is shifted from the imagined, the revisive, to the effort to perceive simply the cruel radiance of what is.

This is why the camera seems to me, next to unassisted and weaponless consciousness, the central instrument of our time.'   (11)

Because Agee here expresses textual and technical problems—his concerns about the "clarity and truth" possible in a certain voice or medium—in moral terms, it is easy to mistake his reflections for attempts at self-expression. Rather, they should be read for the signs of a structure of feeling that documentary made possible, since such expressions of anxiety and alienation were a conventional gesture of the progressive intellectual.

Documentary of the 1930s has often been described in these terms. William Stott argued that documentary "educates one's feelings";[22] Alfred Kazin's foundational study of the period in *On Native Grounds* (1942) pressed heavily on the idea that documentary was a group psychological response. Writers turned toward descriptive nonfiction in part, Kazin said, because the distinction between public and private consciousness that separated literary writing from journalism had been eroded by the Depression, "a series of shattering shocks and tremors that has pounded away mercilessly at the mind."[23] These extended works of reportage allowed the author to address not just public events but also the problem of literary subjectivity itself. Society, Kazin contended, had been "changing too rapidly and violently for literature even to command the necessary detachment for imaginative truth" or the kind of conceptual totality required by the novel form (490); as a result, many authors sought alternatives to conventional prose forms.

One alternative was the political travelogue, the account of the author's impressions of the popular mood, based on his excursions into rural and industrial areas of the country and his conversations with authentic Americans. The itinerant observer, carrying a question or problem from place to place to encounter the rich palette of differences that make up the country, is one of the most venerable figures of American documentary. Setting out among people who are socially or geographically distant from the intellectual's experience, or from whom he or she has been estranged by circumstances of class, profession, or politics, the traveler embodies difference and, through the process of narrating his or her findings, comes to mediate it. Since it submits the author of the documentary work personally and bodily to the pursuit of truth, becoming its instrument—since it requires, in other words, a kind of commitment to the process that is also a kind of self-sacrifice—this particular kind of documentary can seem not just like one kind of documentary among others but like the essential act of American documentary, one connected in a fundamental way to its institutional and national aspirations.

Sherwood Anderson's *Puzzled America* (1935) is an early and striking example of this kind of work. Anderson, who already had a considerable reputation as a literary author, declared his impatience with literature in the book's introduction. There, he announced his intention to abandon a literary position of omniscience. Anderson's declaration turns the general issue of labor and employment into a specific investigation of authorship as a profession, laying out schematically a program of self-correction for the professional author:

> The sketches, attempts at pictures of America now, here being made into a book are the result of a good deal of wandering about. I have tried to be as impersonal as I could.
>
> I am in the position of most writers nowadays. Formerly, for a good many years, I was a writer of tales. It may be that I should have remained just that, but there is a difficulty. There are, everywhere in America, these people now out of work. There are women and children hungry and others without enough clothes. Middle-aged men and women, who but a few years ago felt themselves secure, are now suddenly facing old age, thrown out of their security. They have been thrown out of their houses, off their farms. You see and talk with such people. The amazing thing to the observer is that there is so very little bitterness.
>
> People want to tell their stories, are glad to tell. I blame myself that I do not get more of these stories, do not often enough get the real feeling of the people to whom I talk. I am caught up in something in which all present-day writers are caught. Well, not all. There are some of our writers—they may be the wise ones—who keep themselves in the clear. Such a one says to himself, "What have I got to do with all this? We writers know that government has gone on for a long time. There never was such a thing as a just government."
>
> This is all very well, but there is a sort of blindness, too. I cannot take the impersonal tone. It will not do any more. Government has again grown near to life. It may be that the politicians remain a race apart but the politicians are no longer the government. It may happen that presently they will get lost.
>
> You, the reader, must imagine the writer as going about, constantly puzzled as you are.[24]

If many people want to tell their stories, Anderson observes, the author's professional qualification appears as an obstacle to the general circulation of stories; admitting this ("I blame myself") compels the author to reevaluate his vocation in social and political terms. And he discovers that "government" is constituted *in* the relations of storytelling, not in exteriority to these relations. Government can be thought of as nothing more than the subject's awareness of his or her economic and social relation to other subjects. Politics is distinguished from government, just as authorship is distinguished from the circulation of stories.

Taken as the description of a structure of feeling, the insecurities voiced by Anderson—echoed over and over in allegories of vocation by all manner of intellectuals—can be read as the argument for a particular cultural practice. From this perspective, the subjectivity of guilt-ridden authors was merely a textual puzzle whose solution was lodged in the analogy between their geographical movement and their vacillation between one form and another. Thus, the greater the degree of formal and professional inconsistency, the more authentic the work of representation.[25]

The most typical example of this tendency was perhaps the career of Erskine Caldwell in the late 1930s, which took Caldwell back and forth between one medium or mode and another, often in the same text. In Caldwell's 1935 collection of social sketches, *Some American People,* the point of view of the narrator changes from one story to the next.[26] In some, the narration is delivered in the novelistic third person or with a journalistic detachment ("The crop control plan as it is practiced in the cotton states of Mississippi, Alabama, Georgia, and elsewhere, penalizes the tenant farmer and enriches the landowner" [238]); in others, the faculty of observation is personalized ("The Billings, Montana, autocamp owner was anxious to know if we had heard the story about the banker in a small town in the North Dakota Badlands" [25]); or given to a character who is clearly not Caldwell: "I'm harvesting sixty bushels of corn to the acre this fall, and by the time I get ready to sell it looks like I'm going to make more money this year than I ever did before" (49). And in a few cases, Caldwell moves entirely into the narrative style of literary fiction, dispensing with the first person entirely.

One short piece puts this problem into a narrative frame. "A Country That Moves" is a five-page slice of life at a hamburger stand, where the main event is an exchange between Frank, the operator of the grill, and an unnamed customer. Caldwell is present in the story only as the listener to whom this story has been told, a perspective reflected in the notations "he said" and "he told":

> Twenty miles from Springfield, Illinois, Frank Hanley fries hamburgers in his roadside lunch stand and listens to what is going on in the country. He said he learns more about what is happening, from what travelers tell him, than he does by listening to the radio.
>
> He told about a man stopping in for a bite to eat a few days before and telling him that the Century of Progress Exposition in Chicago was going to run another year. (106)

The conversation between Frank and his customer concerns "the Eighteenth Century": they measure the difference between the current century and the past in terms of the movement of people and information. "'Since the country has started to move,' Frank said, 'everything has changed. Nobody settles down long enough to hold a steady job any more. Everybody gets on wheels and travels'" (107). This is, Frank says, exactly the way it was in the eighteenth century, except for the increased speed of such transit today. He knows that this is the way it was in the eighteenth century, Frank insists, because he gets his information from listening to stories and reading history, rather than from the radio. In his view, this makes the lunch counter—which stands still in the midst of the whirl of progress—a repository of common sense:

> "People zipping up to Chicago, down to New Orleans, across to Los Angeles, over to New York, everywhere in the country, day and night, rain and shine, keeps the country on the move and the tales fresh and reliable. If one man tells me a tale about something that happened in Texas, I can check up on him with the next half a dozen Texas travelers that stop for something to eat. In the Eighteenth Century tales got pretty wild because there was no way of checking up on them." (109)

Frank's final piece of evidence for his position is a story he was told by a traveler from Alabama, which concerned a government camp for transient workers. The workers petitioned Washington, according to the traveler, to be sent a preacher to keep them amused. "'The Government had been sending around tickets to moving pictures every once in a while, but these boogers said they'd rather have a revival preacher than movie tickets'" (109–10). The customer is anxious to know whether the men in the camp got the preacher they asked for. When Frank says that they did, the customer asserts that today is, after all, better than the eighteenth century. No, says Frank, it's just the same. The customer becomes indignant: "'That's what's wrong with the country now. . . . You people flood the country with tales like that, and people have got so they won't believe even their own grandmother any more'" (111). But Frank maintains that the point of the story, improbable as it sounds—transients organizing to demand religion instead of cinema—is not that society has become irrational, or even that the speed of information in a country "on the move" makes for wild distortions that pass for the truth. Rather, the point is that from the proper perspective, the perspective represented by the *collector* of stories, a connection with the past can be established that will allow the nation to move into the future with a common interest. The goal of Frank's scrutiny of stories is not to establish the priority of the present over the past but simply to establish the legitimacy of a structure or system of comparison. Essentially, Frank argues that the literary mode of representation, as a linear mode of narration, is an inefficient way to document the nation. By privileging firsthand knowledge, gained one piece at a time, the national quilt that Caldwell is himself constructing must remain a patchwork. Frank's method, on the other hand, centralizes knowledge. It rationalizes the information brought to the lunch counter by local correspondents, establishing a standard of truth and reliability.

The obvious technical model in this period for this capacity to both gather and disseminate individual voices across the territory of the nation was radio. Caldwell's description of Frank as a sort of human radio transmitter might have in mind Franklin Delano Roosevelt himself, who was described by H. G. Wells as a "ganglion for reception, expression, transmission, combination, and realization."[27] But Frank's disdain for the purely contemporary perspective offered by radio discourages this comparison, and Caldwell seems to be suggesting that the function of the lunch counter is something other than pure communication. He seems also to insinuate—in the inscrutable theme of "the Eighteenth Century" and in the double figure of the listener with which the story begins—that the particularity of individual points of view is meaningless unless they are matched by a faculty of judgment, a perspective from which they can be collected and compared. The nation is imagined here not merely as a roll call of individual voices but rather as a system of incorporating these voices into one. (The documentary medium of the sound film lent itself easily to this sort of polyvocation; an example written by Caldwell is the focus of the last part of this chapter.)

Within such an indirect discourse, the function of the author as originator of narrative, someone who gathers sensual impressions or experiences and puts them into discourse, becomes obsolete. The point of the journeys that a number of writers undertook in the early years of the Depression was twofold: to escape the middle-class location of literary authorship and to develop a true sense of what the "rest" of America was going through. It was as if the motion of these travels would, when narrated, bridge the gap between, in Antonio Gramsci's contemporaneous terms, "intellectual-cerebral elaboration" and "muscular-nervous effort": making authorship socially meaningful, in other words, by identifying it with the physical labor of travel and the migrant worker's experience of dislocation.[28]

The narrative of encounter and estrangement was crucial to the identity of the documentary intellectual, as can be gleaned from the origin story told by Dorothea Lange. Lange's anecdote concerns her memory of a trip to observe agricultural labor with Paul Schuster Taylor, a Berkeley professor of agricultural economics who was then working for the California State Emergency Relief Administration as the field director of the Division of Rural Rehabilitation. Lange had only recently begun to work in social documentary, having established a career in San Francisco as a portrait photographer. Taylor had used some of Lange's earliest efforts at documentary photography, images of the 1934 San Francisco general strike, to illustrate an article in *Survey Graphic* and had arranged for Lange to join his team of investigators.[29] The event began Lange's long relationship with state institutions, one of the most productive public careers in American documentary.[30]

I remember . . . the first day we were out in a car—we'd stopped at a gas station—Paul asked the fellow who put the gas in the car some question about the country around—as we drove off Tom said, "He was a good informant." . . . I thought, "What language! What kind of people are these? 'He was a good informant.'" That really surprised me. I knew then that I was with people who were in a different world than mine.[31]

Because of their use of a technical language to refer to the gas station employee, it is the observers who appear to Lange to be different from herself, and not the employee, whose unreconstructed difference is presumably what Lange and Taylor have come to his "country" to study. Lange's description of the encounter shows how the identity of the documentarist depends upon not only upon difference—the difference between the documentary subject and its audience, or between the subject and the observer—but on an economy of differences: Lange is in a "different world" not only from the gas station employee, the native, but also from the official observers. She occupies a mediating position between science (technology, the professions, the objectivity of the state) and "life." At the same time that she and her camera are present to support the academic and governmental intervention into life, Lange establishes a critical edge between the institutions of social knowledge and their object, signified by the unspoken question "What kind of people are these?" Lange's trip out into the rural working classes, one kind of displacement, occasions another: in her question lies a challenge to the same professional power she wields with her camera. Behind her question is, of course, the image of another "people," the common people, folk, or nation from whom social science and politics draw their authority.[32]

Lange's double-edged question hints at a problem that preoccupied authors and artists on the American left throughout the 1930s, the problem of perspective. Gaining currency in the early part of the decade in the pages of Communist Party organs like *New Masses* and *Partisan Review,* the concept of perspective was derived from Lenin's *What Is to Be Done?* (1909), a text familiar to many leftist intellectuals of the period.[33] In *What Is to Be Done?,* Lenin explained how a truly political consciousness depended on members of a particular class being able to see outside of its own limited sphere of activity. Class-consciousness did not, in other words, come only in the sphere of production and economic existence. "The consciousness of the working masses," he wrote, "cannot be genuine class-consciousness, unless the workers learn, from concrete, and above all topical, political facts and events to observe *every* other social class in *all* the manifestations of its intellectual, ethical, and political life."[34] As was emphasized in Marxist debates on both sides of the Atlantic about the social-realist technique of reportage,[35] such a perspective did not simply mean that the experience of the working class would be represented where it had previously been excluded from representation. Rather, the proletarian consciousness described by Lenin was an abstraction, a theoretical position "from which alone it is possible to obtain this knowledge of the sphere of relationships of *all* classes and strata to the state and the government, the sphere of interrelationships between *all* classes."[36] Whatever proletarian literature was—and the American cultural left debated this question endlessly in the early part of the decade—it would not simply assert the moral or empirical distinctness of working-class experience. But nor would it permit refuge in purely academic objectivity. "Objective writing," Meridel Le Sueur argued in *New Masses* in 1935, "can never provide will or purpose and is related to the liberal formal idea of neutrality and disinterestedness."[37] "You cannot," Le Sueur challenged, "be both on the barricades and objective or removed at the same time" (200). Given their grounding in bourgeois institutions by birth, professional training, and financing, artists who became interested in documentary were placed in a difficult position by this ideology.

As is made clear by Lange's quizzical response to the scene of social inquiry, documentary opened a position of immanent criticism within those systems of representation operated by the state, the left, and the sciences. Michael Denning has suggested that the most important function of documentary for the American left in the 1930s was in providing an alternative to progressivist or teleological social explanation; or, as Denning puts it, as "a sign of the failures of narrative imagination."[38] While it conceives of both narrative and documentary too narrowly, this formulation helps us understand the theme of the itinerant intellectual in 1930s documentary work. The journeys that documentarists seemed to be required to take *in search of* something (true or real) were also journeys *away from* something (false). If these accounts of estrangement, alienation, or displacement could be read as tropes of the failure that Denning regards as central to the Depression-era left, they were also tremendously successful at giving form to its imagination.

Indeed, the success of this antinarrative can be seen, by inversion, in another account of gas-station sociology, a story told by Erskine Caldwell in *Say, Is This the U.S.A.,* his 1941 collaboration with Margaret Bourke-White. The book depicts, in prose and photographs, a nation entering the war recovery that would lift it out of economic and social depression, and this vignette, which Caldwell calls "The Filling Station Circuit," announces the obsolescence of an earlier style of social explanation:

There was a time not so long past when it was the practice of many well-intentioned writers to make periodic tours of the country's gas stations for the purpose of feeling the American pulse. Assuming that it would be unnatural for it to be normal, they tore over mountains and prairies day and night, stopping spasmodically to inquire of filling-station attendants the current state of the nation. The answers they received, which were duly recorded in their notebooks, were to them statistically, sociologically, and esthetically satisfying. In hard times, the country was going to the dogs; in lush times, it was O.K., America!

I know what the answers were, because I have taken a modest number of such junkets. Probably I would have continued touring the filling-station circuit if it had not been for an incident that occurred in Missouri.

We stopped at a filling station and I asked the attendant if he believed that the patriotism, granting its existence, of the American people would arise to the occasion if a foreign aggressor should threaten the peace of the U.S.A. In other words, if an Asiatic or European dictator came over here and attempted to set up another form of government, I asked, would Americans stand up and fight it out, or would they welcome such a change with open arms.

With a business-like gesture the attendant handed me a neatly printed card. It read as follows:

"I am 36 years old. I smoke about a pack of cigarettes a day, sometimes more and sometimes less, but it evens up. I take an occasional drink of beer. I am a Baptist, an Elk, and a Rotarian. I live with my own wife, send my children to school, and visit my in-laws once a year on Christmas Day. I wear No. 9 1/2 shoes, No. 15 1/2 collar, and No. 7 1/4 hat. I shoot a 12-gauge shotgun and have a 27-inch crotch. I like rice, sweet potatoes, and pork sausage. I vote for F.D.R., pull for Joe Louis, and boo Diz Dean. I wouldn't have anything against Hitler if he stayed in his own backyard. I don't know any Japs, but I've made up my mind to argue with the next one I see about leaving the Chinese alone. I'm in favor of the AAA, the CCC, the IOU, and the USA. If I have left anything out, it's an oversight. My business is selling gasoline and oil. If you want your tank filled, just nod your head. If you don't want anything, please move along and give the next fellow a chance. I thank you. Hurry back."

We were getting ready to leave when the attendant came back to the car and, pushing his head and shoulders through the window, leaned towards us.

"Say," he began, "I hope you folks don't think I was rude just now when I gave you that card. I figured I had to get up something like that to hand out, because I was being Q'd and A'd to death by people stopping and asking all sorts of fool things and not buying gas, either."

We shook our heads sheepishly.

"Anyway," he said, "you folks ought to know the answers to all those questions you go around the country asking, especially the one you asked me a while ago, the one about defending the country."

"Why?" we asked.

"Hell!" he said. "This ain't one of those foreign countries! This is America, ain't it?"[39]

The encounter might seem fanciful; Caldwell and Bourke-White had, after all, fabricated typical speech by the subjects of *You Have Seen Their Faces* (1937), their earlier collaboration on poverty in the cotton belt, and had admitted this on the first page of *Faces*. But this implausible encounter touches on a number of ethical and aesthetic preoccupations of the documentary movement of the 1930s that it memorializes. By the end of the decade, documentary had become so thoroughly identified with the narratives and imaginings of the national popular, it seemed, that there could no longer be any distance between the observer and the object. The works examined in the rest of this chapter demonstrate the power of documentary as a social and aesthetic technique for mapping and bridging such distances, before a change in the political climate required their complete elision.

NATIONAL FORMS

In the period of the American left known as the Popular Front—usually dated from the call at the Seventh Congress of the Communist International in 1935 for a united democratic effort against fascism, to the Hitler-Stalin pact of 1939—the focus of left sympathies shifted from the proletariat to the people, from an antagonistic, anticapitalist figure of class to a softer, more general conception that made class and nation roughly synonymous. One can read the effects of this shift in the opening lines of Muriel Rukeyser's epic 1937 documentary poem, "The Book of the Dead," her modernist verse rendering of congressional hearings on an industrial disaster in the rural South, an epidemic of silicosis-related deaths produced in a Union Carbide mining operation and covered up by doctors and scientists employed by the company.

> These are the roads to take when you think of your country
> and interested bring down the maps again,
> phoning the statistician, asking the dear friend,
>
> reading the papers with morning inquiry.
> Or when you sit at the wheel and your small light
> chooses gas gauge and clock; and the headlights
>
> indicate future of road, your wish pursuing
> past the junction, the fork, the suburban station,
> well-travelled six-lane highway planned for safety.
>
> Past your tall central city's influence,
> outside its body: traffic, penumbral crowds,
> are centers removed and strong, fighting for good reason.
>
> These roads will take you into your own country.[40]

The poem begins by considering the variety of abstractions and symbolic forms in which a country can be depicted and suggests that these forms—maps, statistics, plans, wishes—themselves generate an endless series of variations of their object, as many countries are there are readers ("you") to respond to the invitation the poem offers. In the teasing self-reference of the poem's first words, we are enjoined to think of the poem as an interpretive tool, even offering the key to its own interpretation: these lines might serve as the roads down which one has to go to understand how local and personal experience become the matter of a country, or vice versa.[41] The sentimental territory thus constructed ("your own country") retraces the national along the lines of the popular. Describing the act of reading as both a centralizing activity, placing you in the position of the planner, and a decentralizing one, prompting you to leave home, the poem poses from the outset the questions of how textual operations—writing, publishing, reading—are related to this national reconstruction, and of how the creative textuality of the poem might be related to the work done by the other kinds of documents named here and throughout the poem.

The poem thus functions not only as a memorial to the working-class victims and the political process that took up (or impeded) their cause but also as an argument for the political efficacy of documentary. Although "The Book of the Dead" is today regarded as one of the landmark achievements of late-1930s documentary modernism, its style provoked sharp disagreements about the poem's success and value, debates that were made more complicated by the fractious politics of the cultural left at the end of the decade.[42] Walter Benjamin's approving description, from a few years earlier, of Brecht's method as "the use of reality in experimental rearrangements"[43] could equally be applied to Rukeyser's poem, which incorporates a variety of evidentiary forms, including stock reports, interviews, journalism, testimony, and legislative speech taken more or less directly from the public record. By drawing characters and methods from a wide variety of classes, professions, regions, and political positions, the poem synthesizes the progressive strategy of documentary during the Popular Front. These discussions concerned the literal and figurative place of the bourgeois intellectual, relative to the people and the nation, sometimes referred to as the problem of "perspective," and they were decisive for the development of documentary, in the period and after.

By the end of the 1930s, documentary named not only a form but a position. There were enough political variations of this position that to refer to it as a movement would be an oversimplification. Nonetheless, the poem is consistent with what we might call the documentary tendency of the 1930s, insofar as it argues that no image of the world was a neutral one. The figure of the photographer who appears throughout Rukeyser's poem to thread together its views was, unlike the cameraman in *Man with a Movie Camera,* Dziga Vertov's 1929 film, a foil for the poem's politics: "viewing on groundglass an inverted image" (10), this character experienced technological vision as objective truth, an ideological error that the poem, with its panorama of voices and perspectives, seeks to correct. This argument was carried by blunt rebuke ("What do you want—a cliff over a city? / A foreland, sloped to sea and overgrown with roses? / These people live here." [14]), as well as by the kind of dialectical juxtaposition that went, in the period, by the name montage, a term embraced internationally, from theorists such as Vertov and Benjamin to the New York Film and Photo Leaguers with whom Rukeyser associated. On one page, Rukeyser presents the New River valley as an "audacious landscape. The gangster's / stance with his gun smoking and out is not so / vicious as this commercial field, its hill of glass" (28). On the next, it was a source not of profit but of desire:

The quick sun brings, exciting mountains warm,
gay on the landscapers and green designs,
miracle, yielding the sex up under all the skin,
until the entire body watches the scene with love.   (29)

Such contrasts were meant to unearth the contradictions covered by the land, a term that, as we see in this chapter and the next, was crucial to the national politics of documentary in the period. Signifying both people and place, the land becomes the source of an "authentic power" (37) that will call representation to account:

The subcommittee subcommits.
Words on a monument.

Capitoline thunder. It cannot be enough.
The origin of storms is not in clouds,
our lightning strikes when the earth rises,
spillways free authentic power:
dead John Brown's body walking from a tunnel
to break the armored and concluded mind.   (37)

The poem bears an explicit critique of intellectual labor, and those intellectual forms—science, medicine, journalism, law, economics, art—that objectify the material world.[44] This critique was energized by the reflexive question of what kind of work was documentary itself: mechanical labor, art, craft, or career? This question was an allegory for the problem of the American cultural left more broadly, a concept riven by its partisans' multiple identifications and commitments. If the aesthetics and politics of this vexed position, "the left," were shaped by the critique of bourgeois realism undertaken by European cultural Marxists of the period, such as Lukács and Benjamin, documentary was also a specifically American problematic, part of a broad-based progressive attempt to redefine democracy and other "institutional patterns" in terms of popular experience. Part of what Warren Susman argued was a general reinvention of the very concept of American culture in the period, requiring the work of many disciplines, this interest in the folk and their ways was hardly a spontaneous alignment of committed intellectuals and the common people.[45] Rather, it was one of what we might call the professional fictions of the American left, one it shared with other institutions of social knowledge in the period.

LOW-BROW HISTORY

In his 1931 Presidential Address to the American Historical Association, Carl Becker presented a discovery so dramatic that it made the pages of the *New York Times,* despite the fact that, as a piece of historical knowledge, it was utterly banal. "If the essence of history is the memory of things said and done," Becker announced, "then it is obvious that every normal person, Mr. Everyman, knows some history."[46] This "invidious truth," as Becker called it, delivered at the outset of the Depression, might have struck some in his audience as a cruel joke, since it threatened to put the academic historian out of work: Becker suggested that "a professional manner" and a few institutional procedures were all that separated the historian from the ordinary man who labored to remember, on the basis of a document he recovers from his "little Private Record Office (I mean his vest pocket)," whether or not he had paid his coal bill.

But unlike the past of objective history, the traditional purview of academic historians, the "living history" Becker described was a stream of associations, mental and social, that flowed from such artifacts.

> Instantaneously a series of historical events comes to life in Mr. Everyman's mind. He has an image of himself ordering twenty tons of coal from Smith last summer, of Smith's wagons driving up to his house, and of the precious coal sliding dustily through the cellar window. . . .
>
> The picture Mr. Everyman forms of Smith's wagons delivering the coal at his house is a picture of things said and done in the past. But it does not stand alone, it is not a pure antiquarian image to be enjoyed for its own sake; on the contrary, it is associated with a picture of things to be said and done in the future. . . . At four o'clock Mr. Everyman is accordingly at Smith's office. "I wish to pay that coal bill", he says. Smith looks dubious and disappointed, takes down a ledger (or a filing case), does a bit of original research in his Private Record Office, and announces: "You don't owe me any money, Mr. Everyman. You ordered the coal here, all right, but I didn't have the kind you wanted, and so turned the order over to Brown. It was Brown delivered your coal: he's the man you owe." Whereupon Mr. Everyman goes to Brown's office; and Brown takes down a ledger, does a bit of original research in his Private Record Office, which happily confirms the researches of Smith.[47]

When Mr. Everyman discovers that both his memory and his documents led him astray, he reaches important insights about the materials and methods of history: the documentary record can be imprecise, and the archive is often incomplete.

This sense of the document as plastic—artificial and malleable—was an affront to the "noble dream" of an impersonal, scientific history, one made up of "heavy tomes full of actual, self-expressing facts."[48]

The process of historical reconstruction that Mr. Everyman is drawn into by the lapses in his memory and his archive differ from the protocols of the professional historian, as Becker's audience would have understood them, by its subjective, collective, and effective character. With it, Mr. Everyman can "live in a world of semblance more spacious and satisfying than is to be found within the narrow confines of the fleeting present moment."[49] In a gesture of humility designed to save the profession from social irrelevance, Becker argued that with this expanded conception of experience, the American historian placed himself on the same plane as ordinary life: "we do not impose our version of the human story on Mr. Everyman," Becker demurred; "in the end it is rather Mr. Everyman who imposes his vision on us" (235)—a position the *New York Times,* in its approving account of Becker's address, called a "low-brow" approach to history.[50]

The "Ithaca Everyman"—a reference to Cornell University, Becker's home institution—was, according to the *Times,* "more gifted [and] more utilitarian" than other, no less ordinary, Americans, in his ability to see how his history might be applied to the problems of life in the present. An echo of Nietzsche's "effective" history, Everyman's "living history" opposed itself to the "useless history" practiced by academic historians.[51] If his sense of the present should occasionally become confused by the "elfish" memories of a freckled former sweetheart, this would merely serve to remind us that history is grounded in the vicissitudes of subjectivity and experience, "as his physical, intellectual, and moral status, his environment and so on, dictate." The *Times* concluded, with a remarkable openness to the politics of history, that such contingency was only correct: "Each age must have its history suited to its form and pressure." At the outset of a decade in which all aspects of social and political life would be shaped by the "form and pressure" of the problems of classes and masses, the *Times's* excited response to Becker's speech can be seen as the birth announcement of a new form of culture.

Although the term "documentary" was in use by American radical filmmakers as early as 1930—an effect of their exposure to the work of, among others, John Grierson and Dziga Vertov[52]—it would take most of the decade for a cadre of specialists and promoters to make low-brow history into the national-popular form that the AHA and the *Times* had

called for at the decade's opening. Doing so would require an unprecedented collaboration between radical and experimental artists, liberals working in both policy and publicity capacities in state institutions,
and the owners and operators of the communications industry. This
conjoint effort to create an official mass culture from competing aesthetic and political tendencies locates documentary on what Michael
Denning has called the "cultural front" of the 1930s, and it accounts
in part for the remarkable range of documentary forms and politics in
the period.

Denning revives this term, which was used by the cultural left in the
period (and, later, against it), in order to contest the conventional view
that Depression culture was dominated by a documentary aesthetic,
where documentary is taken to be synonymous with social realism.[53]
He argues that the concept of documentary "fails to capture the complexity of the aesthetic ideologies of the cultural front" (119) because of
its legacy in American literary and cultural studies, where the concept
stood for realism, authenticity, and common sense, embodied in the
presentational aesthetic of photographers like Bourke-White, Lange,
and Evans. In its direct address to the middle-class reader, the title of
Bourke-White's photo-textual collaboration with Erskine Caldwell, *You
Have Seen Their Faces* (1937), embodied this aesthetic and the welfare-
state politics that underwrote it. By maintaining that the 1930s were a
laboratory for a variety of aesthetic projects, Denning means to resist
what he calls the "documentary synthesis" of William Stott's formative
1973 account in *Documentary Expression and Thirties America*. Instead,
Denning tells the story of the decade's art and politics in such a way
that a different kind of collectivity is possible, beyond the simpli-
fied notion of democracy, prevalent in many studies of documentary,
which equates it with representational transparency and technological
diffusion.[54]

Within the frame of the cultural front, documentary becomes a
mere symptom of social crisis, "a sign of the failures of narrative imagination" which characterize Depression culture (Denning, *The Cultural
Front*, 119). Denning does not remark on the contradiction between
these two views of documentary, the one in which it serves as a com-
pensatory reaction to crisis, and the one that includes documentary
in the creative and improvisational "aesthetic ideology" of the period,

where it stands for the persistence of modernist avant-gardism into the practice of social realism and the emergence of what the influential leftist critic Harry Alan Potamkin called "an authentic American cinema."[55] But the contradiction may help us think of documentary as a supplement to the cultural front, less a special case of the cultural front than its immanent theory, a mode of expression in which radicals and progressive intellectuals grappled with the problem of how cultural form and social action could be related. Because documentary always begs, if it does not pose, the question of how representation can have agency, its prominence in the cultural formation recounted by Denning means that we should wonder what, exactly, it means to claim that the cultural front "organiz[ed] and mobiliz[ed] audiences" (Denning, *The Cultural Front,* 64).

If documentary could serve to organize audiences, it was just as likely to do so in a hegemonic capacity, announcing crises and managing them on behalf of the state.[56] From this perspective documentary was, in context of the 1930s, an instrument of hegemony. As John Tagg argues, its "claims to retrieve the status of Truth in discourse, a status threatened by crisis," could be understood as part of a larger strategy of state control, wherein "social relations of meaning were to be sustained and national and social identities resecured" (9). Within this regime of representation, the function of the state-produced documentary images Tagg examines is to make social division—the implicit or explicit topic of nearly all New Deal documentary—seem at best interesting and at worst inevitable. It is above all in the movement of photography, from the locations of its referent to the institutions in which photographs are commissioned, produced, displayed, analyzed, consumed, and preserved, that ideological effects are achieved. Taken together, these two operations, reference and circulation, establish what Tagg calls the currency of the documentary image. In the 1930s, the state effectively monopolized this circuit, Tagg argues, and through it, the visual representation of the real. Within this regime, documentary as such functioned as an ideological state apparatus, extending the reach of the state into civil society by means of social and cultural operations.

Clearly, the sense of movement in Tagg's notion of currency, a centralized and transparent means of communicating messages, is quite different from that implied by Denning's idea of a front along which ideas were exchanged among like-minded artists and intellectuals. Yet documentary could support both, a duplicity that was an important aspect of its ideological function in the period, and one that allowed artists to cross with the same techniques among bourgeois culture, the radical left and the liberal state.

PROLETARIANIZATION

"I got to hate the word documentary (though I never devised a better),"
wrote Leo Hurwitz, one of the first American documentary filmmakers
to identify his work with this term, in a retrospective account of leftist
filmmaking in the 1930s.[57] Given that Hurwitz was a founding member
of the revolutionary Workers Film and Photo League, an organization
that did much to establish the aesthetic and organizational mandate
of progressive social documentary cinema in the United States during
its brief existence (ca. 1930 through 1937; it survived until 1951 as the
breakaway Photo League), his ambivalence is a striking indication of
the mixed feelings, forms, and fortunes of documentary in its formative
period, even among its most passionate adherents. Among the many
contending models for social documentary form and practice in the
1930s, which included the narrative ethnography pioneered by Robert
Flaherty, the commercial newsreel, and the public-service propaganda
film that grew out of John Grierson's encounter with Walter Lippmann
and American social science, the radical strain of documentary represented by the Film and Photo League produced the most volatile
mixture of modes, personalities, and motives. Its contradictions were
inherent in its attempt to domesticate the Marxist and modernist inter-
nationals of the 1910s and 1920s.

The Soviet concept of "montage," taken up simultaneously by avant-
garde artists and theorists in Western Europe and the United States,
was a primary inspiration for the Film and Photo League.[58] Its members
were, Hurwitz recalls,

> stimulated by the Russians. I was fascinated by the mosaic character of
> film, by the capacity of documentary film to extract fragments out of
> the matrix of a visual-sound reality, then to weave these fragments into

a form very different from the reality but capable of rending the meaning and feeling of the real event. From this point of view, the documentary film was anything but a document. It did not "document" reality
at all. Its tiny documents in the form of shots and sounds bore the same
relation to the film as the small pieces of colored stone and glass to the
mosaic mural, the brush-strokes to the painting, the individual words
and phrases to the novel. The stuff was document, but the construction
was invented, a time-collage. And it was clear that the question of *truth or
lie* lay not in the stuff you were using but in the thoughts, responsibility,
empathy of the film maker and his capacity to shape a form which could
tell . . . how much of the truth? This responsibility and empathy were
not different from the truth or lie of the fiction film or any other art.[59]

As Hurwitz's phrasing suggests, the conflicts to which documentary as
an aesthetic and social ideal gave rise were in fact dynamic aspects of
the form for its partisans on the left and shaped, as we shall see, its development both *within* and *across* institutions of politics and ideology.
To Hurwitz and his cohort, documentary was a dialectical conception
whose essence was extrinsic: it could only be expressed in terms of the
movement between one form, medium, or social location and another.

Among radicals, documentary was seen as a means of combating
popular alienation from the social and political institutions of American life and of giving the leftist intellectual, through acts of "responsibility and empathy," renewed popular relevance. One typical catalyst of
this process was an act of self-alienation on the part of its makers, who
took leave of their native forms, places, and class positions. Bringing the
cultural intellectual in contact, or conflict, with unfamiliar categories of
craft, occupation, and class was meant to disrupt the traditional relation
of concern between the socially conscious artist and the proletariat.

It was precisely this sort of crisis that Walter Benjamin wished to
institute in his concept of "the author as producer," in his 1934 essay
of the same name. Benjamin's critique of a "new objectivity" in social
realism argued that this style merely described poverty and thus reinforced class structure as a given in modern life. By taking poverty and
the everyday settings of industrial life as its object, this movement not
only objectified class structures, but also posited the transparency of
documentary media, thereby separating art from the historical condi-

tions that made it possible. It was "only by transcending the specialization in the process of production that, in the bourgeois view, constitutes its order," Benjamin wrote, that one could "make this production politically useful" ("The Author as Producer," 230). A symptom of this order was the distinction between the work of the photographer and the work of the writer, a specialization that reinforced and reified a purely aesthetic conception of intellectual labor. "What we require of the photographer," Benjamin demanded,

> is the ability to give his pictures the caption that wrenches it from modish commerce and gives it a revolutionary useful value. But we shall make this demand most emphatically when we—the writers—take up photography. Here, too, therefore, technical progress is for the author as producer the foundation of his political progress. (230)

The recasting of traditional literary structures in the modern mechanical forms of reproduction would, Benjamin argued, make it possible for the leftist author to recognize his place in the sphere of production and, by extension, within the class struggle, rather than outside it, looking on.

These oft-quoted passages fail to make clear, however, just how the combination of image and word would overthrow cultural specialization and the bourgeois conceptions of connoisseurship and professionalism that support it. By the end of the essay, in fact, Benjamin admits that "the proletarianization of an intellectual hardly ever makes him a proletarian," and he is resigned to describing the relation between the committed author and the proletariat as, at best, a "mediated one" (237). In this case, the concept of the specialist can serve as Trojan Horse: the intellectual is most effective when he can betray his class origins, a process he begins by merely observing the material character of his work. Benjamin concludes his address with a series of rhetorical questions, meant to define this cultural praxis: "Does he succeed in promoting the socialization of the intellectual means of production? Does he see how he himself can organize the intellectual workers in the production process? Does he have proposals for the *Umfunktionierung* [functional transformation] of the novel, the drama, the poem?" (238). In his emphasis on the material aspects of cultural work that make it and its products comparable to any social process of production, he outlines a paradoxical strategy for being *against* capitalism, in the double sense of the term: adjacent to it while opposing it.

Many writers on the American left experienced a crisis of vocation in similar terms. Or, rather, it might be more correct to say that at certain moments "the left" seemed to be constituted by such a crisis.[60] The April 1935 American Writers' Congress, for instance, one of the iconic events of leftist culture in the period, was roiled by the questions of where the radical writer should stand, vis-à-vis the proletariat, and what form was best suited to advance the cause of working-class revolution. The published proceedings reproduce the address to the Writers' Congress by John Dos Passos called "The Writer as Technician," in which Dos Passos argued that the professional writer was distinguished from "anybody who can put the words down on paper" by his "discovery, originality, invention" of language.[61] "The professional writer," Dos Passos claimed, "discovers some aspect of the world and invents out of the speech of his time some particularly apt and original way of putting it down on paper" (79). In doing so, he both reflected and inflected the "mind of the group," a social obligation no different from that of the scientist or engineer. Placed immediately after Dos Passos, Jack Conroy's presentation, "The Worker as Writer," argued roughly the same thing in precisely the opposite terms. Conroy lamented that "a semi-private terminology almost unintelligible to the masses" had been the result of a "desperate striving for novelty of phrase and imagery" (83). To achieve an effective literary mechanism for galvanizing revolutionary sentiment, Conroy recommended that writers employ as subject matter "those aspects of American life important to the masses," and "communicate this material as simply and clearly as we are able to the largest body of readers we can command" (83). The difference in language obscured the degree to which the two authors were aiming at the same thing, the same proletarianization of the writer theorized by Benjamin.

The opposition between these two incompatible expressions marks a crucial moment in the formation of the 1930s left. Though Conroy's uncompromising language of popular experience and taste suits a certain stereotype of the left, the rhetoric of the worker-hero that American communists borrowed from Soviet culture in the late 1920s and early 1930s, Dos Passos better captures the ethos of the cultural front with his nuanced conception of a duplicitous professionalism. As Denning explains in his compendious history of this long-lived and highly flexible cultural formation, the concept of the "front" had several meanings. It was used both affirmatively by its partisans, to describe allegiances across political and social lines, and pejoratively by its critics, who meant it in the sense of a deception, when they accused all manner of liberal and left individuals and organizations of masking their communist or Soviet ties.[62] In fact, the value of the front as a metaphor for describing leftist cultural activity was precisely its imaginative character, for this allowed it to accurately describe sites of contradiction within the left. As a concept that prefigured the official communist strategy of the Popular Front, announced in 1935, the flexible notions of "culture" on this front helped make possible the national strategy of the communist left during the Popular Front phase. This was the point made at the Congress by Minnesotan author Meridel Le Sueur, who told the American Writers' Congress that class conflict could also be thought of in regional terms. The Middle West had "*always* been depressed," Le Sueur claimed, and thus knew best how to exploit the "rich and powerful chaos" of the times (135, 137). "Revolution can spring up from the windy prairie as naturally as the wheat" (138), promised Le Sueur, anticipating later generations of Midwestern militants. The Midwestern middle and working classes had been joined as "dissenters, individual madmen, anarchists against the machine." Now, said Le Sueur, a Midwestern intelligence was maturing,

> finding a place, sending a new and vigorous interrelation between himself and others, which at least will give him the free association from the factual bourgeois and decaying reality to the true subjective image of the communal artist, which is already real in Russia: not the spurious subjectivity of the bourgeois artist of personal defeat, subterfuge and apology, but the subjectivity of the communal root image of a rising class that has no reason for entrenchment and subterfuge, and links him further and deeper to all. (138)

In a 1935 essay published in the pages of the American communist journal *New Masses*, Le Sueur issued a wrenching challenge to middle-class intellectuals like herself, titled "The Fetish of Being Outside."[63]

Le Sueur described the situation of the committed writer in terms somewhat more anxious and tentative tone than those of the Writers' Congress addresses:

> I do not care for the bourgeois "individual" that I am. I never have cared for it. I want to be integrated in a new and different way as an individual and this I feel can come only from a communal participation which reverses the feeling of a bourgeois writer. What will happen to him will not be special and precious, but will be the communal happening, what happens at all. (202)

In this plaintive appeal, Le Sueur assumes, as did many left intellectuals during the Depression, the self-evidence of a difference between popular feeling and intellectual knowledge.[64] If the intellectual has an abstract kind of knowledge, the people have real experience, marked with particularity. The encounter with the common people and their feelings these writers called for was intended to dislodge the literary intellectual from his or her traditional location and vocation. Embedded in this expression of a desire to experience "what happens at all" is the vision of a new function for the American public intellectual, a movement from one kind of social function to another, from the traditional function of manufacturing consent for the policies of the class in power to the enunciative service of the dominated class, helping it to express itself to itself. If there was a typical gesture of front intellectuals, it was the kind of betrayal Benjamin recommended, calling it the service of mediation. It was the same ethic that Dos Passos named in his conception of radical professionalism, and it was present in the anxious character of Le Sueur's self-reflection. But the front extended, as Denning notes, well beyond the official institutions of the communist left, and one finds similar impulses in other sites where attempts were made to decentralize and democratize the professional production of social knowledge. It was in cinema that this strategy of proletarianization could be most fully tested because film offered the means for the most thorough and diverse fabrication of a social text. The last section of this chapter takes up one such production, the Frontier Films group film about the Highlander Folk School in Mount Eagle, Tennessee, *People of the Cumberland* (1938).

PEOPLE OF THE CUMBERLAND AND THE NATIONAL FABRIC

Incorporated as a nonprofit production company in March of 1937, Frontier Films continued the work of Nykino (as in New York *kino*, after Vertov's *kinoks*), the group of filmmakers who broke away from the New York City branch of the Workers Film and Photo League in 1934, including Leo Hurwitz, Irving Lerner, and Ralph Steiner. Nykino intended to experiment with narrative structures and dramatic techniques borrowed from theater and fiction film, while maintaining the left-documentary commitment to the critique of capitalism and the true depiction of class-based reality. Its interest in dramatic reconstruction had been inspired by the methods of the Soviet filmmakers, as well as by the March of Time newsreel and the experiments in psychological realism of the Group Theatre, where Nykino members attended classes. In addition to hosting various lectures and workshops on writing, acting, film and photography, sometimes in collaboration with the Group Theatre or the leftist theater journal *New Theatre*, Nykino edited and released a number of films begun before its formation by group members, and the group planned an ambitious schedule of original productions. But Nykino had trouble finishing films and completed very few of the projects it originated. These included an installment of *The World Today*, intended as a leftist answer to the March of Time; *Sunnyside* (1937), a documentary about a strike by owners of low-cost houses in Queens against exorbitant mortgage fees; and *Black Legion* (1937), a docudrama about the Michigan hate group that had terrorized ethnic and religious minorities and union members.[65] With a new administrative structure, an infusion of new collaborators, a high-profile advisory board, and, most important, backing from liberal philanthropists, artists and arts patrons, and social and labor organizations, Frontier Films was meant to solve some of the organizational and financial problems that Nykino faced and to allow group members to devote more time to making films.[66] The group began by completing two documentaries based on footage previously shot or acquired by group members: *Heart of Spain* (1937), a film about Republican blood clinics in the Spanish Civil War; and *China Strikes Back* (1937), about Chinese communist resistance to the Japanese invasion. At the same time, production began on *People of the Cumberland*, a commission that had been arranged by

Ethel Clyde, the steamship heiress, patron of progressive causes, major Frontier donor, and supporter of the Highlander school.

The question of how specialized intellectual labor could refashion itself and the class system that it supported was central to *People of the Cumberland,* and it was worked into the texture of the film itself, starting with the presence of Erskine Caldwell, who wrote the film's narration. Caldwell had been associated with radical documentary since the early days of the Film and Photo League, when he had served on the League's National Advisory Board.[67] Caldwell's credited role as the author of the commentary for *People of the Cumberland* was later questioned by other members of the group, but this should hardly be seen as a serious challenge to the film's capacity for truth.[68] The credits already pose a kind of puzzle, a result of Frontier's collectivist character and of red-baiting: some of the names listed are pseudonyms, and there is some disagreement about what the attribution of directorial responsibility, to "Robert Stebbins" and "Eugene Hill," means.[69] More to the point, the film is keenly aware of the problems of aesthetic and social mediation, a concern that is underscored by the person and content of the narrator's speech, as well as by the sound-image structure into which the narration is set. Fabricating authentic speech and employing multiple voices were, of course, techniques Caldwell had used in earlier nonfiction work. But the consistency of Caldwell's signature is of less importance than the continuity of these techniques with the collective nature of documentary film as a formal and political practice that Frontier was attempting to establish. *People of the Cumberland* marked the group's definitive turn toward a mixed mode of documentary film that would be their undoing, culminating in the ill-starred *Native Land* (also begun in 1937, and not released until 1942).[70]

An exemplary work of the cultural front, the film was one of many in the period to take up the problems of rural poverty and the exhaustion of human and natural resources, including Pare Lorentz's films for the U.S. government, *The Plow That Broke the Plains* (1936) and *The River* (1937), films that the group set out explicitly to oppose, even though Frontier members had helped make them,[71] *Men and Dust* (Sheldon Dick, 1939), *Valley Town* (Willard Van Dyke, 1940), and *The Land* (Robert Flaherty, 1941). While all dealt with the industrial and social causes of rural and agricultural troubles, only *People of the Cumberland* approached them through the problem of culture. At the center of the wide-ranging twenty-minute film was the Highlander Folk School, an institute established in 1932 to train local labor leaders in an effort to combat the exploitation of the local population by mining and lumber-milling companies who had cleared the region of arable land and forced wages down to starvation levels. The founder of the school, Myles Horton, was a Tennessean who had attended Union Theological Seminary, where he had studied with the socialist theologian Reinhold Niebuhr, as did others who followed Horton to Highlander. After several years of working to collectivize labor and to reinvigorate regional traditions in the Cumberland Plateau, directors of the school sought to broaden the its reach and financial base, and they asked one of their financial sponsors to provide funding for a film about the school's activities.[72] Acclaimed in its time as the "most popular labor film ever made," the film would seem to have achieved the school's publicity goals.[73] Screened in a wide range of venues, from commercial theaters to the historic nonfiction program at the Museum of Modern Art at the end of 1939, the 1939 World's Fair, and the typical nontheatrical variety of community groups, labor organizations, churches, and scientific societies, the film's circulation described a diffuse public domain in which the concerns of philanthropists, artists and aesthetes intersected with those of labor and the left.[74] The film works with a set of familiar oppositions—north and south; educated elites and common people; capital and labor; skilled and unskilled trades (or in the terms of the moment, AFL and CIO)—which it progressively undermines in its narrative and aesthetic registers, using a hybrid of fiction and documentary techniques.

From the very first image, the film announces its intention to recast these oppositions as a dialectical synthesis of counterbalanced forces. It is a composite image: the words "Frontier Films presents" are set against a textured background that brings to mind burlap or other coarse textile and that appears behind the titles separating each of the film's four sections. (The contents of these sections can be roughly outlined as: the despoliation of the Cumberland Plateau and the desperation of its people; the education and organization of the people within regional and national collectivities; the violent forces of reaction; the resilience of the people, their health and humor, and the promise of youth.) The thatched backdrop suggests, of course, the textile crafts and industries of the region. But the visible warp and woof of the lines that make up this visual field also announce the film's own intention to work allegorically and poetically, turning the traditions and history of the location from mere themes or topics into the text or, more accurately, the subtext of the film. Here the film announces a method of creating image-texts that is in keeping with Benjamin's call, in "The Author as Producer," for a "recasting" of forms, one that would lift the matter of production from the inert status of content and weave it into the work as an element of its structure.[75] But as is made plain by Benjamin's thoroughly high-cultural points of reference (Soviet Constructivism, dada, Brecht, Hans Eisler), the European modernist context was quite different from that of Depression modernism in the United States. In a country where the economic and social structures of the cotton and textile industries conspired to keep vast segments of the population illiterate, textile is not only an etymological resonance in the concept of the text but also the symbol of historical forces in conflict with it.

Thus, this opening hieroglyph hints at a conflict between verbal and nonverbal forms of culture that the film will hope to resolve, which in fact it must resolve, if it is to extend and not simply memorialize the work of the Highlander School. This goal requires that the film not only make common cause with the workers in the film, honoring and spreading word of their efforts at self-organization—a properly revolutionary goal—but also, in keeping with the dictates of the Popular Front, that it explain how the specialized labor of the bourgeoisie might advance this goal and how the efforts of both blue- and white-collar labor can be located within the national fabric. The latter aim is signaled aurally and visually in a variety of ways throughout the film, some of them exceedingly subtle: shots in which the arms of square-dancers intertwine, for instance, extend the visual motif of weaving into the cultural practices of the region. Its most blatant manifestation, however, is the frequent appearance of a literal embodiment of national fabric, the American flag. The rest of the credits involve several fabrications, including pseudonyms and vague or incomplete attributions of responsibility for the craft elements of the film. The final revolutionary gesture of the opening titles is therefore simply to invert

Figure 1.1. *People of the Cumberland* (Robert Stebbins [Sidney Meyers] and Eugene Hill [Jay Leyda], 1938). Still capture from DVD. Courtesy of the Highlander Research and Education Center and the Tennessee State Library and Archives.

the very meaning of literacy in the cinematic text: being able to read the credits does not necessarily help the viewer know who contributed what to its construction. Later passages on the audio-visual forms of instruction employed by Highlander—posters, forms of role-playing, cultural demonstrations—will substantiate this point.

After the opening credits, a short prologue sets out the social problem the film will address: a regional culture and economy destroyed by industrialist greed, forcing families out of their homes and communities to search for work and food. Then the film introduces the film's central historical character, Myles Horton, the founder of the Highlander School. Smoking a pipe and reading in a book-lined study, Horton offers a striking visual counterpoint to the bedraggled men, women and children of the first section (see figures 1.1, 1.2). The class difference signified by the contrast is underscored in the music accompanying the beginning of the second section, a jaunty and slightly discordant

Figure 1.2. *People of the Cumberland.* Still capture from DVD. Courtesy of the High-lander Research and Education Center and the Tennessee State Library and Archives.

modern composition. In themselves, these visual and aural markers of bourgeois and professional culture remind us of the class antagonism that produced the misery documented in the previous section. The film thereby begs the question crucial to the ideology of the Popular Front: how will the history of these class differences be overturned by a culture uniting rich and poor Americans? And how, furthermore, can ideological apparatuses like education be refashioned to serve the ends of social amelioration, rather than social division?

The narration informs us that Horton and Highlander offer a "new beginning" to the people of the Cumberland, "a link between the towns and the mountains," a statement that emphasizes what has already been made clear in the montage, when the film shifts abruptly from pseudo-photographic images of the impoverished hillside and valley communities, imitating the aesthetics of FSA photography and Pare Lorentz's films, to the clean and dynamic compositions of the sec-

Figure 1.3. *People of the Cumberland.* Still capture from DVD. Courtesy of the Highlander Research and Education Center and the Tennessee State Library and Archives.

tion introducing Highlander. The same kinds of people we saw in the opening are now shown happily engaged in ordinary tasks, in marked contrast to the morose and static dispositions of the earlier bodies. The school and the local population are now described as "neighbors" and a "community." The image of a folk-dance lesson at the school, one of the dances "of a long time ago, when the community was happy and prosperous," is evidence for the claim that "the school took roots among the people" (see figure 1.3).

If folk culture, remediated by the school's enthnologists, is the mechanism for binding this community, labor education is presented as the means for expanding it beyond the southern Appalachians. In an upbeat series of short sequences, the film expresses the idea that labor unions are both the outgrowth of these local forms of community and the means of their dispersion onto the national scene. Students at the school are shown learning about the merits of unions and the protocols

Figure 1.4. *People of the Cumberland.* Still capture from DVD. Courtesy of the Highlander Research and Education Center and the Tennessee State Library and Archives.

of civil discourse, and emphasis is placed on the active nature of their learning (see figure 1.4). In an innovative application of mise-en-scène, they discuss the benefits of unionization while attending to a garden at the school. Then they test their knowledge by debating and making speeches (see figure 1.5). In these educational units, the school's pedagogical method is adapted for the medium of film, and in accordance with the principles of documentary as a "moving document of life" that Steiner and Hurwitz had developed in their Nykino phase.[76] These sequences show the students of Highlander learning and articulating ideas themselves rather than giving these ideas the voice of the narrator, as would be conventional. While the flat sonic texture and imprecise lip-synching of the labor-organizing lessons give away that these discussions were concocted in postproduction, this pantomime of discourse answers the question posed by the narrator's blunt assertion that the school had rooted itself in the lives of the people and suggests that cinema can assist in this incorporation. If the school is

Figure 1.5. *People of the Cumberland.* Still capture from DVD. Courtesy of the Highlander Research and Education Center and the Tennessee State Library and Archives.

necessary because the folk have lost their ability to speak and commune with one another, film can help reconstruct their voice. That it does so in both staged actions and newsreel footage of strikes and marches from around the country, set to audio recordings of protest singing, should strike us less as stylistic inconsistency than a refusal to hierarchize styles of knowledge that is in keeping with the Popular Front politics of social diversity.

Indeed, this section features one of the few sequences in any progressive documentary of the era that does not condescend to women. Women figure prominently in footage of UAW marches and sit-down strikes. In a sequence focusing on the Amalgamated Clothing Workers of America, women are seen and spoken of as leaders of a technologized national movement, presented in a series of heroic close-ups at their cutting and sewing machines and shown in groups, composing and distributing the ACWA newsletter (see figures 1.6–1.9). Images of this sort, of course, cannot help but raise the question of women's role in

Figures 1.6-1.9. *People of the Cumberland.* Still captures from DVD. Courtesy of the Highlander Research and Education Center and the Tennessee State Library and Archives.

documentary filmmaking, and the significance of their absence—from the production of *People of the Cumberland,* besides the sound editing of Helen Van Dongen; from the Frontier group, other than in advisory or supporting capacities; and from left documentary film of the period and for decades after. The passage is an aberration in the masculinist image repertoire of the genre, which can perhaps be seen as consistent with its makers' devotion to Vertov and his aesthetic of gaps and intervals. Associating women with action, and with the production of both goods and knowledge, the film remakes the largely static images of women in the first section, which already restage well-known images by Dorothea Lange and Margaret Bourke-White.[77]

Amplifying the dynamic interval introduced into the film by the theme of women's role in the movement, the following section appears stylistically inconsistent, within itself and with the surrounding sections. Based on an actual incident of antiunion vigilantism, the section uses dramatic techniques to imagine the murder of a United Mine Workers of America organizer; these techniques include a voice-over that switches from the perspective of the antiunion forces to that of the doomed organizer, recalling his murder from beyond the grave. Crosscut with a scene of miners being sworn into the UMWA, the vignette of the organizer's murder stands out in its emphatic use of continuity editing, which distinguishes it from the presentation of the union ceremony and from the rest of the film. Precisely because of this contrast, the visual continuities from one shot to another and the character-based interior monologue act here as a sign of trouble and a source of anxiety, expressing the violence of capitalism in the form and structure of the conventional narrative film. These narrative devices recall the arguments made against the "fascist" propaganda of Hollywood film in the Film and Photo League journal *Filmfront*, putting them into practice by a technique of inversion. Contemporary viewers seemed unprovoked by this section and likely saw it as less of a disjunction than do more recent viewers habituated to the *vérité* aesthetic. (Vlada Petric's 1973 description of the reenactment as "histrionic" and "in total stylistic dissonance with the strongly documentary fashion of recording reality in the remaining portion of the film" says more about the conception of documentary in the United States in the mid-1970s than it does about the film.)[78] If the noir look and fictional subjectivity of this part of the film is out of step with the aesthetic of other sections, this is not because other sections of the film eschew constructivist techniques in favor of literalist realism. And the patchwork quality of the entire film text testifies also to the flexibility of the documentary concept on the left in this period. As a front of cultural struggle, documentary could not be reduced to a singular perspective on a social reality that was in itself a collection of diverse, often disjunctive parts.

Isometric social force is a pronounced theme in the last part of the film, centered on the 1937 Fourth of July celebration in La Follette, Tennessee. This section deploys the full resources of what Kenneth Burke called the "revolutionary symbolism" of the left to elevate the specific struggles the film has addressed—of labor, of the Cumberland region—to the status of a national mythology.[79] Featuring speeches by the heads of the local branch of the UMWA, the Highlander School, and the TVA, the La Follette event becomes an opportunity to weave together the forces of the workerist and intellectual left with those of the liberal state. This montage compares the power managed by the government, visualized in the turbulent waters of a TVA dam, with the raw social power of the people. The cinematic resources of mise-en-scène and montage allow the film to demonstrate how its own creative faculties can be crucial to the mythology of this political front.

Although the section begins with images that seem, as Petric says, merely to inscribe reality—signs advertising the July Fourth rally and groups of marchers assembling—these are soon interspersed with images staged for the camera, in which marchers' movements are choreographed to end in dramatic compositions. The posters we see in the opening images promise a series of speeches by labor and government leaders, followed by festivities, but the film mixes the speakers together with games, races, and a hog-calling contest, even going so far as to admonish "no more speeches—this is a holiday!" This emphasis on play and fitness is reminiscent of the Soviet revolutionary cinema that Frontier members would have viewed in the early 1930s, and the contention that revolution is a form of physical as well as mental conditioning recalls the hygiene newsreels made by Medvedkin and the exercise sequence in Vertov's *Man with a Movie Camera* (1929). Extending the stylistic tension produced by the previous section, the idea that solidarity is formed in contest is threaded through this section as theme and form. A marriage, a boxing match between friends, a tug of war between miners and mill workers, and the rift between the American Federation of Labor and the Council of Industrial Organizations are strung together as examples of dynamic tensions and reversals. "These lads are buddies on weekdays, but on holidays they slug each other" is the caption the narrator offers for the boxers, inverting the usual opposition between workplace and site of leisure and between workday and holiday; and speaking for a UMWA representative, the voice urges "AFL or CIO, we've got to get together—that's what union means."

Keyed by the statement "youth takes over," the final minutes of the film enact a frenetic series of combinations and reversals. Russell

Figure 1.10. *People of the Cumberland.* Still capture from DVD. Courtesy of the Highlander Research and Education Center and the Tennessee State Library and Archives.

Campbell notes that the staging of events in *People of the Cumberland* that were not and could not have been filmed, like the killing of the UMWA organizer, was consistent with the desires of Nykino members, from the time of their split with the Film and Photo League, to be able to document what capitalist control of the media prevented from being recorded.[80] The final section of the film, however, constructs a future vision from fragments of the past. Images from minutes or even seconds earlier in the film reappear and are given new meaning. One may see this as resignifying; a stronger reading would say that Frontier's aim was to show that images have no inherent meaning and are in constant flux, like the flows of water harnessed by the TVA dam, which is the source of new energy for the region. The film's opening images of gaunt mothers, barren mines, and dirt graves are reprised as a reminder of the past that may always return. In its place, the film unsentimentally suggests, "daughters of miners, daughters of lumbermen" will provide energy "to bring out of the stony ground: light—

TVA—light for the dark valley," a series of terms that connects the potential energy of nature to the power of the welfare state (in the form
of the Tennessee Valley Authority and its hydroelectricity) and the lu-
minous power of cinema. Channeled back into those collectivities who
are both the film's subjects and its addressees, this power is symbolized
by the group of young men in a shot-put competition on whom the
film ends. Given heroic stature by the low-angle framing, the final shot
captures one in an iconic pose, clenched fist raised toward the camera.
But equally impressive is the crowd of young boys who lean into the
frame around him, watching for his shot to land (see figure 1.10). The
incorporation of this organic audience into the film is one more form
of synthesis. This striking image not only brings together an action
and its reception within a single frame, but it also confronts us with an
image of ourselves, watching and waiting for the effects of a projected
object. In this way, the film attempts at its conclusion to symbolize
its own future: the horizon or *frontier,* one might say, of the audience,
which it might energize as a public sphere. But as a tableau, this image also marks the uncertainty of this future and the anxious temporality of all progressive documentary, as it "memorializes the present
for the future."[81] (This group of ordinary, anonymous young men, one
becoming several, prefigures the statistical sublime of *Fahrenheit 9/11's*
audience, the number so big, according to Moore, that no one could
remember it.) In order to understand why the outcome of this narrative
was so difficult to imagine, and has since become so difficult to recall
and to view, we must turn to the other major partner in the cinematic
cultural front: the New Deal state. That documentary enterprise is the
subject of the next chapter.

2 / VOICE-OVER, ALLEGORY, AND THE PASTORAL IN NEW DEAL DOCUMENTARY

THE POLITICAL ALLEGORY OF THE VOICE

The totalizing state projects of social welfare, land management, and economic regulation carried out by Western industrial nations in the 1930s have often been described in terms of an all-powerful vision that mapped both space and social relations. Documentary photography and cinematography were perfectly suited to the optic of social, scientific, and economic rationality that James Scott identifies as a hallmark of the high modernist state.[1] These modes of visual representation gained prominence in the period as means to document and promote state efforts to transform natural and social space. Fusing the symbolic registers of art and science, the new medium of the social documentary film provided a model for the processes of abstraction crucial to the new mode of governing.

This modeling started with the empirical methods of documentary, which often entailed vast projects of mapping and collecting. One of the grandest examples was Robert Flaherty's two-year, twenty-thousand-mile trip to gather raw materials for *The Land* (1941), his government-sponsored film about agricultural reform. On the screen, this affiliation could produce images that were at once artistic and ideological, like *The Land*'s abstractionist patterns of curving furrow lines of contour plowing. Seen from a plane flying high above, this landscape could be made to resemble its opposite, the highway cloverleaf taking commuters to and from the suburban greenbelt idyll that appears at the end of Willard Van Dyke and Ralph Steiner's 1939 film *The City* (see figures 2.1 and 2.2). In these strange and beautiful images, an entire

Figure 2.1. *The Land* (Robert Flaherty, 1941). Production still. Courtesy of The Robert and Frances Flaherty Study Center, Claremont School of Theology.

Figure 2.2. *The City* (Ralph Steiner and Willard Van Dyke, 1939). Publicity still.

program of political and environmental change was projected. Not just the "matter of taking care of the spectacular erosion phase by use of big machinery" that *The Land*'s state sponsor worried Flaherty would produce—thinking, perhaps, of the big parade of tractors and threshers in Pare Lorentz's 1936 government documentary, *The Plow That Broke the Plains*—but a dramatically stylized image of the "quieter form of conservation" the government thought the film could promote.[2] That these images remained virtually unseen in the United States—the film was shelved by the government when the American entry into World War II made its grim view of agricultural capitalism untimely—only accentuates the analogy between documentary and state apparatuses for turning the world viewed into the world catalogued and stored.[3]

Vision was only one aspect of the allegorical structure of documentary in the period. Equally important was the complementary function of audition. Typical of this counterpoint was the narration that accompanied *The Land*'s spectacular images of contour farming. These images were, in one sense, brought down to earth by the conspicuously pedestrian voice-over, Flaherty's own, which remarks: "It is a new design. The farmers talk it over. It looks practical. It is practical. . . . The face of the land made over. Made strong again. Made strong forever." But in another sense, this drumbeat of assertions was the ideological rhythm of the film, and of American documentary during the New Deal. Moving from simple statements of fact to grandiose national projections, the voice in these films was no less visionary than the image.

With the conversion to sound gradually making its way to nontheatrical and 16mm production and exhibition, the rhetorical capacity of documentary changed in the 1930s and, along with it, so did the form's social function. With the addition of sound to the range of elements under the producer's control, the application of documentary to technical or humanistic instruction, propaganda, advocacy, and artistic experimentation was significantly expanded. Above all, the potential to pair images with particular voices, both authentic and imaginary, changed the way documentary was conceived as a means of public address, generating paradigms of representation that filmmakers would use for decades to come. This was not merely a formal or technical change; it also entailed a rethinking of the American public sphere and of the nation out of which it was crafted.

Such a change was in some sense anticipated by the expansion of radio in the previous decade. The vast expansion of this local and regional medium made radio into a properly public sphere in the late 1920s and early 1930s, one of essential importance to American identity. As the head of NBC claimed in 1930, radio could prevent "our now vast population from disintegrating into classes" and help Americans "realize our common interest in our national problems."[4] But if this nationwide linkage promised to level differences, it also raised the question of just what identity was in America and how it could be generated and preserved. Faced with the sounds of unfamiliar accents, dialects, and speech patterns, listeners might wonder not only how their own voices fit into the national public but also whether such differences were authentic and permanent. Without visual cues, listeners might not know for sure whether the person speaking to them over the radio was really a native of the group or region they sounded like. Thus, voices marked with particularity were a sign of the ambivalence and anxiety of radio's public.[5]

Radio was, of course, only one of many cultural antecedents for the voice-over style of classic documentary, but it was one that provided many of its earliest and best-known styles and performers. And placing it in this historical frame helps us grasp how voice-over was not merely a technological necessity in the awkward infancy of the American sound film but an aesthetic and ideological option to be exercised in various ways. Moreover, the conventional description of classic documentary voice-over as pedantic and monotonous is no less ideological. (The very hyperbole of the term "Voice of God," which is used with both bemusement and scorn, belies an elitist fear of documentary's mass audiences, implicitly characterizing them as dupes of ideology.) Instead, I want to suggest that these forms of narration serve, even or especially in moments of stylistic excess, as an index to the political factions and functions of social documentary in the 1930s.

The films discussed in this chapter belie the conventional description of classic documentary enunciation as a monolithic leveling of social topographies of class and region. Although nearly every analysis of documentary sound film in the 1930s remarks on the phenomenon of the voice-over, the relationship of this ideal speech to the world it represents has remained largely unexplored. Critics of the prolix type of classic documentary represented by *The Plow That Broke the Plains* and *The River* (1937) complained that the voice in these films was pedantic and redundant, merely repeating what viewers could learn from their images. Typical and paradigmatic is Siegfried Kracauer's attitude in *Theory of Film: The Redemption of Physical Reality* (1960), where he laments the undermining of the image in American documentary by commentary. Kracauer objects to the redundancy of the "lyrical tirades" of Lorentz's *The River,* comparing them with the "deluge of words" with which newsreels overwhelmed their images.[6]

The apparent redundancy of this epic speech was central to its pastoral power. The world depicted in these films is described and spoken for by this voice, making it at once mute and suffused with sound. These silences can be written off to factors of technological and economic necessity, including the gradual and belated conversion of documentary production to the synchronous sound techniques that commercial filmmaking had adopted before the end of the 1920s; the expense and difficulty of sound filming, especially on location; and the relative poverty of documentary filmmakers. But the audio-visual cosmology of voice-over has broader implications for understanding the ideological function of documentary in the period. What from one perspective looks like uneven development in the history of cinematic modes, with sound documentary falling behind the pace of technical and textual innovation in the commercial narrative industry, can also be seen as an expansive moment for what Michel Chion calls the "audiovisual illusion."[7] The mysterious and alienating qualities of this voice add value to the image, argues Chion; only in a rigorously visual ontology of film could it be said that voice-over detracted from the cinema rather than adding to its powers. Indeed, the separation and recombination of voice and image puts the latter in the position of being structured and animated by the former.[8]

This animistic (or, as Chion calls it, "acousmatic") speech must be read, in the films of the New Deal, as a kind of political ventriloquism. In that guise, it becomes a volatile agent of hegemony. "When we hear a voice from nowhere," observes Steven Conner in his history of ventriloquism, "we hear something which our eyes assure us is not possible."[9] Separating voices from bodies is a mark of power, and the primary objection of both critics and subsequent generations of filmmakers to 1930s documentary was that, through voice-over, this form imposed a single and obvious meaning on the documentary image. But these complaints about the excessively obvious character of this mode of commentary identify what is most effective about the voice as a means of projecting state power. State voice-over is meant to galvanize mass attention: it is an address in which the form of the instruction supersedes its content. It is no accident that New Deal voice-over frequently developed the pedagogical topic of place and displacement. The state that speaks in these films was one that gained its authority by an uncanny ability to produce and fill empty spaces: in the land, but also in the American character. This voice projected itself into both places in an uncanny ventriloquizing of the American people, in whose name the state claimed its new powers.

The dislocation of sound from the image in space and time was crucial to its use as an allegory of legitimate and rational application of state power, even when these sounds have an excessive and imaginary character, as music that speaks or voices that detach themselves from bodies. Insofar as it raises the problem of how voiceless subjects will be represented to, in, and by the state, American documentary of the 1930s testifies to the complicated negotiations in the period among the left, its vanguard intellectuals, and the institutions of government. The public address formed through these negotiations marks a quite different sense of government than the operations of visual and graphic supervision that mark the social and environmental reform projects of welfare and socialist states in the 1930s. The country that is heard is governed differently than the one which is merely seen.[10] Acoustic space, claimed Walter Ong, is "a vast interior in the center of which the listener finds himself together with his interlocutors."[11] "Sound," writes Ong, "situates man in the middle of actuality and in simultaneity, whereas vision situates man in front of things and in sequentiality."[12] Their combination in the sound documentary makes possible, as we will see, competing but complementary logics of totality and even, I will suggest, a totality that includes its opposite, particularity.

Allegory is the term for this dialectical operation. In its submission of the detail to the ends of narrative, the classic documentary follows the modernist model of state power described by James Scott, dislodging fragments of experience from their particular time and place and converting them to a form of expression that can be read topographically or aesthetically, as scientific data or art. At the same time, however, this operation makes it possible to understand the epic narratives told in New Deal documentary as fictions. Within the regime of allegory, according to Walter Benjamin, anything can mean anything else. But for Benjamin, the "world in which the detail is of no great importance" is at the same time a world in which these details, made into signs, must gain "a power which makes them appear no longer commensurable with profane things, which raises them onto a higher plane."[13] This tension is felt constantly in the expository documentary. The mundane facticity of the detail must be maintained for the film to function as explanation, but the detail must also be, as Benjamin says, "sanctified" for the film to function as persuasion or expression, rather than simply instruction. "Allegory," writes James Clifford, "prompts us to say of any cultural description not 'this represents, or symbolizes, that' but rather, 'this is a (morally charged) *story* about that.'"[14] In this respect, New Deal documentary is meant not only to instruct a specific population, as small as a community or as large as a class or nation, about the political or scientific initiatives depicted but to instruct its audiences, as well, in the interpretation of the cinematic text, and thus in the ideational and ideological power of documentary representation itself. (Although it cannot be claimed that documentary was invented in the 1930s, the last years of the decade were undoubtedly a period of heightened visibility for the form, which was the subject of unprecedented attention in the custodial institutions of American culture, including newspaper columns, museums, scholarly discussions, and philanthropic foundations: through their efforts, documentary became visible and debatable as a distinct form of American culture.)

Recent applications of Benjamin's concept of allegory to ethnographic description emphasize its capacity to redirect, and thus critique or resist, the ethnographic gaze. While state propaganda would hardly seem like the place to find either ethnographic knowledge or its deconstruction, certain aspects of the New Deal project in documentary cinema can be read in the terms that Catherine Russell, following Benjamin and Clifford, uses to describe critical ethnographic cinema: as an experiment in the sacralization of everyday American life, in the ruins of which we can discern "utopian desires for historical transformation" and a "critique of modernist progress."[15] The ethnographic character of these films extends beyond their experimental use of the cultures and places they survey to the state from which they emerge, and which they helped a public to imagine. From them, we can reconstruct an image of the cultures—political, professional, intellectual, bureaucratic, folk—that intersected in New Deal documentary.

TALK OF THE TOWN

Nonfiction film had long been regarded within the U.S. government as a way for state agencies to directly address the users or potential users of government services.[16] This instrumental address was modified under the aegis of the New Deal to serve a related but somewhat different end, the creation of publics. These forms of association took as their subject (and sometimes their object) those directly and indirectly affected by the social, agricultural, and economic crises befalling the country. Through documentary work, intellectuals from across the political spectrum exerted corrective pressure on the institutions that spoke for the masses, from organs of capitalism to the government and the left in its organized forms. In this sense, American social documentary of the 1930s may be said to serve not only the didactic function of pedagogy or promotional functions of propaganda or publicity but also the generative function of a public sphere.

Metaphors of voice and its cognates—appeal, vocation—were most immediate and reflexive in sound cinema but were not found only there. Indeed, the appearance of these figures in many documentary media forms added to the impression these forms drew on a diverse and widespread social imaginary. The literary prose and poetry of Sherwood Anderson, Erskine Caldwell, and Muriel Rukeyser featured a quilt of hinterland voices that challenged the representative and singular authority of the social scientist, the politician, and the author. In works that combined literary enunciation in lyric and narrative forms with documentary photography, this critique was placed in the hands of the reader. It was in the difference between forms of expression and media these books employed—in some cases, a palpable gap between the left-hand page and the right—that a space was created for the read-

YAZOO CITY, MISSISSIPPI. "I think it's only right that the government ought to be run with people like us in mind."

Figure 2.3. Erskine Caldwell and Margaret Bourke-White, *You Have Seen Their Faces* (1937).

er's engagement with the questions posed by the text. The very title of Erskine Caldwell and Margaret Bourke-White's best-selling *You Have Seen Their Faces* (1937) indicated the effect Bourke-White's photographs were supposed to have on the viewer (see figure 2.3). In the manner of a voice of conscience, they asked the reader to silently fill in the rest of the sentence. You have seen their faces: what are you going to do about them? This appeal was the return of a specific repressed, a collective voice stifled by a failure of political representation. In *American Exodus: A Record of Human Erosion* (1939), the product of a collaboration between sociologist Paul Schuster Taylor and photographer Dorothea

Lange, Taylor writes that "those whose cry of distress is most anguished are ciphers politically to those who sit as representatives in Austin and Washington."[17]

In attempting to figure this cry, however, the photo-text made it even more of a cipher. Caldwell's captions for Bourke-White's photographs in *You Have Seen Their Faces* have a similar effect. Appearing in quotation marks, as if they were the recorded speech of the farmers, bait sellers, worshippers, prisoners, and bosses who are the subjects of the photographs, these words approximated authentic folk voices, an effacement the authors claimed was necessary "to avoid unnecessary individuation." "The legends under the pictures are intended to express the authors' own conceptions of the sentiments of the individuals portrayed," they wrote; "they do not pretend to reproduce the actual sentiments of these persons."[18] In *Land of the Free* (1938), Archibald MacLeish took this gesture a step further. MacLeish reproduced existing, and in some cases famous, documentary images and added to them what he called a lyrical "soundtrack." But the "voice of the people" that MacLeish fabricated for them was not only an imposition on them, in the manner of Caldwell's captions for *You Have Seen Their Faces*. It also presented this "people" as racked with doubt about their principles and the country's direction. The poem's refrain is that the people "don't know" or "aren't certain" anymore about the security of the Jeffersonian foundation: "We wonder if the liberty was land / We wonder if the liberty was grass / Greening ahead of us: grazed beyond horizons. . . . / The dust chokes in our throats and we get wondering."[19] The coordination of image and text allows the people displayed by the photographs to appear literally self-reflective, synchronizing the collective voice of "the people" (the ostensible author of the lyric that appears on the left-hand pages) with the well-worn images of drought, erosion, and struggle on the right-hand pages—asking, in effect, what consequences the mass circulation of these images would have on their subjects and making clear that the voice of the people could not be distinguished *from* this circulation (see figure 2.4).

That the idea of the vox populi could be employed for distinct or even antithetical effects is attributable, in part, to the period's complex conception of the voice and its emergence as the fundamental problematic of documentary. Under the sign of the voice, documentary

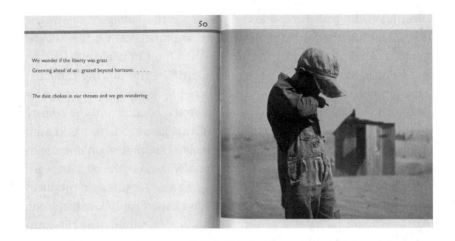

We wonder if the liberty was grass
Greening ahead of us: grazed beyond horizons. . . . .

The dust chokes in our throats and we get wondering

Figure 2.4. Archibald MacLeish, *Land of the Free* (1938).

brought together issues of representation and responsibility with problems of aesthetics and culture, including the question of how progressive authors, artists, photographers, and filmmakers should deal with
the increasingly broad appeal of documentary to the architects of public opinion. The incorporation of documentary representation into the
state apparatus, which involved as well the incorporation of progressive intellectuals (and the left more broadly) into the state, required
the invention of what Gilles Deleuze and Félix Guattari call a "collective assemblage of enunciation," those socially effective statements—
promises, questions, commands, instructions—that create subjects as
an effect of their circulation.[20] Adopting an inflection at once universal
and highly localized, New Deal voice-over aimed to bring such a collective subject into being. As projections of the folk, these assemblages
also served to project an image of the forces competing for popular
authority: the left and the welfare state.

In *The Public and Its Problems* (1927), John Dewey called the town
meeting the original American "political medium."[21] But Dewey also
recognized that this ideal was now something of a historical fiction.
It thus lent itself to creative treatments like James M. Cain's tongue-
in-cheek primer on American politics, *Our Government* (1930). Though
Cain would soon be better known as an author of crime fiction and

screenplays, he had worked as a reporter for the *Baltimore Sun* in the 1920s, and his first piece for a magazine was an article for the *Atlantic Monthly,* based on reporting for the *Sun,* on a topic of perennial interest to American documentary, labor organizing in the mining industry. Cain presents *Our Government* as an example of a popular science of American political institutions, from the town council and the county sheriff to Congress and the presidency. Cain claims to have based each of the seriocomic vignettes that compose *Our Government* on documentary evidence of the problems conventionally faced by each of these institutions. (In the chapter on the U.S. Congress, he simply reproduces a section of the *Congressional Record.*) Each chapter captures an episode of discourse on political or governmental process, simulating the transcript of a speech or discussion taking place in an arena of formal politics. His ambitious claim for this method of "complete verisimilitude" is that it will make the United States "unique among nations," in being a country that knows "what its government actually is."[22]

Using his ear for American vernacular to render the particularities of utterance within each deliberative body, Cain depicts all of these official orders of speech as equally beset by the gap between the particular case of language or voice and the ideal of the political speech act—legislation, policy, verdict—that it exists to pronounce. Cain's withering tone is established by the first of the dialogues, in which the civic leaders of a fictional Ohio town that has hosted a visit by the president discover that the speech has been plagiarized, incompetently, from reference books and Chamber of Commerce materials. The men squabble over the meaning of this revelation, only to agree that the real significance of the speech was that it happened in their town and that they witnessed it. "The main thing is," the men chorus at the end of the scene, "He's been here!"[23] In other scenes, an inebriate governor presides over a pardons hearing; a jury hears a florid speech by a prosecutor, defending the Christian virtue of the Ku Klux Klan; and so on. At first glance, this collection of bathetic scenes seems patently comic, a work of parody and critique, rather than the work of realism and education Cain sets out in his introduction.

But *Our Government* can also be read as espousing political principles, the same ones that social documentary of the period would pursue. At every level of government, Cain suggests, the ideal of the institution must be adjusted to fit the individuals who constitute the institution. This juxtaposition displays itself in the spoken events that effect acts of governance. Cain's pragmatic outlook echoes Dewey's contemporaneous view that American democracy is essentially local, having "developed out of genuine community life, that is, association in local and small centers."[24] For Dewey, the possibility of an actually existing democracy depended on tensions between the democratic ideal and the "fact" of community.[25] The frustrating scenes of political, legal, and administrative procedure that constitute *Our Government* appear, from this perspective, as a provocation to the reader's political sensibilities, in line with Dewey's injunction, "change men's estimate of the *value* of existing political agencies and forms, and the latter change more or less."[26]

The attitude of realism that Dewey suggests is essential to progressive politics and was fundamental to the American conception of social documentary in the 1930s, in its charge to the spectator no less than in its code of representation. Documentary was a way to illustrate the relation of the particular—the fact, the local, the individual case, the utterance—to social generalizations and abstractions. Community, Nation, Democracy, Public: these were all, according to Dewey, social forms that existed only as ideas.[27] In its topical orientation to life at the regional and urban margins of technological modernity, documentary tested these abstractions, even as it supported and promoted them. Cain's use of the styles of American speech exemplified a crucial problem in the documentary ideology of democracy, even before documentary had been codified as a cultural practice. On the one hand, the idioms of informal speech signified the ordinary and authentic character of American political institutions. The method Cain proposed would not only let the country see "what its government actually is" but would also encourage readers to recognize themselves in the government. On the other hand, people and their speech appeared to be the greatest impediment to the operation of representative government and to its function as authentic expression of the popular will. Thwarted constantly on the narrative level, the political ideal of democracy re-emerges at the level of the text. The measure of Cain's idealism is, paradoxically, his fidelity to the way Americans might actually speak when taking positions, making decisions, and confronting their differences. This cacophony, Cain suggests, is what democracy sounds like. What initially seems to be a cynical contradiction between the text's stated intentions (to inspire faith in the American political system by helping make it transparent to ordinary Americans) and its method can instead be seen as a lesson in the interpretation of foundational statements—documents—like prefaces and constitutions for use in everyday life.

As they did throughout documentary in the 1930s, voices stood in Cain's text as the embodiment of a critical problem. How to preserve the integrity and idiosyncrasy of experience while submitting it to textual manipulation, as example or evidence, in an address to a diffuse public? From the moment when sound was added to the palette of textual means in cinema, the voice became a figure of this enduring question for documentary cinema. Whether and how documentary should speak for and about, as well as to, others were versions of another crucial question for American progressives, the problem of how the individual was to be incorporated into a public, especially one constructed through the alienating technologies of mass communication, without losing his or her particularity and independence.

Whenever the figure of the vox populi appears in the subsequent history of American documentary, it brings into relief the process by which film and other reproductive media borrow or extend the representational power of mass politics. Group discussions *of* documentary films, videos, and television programs, whether formally instituted or ad hoc, are an important aspect of this process, one whose history is largely uncollected and unexamined. This history would include a range of discussion contexts, formats, and functions, including the workers' groups in which leftist newsreels were screened in the 1920s and 1930s; the feminist consciousness-raising sessions of the 1970s, where women viewed films like *The Women's Film* (1971) or *Self Health* (1974); the activities suggested to teachers who used the state documentary *The Plow That Broke the Plains* (1936) or episodes of the HBO miniseries *Pandemic: Facing AIDS* (2003) in their classrooms; or the conversations orchestrated for television after the broadcast of controversial programs, like the February 2003 "town-hall meeting" put on by ABC News and PBS after the PBS broadcast of *Two Towns of Jasper* (2003), a documentary film about the murder of a black man in Jasper, Texas. And recent scholarship has found evidence of an entire educational subgenre of mid-century films *about* discussion, including films that teach viewers how to discuss a film.[28]

These actual situations of discussion moderate the persuasive power of the film screened and of the mass medium and adapt both to local structures of collectivity. But where the people's voice appears as a scene *in* documentary films, it can be said to depict the appeal of documentary cinema itself. The conventional form of this voice is a scene of ordinary people expressing and exchanging views on matters crucial to their identity as a collective body. This body—which could look like a public, an insurgent proletariat, or a diffuse mass—is given form by narration, either written or spoken, that collects its various voices. In the classic period of American social documentary, these depictions tended to reverence and idealization. Rarely did they display any doubt about the ability of the people to address themselves, especially if a committed intellectual was available to help channel or collect them. Such scenarios were remarkably optimistic about the technics of democracy, even when they shared the nostalgia of Dewey's description of the town meeting.

Perhaps the emblematic expression of this optimism appears in *The City* (1939), a sponsored documentary made by two veterans of the various documentary movements of the 1930s, Ralph Steiner and Willard Van Dyke. *The City* was commissioned by the American Institute of Planners for screenings at the New York World's Fair of 1939 and 1940, an event that marked a significant step for documentary film as a category of public art in the United States. One public relations professional imagined the upcoming fair in terms of documentary film, promising that the fair would provide business and industry with modern propaganda tools, "just as the government is making use of such means as Pare Lorenz's [*sic*] *The River* on the screen."[29] *New York Times* film critic Bosley Crowther described the fair as the opportunity for American producers of social documentary to consolidate as a professional institution. Reviewing recent developments in state and independent documentary production, Crowther pointed to the founding of the Association of Documentary Film Producers, a response to programming opportunities presented by the fair, as a watershed, noting that prior to this event documentarists "had been in a thoroughly disorganized state, unrelated, suspicious and critical of one another and mainly in-effectual as a group."[30] According to Richard Griffith's report in the inaugural issue of *Films,* the fair was "the best opportunity documen-tary has ever had."[31] *The City* represented to Griffith (who managed the Science and Education Theater, where the film was shown, in 1940) the great, if unfulfilled potential of "fact films" at the fair, and of docu-mentary at the end of the 1930s. The cinematic comparison of the old American village and the city of tomorrow was the film's most "valid film idea."[32]

Near the beginning of the film, a few silent shots of people at a country meeting are narrated with the following voice-over, written by Lewis Mumford (and based on his book *The Culture of Cities* [1938]):

> A century or two ago we built our church and marked the common out. We built our town hall next, so we could have our say about the taxes, or whether we need another teacher for the school. When town meet-ing comes around, we know our rights and duties, and no harm if we disagree. In all that matters, we neighbors hold together.

Where the serial logic of voices in Cain's *Our Government* laid out ut-terances one after another, highlighting the gaps between them, *The City* uses the audiovisual syntax of cinema—silent images of talking people, an unseen voice speaking at once for them and to us—to al-legorize representative democracy, rationalizing it in a timeless figure of speech: "we . . ." Although this kind of voice-off has conventionally been referred to as "Voice of God," the version we hear in *The City* and the other films of its moment is more accurately described as the "voice of the state." While it is true that the narrator monopolizes the authority to speak, and does so from a disembodied position of author-ity, the narration's role is to imagine the speech of the anonymous folk depicted in the images and to collect and redistribute it. And in its rhetoric, its use of the present tense and the collective first-person, the film invites the viewer's active participation. As Charles Wolfe writes, "the idea of 'voice-over' depends upon our sense of the film as a text, capable of being partitioned in ways that are conceptual or structural." The voice-over can thus be read as "governing the formal construction of a work."[33]

As the interpretive key to the textual operations of classical documentary, the governing voice also marks a historical shift in documentary form and practice. When recorded sound was added to the faculties of cinema, it surpassed other indexical media as a document of experiential reality. The addition of sound to the moving image makes documentary cinema more believable and persuasive when it describes experience. But this very same development also enhanced the expressive capacity of documentary. Adding dialogue, voice-over commentary, or the emotional shading of a musical score to images could both deepen and undermine the authenticity of those images, depending on how the sound was produced, manipulated, and positioned.[34] Charlie Keil suggests that film sound, the voice in particular, is as important to American documentary in the 1930s for its figural and textual qualities as for its physical and phenomenological ones, becoming much more than an element of evidence or composition.[35] Especially in the ways that it staged and structured speech, the use of sound in the documentary film text allowed American documentarists of the period to work out a politics of representation.

By contrast with the feature-film industry, where recorded sound tended to be used to shore up the illusion of realism, turning narrative film into canned theater or audio-visual novel, the independence of sound from image opened documentary filmmaking to entirely new possibilities of assemblage, in both the artistic and social senses. The mobility of the aural signifier, with respect to the indexical image and its place on the screen, can be read as itself a metaphor for the political situation of leftist and liberal documentary in the period, shuttling among art, science, and agitation, as well as between the New Deal state, the independent left, and the various forms of "the people" for which both political institutions claimed to speak. Documentary cinema offered progressives within the state and adjacent to it a medium in which to imagine new social and political configurations. This utopian capacity was tied to the specifically figural and allegorical character of documentary in the period. Documentary form became a kind of social imaginary for the period, a model of what Mumford called, in the introduction to *The Culture of Cities,* a "collective art and technics."[36]

The City (1939) exemplifies this technocratic dream of coordinating, through the arts of mechanical reproduction, social forms and aesthetic ones. Originally offered by the film's sponsors to Pare Lorentz, the key figure in New Deal documentary cinema, *The City* was a work of liberal modernist concord, bringing together the wealth of the Carnegie Corporation and the Rockefeller Foundation, which contributed funding, with well-established cultural intellectuals like Mumford, the composer Aaron Copland, and members of the influential leftist filmmaking collective Nykino.[37] The first part of the film, which includes the town-hall meeting, presents the town of "a century or two ago" as the ideal of American social life. Opening images of circularity and flow (a water wheel, boys swimming in a river, men turning wagon wheels out of steel) suggest the organic integration of work, culture, and government lost in industrial capitalism and rediscovered, the film will argue, in the greenbelt suburb. "The city," writes Mumford in *The Culture of Cities,* is a "fact in nature, like a cave, a run of mackerel or an ant-heap. But it is also a conscious work of art, and it holds within its communal framework many simpler and more personal forms of art,"[38] a claim that also captures the aspirations of social documentary in the period. It is a point reiterated in the images of women sewing and weaving, accompanied by the narrator's assertion that this, too, is a form of art. "Art isn't something foreign we look at in a showcase," Mumford's narration insists, "it's in the blankets we've spun and woven right at home."[39] But the most important image of weaving doesn't appear in the image at all. It is the aural image of political discourse, of "neighbors" agreeing to disagree. In the narrator's voice, differences are reconciled. And in the shift from the historical past of "a century or two ago" to the present tense, the differences between periods of American democracy are also resolved, woven into a continuous unfolding of the original idea.

Although it is tempting to think of voice-over as synonymous with domination, the technique was used by all manner of political filmmakers, both inside and outside the state. The use of a narrator (or, in some cases, more than one narrator) to play the many voices of a political community could be found in films as different as Van Dyke's *Valley Town* (1940), a film about industrial labor made in collaboration with New York University and the Alfred P. Sloan Foundation; *People of the Cumberland* (1938), Frontier Films' collectivist film about the Highlander School; and documentary works of state propaganda from

World War II, both racist (*The Battle of Midway* [1942]) and antiracist (*The Negro Soldier* [1944]). As was the case with progressive ideology throughout the New Deal political landscape, this particular modality of the voice can be thought of as a state institution whose effectiveness required its distribution beyond the offices of the government.

ENUNCIATION AND STATE CINEMA

Charles Wolfe has suggested that the common term for documentary voice-over in the classical period, "Voice of God," is both formally and ideologically imprecise. Rather than a position of omniscience, the place of the voice in many films of the period, both state-produced and independent, is an indefinite and unstable "elsewhere," relative to the world of the image and the screen.[40] Applying Wolfe's corrective to the domain of state cinema helps us understand how the appeal of documentary cinema was important to the self-imagination of the American welfare state and how this appeal relied, in a particular way, on a specifically documentary enunciation. While it is true that the voice-over commentary that accompanies many examples of classical documentary tended to the grandiloquent, to simply dismiss this element of the soundtrack as superfluous to the images, as many critics did, is to miss something important about these films and their publicity function. In fact, the redundancy of the voice in these films is one of the main devices by which these films enunciate. Enunciation can be described as the way that "some parts of a text talk to us about this text as an act."[41] If enunciation breaks down the difference between the inside of the film and its outside, it describes also the function of the documentary voice in the New Deal, giving the awesome phenomenon of state power a local and familiar character. Its aim was to reduce the sense of the state as a transcendent authority over the people and establish, in its place, the immanence of governmental power.[42] To play this public relations role, New Deal documentary did not so much invent as modify a conventional documentary voice, one developed through thousands of films and film screenings in years previous.

By the mid-1930s, the federal government had been producing educational and factual film for more than two decades, through filmmaking operations in the Department of Agriculture, the Department of the Interior, the Signal Corps, and many other bureaus and offices. Films like *The Work of the Bureau of Mines* (1916), *Helping Negroes to Become Better Farmers and Homemakers* (1921), *In Madagascar with Uncle Sam's Agricultural Explorers* (1931) made by the Department of Agriculture and its Bureau of Plant Industry, or the Treasury Department film *The Story of the U.S. Coast Guard: Service Ashore* (1935), served to explain what different agencies did and to extend the reach of government services through nontheatrical screenings, often organized by the viewers themselves. To grasp the ideological significance of style and voice in the later New Deal documentary, it is useful to examine the didactic tone and function of this earlier form of government educational film. One of what Ronald Greene calls the "mundane genres" of documentary, these films nonetheless performed a sophisticated manipulation of visual and aural address.[43]

The informational short *The New Frontier,* made in 1934 by the Extension Service of the Department of Agriculture to promote the work of the Federal Emergency Relief Administration, a film which circulated in both sound and silent versions, provides a typical example of documentary in its most instrumental form. This ten-minute film explains how depressed rural areas can be revived by federal relief programs that promote self-sufficiency, collective labor, and conservative use of land and resources. The film describes Woodlake, an experimental community in east Texas, one of a number of FERA projects to resettle farmers and residents of rural areas and introduce them to cooperative ways of work and life. It begins with a short introductory sequence depicting a typical instance of the kind of privation that New Deal agricultural programs were meant to overcome. "All of you," the commentary asserts, "have seen shacks like this one," while the screen presents views of a young family who have set up a rough camp (see figure 2.5). The place or identity of the shack dwellers is never given with any more specificity than this, and it is apparent that their isolation in the opening shots as mere icons of poverty is meant to mirror the social isolation of the poor from others of their kind before the arrival of the New Deal. While a man attempts to plow an unruly piece of land in another single shot,[44] the voice explains that FERA is "building rural communities where new industries may find workers and where these people may

Figure 2.5. *The New Frontier* (H. P. McClure, 1934). Still capture from DVD.

grow their own food in place of the direct relief paid for by the more fortunate." The story of the community at Woodlake, which appears both socially and rhetorically more cohesive than the scenes presented in the prologue, is presented through a series of minimal narrative sequences as brief as two shots, and more extended use of the expository devices that in the prologue served only to remind the viewer that he or she is well acquainted with such images. (Two shots from the prologue do not fit this explanation; I will explain why shortly.)

The rest of the film uses two basic strategies to bring together the form of communication with its content—to duplicate, that is, the effect of social integration modeled by the Woodlake project in the communication between enunciator and addressee. One strategy is the film's use of simple syntagmatic units of narrative, building the success story of Woodlake from short episodes that demonstrate the variety of life and work opportunities offered by the FERA settlement. This rhythm of episode and narrative echoes the process by which the Woodlake "colonists," as the film calls them, literally reconstruct their lives from natural resources. These resources include their own physical capacities, which must serve a variety of functions. Resourcefulness is the byword of the project. The narrator emphasizes the importance of the wood-shop, in which not only housing and farming materials may be made but also future spending power, as well. One episode presents a group of white-collar workers who have learned to grow corn and sugar cane.

Another strategy is the extensive use that the film makes of the deictical voice. In deixis, the speaker makes overt reference to the physical context that joins speaker and listener, by a set of markers that include personal and demonstrative pronouns, adverbs marking time and location, and verb tenses.[45] Deictical speech, which Christian Metz describes with the formula "I-Here-Now," emphasizes the immediacy of communication and the reversibility of the speaker's and listener's positions. A deictical utterance is one in which the identity of the "I" and the "you" are determined only by the present act of speaking: at any moment, the you *could* become the I. The chatty irreverence of the commentary in *The New Frontier* ("While we're down this way, we'll drop in on one of the neighbors"; "Wanna know where the water comes from? All right, we know all the answers: here's the community water works") exploits the necessarily political aspect of deictical speech, the merely temporary hierarchy of speaker and addressee.[46] The same could be said of most of the images in *The New Frontier:* large, loosely framed frontal shots that show as much as possible of the activities and environs of the Woodlake community. One way to read these shots would be to say that they balance out the insistent directing of the viewer's attention by the voice-over. At the same time, the demonstrative capacity of these large, plain shots, taken from an objective and frontal perspective, is unmistakable. In its extensive use of such shots, and descriptive sequences that bring together a number of visual examples of a particular feature of the project, the film seems designed to argue for the fairness and reason behind such a plan.[47]

Occasionally, the film combines these two strategies, as in the sequence titled "Bringing in Their Women and Children," the only sequence in the film that develops distinct characters and a conventional cause-and-effect narrative progression. Introduced by a title card and the narrator's invitation to "look in on a Woodlake arrival," the sequence tells the story of an unemployed accountant from Houston who is reunited with the family he could not support there. But after the choppy series of images that announce the arrival of the family and their truck, the film abruptly turns from this miniature narrative to a discussion of the east-Texas style of architecture and the wisdom of FERA planners in adopting it in the colony. As the voice-over explains the merits of the open-porch design, the screen presents a selection of views of homes and porches, the most extended descriptive series in the film. Here the film invites the viewer, perhaps more emphatically than anywhere else in the film, to observe with two different senses: to listen to the voice but at the same time to attend to the logic of the group of images. One is asked here to *listen* to the image, insofar as what appears on-screen gives the viewer an imperative: *compare these different houses and see the similarity among them.* When the commentary returns to the case of the family from Houston with an exaggeratedly self-reflexive good humor ("Oops! Almost forgot our stranded public accountant from Houston. Well, here he is, turning into the yard of the house he has picked in Woodlake"), it is as if the voice track must reassert itself as a personality to compensate for the brief rhetorical independence of the image from the voice-over. The narration seems to be saying: you and I were having a conversation when we were interrupted by that group of images that had a logic of their own. What the film seems to assert here is that the narration of government or instructional cinema is uncomplicated, colloquial, ad hoc: an act rather than, as it is in the well-established Hollywood style of narration, a system. What must be suppressed for this congenial arrangement to order the narration is the presence of what Metz calls a "*Grand Imager,*" an enunciator behind the personable Morse Salisbury, who speaks the narration of *The New Frontier.* This *Grand Imager* would be a metaphorical sense of the voice, an immanent aspect of the filmic text, capable of speaking visually and producing figures, not just literal meanings, from the images and sounds recorded by the cinematic machines.[48]

Whether we regard its inhumanity as the effect of the technological mediation which delivers the film to the cinema audience, the effect of the textual system that allows for codes and conventions, or both, its stigma is audible in the two shots from the film's introductory sequence to which I referred above. This brief passage is unlike anything in the

Figure 2.6. *The New Frontier* (H. P. McClure, 1934). Still capture from DVD.

rest of the film; it is so disjunctive that it asks to be considered as a sort of commentary on the rest of the film. At the end of the three opening shots of mother and children at their makeshift home in a clearing, the voice-over explains that, like many other families, "their jobs were taken by machinery." On "machinery," the film presents a close-up, one of the few in the film, of a hand dialing a telephone (see figure 2.6). The commentary continues: "Every time a dial system is installed, it takes jobs away from two-thirds of the telephone operators," as if the example of the telephone was a merely convenient or natural one. But it is not merely an ironic coincidence that the example of the mechanization responsible for displacing families is a communication technology, one used to extend the relationship between speaker and listener over great distances. The next mise-en-scène suggests that what is at work here is not irony but overdetermination. Over a shot of what appears to be a sound technician replacing tubes in a large recording cabinet, the voice-over explains that "when sound was introduced into motion pictures, it forced out half of the nation's actors and musicians" (see fig-

Figure 2.7. *The New Frontier* (H. P. McClure, 1934). Still capture from DVD.

ure 2.7). Given the effort in the rest of the film to make the voice-over commentary human and sympathetic, this sudden, reflexive reference to an immanent antagonism between the film's means of speech and its subjects, the unemployed, this particular choice of example cannot simply be dismissed as an inside joke on the part of the filmmakers.[49]

In this simple example, we glimpse the germ of the New Deal documentary cinema of 1936 through 1940: the creation of an ideal form of American government or state through technological enunciation. The textual qualities of documentary film are important to this enunciation. Indeed, despite Metz's ambivalence about the critical interest of nonfiction cinema, they give a particular form to the definition Metz borrows for "impersonal" enunciation from Pierre Sorlin: " 'the film indicates its relationship with the public by emphasizing that it is a film (an object fabricated from shot images and recorded sounds), without involving the slightest trace of subjectivity.' "[50] That this New Deal documentary project never quite came to fruition and remained an ideal is an important aspect of this enunciation and its figures.

THE UNITED STATES FILM SERVICE

Between *The New Frontier* and the establishment, in 1938, of the short-lived United States Film Service, an important transformation of the public nature of American nonfiction cinema took place. Comparing *The New Frontier* to the Film Service productions gives a sense of the rhetorical and historical differences between a nonfiction film that seeks, above all, to inform its audience and one that carries a broader sort of appeal. If the former is characterized by an instructional voice that urges the audience to direct its attention to the image, in order to derive a certain meaning from it, the latter adds an implicit command to this lesson; it serves the disciplinary function Deleuze and Guattari call the "order-word."[51] The state documentary addresses its viewers as citizens: it invites viewers to recognize that by interpreting the documentary text, or code, they take part in an ideal form of national community. Before turning to a central example of this discourse, Joris Ivens's 1940 film for the Film Service, *Power and the Land,* I want to set out the ways that this particular form of the social imaginary was structured by the historical conditions from which it emerged, as a project in bureaucratic cultural production. These included: the encoding of agriculture within the nascent discourse of the welfare state, as both tradition and invention; the spread of documentary into the commercial sphere of narrative fiction film; and the doctrine of quality and efficiency inside the Roosevelt bureaucracy.

By converting the local practices of farming into a figure or code that could be read by technocrats far removed from the fields, states have been able to centralize agriculture in the manner of any other modern form of production. Such operations ensure that the nation is grounded in ethnic, racial, or precapitalist soil. The New Deal agency of documentary cinema can be viewed as an example of this high modernism, insofar as it represents an attempt to convert crisis-ridden landscape to an efficient textual apparatus.[52]

A bureaucratic vision mediated between government projects and the people the projects were supposed to serve. Funding for *The Plow That Broke the Plains* and the other governmental documentaries that followed was based, in part, on the administrative function of the films. In requesting funding for *Plow*, Rexford Tugwell, the Brain Truster who headed the Resettlement Administration, referred to the "necessity of educating its employees and the employees of cooperating agencies of the government with respect to these problems [erosion, drought, over-production]." Tugwell argued that a "moving picture of the character described above will be one of the most effective, quick, and inexpensive means of explaining some of these problems of the [Resettlement] Administration to its employees and to the employees of these agencies," and that "the motion picture will clearly reduce the need for sending people into the field to explain the work of the Resettlement Administration and the need for calling people to Washington to receive explanations."[53] It is clear from the films themselves and from the record of their success in general circulation that they weren't addressed exclusively to the bureaucracy. But if we are to understand the films as a form of social mediation, it is important to keep in mind this original addressee. Working with the medium of the feature film gave these same bureaucrats a very different sense of their vocation, orienting them in an unlikely way toward the public sphere. The power of this address to compel national identification is clear from an impassioned memo about the final Film Service project, *The Land,* sent by Van Rensselaer Sill, a staff person in the Department of Agriculture, to the information director of the sponsoring agency within the department:

> I don't know if you fully realize what we have in this film; you have been so close to it that possibly you find it difficult to stand off at a distance and just feel and think about it. To me it is a social document that belongs to all the people, not the AAA or the government, or Paramount, or RKO. I believe it would be dishonest not to make a very strong effort to get as wide a distribution as possible. Somehow, I don't feel that we could call ourselves Americans if we took an indifferent stand on distribution of this picture, or if we felt that internal problems involving the field etc were more important than the contribution this film can make to life here in this country.[54]

The force of Sill's national sentiment precipitates a striking reversal of Louis Althusser's "hailing" model of ideological interpellation, where receiving a call from the state converts the anonymous individual into the responsible subject. Here, the orientation to a public sphere of film generates a bureaucratic fantasy, one in which the state agent blends into the mass of Americans. It is the state, in other words, that is hailed by the walk-ons populating Althusser's "little theoretical theatre," the ordinary people out of whom Althusser's cop hails the subject.[55] (And what is a bureaucrat, if not the state played by an extra, a nobody?)

Embedded in Sill's fantasy is a memory of documentary in its exploitation mode, commercially financed films that documented the filmmaker's encounter with exotic lands and cultures. (Well-known examples include *Grass: A Nation's Battle For Life* [1924], *Africa Speaks!* [1930], *Bring 'Em Back Alive* [1932] and *Congorilla* [1932], as well as travelogue series like "The Magic Carpet of Movietone" and "Traveltalks.") While the New Deal social documentary adopted a distinctly different attitude to the exploitation of nature, it borrows some of these earlier films' sense of documentary as a form of cinematic attraction. Pare Lorentz, who had a hand in all of the feature documentaries produced by the Roosevelt administration, boasted that for *The Plow That Broke the Plains* "we had a special lens made to get the largest possible spread. The motion in our motion picture was going to be *architectural,* the ominous changes in the land itself."[56] The view afforded by this lens was not to be simply a depiction of the natural world in crisis, but a masterful representation and, as Lorentz suggests, a learned and structured view. The focus of this motion picture and the series of films that followed it was a changing Nature, or, to be more precise, Man's social, economic, and technological attempts to come to terms with a Nature in which he had interfered. Lorentz's metaphor suggests that the state *was* a form of nature: the viewer imagined by Lorentz was meant to experience the structural effects of design, planning, measurement, and engineering on the land. The metaphor of architecture suggests a displacement of the spectator, the creation of a space through which the spectator moves while viewing. This displacement would presumably complement the efforts of New Deal agencies at resettlement and modernization of the underclass depicted in the films. The New Deal documentary was to be a way the general public might experience what those changes signified for the American people. The architect of Lorentz's vision was the state, and what the viewer would grasp through these films was the condensed effect of state intervention in human and physical nature.

The agricultural disaster that faced whole regions demanded a broad and contentious series of governmental measures: not only measures of relief, as in the early phases of the New Deal, but wholesale rethinking of major industries and institutions. To restore the vitality of the agricultural branch of the economy would require the government to take a much more active part in relations of production and the ways of life that depended on those relations, including the redistribution of the population throughout city and country.

Liberals in Roosevelt's Brain Trust argued that "existing farm programs placed excessive faith in business recovery and emergency relief and that they had failed to help rural America's poorest residents."[57] They pushed Roosevelt to implement measures that would allow farmers to take a more active role in their recovery, measures at once more bottom-up and top-down than the consumption-based relief programs of the so-called First New Deal of 1933 through 1935, initiatives that left the social principles of capitalism largely unquestioned. Under Rexford Tugwell, for instance, the Resettlement Administration, created in April 1935, attempted to deal directly with the exhaustion of arable land and the isolation of farming communities by resettling farmers on government land and by cultivating solutions to the problems of scarcity created by existing property relations. The RA helped establish cooperatives, constructed model communities, and gave grant and loan money to small and tenant farmers. Because these measures would put the administration in political and philosophical conflict with elements in Congress and in the private sector, it turned to public relations to create political leverage for them in an unprecedented federal application of the mass media. The goal of this campaign was to create a sympathetic image of the crisis and of the government's efforts to combat it. "Every citizen must play his part" in the struggle to return the United States to prosperity, one government report urged. Agricultural capital was "a vital concern of everyone. It is as significant to merchant, manufacturer, and banker as to those who work immediately on the land. . . . Progress or decadence of a people is determined by the manner in which it accepts and utilizes these gifts of nature. . . . A people must choose."[58] This campaign included a cinematic branch, an enterprise known primarily through a small group of documentary features made for general distribution between 1936 and 1942. Making use of many of the resources of conventional narrative cinema, these films turned the mundane topic of social reform and its political process into miniature epics of the struggle between tradition and modernization.

In 1938 the Roosevelt administration gave its support to the nation's first federal program in documentary cinema. This controversial initiative would be dogged by strong opposition in Congress until its demise in an appropriations bill two years later. In forming the United States Film Service, the Roosevelt administration had hoped to duplicate the critical and popular success of two previous government-sponsored documentary films, *The Plow That Broke the Plains* and *The River,* and to capitalize on the positive publicity the government had generated with those films for both its policies and its image-making capacity. The actual mandate of the Film Service was as much bureaucratic as creative, however. The establishment of the Film Service also entailed a number of administrative actions meant to consolidate the various cinematic apparatuses of the information, propaganda, and education bureaus of various departments and agencies into one system of distribution to other areas of the government and to the general public. Its advocates claimed that a streamlined Film Service would be better able to serve the users of government films, in both the general public and the government alike, than the variety of services within individual bureaus operating independently of one another.

In its day-to-day operation, the service was to function primarily in a curatorial and advisory relation to other government agencies and departments, some of which had well-established filmmaking operations of their own. In addition to distributing *The Plow* and *The River,* the service's two most popular titles,[59] the service acted as a clearinghouse for the distribution of around four hundred government-produced films to schools, community organizations, business and professional organizations, labor groups and farmers' cooperatives, religious organizations, libraries, and other civic institutions. The Film Service was also responsible for the design and publication of study guides and other pedagogical materials to accompany film screenings and for the development of a Latin American "Good Neighbor" film program. The service would have three main virtues: it would save the taxpayers money, simplify the distribution of government-issue motion pictures, and increase the spectator's enjoyment of government film by instituting a set of aesthetic standards in line with those of the American entertainment cinema. A subsidiary goal of this quality initiative was to increase the presence of government film in commercial theaters, where it had previously been represented only by informational shorts in the program of newsreels and other short subjects that preceded the Hollywood feature. In his instructions to the heads of the National Emergency Council and the Office of Education, the agencies that housed the Film Service during its brief tenure, Roosevelt asserted these goals:

> It has been found advantageous for these agencies to produce motion pictures, sometimes with sound accompaniment, illustrating the physical and human problems confronting the country and the methods adopted by the Government for their solution. Such pictures serve a double purpose. For the people as a whole they make understandable the basic causes of present conditions. For the government employees in the relief and work relief programs, there is provided, not only the invaluable aid that results from this understanding by the general public, but the clarification of the purposes of the relief statutes which they are engaged in administering.[60]

The controversy over the service's activities emerged largely in relation to its production of what in the Hollywood system were called "prestige pictures," feature films with high production values, famous talent, relatively large budgets, and, frequently, a sweeping narrative scope. In addition to Lorentz, the filmmakers recruited to direct Film Service productions included Robert Flaherty; the Dutch socialist filmmaker Joris Ivens and his editor Helen Van Dongen, already well-known in the United States by leftist filmmakers and critics; and cinematographer Floyd Crosby, who had worked with Flaherty and F. W. Murnau on *Tabu* (1931), with Lorentz on *The River,* and had served as president of the antifascist Motion Picture Guild.[61] These prestige productions—Lorentz's *The Fight for Life* (1940), Ivens's *Power and the Land,* and Flaherty's unreleased *The Land,* finished in 1941 under a branch of the Department of Agriculture after the suspension of the service's operations—also employed prominent American composers, musicians, and poets to create distinctive sound tracks, such as Virgil

Thomson, Aaron Copland, and the Pulitzer Prize–winning poet Stephen Vincent Benét. The Film Service was certainly not the first agency to concern itself with the issues of style and quality in nonfiction filmmaking; in a 1938 speech, Fanning Hearon, director of the Division of Motion Pictures at the Department of the Interior, called for "professional titling, background music with subject feeling, interesting, rhythmic narration; social implications; camera angles and special photographic effects; a little drama in the story; a little humor and perhaps a lively girl in a white bathing suit. In short, if such an expression makes sense, a factual improvement on reality." [62] But the vision of the Film Service and of the modernists it employed went well beyond such modest demands to make government film less boring and put the service in a precarious position from its inception.

Opponents in Congress used a variety of arguments against these productions to call the service's legitimacy into question. They argued that these films were a waste of money since they unnecessarily duplicated existing filmmaking operations and that they put the federal government in the position of competing with Hollywood, an impression it could not afford to risk since the Justice Department had been trying for several years to build an antitrust case against the Hollywood studios. Some in Congress also held that the government was using for propaganda purposes funds that had been set aside for the administration of relief programs and, further, that the service was unconstitutional since the federal government was usurping the authority for education given in the Constitution exclusively to the states. The Film Service's critics also argued that making mass appeal the aim of government films transformed the narrowly informational work of publicity performed by these films into a propaganda campaign, a manipulation of public opinion designed to reassure the nation of the timeliness, intelligence, and benevolence of the Roosevelt administration's programs.

The concept of quality filmmaking, which was often used to describe the Film Service's objective, was at the heart of these problems. To the administrators, quality could serve as a synonym of efficiency, as Roosevelt's own instructions on the matter suggested: "in order that all proposed pictures to be produced by departments or establishments of the Government might be improved, wastage prevented, and real economies in production effected," Roosevelt proposed that "a system of minimum standards of quality in motion pictures produced, exhibited and distributed by the Federal Government" be established.[63] To the filmmakers, however, quality might mean something else. In his defense of the service's use of relief funds, Lorentz claimed that formal and technical standards demanded that the service use filmmakers trained in factual film, rather than, as was the case with the federal cultural programs funded through the WPA (the Federal Theatre, Art, Music, and Writers Projects), making work for unemployed filmmakers. "It is not easy," Lorentz argued, "to step out and find men who are trained in the recording of facts. There is a great deal of difference between recording facts and recording fiction and drama."[64] But the reason Lorentz gave before Congress for this impolitic adherence to professional standards clashes with the finished form of the service's productions, which rely more heavily on dramatic and narrative effects than American factual films had to that point. In fact, it was for this blending of fiction and nonfiction effects that the films were celebrated. A *New York Times* reviewer of Lorentz's *The Fight for Life* described wryly what was distinctive about these films:

> Pare Lorentz makes films for the Government. By all governmental film tradition they should be dry as dust, jam-packed with statistics and graphs, as stirring as a Department of Agriculture bulletin on the boll weevil. . . . Something must be wrong with Mr. Lorentz. His film about soil erosion was a splendid documentary called *The Plough* [sic] *That Broke The Plains.* His film about floods emerged as the poetic and magnificent epic, *The River.* His film about maternity arrived at the Belmont yesterday as *The Fight for Life,* and it's as dramatic as life itself.
>
> We don't know what it is that's wrong with Mr. Lorentz for thinking there is drama in the greatest adventure of life . . . for thinking any of us may be interested—no less fascinated—by the workaday routine of visiting nurses and physicians on maternity duty in the slums.[65]

The pursuit of quality can be seen as the inscription, at every level of the cinematic enterprise, of an ideal, an answer to the question that William Guynn says is implicitly posed in all classic documentary form: "In the absence of filmic pleasure that the fiction film exists to produce, why does the spectator go to see a documentary?"[66] From the place its documentaries occupied in the cinematic marketplace to the organization of the cinematic text and its appeal to the viewer, the Film Service held itself out as an ideal form of mass culture, one that combined entertainment with the didacticism of government publicity and the social conscience of the radical-left newsreel and documentary collectives, whose members worked on Film Service productions. Film Service documentary engaged both the state and commercial public spheres, and it did good for both its spectators and its subjects. This sense of responsibility to serve and unite various publics of makers and viewers—an especially strong calling for filmmakers aligned with American communism in the period of the Popular Front—is inscribed throughout the service's films in both theme and address.

POWER TO THE PEOPLE: ELECTRICITY AS ALLEGORY

"Entertainment of a sort that excites the mental powers, calling forth effort and concentration, is the obvious antidote to pointless fantasy," wrote a Film Service supporter in a 1940 book on film and education.[67] But if the service's films were films with a point, they relied nonetheless on techniques of narrative fiction, what Thomas Waugh calls the method of documentary personalization.[68] Although Lorentz had eschewed characterization in his two previous films, three of the four Film Service projects relied heavily on highly condensed personae, what Soviet film theorists called "typification" or "typage," and what Waugh, referring to the work of Joris Ivens, calls "personalized didacticism."[69] From this perspective, the character-driven narrative form of the films completed under the authority of the service, *Power and the Land* and *The Fight for Life*, gave a human face and voice to abstract processes of interpellation.

The source of this interpellation was not explicitly or exclusively the state. In *The Fight for Life*, which follows the reeducation of a young obstetrician at a city maternity clinic, the main character responds to the professional obligation—frequently personalized in his teachers—that he learn and heal, and he only belatedly interprets these as the call of civic or national responsibility. The two calls are conducted in series: the

Figure 2.8. *The Fight for Life* (Pare Lorentz, 1940). Still capture from VHS.

young doctor has, like the film's audience, experienced his professional indoctrination as a series of voice-overs, including a film within the film at the maternity clinic, narrated by one of his instructors. Not all of these voices of supervisory authority are male: the most regular voice in the film is that of the maternity center's receptionist, who is heard frequently over the image of a large gridded chalkboard, calling out the locations and details of active cases (see figure 2.8). Identified at once with the technological network of the telephone system and the supervisory agencies of the social and medical sciences, as well as, in an unspecified way, the local welfare agencies funding the center, this voice-of-grid is the most potent symbol of the technocratic ambitions behind the service, and the New Deal itself. Late in the film, the young protagonist observes the squalor of the neighborhoods in which he has been training, and he wonders aloud, over footage of vacant lots and gleaners sifting through trash, why "we" allow people to live and starve in such conditions. Despite his transformation into a voice of civic responsibility, his appeal remains philosophical and humanist. At no point does the film suggest a political cause or solution for the problems of urban poverty and illness with which the film is ostensibly concerned.

But in *Power and the Land,* the nature of this calling and the transformation it effects in the characters and viewers who receive it is unavoidably political. *Power and the Land* is about the work of the Rural Electrification Administration, a bureau of the U.S. Department of Agriculture, to bring electricity to farms and rural areas and to encourage the establishment of rural power cooperatives. But rather than being a lesson from the perspective of the state agency, in the mode of *The New Frontier, Power and the Land* is primarily a nonfiction story about one particular case, the Parkinson family of St. Clairsville, Ohio. The link between "social relations of meaning" and aesthetic or textual strategies is especially profound in the example of *Power and the Land,* where the attempt to model a new social contract was so thorough that this textual strategy bled over into the real lives of the film's subjects. During the making of the film the Parkinson farm was in fact wired for electricity and supplied with some of the new appliances we see at the end of the film (others were only lent to the family for the duration of shooting), in exchange for their participation. Presented in the film as both an authentic example of the need for a welfare state and an ideal of democratic citizenship, the Parkinsons became a literally model family through the production of the film, as Mrs. Parkinson indicated in a letter to the director, Joris Ivens, after filming:

> There is a separate meter on each piece of electrical equipment and I am keeping a record for the Rural Electrification Administration. How many pieces of washing each week, the number of persons for each meal, amount of and so forth, so by the next meeting our friend Mr. MacAllister will be able to tell exactly how much it costs to have a clean shirt or make a pot of coffee. They put the outside meter on yesterday.[70]

A written prologue announces the synecdochal relation between the Parkinson family and the country at large: "Here is one American farm, one American family—the Parkinsons, there are thousands like them, all over the union." (This is, incidentally, one of the few times a demonstrative phrase like "here is" is used in the film.) The film then embarks upon a story designed to raise and subdue the tension between two seemingly antithetical ideals, primitive community and technological development, a dialectical desire for what Lewis Mumford called, in *Technics and Civilization* (1934), the "new objectivity" of technologized, and technocratic, societies.[71]

In the first part of the film, we see one complete day of farm work and life and are led to understand both the difficulty and the pastoral charm of life without electric light and power. The family gets up in the dark and does the morning chores by the dim light of kerosene lamps; the sons harvest an alfalfa crop with a horse-drawn thresher; an order of the Parkinsons' milk is refused by the dairy because of spoilage that is the result of insufficient cooling; Hazel Parkinson and her daughter do "the women's work" of laundry and filling the lamps, jobs that take all day. After dinner, the children do their homework, and mother tries to sew in insufficient light (see figures 2.9 and 2.10). The second part of the film is organized around the theme of "neighbors, working together," and demonstrates how cooperation, community, and government are linked: the men of St. Clairsville get together to help Bill Parkinson cut his corn crop with machetes and then sit on the ground and discuss the merits of electricity and electric appliances. This leads to a town meeting with an REA representative, where the men and women of the community consider the government's offer of assistance in acquiring generators and power lines. (These "dialogue" scenes were, like the rest of the film, shot without sound, so the roles of the participants in the discussions are all played by the voice of the commentary, William Adams, who reads a script written by Stephen Vincent Benét.) In the third section of the film, the community installs its power lines. The film breaks away briefly from the story of the Parkinsons and St. Clairsville to present a graphic representation of the work done nationally by the REA since 1935 and to show, by images of power lines, the connection between the city and the country. It returns to the Parkinson farm to compare their lives after electrification to what we saw of them in the first part of the film. Now they have adequate light in the barn, reliable cooling for the milk, and all the ame-

Figure 2.9. *Power and the Land* (Joris Ivens, 1940). Frame enlargement from 16mm filmstrip.

Figure 2.10. *Power and the Land* (Joris Ivens, 1940). Still capture from DVD.

nities of a modern home, including lights that come on with the flick of a switch, running hot water, a washing machine and electric iron, a radio, and the electric oven that allows Hazel Parkinson to prepare the dinner that ends the film.

The relation of these events to one another, as elements of both a quotidian account of rural life and values and a historical narrative of change and modernization, is suggested to us by the voice-over, which remarks from time to time on the significance of a depicted act or scene. Over shots of Hazel Parkinson's early-morning routine of bringing water to the kitchen and starting up the wood stove, the voice-over comments: "This is 1940. But the farm woman's day is long. They don't complain, the women like Hazel Parkinson, but they know on an August morning how hot the stove was going to be at noon. They might not say much about it, but they wish you could just turn on a faucet to get your water the way you can in town." And later in the film, after the power lines have been installed, the commentary points out that now, instead of "minutes at the pump," it will only take "a turn of the hand" to provide water for the horse: "power at cost" will mean "better living. We've got the power from the high lines now. It'll help us out, through night and day."

The voice-over and its figures of speech guide the viewer to a general understanding of these ordinary acts. But voice is not the film's only allegorical device. In contrast to the utilitarian composition of *The New Frontier, Power and the Land* also makes use of a wide range of expressive devices, including camera angle and movement, shot size and lighting, and physical gesture and expression, along with the musical score, to underscore certain pedagogical dimensions of the narrative. Thus, Floyd Crosby's chiaroscuro shots of Bill Parkinson working in the barn before sunrise aren't just aesthetically pleasing; they also serve the purpose of presenting a contrast to the later images of the farm evenly lit by electric light. In fact, the film here seems to suggest that the rural landscape, or the passive appreciation of its beauty, contributes to the social and political problems of those living there: the aspects of farm life that appear romantic to the outsider are in fact the most urgent causes for modernization. The film in this way creates a cinematic excuse (in the sense of alibi, or other place) for the active intervention, by the filmmakers and, by extension, the New Deal, in the lives of the inhabitants of this picturesque region.

Power and the Land abounds with such moments, where an aural or visual pun on "lighting" or "power" or "lines" reiterates the theme of the film. The resonance can be as slight as the play between a shot and a line in the commentary, as when, during the conventional scene of the common folk speaking their minds (in this instance, about electrification), the voice-over, speaking for one of the men, says "I'd sure like to light up the barn": during this line, we see a close-up of one of the men's hands rolling a cigarette. And sometimes the structure of the double meaning is much more elaborate, as in the sequence of nine shots following the flow of power, via electrical lines, from a generating station in the city to the Parkinsons' house in the country. Benét's commentary tells the viewer, over a pan along the overhead lines, that "there's a tune as the wind blows through the wires, power for the Parkinsons," and as the lines reach the Parkinson home, it is difficult not to see the lines as the scriptural structure of the "tune" itself. The diagonal left-to-right and top-to-bottom pan that reaches the side of the house is accompanied only by the score, heavy, at this moment, on strings, making the five lines of the wires look suddenly like the five lines of the musical staff. The denotation of the sequence is simply that power lines create a link between city and country. But the connotation makes reference to the materials of the film itself as a means of continuity between one location and another, conducting social relations across distance through the materials of cinematic expression.

Such moments are one of the ways that the film links the specific narrative of the Parkinsons and St. Clairsville to the general narrative of the United States under the New Deal. As a representative of the general public to whom the film was addressed, the spectator is the linchpin of this interpretive structure. The implicit claim of state documentary to communicate the ideals of the state and to engage spectators as citizens depends upon the spectator's interpretation of the film text: not just the spectator's enjoyment of its content, but his or her comprehension of the relation between this content or story and the documentary form. In trying to make the relation between form and content a significant one, documentarists faced the hegemony of classical Hollywood film style, where form merely made possible the comprehension and enjoyment of the narrative. In classical Hollywood narrative, form was subordinate to the logic of narrative and character psychology, which appeared to motivate form. Documentary was hardly immune from this problem. As is still true today for many critics, a documentary had form only insofar as its content was reality. In response to American reaction to his Spanish Civil War documentary, *The Spanish Earth* (1937), Ivens complained that

> film critics, especially in America, were at this time so exclusively involved in the fiction film that there was even difficulty in establishing a workable viewpoint from which to criticize a documentary film. I believe that if these critics had worked out a solid esthetic for the fiction film they would not have been at such a loss before an unfamiliar film form. Thus, occasionally, they talk about form, when they actually mean content, making a complete distinction between picture and the commentary.[72]

The use of allegory in *Power and the Land* is, in part, a response to this situation.

Power and the Land presents electricity as a metaphor for the mediating role of the government. But it is not only the present and potential tensions among bodies politic—the left, the people, the government—that are mediated in this allegory. Allegory is a way to relate the life of the individual to transpersonal realities, and the story of the Parkinsons' modernization also establishes connections between the kinship group and the social, the local and the national, the rural and the urban, traditional values and progress. These oppositions are paralleled by the hermeneutic opposition, between the particular historical example and the general ethical lesson, that structures the film. Government is nowhere seen intervening in a direct way in these tensions but consists in the mediation between them. And in turn, the narrative is structured along the lines of the electrification metaphor. Like electrification, narrative allows information to travel across distances and yet still unite a population as a community.[73]

The problems addressed and mediated by the film are figured throughout the film as matters of power. The country people are literally without power. They get together and discuss this problem; as the commentary says, "they talk it over the country way, the slow cautious decision of the people." They see that there is something wrong with their situation. In coming to this understanding, they gain *political* power. This process of "slow, cautious decision" makes them an ideal form of democracy, but how does it help them with their initial problem? In order to gain the (electrical) power they lack through the (political) power inherent in them as a community—in order, that is, to modernize their farms—the farmers need the help of the government, which, unlike the private utilities, will treat this problem objectively. Where the utility industry has no motivation to provide power to rural communities, the government sees modernization as a public need. In keeping with the deficit spending model of the New Deal, the government is able to see the farmers' lack of purchasing power as an opportunity to expand capitalism into a new territory.[74] The effort of the film is to show the relation between the two kinds of power, and to show how, with the help of the government, lack is transformed into opportunity and idealism generates responsible government.

In order for the film to be in this way about mediation, some narrative progression is necessary: not just of the story of the modernization effort but also of the reflexive subtext of this story, the conversion of the film from a simple case study of a rural community to a lesson in the ethics of government for the general viewer. So, for two reasons, it is not enough for the lyrical depiction of milking by hand early in the film ("Milk, ringing in the pail, white and clean, fresh milk for the town and city, fresh milk that makes bones and muscles for the children of the nation") to announce a connection between the farm and the rest of the country, a natural or harmonious relation that is underscored by the correspondence between the rhythm of the milking action and the rhythm of the tune on the soundtrack. First, because of a fundamental disease at the heart of the natural relations of production and reproduction depicted in this scene. It turns out that some of the Parkinsons' milk has soured in storage. Though it stands for a pastoral ideal, the manual labor of dairying (an activity that involves both Bill and the sons who, it is suggested, will inherit the farm) is nonetheless an impediment to modernization, and consequently a threat to the nation's health. How will this purely market-based relation between city and country, producer and consumer, one family and others, be healed? Through the construction of a public sphere that is depicted in, and eventually embodied by, the film itself. Thus, the second reason that the link between farm and nation cannot simply be announced by the voice of the film is that it is through the spectator's comprehension of the allegorical narrative that this connection will occur in its healthy form. That is to say, the film itself will demonstrate a principle of social organization besides those—the family; the market—based entirely on relations of production and reproduction.

It is because the import of this new principle, the welfare state, is so great, and implies such a large-scale reformation of "life," that the New Deal documentaries eschew the direct instruction style of voice-over associated up to this point with government instructional and promotional film of the sound era, an example of which we hear in a film like *The New Frontier*. This tutelary voice must be faded down or muted. Hence the puns, the repetition and redundancy, the use of indirect and lyrical discourse rather than the direct address typical of narrowly instructional cinema. If direct speech constituted the major role of text as act, then the interpellative function of this particular kind of state documentary demands that it not instruct so much as enunciate, or "talk to us *about* this text *as* an act."

One form that enunciation takes in *Power and the Land* is the intratextual relation between the soundtrack and the planes of narrative and image, in which the music and the commentary announce the effort to convert the merely documentary images to characters, figures, and story elements. The tone of the commentary, as I have already said, is often that of a novelistic narrator, employing the psychological device of free indirect discourse. In the scene of the "slow cautious decision of the people," this intratextual voice presents the film with both a problem and an opportunity. This scene is the crux of the narrative, insofar as it represents an instance of the organic public sphere, wherein men of St. Clairsville meet on the basis of a mutual interest in order to make an appeal to the government. But because it is technically unfeasible and stylistically inconsistent for them to speak in their own voices in this scene, the voice-over provides this dialogue for them. Given that the point of the scene is that the men find the voice with which they will address the state, and that they find this collec-

Figure 2.11. *Power and the Land* (Joris Ivens, 1940). Still capture from DVD.

tive voice by, as the commentary points out, listening to one another carefully, the monopoly on speech by the voice-over has to be viewed as something of a contradiction. Ivens deals with this contradiction by highlighting it visually: he organizes the men in such a way that the tracking shot that takes in the men as a group, a set of talking heads in profile, emphasizes their ears (see figures 2.11 and 2.12). If it is initially disturbing that a scene devoted to the men talking and listening to one another depicts them as unable even to hear themselves, the film turns this lack to ideological ends. Government, it seems to say, helps us bridge distance and divisions of class and geography that become more, not less, significant with the technological modernization of national space. The rational application of technology to problems of society will not only decrease the alienation and social fragmentation threatened by the mechanization of work but will promote reflective citizenship.[75]

Figure 2.12. *Power and the Land* (Joris Ivens, 1940). Still capture from DVD.

In fact, it is insufficient to call electricity a metaphor in the text of *Power and the Land*. It is, rather, the model for the text, as present in the film's form of expression as in its contents and their thematic harmony. Electricity transmits and is transmitted; it transforms and is transformed. These functions are coextensive with the film's language, operating like the free indirect discourse of ideology that Deleuze and Guattari call the order-word, which "goes from saying to saying."[76] Along these lines, the scene just described, of a voice that channels the popular vocation of politics, the call to democracy and to national responsibility, raises the question of how the film's address is felt beyond the film. How do we in the audience, at a different sort of distance from the discussion, hear these discussions as related to our own lives, as instructive to us in our own communities?

If this question drives the organization of the film text in *Power and the Land* and the other ventriloquist works of the Film Service, its enunciation extended beyond the borders of the film itself, as is clear from the Service's 1938 study guides to *The Plow That Broke the Plains* and *The River*, then being distributed by the service. The writers of the guides imagine an amazing range of activities that educational screenings for both children and adults will generate. The repeated viewings that the guides prescribe might compel not only the democratic activities of voting in federal elections (government legislation supporting sensible use of natural resources, the guide to *Plow* insists, "can only be carried out if a large majority of the local people are in favor of protecting the land and will express their opinion in an election held for that purpose") or participating in local government (protected areas "must be formed by local people under state laws, and the associations must be local in origin"), but also a wide range of forms of civil association. School children might correspond with children living in the Dust Bowl ("Get them to tell you of their experiences during the bad storms") or form social groups interested in land use ("Are there any clubs or organizations in your neighborhood working on a conservation program? . . . If there is no club, could you help to start one?").[77] And the guides provide a whole range of suggestions for applying *The Plow* and *The River* to group activity in the classroom ("The subject matter of the Great Plains is rich in dramatic significance. . . . The whole sweep of the subject, presented chronologically, should make a most stirring pageant" [43]). The study-guide idea seemed to suffer from the same frustrated idealism of the Film Service itself: no guides appear to have been produced for the four films actually produced under the aegis of the service. Instead, the suggestions that the guides make for further reflection are made implicitly in the enunciation of the service films.

To conclude that there is an enunciation specific to documentary that can be placed in the service of these democratizing or civilizing functions, we would have to be able to say that the documentary narration did not close off the question of the viewer's relation to the text as firmly as does classical narrative. The viewer of classical narrative is engaged with the film primarily by working out the story and by the acts of identification that put the viewer in the position to assimilate the psychological logic of the narration. Classical narrative is by no means thoughtless or mechanical but is structured, as William Guynn puts it, around the "gradual and halting resolution of enigmas, a suspense that creates expectation in the reader and dispatches him along the labyrin-thine pathways that lead to 'truth.'"[78] In order to perform a different function, the classical documentary narrative must more or less dis-pense with suspense as a motivation. It does not, according to Guynn, "hold us in suspense or generate expectation. It discloses itself: there are no enigmas to resolve."[79] But the story of the Parkinsons and their encounter with local cooperation and government regulation nonethe-less must end. In the final section of the film, illustrating the benefits of life with electricity, the film reiterates that its operative principle is not simply the production of hermeneutic desire but the production of interpretation—less the closure of the narrative than the disclosure of the discursive logic.

In the last eight and a half minutes of the film, after the power lines arrive at the Parkinson farm, the film picks up where it left off, before the interlude on government and the public. In returning to the con-ceptual frame of daily life on the farm, however, the film dispenses with the temporal structure around which the "before electrification" open-ing section was organized. Rather than taking us all the way through the work day, as the opening section did, the film picks up at the Par-kinson home in the late afternoon and enumerates the various changes brought by electrification. The narrative structure of the film suddenly appears very simple, even schematic: everything that happens in this fi-nal section forms part of a set that could be titled "after electrification." In this catalogue of brief scenes showing the Parkinsons learning to in-corporate modern conveniences into their lives, three pieces of visual play underscore and reiterate the themes of the film.

As I suggested earlier, the concept of the line is quite significant in the film, and it appears as both a visual and narrative figure. This preoc-cupation is worked into the final section in a scene with Bill Parkinson and his youngest son. We see the son getting into the shower, a con-tinuation of the statement made by showing Bill adjusting and testing the water heater, proving that the house now has hot running water. Hearing his father come upstairs, the son closes the shower curtains, and hides while Bill washes his hands. In a shot/reverse-shot sequence, the son sticks his head out of the shower and surprises his father. In re-turn, Bill splashes his son with water from the sink. Reiterating a scene from the first part of the film where Bill and his young son engage in some play with the machete Bill is using to cut cornstalks, this sequence is, from one perspective, simply a piece of visual shorthand to show that, despite the addition to the home of labor-saving devices, electrical gadgets, and other ways of life imported from the city, the Parkinson home retains the closeness between family members born from hard work and necessity.[80]

But the creative choices that Ivens and the film's editor, Helen Van Dongen, make in constructing the sequence suggest that more can be squeezed from this scene than sentimentality. The film has already emphasized the contradiction of the lines: the power lines both increase and threaten essential forms of relation and continuity between people. All of the old-fashioned ways and values represented by the farm in the romantic-popular imagination, clichés that are cited throughout *Power and the Land,* are threatened by the encroachment of modern urban life and the unrestricted pursuit of profit that the private electrical industry is gently accused of. But at the same time, the link to the city and the rest of the nation promised by the power lines and, by implication, the return of prosperity, increases the strength of certain social and cultural bonds: the primitive democracy in which the men of St. Clairsville assemble to discuss a power cooperative and the patriarchal line of inheritance through which the farm came into Bill Parkinson's hands, and through which the farm will be maintained after Bill Parkinson, like lamplight, disappears.

These dilemmas of modernization give added resonance to a syntactical eccentricity in the washing scene between Bill and his young son. The water play between the two of them takes three shots. In the first, Bill is at the sink, and his son sticks his head out of the shower; in the second, a closer reverse of the first shot, Bill throws some water from the tap at his son. When we return to a close-up of the son, we expect the pay-off, the water hitting him. Instead, the film presents us with the son's face, still teasing his father. Only after what seems like far too long for realism does the water hit the son in the face. Given that Van Dongen was an experienced editor, and that there are many examples in this film and in *The Spanish Earth,* her previous film with Ivens, of shot combinations that deliberately break with the conventions of continuity editing, it is hard to see this temporal extension merely as a mistake. Instead, it could be read as a reiteration of the productive par-

Figure 2.13. *Power and the Land* (Joris Ivens, 1940). Still capture from DVD.

adox of "line." Electrical lines allow power to overcome distances that seem insurmountable, even the gap that threatens to emerge in the patriarchal line because of the encroachment of technological society on the traditional ways of work and life.

Two other pieces of visual play from this final section exploit the idea of the obsolescence of the Parkinson parents and the transformation of their old ways and old bodies into a source of life for the community and the imagined community constituted by the film's viewers. The first is the shot near the beginning of the final section where Bill Parkinson comes home for dinner, entering the house through the kitchen door. He enters the shot on the right, takes his hat off, and puts his hat on a kerosene lamp sitting on a table in the foreground of the shot (see figure 2.13). Before exiting the frame on the left, he looks down with amusement at the hat and smiles slightly, not only drawing our attention to the lamp but showing that he understands the significance of this image, which lingers after Bill leaves the shot, before cutting to one in which he is capping off the lamp, which is now a useless ornament. To the spectator, this pun has a double meaning because the image, representing the successful conversion of the Parkinson farm to electricity, caps off the story. In the overt look down at the hat, which Ivens no doubt called for in his direction of the scene, the two meanings are tied together.

In his look down at the lamp in acknowledgment of the fanciful nature of his gesture, Bill acknowledges as well his transformation from historical subject to actor or allegorical figure. In other words, the pause to "say" to the audience, "I know that you know that that was a heavily weighted gesture," figuratively snuffs out not just the lamp but the old Bill Parkinson, too: he is no longer Bill Parkinson, struggling farmer, but now Bill Parkinson, symbol of progress, the American equivalent of Marfa, heroine of Eisenstein's *The General Line* (1929), through whom the stubborn peasants and *kulaks* are modernized and collectivized. Hazel Parkinson is likewise elevated to an allegorical figure at the end of the film. At the beginning of the final section, Hazel is in the kitchen, demonstrating the new fixtures to her older sons. When one of them turns on the new overhead light, Hazel is shown in a close-up raising her eyes to look at it (see figures 2.14 and 2.15). For the attentive viewer, this shot recalls the sequence at the end of the first part of the film, where a close-up of Mrs. Parkinson straining to sew in the dim lamplight emphasized the mother's sacrifice for her children and the tight bond between family members. In recognizing that the later shot rhymes with the earlier one, the spectator takes an active part in the articulation of the allegory. To notice that the close-up of the mother emphasizes her eyes is to "get" the relation between the narratives and to have been "enlightened" by the film. The mother's glance at the off-screen source of her satisfaction suggests that she is acknowledging a higher authority for its divine intervention into their lives. The whimsical overtone is that she does indeed have a higher authority to thank for her transformation, though whether this invisible force is the state or the audience, agent of the allegorical operation, is left unresolved. Therein resides the social power of the cinematic order-word.

If the town meeting was the emblem of New Deal documentary, it was also its symptom. While Steiner and Van Dyke, Ivens, and Flaherty

Figure 2.14. *Power and the Land* (Joris Ivens, 1940). Frame enlargement from 16mm filmstrip.

Figure 2.15. *Power and the Land* (Joris Ivens, 1940). Frame enlargement from 16mm filmstrip.

were filming their "little theoretical theatres" of men gathering to talk things over, Congress was gutting the Film Service, herding its staff from one department to another, and laying the grounds for the transformation of state-sponsored social documentary into war propaganda, replacing the liberal-left teams responsible for Film Service productions with routinized Hollywood filmmaking under the direction of figures like Frank Capra and John Ford. But while the Film Service was undoubtedly the victim of political cynicism, it is tempting to read its failure as the fullest expression of its own idealism; its commitment to an ambiguous "quality" style of cinema; and its commitment, behind this aesthetic, to the New Deal stew of organic forms of community and scientific management.[81] In this way, the ruins that appear throughout service films—the obsolete practices and tools in *Power and the Land;* the death that opens and haunts *The Fight For Life* and the slums in which it closes; and the abandoned mansions and derelict farmers in *The Land* and, indeed, the very pointlessness of that film, an untimely echo of earlier New Deal films—seem the most fitting epitaph for the Film Service itself and for its formal experiment in contemporary public history. Epitaph or allegory: for, as Benjamin reminds us, the ruin is the presence in reality of the failed aspirations of the past.[82]

PART II

Lyrical Tirades

New Documentary and the New Left

3 / REVOLUTIONARY SOUNDS

Listening to Radical Documentary

"Hot" history, history in the course of being made, is an auditive history . . .
—ROLAND BARTHES, "Writing The Event"

The dynamics of sound in various forms were no less important to radical documentary in the 1960s and 1970s than they were to the development of the New Deal and Popular Front versions of social documentary, with their oracular voices and dramatic modern scores. The methods and concerns of European and North American *cinéma vérité* documentary promised a cinema of social commentary that would be freed from the imperious voice-over exposition of classical documentary. The political goals of radical filmmakers aligned with the civil rights, antiwar, feminist, and gay liberation movements—above all, of giving voice to those whose struggle was carried out on terrain at once too local or too international to be considered American in the terms established by the national media—were therefore linked to the aesthetic challenge of finding an appropriately particular language for the representation of these struggles, one that also reflected the economic, technical, and organizational problems of film as a medium.[1] Fidelity was the dialectical principle of this filmmaking: the less elaborate the technology of representation, the higher the fidelity to politics.[2] The amount of what, under the conventions of mainstream film and television, would be regarded as noise in these documentaries was directly proportional to the filmmakers' commitment to political causes. These sounds, and the cinema that emerged to disseminate them, are the focus of this chapter. Yelling, immoderate proclamations, ear-splitting rock music, electronic feedback, bad singing, untranslatable speeches and songs, accented English, and all manner of sounds unmoored from visual referents: these were not just aural icons of a radical style of politics. Incorporated into the films as expository devices, they were signs of a problem in the public sphere of cinema.

D.N. Rodowick writes that 1968 was the moment at which the cinema became free to work with the "inexplicable" and the "undecidable" and in which *"incompossible* worlds proliferate as incongruous presents."[3] This kind of statement has tended to refer only to narrative and art film of the period, as well as to the development of an academic discipline of film theory, one that largely ignored documentary. But the goal of many Movement filmmakers and organizations was to infuse the present time observed by documentary with a sense of incompossibility, the sense of a time out of joint. In this way, the concept of dissonance might be taken as an epistemological principle, extending to the historical analysis of documentary and its periods.

ECHOES OF '68

Positing a historical dynamic in American documentary film, Paul Arthur describes three "interludes of high visibility" for American documentary, moments when a variety of factors conspired to give nonfiction modes of film and television the appearance of social relevance.[4] However briefly, these modes came to seem a new frontier of politics on which responses to crisis can be aired, and solutions explored. Observing certain philosophical and ideological continuities between otherwise very different forms and ages of American documentary— New Deal documentary, the independent *cinéma vérité* movement of the 1960s, and the ironic postmodernism of first-person documentaries like *Sherman's March* (Ross McElwee, 1986) and *Roger & Me* (Michael Moore, 1989)—Arthur argues that the "undulations of American liberalism" can be felt not only within each period but in the intervals between them. Each moment produces "figures through which to signify the spontaneous, the anticonventional, the refusal of mediating process," argues Arthur.[5] That these periods of invention can all be said to pursue the goal of greater authenticity and a vaguely defined "fidelity to the Real"[6] makes them seem less like phases of an evolving artistic discipline, or historically specific social interventions, and more like another of the cycles and patterns that typify cultural life under the conditions of consumer capitalism. Arthur concludes that "for better or worse," American documentary will always pursue the goal of "historically specific legitimations of authenticity."[7] Each of his three moments in the history of American documentary comes to serve as an example of a merely functional opposition between the present form of documentary and a past one. This timeless process resembles the movement of ideology, in Louis Althusser's well-known formulation: even if specific ideologies have histories, ideology "in general" is eternal.[8]

This analysis appears to be borne out by *The Weather Underground* (Sam Green and Bill Siegel, 2002). *The Weather Underground* tells the story of Weatherman,[9] the radical faction of Students for a Democratic Society (SDS) that tried to force the organization to take a more militant position on the Vietnam War, which it considered the flashpoint of an international revolutionary movement against racism and imperialism. In 1968, at the height of its visibility, SDS membership numbered around 100,000.[10] But by 1969, the group had begun to fall apart under the pressure of months of internal squabbling. One of the final straws was the negative publicity the Weathermen generated for the Movement during the Chicago "Days of Rage" action in October, during which several hundred people—a much smaller group than organizers anticipated—took to the streets to smash windows and battle with police. Soon after, the Weathermen abandoned the failing organization and went underground as a small, scattered cadre committed to the violent overthrow of the state. Composed of interviews with former Weathermen and SDSers, a rich mixture of archival and stock footage and audiotape, and excerpts from diaries and memoirs of the underground life (read by Lili Taylor, the actress who played guerrilla feminist Valerie Solanas in Mary Harron's biopic *I Shot Andy Warhol* [1996]), the film paints a vivid picture of these years and the individuals who survived them.

To tell this story, Green and Siegel gathered a wide variety of archival and stock materials, including television news broadcasts, news and surveillance photography, documentary and propaganda films, and generic commercial and private images of mainstream life. In their energetic style of montage, the filmmakers treat all of this pictorial matter as equally valid, or equally suspect, images of history, regardless of its original function. In such an amalgamation, an old television ad or a clip from a porno film does just as well to visualize the 1970s as does newsfilm, documentary photography, or eyewitness testimony. This apparent discrepancy between the meticulousness of the filmmakers' visual research and the irreverence of their editing style is reflected in the film's soundtrack, which eschews the usual selections from popular music of the period in favor of an ambient electronic score that pulses and whines, enhancing the historical separation that infuses the filmmakers' treatment of images.

While this highly mannered manipulation of audio-visual form suggests, at first glance, a break with the logic of truth that, according to Arthur, defines American social documentary, it also places *The Weather Underground* and retro-revisionist films like it within the cycle of authenticities that Arthur describes, on the principle that each succeeding mode must invent techniques of representation and enunciation that challenge and displace those of the previous mode. Returning to the montage constructions and modernist textual layerings of 1930s documentary, including the use of stylized, plural voice-overs, the film rejects the axiom of transparency that marked both *cinéma vérité* and the first-person documentary of the 1980s and 1990s. At the same time, however, it embraces history precisely as stylistic excess, as a way to declare its fidelity not only to the ideas and experiences of its subjects but to the present as well. To bind together its collection of images and sounds, the filmmakers borrow the formal heterogeneity of the state-modernist documentary of the New Deal era, stripping out the confident overtones of scientific and technological rationalism and of the centralized political authority of the welfare state.

The discord that is audible on the soundtrack and visible in the images stands, in other words, for both the present state of the left, a movement in disarray, and the fondly recalled cacophonous period around 1968, when it was in full voice. The dynamics of sound in various forms—music, speech, and noise—were important to the development of radical documentary, as they were to the organization and the self-image of the New Left itself. Weatherman took its name from a line in Bob Dylan's 1965 song "Subterranean Homesick Blues," and the group used lyrics and titles of songs by Dylan, the Lovin' Spoonful,

the Doors, and other popular musicians in its policy statements, com-
muniqués, and publicity materials. Kirkpatrick Sale's description of
the foundational public act of Weatherman, the pointless destruction
of Gold Coast storefronts and cars on the first night of the Chicago
Days of Rage in October 1969 underscores the dissonant quality of the
Movement and its public spheres:

> The crowd swarmed down the streets, shouting and ululating and trot-
> ting with a supercharged emotion and a flush of unleashed energy—"I
> saw and felt the transformation of the mob," a New York Weatherman,
> Shin'ya Ono, wrote later, "into a battalion of three hundred revolution-
> ary fighters"—and then within moments they began the assault—"*Ho!*
> *Ho! Ho Chi Minh!*" . . . "Each one of us," Ono said, "felt the soldier in
> us." Their courage fed on the noise, the almost tangible vibrations of
> the chants and yells echoing off the buildings on the narrower streets,
> sending a tingle up the spine, creating for moments on end the hyp-
> notic sense of vast and unstoppable numbers, invincible and righteous
> power. Their adrenalin rose at the forbidden, musical sound of breaking
> glass.[11]

One mark of *The Weather Underground*'s fidelity to its subject is its use
of similarly jarring and dissonant sounds. Mainstream documentary
convention dictates two kinds of sound to accompany historical images: direct sound, taken from the space and time of the profilmic; and
the nostalgic use of period-specific pop music. Like the irreverent treatment of historical images in the visual register of the film, however, the
use of discordant and anachronistic music and noise on the soundtrack
expresses, by its very resistance to conventions of documentary sound,
a kind of solidarity with Weatherman's radical mission.

Suspending the historical conventions of sound, the film instead develops what Joan W. Scott calls a historical "echo." As an aural metaphor, echo stands for the question of how the present and the past are
related in the work of the historian:

> For historians, echo provides yet another take on the process of estab-
> lishing identity by raising the issues of the distinction between the
> original sound and its resonances and the role of time in the distortions

heard. Where does an identity originate? Does the sound issue forth from past to present, or do answering calls echo to the present from the past? If we are not the source of the sound, how can we locate that source? If all we have is the echo, can we ever discern the original?[12]

Sounds are not perceived, as Christian Metz pointed out, the same way that images are. We always know exactly in what direction we are looking: images have a clear location (the screen) and source (the thing in the world that the image resembles). But it is never quite as clear where a sound is coming from or what produces it. The aural object loosens the bonds between the subject and what it perceives, suspending, as Metz says, the "'adverse spectacle' of subject and object."[13] As is exemplified by the use of certain sounds in *The Weather Underground*, this loosening contributes to the phenomenon of historical echo, allowing the film to pose the question, "Who (and where) am I in relation to this past?" The function of such sounds is to make viewers reflect upon the difference between the present and the past and, indirectly, to reflect upon the privileged status of documentary film as a bridge between past and present, as a tool of historical understanding. This is true in particular of the melancholic sounds that linger from the film: the airy, minor-key bleeps of the musical score and the tones of shame and regret in the reflective interviews.

By using retrospective interviews shot at close range to structure its argument, the film becomes preoccupied with the very logic of historical continuity it otherwise means to challenge, reverting to the evidence of experience.[14] Using cinematic tropes of interiority, it individuates the former Weathermen as psychological and moral subjects. This subjective dimension is noticeably absent from their appearance in Emile de Antonio's earlier film about the group, *Underground* (1976), where the filmmakers base their approach on the social and political form of the tactical collective, on the model of the guerrilla cell. In their interviews, the former revolutionaries reflect on the consequences of their actions and explain them not only in terms of what they believed then but how they live now. Not all of these interviews have the tenor of apologies, and many of the subjects speak movingly of their ongoing commitment to radical social change, even when this belief has come at the cost of their freedom or their sanity. But the dominant tone of their testimonies, and of the film itself, is one of regret: regret for the hardships the fugitives caused their families, who had to endure years of secrecy about their existence, and regret for the damage that Weatherman did to the student movement and the causes of the radical left. In his scathing contemporary assessment of Weatherman, Kirkpatrick Sale echoed many on the left, from feminists and the Black Panthers to the displaced old-line Marxists in SDS, who felt that, for all its dogmatic criticism of the white bourgeoisie, Weather's Third World–ism was built on the disavowal of privilege: the group's only real principle, according to Sale, was contrition, its members' regret that they had not been born black or poor.[15] From this perspective, the remorse displayed in *The Weather Underground* by the former radicals is historically accurate and consistent.

But the feeling of distance and loss in relation to the past is not the exclusive province of the film's subjects. Its cutting and manipulation of historical footage suffuse the viewing experience with a sense of separation between past and present, while the moody electronic score and expressions of remorse on the faces and in the voices of the film's interview subjects give this distance a sentimental shading. The film appears to share its subjects' disappointment at the failed promise of the Movement, and it requires of its viewers that they, too, feel sad about this loss. In the texture of the film, specific regrets—about tactical political errors or about the personal costs of life underground—become a generalized lament for the passing of the radical left. This identification of the film with its subjects takes the paradoxical form of a disavowal, the acknowledgment that we no longer live in that past that they inhabited. If it is sad to be a former member of the Weather Underground, it is sadder to inhabit a present in which their beliefs and actions seem outdated.

The film's ironic treatment of its archive of visual artifacts hardly diminishes this pathos. This irony serves, rather, as a sign of the melancholy that suffuses the film and many other, similarly sympathetic accounts of oppositional culture in the 1960s and 1970s. Nostalgia does not accurately name this feeling because the filmmakers are obviously leery of the idealization of the Sixties that is commonplace in leftist documentary. Rather, the film engages in a form of fetishism that Walter Benjamin called "left-wing melancholy."[16] The left melancholic,

Benjamin writes, is acutely conscious of the "empty spaces where . . . feelings—nature and love, enthusiasm and humanity—once rested. Irony is the left melancholic's defense against loss."[17] In this vein, we might say that the real topic of *The Weather Underground* is less the radical group of its title than the embarrassing discrepancy between the documentary evidence of a once-vibrant radical movement, in a time of widespread social and political upheaval, and the notable absence, in the present, of the effects of this movement. The film's reliance on a particular affective palette makes this defeat seem inevitable. The dissonance between the methods or goals of the Movement and their defeat at the hands of the establishment (or simply of time itself, which ages the young revolutionaries or passes without shape in the prison sentences they eventually received) is resolved in the melancholy that the viewer and the film finally share.

The sounds of revolution are ultimately reduced in *The Weather Underground* to a theme or figure in the larger metaphorical structure of the film's melancholic voice. When it is measured against the reasonable voices of the film's subjects speaking in the present, this noise functions as the sign of a radical vision that proved to be an illusion, a fantasy in the simple sense of an unrealistic idea.[18] In keeping with what is ultimately a liberal view of history, one based in the individual, the film reestablishes a hierarchy of sounds, in which nonverbal noises are subordinated to self-possessed, reflective speech. Returning to the films of the period, however, it is not clear that sound has to be narrated and historicized in this way. As both theme and textual element, sound served as the basis for a wide-ranging debate amongst filmmakers and critics about the form and function of left documentary.

CINÉMA VÉRITÉ: THE PARADOX OF FIDELITY

"Subterranean Homesick Blues," the song from which the Weatherman organization took its name,[19] opens D. A. Pennebaker's 1967 film *Dont Look Back* [*sic*], a chronicle of Bob Dylan's 1965 concert tour of England, in a long pre-title take that was meant to function as a musical short. (Pennebaker credits Dylan with the idea of the short: Dylan had asked Pennebaker to make him a scopitone, a kind of jukebox film.) Dylan

Figure 3.1. *Dont Look Back* (D. A. Pennebaker, 1967). Still capture from DVD.

stands in an alley holding a stack of cue cards on which selected words and phrases from the song's lyrics are handwritten (see figure 3.1). He lets the cards fall one after another to the ground as, on the soundtrack, he is heard singing the tongue-twisting song, which was then rising in the British pop charts. The contrast between Dylan's placid image and his canny voice sets the tone not only for the film but, as Paul Arthur and others have argued, for the American institution of *cinéma vérité* itself. Although the historical significance of *vérité* is usually described in terms of the technological achievement of lightweight synchronous recording, one can also say that the ironic juxtaposition of the silent image and the prolix soundtrack in this sequence is characteristic of the antiauthoritarian ideology of American *vérité*, what an early historian of the form referred to as its "uncontrolled" aspect.[20] As Arthur puts it, this "denial of conventionality" took the textual form of an opposition between "fulsome speech and reticence."[21] If at the level of mechanical representation, the claim of *cinéma vérité* was a unique fidelity to the real, this principle was upheld by a paradoxical inversion at the textual level: by breaking the genre's own rules of authenticity, the film was attempting to be faithful to its skeptical subject. The film's dispassionate and ironic politics consisted of such gestures, which easily converted to sociological generalizations of the sort American documentary had been content to make for decades.

The opposition between a private Dylan, filmed by Pennebaker, and the misrepresented public Dylan is played out throughout the film. Early on, Dylan reads aloud an account of his chain-smoking in a British newspaper (" 'Puffing heavily on a cigarette—he smokes eighty a day . . .' ") and exclaims, with a laugh, "I'm glad I'm not me!" Although the rhetoric of *cinéma vérité* maintained that everything viewers saw and heard was captured in a happy coincidence of the subjects' honesty and the filmmakers' attention, it is no accident that this remark appears early in the film, since it announces the premise of the film: that the "I" recorded by the film crew is more true than the "me" presented in the mainstream press. This argument is underscored by the numerous sequences in which Dylan is asked inane questions by reporters, to which he responds with a mixture of scorn and bemusement. Subtending this argument—that documentary is an independent institution of social knowledge and freer to tell the truth than the heavily capitalized corporate media (often represented in these films by publicists or by reporters from newspapers, television, or magazines such as *Time* or *Newsweek*)—is another sociological thesis, one central to *vérité* as an American form: that everyone can be a celebrity.

In fact, the film's argument hardly depends upon the particularity of Dylan. The opposition between the public and private faces of celebrities was a habitual theme of the *cinéma vérité* films Pennebaker, Richard Leacock, and Albert and David Maysles worked on under producer Robert Drew, starting with the Drew Associates films about the Kennedys and other public figures (including *Primary* [1960]; *Nehru* [1962]; *Jane* [1962]; and *Crisis: Behind a Presidential Commitment* [1963]). When these cameramen broke away from Drew to make their own films, they continued to work in the vein of the celebrity portrait. This preoccupation with well-known personalities was in part pragmatic. A well-known subject helped build an audience for works that could not command the viewership guaranteed for documentary television.

But it was also an expression of a social philosophy. The individuals scrutinized in American *vérité*, famous or not, appear to the viewer as performers for a number of reasons: because many of them are used to being seen by a large audience; because, if we see them on film, we can assume that they have agreed to be filmed and are conscious of the presence of the camera and microphone; and, moreover, because the distinction has ceased to be meaningful. If ordinary people could be made into representative characters by their appearance in a work of *cinéma vérité* (as was the case for the small-town South Dakotans in Leacock and Chopra's *A Happy Mother's Day* [1963], the inmates and guards in Frederick Wiseman's *Titicut Follies* [1967], or the Louds of Craig Gilbert's *An American Family* [1973]), then by the same token, we learn that professional performers are, behind the scenes, ordinary people: they stumble for words, they are given to petty or ugly emotional reactions, they mumble, they take naps. Celebrities can serve as allegories of ordinary people in these films precisely because their apparently natural ease with cameras and audiences helps, as Arthur points out, "maintain the fiction that camera observation is part of a natural landscape of behavior."[22]

Indeed, one could say that in these films being filmed is merely allegorical: the performer's filmed image reminds viewers that everyday life and the institutions that make it possible are just a series of stages for self-presentation. Though it means to demystify spectacle and the cult of personality it generates, this logic serves to reify individual personality as the site of social truth. Using professional entertainers and other public figures to model character, films like *Dont Look Back* suggest that social truth is reducible to the embarrassing secrets that we reveal in unguarded moments of speech or gesture.

An example of this principle is the scene where Dylan is interviewed by a journalist from the African service of the BBC, the rare interviewer he seems to respect. In response to the question "How did it all begin for you, Bob? What actually started you off?" Dylan pauses and then begins to answer. But he only gets out a tentative "Um . . ." before the film cuts abruptly to a different time and location. Because adherents of American *cinéma vérité* insisted that the scrutiny of social situations in the present was the only tool documentary needed, it is a shock not only to leave Dylan in mid-utterance but to be transported back in time, to very rough footage (shot by Ed Emshwiller) of an earnest-looking Dylan on a Mississippi farm in 1963, playing "Only a Pawn in Their Game" at a voter registration rally. "Um" is the sort of meaningless utterance on which *vérité* filmmakers established the authenticity of their recordings. Likewise, the film seems here to catch itself backsliding on its own methodological premise to remain in present time. This betrayal apparently provides its own excuse, insofar as it demonstrates that even cinematic narration is inconsistent and unreliable. And it thus reinforces the film's fidelity to its subject, which, like all *vérité* subjects, is authentic to the extent that it comes apart under the pressure of convention. Even the spelling of the film's title, which reviewers and historians insist on correcting with an apostrophe, is a kind of public inside joke about the value of mistakes and inconsistency in the historical record.

The retroactive cut and the historical footage also have a rhetorical function. By leaving the scene of the BBC interview before Dylan responds to the question and providing audio-visual evidence of "how it all started" for Dylan, the filmmakers assert the priority of documentary film over other methods of investigation. In fact, as is emphasized by the film's title, taken from a new Dylan song, "She Belongs to Me" ("She's got everything she needs / She's an artist, she don't look back"), Dylan was meant to exemplify a historical shift, from the folk singer to the rock artist. But the question of where Dylan's art came from is less important, the film suggests, than where it was going. The smattering of applause at the end of the Mississippi performance is replaced, over the course of a cut, by a huge ovation that greets Dylan as he begins another performance on his British tour. The difference in venue and size of audience is meant to indicate the changing fortunes of American folk music. And it implies that Dylan is an artist capable of bridging the traditional and collective aesthetic of folk and the romantic individualism of rock, and capable of putting rock's mass appeal to socially responsible uses. The relentless stare of the *cinéma vérité* camera serves as an analogue of Dylan's own performances of social observation and progressive conviction. Along with the grain of the high-speed film stock, the jerky movements of the camera and the lens, and the aural murk of the soundtrack, this gaze is meant to translate the unpolished and urgent manner of Dylan's singing and the unpretentious charm of his on- and off-stage personae into a cinematic style.

In applying this principle of fidelity to the sound of popular music, the rock-themed documentaries that followed *Dont Look Back* exploited the capacity of *cinéma vérité* to translate social phenomena into individual experience on a mass scale: to convert the social, in other words, to spectacle. These close-up images of commercial popular culture and its mass audience illuminate what Guy Debord called "the society of the spectacle," in a tract published the same year that *Dont Look Back* was released. Debord argued that spectacle is a form of violence, insofar as it separates people from their experience and from one another precisely by formalizing experience and re-presenting it in a simulation of intimacy.[23] In her *New Yorker* pan of *Gimme Shelter,* the Maysles brothers' film of the disastrous free concert the Rolling Stones performed at Altamont Speedway in 1969, where a fan was killed by the Hell's Angels, Pauline Kael argued in essentially these terms that *cinéma vérité* was a form of exploitation. Reviewing the film was "like reviewing the footage of President Kennedy's assassination or Lee Harvey Oswald's murder," Kael argued.[24] Worse, Kael wrote, the film functioned as an alibi for the filmmakers and their subjects by combining *vérité*'s naïve, observational style with a reflexive frame in which the Stones watch the footage of the killing at a Steenbeck editing bench, expressing surprise and remorse at what they see. Her review is an attack on the *vérité* movement itself. The "sham" of *cinéma vérité,* she argued, was its pandering to a commonsense phenomenology: it "appeals to an audience by showing it what it wants to believe."[25]

Kael's objection to *cinéma vérité* was predicated on a typical audiovisual application of this method, one whose formula was to "let the event speak." In a 1975 article, one of the few attempts to theorize documentary film sound, Pascal Bonitzer writes:

> This is an interesting formula, not only because in it can be read the elision of (the author's) point of view toward the event in question, but also because it displaces this "question of point of view"—which is so important for "politics"—to a problem of *speech.* It is because it is inscribed there that "it speaks," that the just vision of an event depends on what the latter *says,* that the eye is carried by the voice, and under the circumstances, a voice which, if not silent, is at least without *subject.*[26]

Films produced under this mandate made the viewer express the meaning of their sounds and images and of the events they documented. If this ventriloquism could be described as passing from the "eye" of the film to the "voice" of its viewer, this was because no speech of this magnitude was meant to appear in the film itself. Whether made according to French or North American ideas of *cinéma vérité* or in the style of historical dossier Bonitzer describes, which pieces together materials on a single event, such films claimed to offer viewers the freedom to experience history and its contradictions directly, free of the comprehensive perspective that had formerly governed social documentary films. (If, as critics never tired of pointing out, many early works of *cinéma vérité* included narration, this aberration was dismissed by their makers as a hazard of their principles, which included drawing socio-drama from life, where speech was often unclear, and prioritizing image over language.)[27] The speech that did appear in such films retained some of its semantic value, but this aspect of its textual function was balanced against its material qualities, as one aural element among others in the sound mix and as one formal component of a larger system. The pursuit of a properly filmic politics of documentary would entail attention to these material dimensions. Even though filmmakers and theorists had recently mounted a variety of challenges to the cinematic apparatus and its effect of "suture," their critical force, Bonitzer suggested, was still in doubt: even "perversion of the apparatus" could still lead back to "representation." It was still necessary, Bonitzer said, to address "the question of the object: what to do . . . with the look and the voice?"

One early example of the profound force this question had on some documentary producers is *Cicero March* (1966), a little-known short film by a Chicago-based company of filmmakers who called themselves the Film Group. Formed as a commercial production studio around 1963 by Mike Gray, then working for a Chicago advertising agency (but known later for *The Murder of Fred Hampton* [1971] and his script for *The China Syndrome* [1979]), with photographers Lars Hedman and Mike Shea, the Film Group turned to documentary primarily as a means for testing Gray and Hedman's ideas for freshening the visual style of television advertising.[28] Shea had worked for *Life* as an editorial photographer and had brought to Chicago one of the first *cinéma vérité* cameras, a 16mm Auricon news camera converted (by technical wizard Mitch

Bogdanovich) to make it easier to carry on the shoulder and to synchronize with the Nagra reel-to-reel audiotape recorder then favored by documentary filmmakers, sidestepping the cumbersome double-system optical sound with which the Auricon was outfitted in the factory.[29] The Film Group operated a large studio on West Grant Place and was successfully occupied with corporate accounts such as J. Walter Thompson, Commonwealth Edison, and Kentucky Fried Chicken, when Shea insisted that they take note of the racial and political tensions roiling Chicago. Never intended for wide commercial release, and used by the Group primarily to showcase their methods and their equipment to potential clients, *Cicero March* documents an African American civil-rights protest against housing policies and real estate practices in Cicero, an all-white suburb that had been the site of racist mob violence fifteen years before. The film captures the charged atmosphere of the two-hour event, which editor Jay Litvin reduced to a seven-and-a-half-minute series of impressions without commentary and with a bare minimum of explanatory titles. (The only words to appear on screen are the date of the march and the filmmakers' names at the beginning of the film, and the title and the Group's name, at the end.)

The march itself came at the end of a summer of protests against racial bias in the Chicago housing market, led by Martin Luther King Jr. and the Southern Christian Leadership Conference. Under the auspices of the Chicago Freedom Movement, which brought SCLC together with local groups, King had intended to lead about three thousand marchers across the city line, from the Westside neighborhood into Cicero. But two days before the march, King reached an agreement with Mayor Daley and the head of the Chicago Real Estate Board on a plan to end discrimination in rental and sales practices, and he called off the march.[30] A number of African American rights organizations, including the Chicago unit of the Congress of Racial Equality, led by Robert Lucas, the militant West Side Organization, and several other groups pledged to go ahead with the demonstration. Two hundred marchers, accompanied by more than ten times that number of National Guardsmen and police officers, as well as hundreds of white hecklers and counter-demonstrators, thronged the streets of Cicero on Sunday, September 4. The two-hour march ended, as organizers and state authorities had feared, in violence. In addition to epithets, hecklers threw stones, bottles, and firecrackers at the marchers and police. Some marchers fought back. Dozens were arrested.[31]

Cicero March—which was never released commercially—provides no background or explanation for the events it witnesses, makes little attempt to distinguish individual participants in the conflict, and begins and ends in medias res. It is in this respect as much an experiment in form as a social document, and its relation to the conventions of liberal documentary, even of its time, seem strained when it is viewed next to other examples of *cinéma vérité* on similar subjects. Compared to, say, the Robert Drew Associates' television documentary *Crisis: Behind a Presidential Commitment* (1963), made for ABC News during the Kennedy administration's battle of wills with George Wallace over the integration of the University of Alabama, *Cicero March* makes little attempt to explain racial violence or the state's role in it, or to make these seem like problems on which there could be an objective perspective. Filmed with a number of camera units, some of whom had unprecedented access to the inner circles of power at the highest levels of state, *Crisis* employs the tools of documentary observation and narrative cinema, honed in earlier Drew projects that used the same "crisis" structure, to fashion a compelling study of political character and drama. *Crisis* presents an appreciative picture of the Kennedy brothers' handling of Wallace, and of the civil rights movement itself, but one that is so focused on developing its characters and its story in novelistic detail that the historical complexity of events largely disappears and the conflict becomes entirely symbolic. African Americans are present only in the token form of the two students attempting to register at the university. As with many of Drew's films, the implicit argument of *Crisis* was finally a circular one: that a true understanding of American social and political life came from the apprehension of the intimate and interior structures of its most visible avatars, those public figures most recognizable and least accessible to the mass audience. Since it claimed to put viewers in more direct contact with their political leaders than other journalistic media could, it was not surprising that the press disdained the film, even while it was in production. In its second editorial on the film, the *New York Times* objected that "it is improper to make a stage-show of the inside processes of Government." The *Times*'s television critic, Jack Gould, singled out a sequence of peculiar aural clarity to make this point, one in which Deputy Attorney General Nicholas Katzenbach orders reporters away from his two-way radio, so that he can have a private conversation with Robert Kennedy: "he must talk in private," objected Gould, "so viewers of last night's managed news film could clearly hear his words."[32]

By contrast, *Cicero March* presents its viewer with a quilt of sound. Helicopter noise suffuses the film. Other sounds, captured by Gray with a Nagra shotgun microphone—songs, chants, and cheers from the marchers and the neighborhood counterdemonstrators; taunts and obscene epithets hurled by one side or the other; commands by the march organizers or the police to "get on the curb" and "keep it moving"; and an occasional cherry bomb explosion—rise and fall in and out of this din. Shea's camerawork, constantly reframing the faces and bodies of the protesters by movements of his own body or the lens barrel, creates a fluid position within the events the film covers. Although it would be hard to argue that the film has any sympathy for the position of the white counterdemonstrators, whose displays of racist hysteria are frightening to observe (see figure 3.2), the film does attempt to loosen the Manichean oppositions favored by the Drew films. This dialogic conception of the social field is underscored by the sound Gray records. Enhanced by the pickup pattern of his microphone, the film's undifferentiated and unhierarchized arrangement of sounds complicates the question sung by the protesters near the opening of the film, "Which side are you on?" a song that comes, of course, from the unionization battles at West Virginia coal mines in the 1930s.

If this echo of the laborist old left links the film to the political heritage of American progressive culture, other sounds mark a definitive break with these traditions. One of these is the profanity tossed up frequently in the sea of voices and noises. Over the image and noise of a police helicopter surveying the march from overhead, the very first words in the film are "let the police guard your march, motherfuckers." Commenting on the use of obscenity in Movement rhetoric, Herbert Marcuse remarked that it constituted a "methodological subversion of the linguistic universe of the Establishment," one that "breaks the false ideological language and invalidates its definitions."[33] If the epithets hurled at the marchers by Cicero residents seem, on the contrary, to uphold those definitions, their very audibility in a documentary film

Figure 3.2. *Cicero March* (The Film Group, 1966). Still capture from DVD.

of the period could be considered evidence of a certain kind of break with convention. Even if the content and intent of such speech was plainly conservative, its uncensored reproduction in *Cicero March* was meant to perform a liberating function. In the linguistic terms then in use by semiotic film theorists, the sounds of these words evinced the distinction between the content of a statement and its enunciation. Hearing these sounds allowed this difference to be articulated as a political dialectic. Contrary voices could coexist at different levels of the same text at the same time.

Shea and Gray didn't ask the march organizers for permission to film the march or to join it, but it is clear that everyone involved, including the police and the hecklers, expected to be filmed and photographed. Amateur and professional cameras show up repeatedly in Shea's frame, wielded by reporters, marchers, counterdemonstrators, and bystanders, as do microphones, tape recorders, and the notebooks of print journalists (see figures 3.3 and 3.4). These specular images were a trope of *cinéma vérité*. Revealing the presence of competing documentary sources

Figure 3.3. *Cicero March* (The Film Group, 1966). Still capture from DVD.

Figure 3.4. *Cicero March* (The Film Group, 1966). Still capture from DVD.

made two points: that the mere recording of events wasn't enough to guarantee the truth of their representation; and that all representation, including the film in progress, comes from a particular position. Showing other means of recording within the frame of the film was a way of making the limits of that frame, in a manner of speaking, visible. One point to be taken from the Film Group's application of the techniques of *cinéma vérité* to the Cicero march is that the line demarcating the edge of the event and its just image can always be moved.

Indeed, the motility of the film's audiovisual frame calls into question the very notion of the historical break that Marcuse invokes in his analysis of radical speech, even as the film seems, in its explicitness, to inscribe a sharp division between sides: if not exactly black and white (since many white faces can be seen among the prointegration marchers), then at least between right and wrong, progress and tradition. Which side *are* the filmmakers on? In the end, this may not be so easy a question to answer. This is true of the film's final image, of police roughing up a Cicero heckler. If the film seems to pit the viciousness of the racist crowd against the nonviolence of the civil rights marchers, these images put the liberal viewer in the position of questioning his or her opposition to violence. It is striking to see such an ambivalent image of state power in a film at the outset of a decade of anti-state documentary. Freeze-framing this image, the film here performs its own arrest on reality (see figure 3.5). That it takes this moment as the opportunity, finally, to provide the viewer with the title of the film seems to underscore the filmmakers' identification with this position between good and evil. The power of the film comes in part from its refusal to comment on the violence it observes, to the point that *Cicero March* is nearly incomprehensible to any viewer without a sense of the march's historical context.

In fact, it was only later, during the production of *American Revolution II* (1969), the Film Group's feature documentary about protests at the 1968 Democratic nominating convention in Chicago, that *Cicero March* was even treated by the group as a documentary at all. In order to raise money for *American Revolution II,* a number of shorts drawn from the group's filmmaking, including *Cicero March,* were repackaged as part of an educational series and marketed to local schools. Before this, *Cicero March* functioned merely as a calling card for the Film Group and

Figure 3.5. *Cicero March* (The Film Group, 1966). Still capture from DVD.

its equipment. This industrial history does not negate the value of the film as a document. It does, however, emphasize how difficult it is for documentary to speak for itself, as it was hoped by many that it could finally do with the arrival of the hand-held 16mm camera and the synchronous-sound reel-to-reel tape recorder. A film of a political demonstration, meant merely to demonstrate technology and technical skill, *Cicero March* suggests what Roland Barthes called, in 1968, the "reality effect," "mak[ing] notation the pure encounter of an object and its expression."[34] But precisely because it fuses two quite opposite senses of demonstration, this little film shows instead the difficulty of enforcing a distinction between documentary and its others—in this case, commercial realism—in terms of style, mode of production, personnel, or technology. If the film now can be heard to say more than one thing at a time, this aural history testifies to the discursive complexity of documentary even at those moments when, as Paul Arthur argues, it seems to speak most directly.[35] That the film is itself the product of competing motivations—marketing and social justice—can be taken as evidence of the traditional difficulty of separating art, commerce, and politics in the practice of documentary. But it can also be attributed to a politics of media specific to the era, one that took advantage of the increasingly unstable relationships between soundtrack and image.

REVOLUTIONARY SOUNDS

With the breakup of the studio system in the 1960s and the development of new recording technologies and postproduction techniques (including the increased use of Foley artists and ADR techniques and experiments with perspective and synchronization) had come a loosening of the conventions of sound-image relations. The sometimes jarring mixes and correspondences that resulted from these innovations provided another means to express the social discord of the period. The intentional sound mismatches in *The Graduate* (1967), for instance, could be read as analogies of the generation gap. The gunfire in *Bonnie and Clyde* (1967), which was instrumental in establishing the film as an emblem of student and youth rebellion against the establishment, was so loud that projectionists frequently regarded its level as a mistake and compensated by turning it down.[36]

Thus it was not surprising to find movies as different as *Medium Cool* (1969), Haskell Wexler's docudramatic exploration of late-Sixties politics, and *Head* (1968), the big-screen vehicle for the pop group the Monkees, making use of noise as a way to claim solidarity with oppositional culture. *Medium Cool*, which follows a television news cameraman through Chicago in the days leading up to the Democratic National Convention, opens with a terrible sound, which we hear even before we see an image. The noise comes from a car horn that has been jammed on during an accident. The sound recordist who accompanies the cameraman reaches under the hood and unplugs the horn, in order to get a better level from the groans of the accident's victim, still lying next to the car. (Only after the crew has their footage do they call for an ambulance.) This scene is meant to set the tone for the film, which explores, in its roundabout, episodic way, the tensions of the summer of 1968 and the fraught relation between oppositional political groups and the mass media.

The year 1968 was defined by scenes of violence. It was the year when the tide began to turn decisively against the U.S. military and its allies in the Vietnam War. After the spectacular miscalculations and defeats that came to be known as the Tet Offensive, the government began to lose the battle to convince the American public that the war could be won. Martin Luther King Jr. was assassinated in April, leading to days of rioting in a number of American cities. In the space of two days in June, Andy Warhol was shot and Robert Kennedy was assassinated. Emboldened by the embarrassment of Tet and Johnson's apologetic refusal to seek the Democratic nomination for the presidency, students and others on the left began to stage highly visible protests, including the takeover of several buildings at Columbia University, effectively shutting the university down for weeks, and the bloody confrontation between law enforcement and protesters at the Democratic National Convention in Chicago in August. These violent images were matched by scenes from France, Germany, and elsewhere in the West, where students joined with striking workers to shut down factories, institutions, and whole city districts.

One of the clarions of the culture of '68 was the squeal of guitars, at the point of distortion or destruction. In *Miami and the Siege of Chicago*, his account of the presidential nominating conventions of 1968, Norman Mailer makes the guitar the antidote to the distress brought on by the political process, symbolized by the Democrats' hotel itself. "Nothing worked well in the hotel, and much didn't work at all," Mailer complains.

> There was no laundry because of the bus strike, and the house phones usually did not function; the room phones were tapped so completely, and the devices so over-adjacent, that separate conversations lapped upon one another in the same earpiece, or went jolting by in all directions like three handballs at play at once in a four-wall handball court. Sometimes the phone was dead, sometimes it emitted hideous squawks, or squeals, or the harsh electronic displeasure of a steady well-pulsed static.[37]

The tension between the "electronic displeasure" caused by the broken democratic communication system and the "wonderful power" of the electric guitar was an important element of the political imaginary of '68.

The juxtaposition of both sorts of sounds—of system overload and of harmony, noise and music—characterized the movement's mass spectacles, gatherings like Altamont and Woodstock. The disorder for which these events were famous was at once a discouraging sign that they were heavily capitalized, demonstrating that, like everything else connected with "youth," the counterculture was simply one more field for exploitation, and, at the same time, the mark of their challenge to the prevailing social order.

The rock festival was a utopian version of commercial public space, according to Simon Frith: its function was to "provide materially the experience of community that the music expressed symbolically."[38] The *cinéma vérité* style in which *Monterey Pop* (D.A. Pennebaker, 1968), *Woodstock* (Michael Wadleigh, 1970), and other films of this cycle were made invited the viewer's participation in this community. But their intimate style had the effect of further mystifying cinematic production, as even the *Wall Street Journal* noticed: "One thing Woodstock proved is that young people are commercially exploitable," remarked the *Journal*'s film reviewer. Because the festival itself had lost money, the film would help the festival organizers recoup their costs: "In that sense, *Woodstock* should be even more successful than Woodstock."[39] For this reason, the rock-festival film was the antithesis, to a number of critics, of the "anger and contention" they felt was the proper object of documentary in the 1960s.[40] What such critics meant was that the experience of watching these films was inconsistent with the spirit of collectivity that attached to the noisy gatherings depicted. In a symptomatic way, the utopian scene of the rock festival in *Monterey Pop* does express the "anger and contention" of the Sixties in its evocation of the pure, liberated space of the performance. If the spectacular aspects of the rock festival cancel out whatever utopian potential for community this sort of gathering promises, the artlessness with which Pennebaker and Ricky Leacock record these events testifies to the scarcity of terms for similar experiences of collectivity in ordinary life. By investing the spectacle of Hendrix's libidinous and self-contradictory performance with intimacy—the impression of the front-row seat we get from close-up shots of the audience—*Monterey Pop* evacuates this noise of its symbolic force. For all its spontaneity and "uncontrolled" energy, the *cinéma vérité* documentary style was not so different, as a vision of society, an evocation of a community of viewers, from the classical documentary it claimed to replace.

Although it seems, next to such earnest accounts of musical experience, like an affront to the youth movement's principles, the Monkees movie, *Head,* is in its own way a more authentic record of the politics of discord. Like *Medium Cool,* the film opens with an aural shock—feedback from a microphone—and an illegible image, a bright red screen that is subsequently revealed to be the extreme close-up of a ribbon-cutting ceremony. The P.A. system is only one source of the noises disrupting the ceremony: wind, boat and car horns, and helicopter blades all prevent the mayor from being heard clearly as he performs his ceremonial function. And when the mayor finally masters the sonic environment, the Monkees themselves race through the scene, preventing him from completing his official address. The presence of the cinematic apparatus in the scene and throughout the film makes the same argument as the more explicitly McLuhanite *Medium Cool:* that politics is a form of media spectacle; that there was no dimension of experience that could not be mediated electronically; and that these ideas no longer had the potential to shock.

Head was an attempt by producers Bob Rafelson and Bert Schneider to salvage some commercial potential from the Monkees before their star faded from view. Rafelson and Schneider, whose company, BBS Productions, would make possible the most successful 1960s exploitation of the counterculture, *Easy Rider* (1969), and the most widely seen antiwar documentary, *Hearts and Minds* (1974), had created the group in the Richard Lester image of the Beatles. The Monkees had enjoyed two successful seasons on American television and the pop charts, despite merciless critical reception.[41] The film was essentially a series of skits poking fun at the group's plasticity, braiding the altered states of psychedelia and free love with their subjection as commodities. In a studio canteen on the Columbia lot, a transvestite waitress addresses the group as "God's gift to the eight-year-old." "Changing-your-image time?" she asks sarcastically. "Why don't you have them write you some talent?" By fully embracing their exploitation, the Monkees, it appeared, would free themselves from their (critics') hang-ups about authenticity and originality. At one level, this liberatory logic merely inflates the commercial potential of spectacle, allowing the producers to put the Monkees in as many costumes and picturesque locations as possible, to fill the film with musical performances and dance numbers, and to permit a stream of cameo appearances by Sonny Liston, Annette Funicello, Frank Zappa, Dennis Hopper, and Jack Nicholson, who all pass through scenes, with or without lines. But in the context of 1968, these displays must also be read as the expression of significant changes in the form and meaning of cinema, the shift to a cinema in which imaginary and real are indistinguishable in the image.

Head was met with scorn from serious viewers and disinterest from Monkees fans, whose numbers were already dwindling. The symptom of its producers' double miscalculation, in attempting to exploit both the art-house and teenybopper markets, was its generous use of documentary footage and, above all, its use of violent images of the Vietnam conflict. For Pauline Kael, such images were the sign of the film's "doubling up of greed and pretensions to depth" and were "enough to make even a pinhead walk out"; the ellipsis that ends her review suggests that she did just that.[42] If the film was equally unwatchable to viewers who could appreciate the radical gestures of *The Graduate* or *Bonnie and Clyde* and to viewers who had enjoyed seeing the Monkees on their television screens at home, the documentary images of violence marked this negative correspondence. Images of fatal violence functioned like the images of explicit sex that were increasingly visible as signifiers of the new American cinema, guarantors of its power to speak truthfully and directly about experience despite—or through—an image that was demonstrably false. These images are used in *Head* as a touchstone of the Monkees' authenticity. But if the Monkees fail that test because they are products of television, then the reality of "Vietnam" was itself in question. Television was where viewers had become familiar with the images of the Monkees. But it was also the venue for the American public experience of the war, and the screen on which images of dead and dying Vietnamese citizens and U.S. soldiers had become a familiar nightmare.

The most striking instance of the documentary problematic comes a few minutes into the film, when the field of the image divides into a series of smaller images in the shape of television screens, each featuring a shot or sequence from the film to come. Behind this series, the Monkees frantically sing a song in which they celebrate their superficiality ("You say we're manufactured / to that we all agree / so make your choice

Figure 3.6. *Head* (Bob Rafelson, 1968). Still capture from DVD.

and we'll rejoice / in never being free!"). The very last of these images is the only one that is not from the film's plot: it is the infamous NBC footage of a prisoner being assassinated at point-blank range by Nguyen Ngoc Loan, the South Vietnamese police chief, in February 1968 (see figure 3.6).[43] As this shot appears on the screen, the song's last lines are heard: "The money's in, we're made of tin, we're here to give you more." When the line is repeated, the last word is replaced with a gunshot. The screens are then filled with images of the execution, blood spurting from the fatal wound as the body falls to the ground. A woman's scream abruptly takes over the soundtrack from the Monkees' voices and is quickly attached to the slow-motion image of an ecstatic young Monkees fan. While the band performs one of its few original compositions, "Circle Sky," the film amplifies the analogy between American ecstasy and Vietnamese pain, intercutting images of Vietnamese civilians in dispositions of fear and suffering with views of the band and its fans.[44] Near the end of the song, while Mike Nesmith sings the lines "what you've seen you must believe / if you can," we are again shown the image of the Saigon street execution. This time, its effect is different.

Where the juxtaposition of war and entertainment first suggested a parallel between the two, the film now exhorts us to treat the image of violence as real, against the powers of fiction that commercial film and television exploit. What can such a demand mean in a film that works hard to convince its audience that precisely the opposite is true of images: that they are unbelievable and are the source, like drugs, art, and advertising, of a fantasmatic escape from grim reality? The frequent use of superimpositions, reversed images, oversaturated and solarized colors, the discontinuous editing within and between sequences, and the associative passage from one parodic or fantastic scenario to another: these effects, drawn from the methods of Busby Berkeley and contemporary experimental cinema alike, undermine the viewer's faith in the ontology of the photographic image. In this textual and historical context, the demand that we regard the documentary image as an index of reality, as something we "must believe," is itself an incompossible demand. The documentary image appears at once as the limit of experimentation and as just another plastic ploy. If the Monkees are a prefab product of television, it is precisely this iconicity that allows them to bring to our attention the force of "Vietnam" as an image. So the demand that we regard the documentary image as index of reality appears, in this context, dissonant, just as difficult to incorporate into the American mind as the conception of American defeat in Vietnam— which, for many, was the meaning of Tet, just as the image of the street execution in Saigon made the concept of just war unpalatable.

In patently inauthentic products of mass culture, the authenticity of the documentary image functioned not merely as the truth but as a marker of larger contradictions. This tension operated in filmmaking at the other end of the production scale as well. Filmmakers in the New Left aimed to create an authentic relation to oppositional politics by challenging the actuality of the image, the very tool by which documentary had claimed priority over other genres as a representation of social reality. This dissonance, instituted within the text as a contradiction between aural and visual signs, came to function as a form of political authenticity.

HATE IN THEIR VOICES

The distinction between the form and content of noise was precisely what the radical documentary organization Newsreel tried to avoid in its attempts "to provide an alternative to the limited and biased coverage of television news."[45] Revamping the didactic structure of classical voice-over documentary while rejecting as well the pseudo-ethnographic social observation of American *cinéma vérité*, the Newsreel films I consider here use voice, noise, and music to unsettle the social relations presumed by liberal documentary. Although off-screen voices are an important textual element of early Newsreel works, these voices are explicitly partial and are situated at an uncertain distance from the images they accompany. But if they are not exactly "over" the images, nor are they subjectively "in" the images. The soundtrack voices, often chosen precisely for their lack of expertise or objectivity, do not lecture their audiences. But neither do they appear as merely spontaneous expressions of a social reality that is commonsensical and that can be gleaned from the recorded surfaces of everyday life. Rather, the tension in these Newsreel films between wild sound, recorded in the heat of struggle, and voice-off, imposed during the process of mixing and editing, suggests a social contradiction at a higher level, between perceptual reality and the structures and schedules of production.[46] By using particular voices in unfamiliar ways—disconnected from individual bodies but without the omniscience and objectivity of classical voice-over—Newsreel filmmakers meant to create, quite literally, new spaces for debate about the issues they covered, going so far as to adopt the old workers' technique of sending speakers to newsreel screenings to field questions and comments afterward. But the organization had no illusion about how "free" speech was; if nothing else, its use of voices was meant to undercut the platitude that every American was entitled to his or her opinion. The early Newsreel films resisted, on the one hand, the authoritarian voice of the state and of the official news sources and, on the other, "that sterile game" of left documentary, "speaking your language your way."[47] The group had little interest in consensus or such simple metaphors as dialogue; they were, indeed, happy to claim that "Newsreel must make half the decisions for" audiences who would not, of their own accord, take an interest in their subjects. Above all, these contradictions were meant to provoke audiences' reflection on the relation between film and action. Pascal Bonitzer's formulation about the sound of French political cinema in the wake of 1968 is appropriate here: "it is the spectators," Bonitzer writes, "who, 'in the last instance' utter (contradictorily) its truth."[48]

Initially, Newsreel was a national network of production collectives based in Boston, New York, Chicago, San Francisco, and Los Angeles. Its members aimed not only to make images of social discontent but to make films that served as models of media critique, challenging mainstream media practice. In contrast to the moderate, paternal tone of mainstream news sources, through which the perspective of the corporate media could be presented as fact, Newsreel's members aligned themselves with their subjects, attempting to use the cinematic medium as an oppositional and agitational tool. "In our hands," wrote two members of the San Francisco branch, "film is not an anaesthetic, a sterile, smooth-talking apparatus of control. It is a weapon to counter, to talk back to and to crack the facade of the lying media of capitalism."[49]

Newsreel's logo was a rapidly flickering image of the group's name, accompanied by a sound that could have been either a machine gun or the chattering of a projector. The ambiguity was, of course, crucial to Newsreel's self-image as a weapon against spectacle and the passivity that spectacle produces. At the heart of the Newsreel method was the idea that cinema, as an economy of both images and labor, could be placed in the service of diverse, dispersed challenges to an authoritarian social order. The work produced by its members and collectives, particularly in the first year or two of the organization's existence, was by no means consistent, either formally or politically. In keeping with the organization's generic namesake, its earliest films focused on particular events or groups, though with no pretense to comprehensive or even accessible reporting: "don't talk to me about 'content,'" Robert Kramer, one of the principal organizers of the New York branch, wrote in a 1968 collective statement of the group's methods and goals that appeared in *Film Quarterly*.[50] "I think we argue a different hierarchy of values. Not traditional canons of 'what is professional,' what is 'comprehensive and intelligent reportage,' what is 'acceptable quality and range of material.'"[51] These works ranged from shorts like *No Game* (1968), a sixteen-minute account of the October 1967 march on the Pentagon, and *Up Against the Wall, Ms. America* (1968), a six-minute film about a feminist disruption of the 1968 Miss America pageant, to more sustained treatments of Movement actions, like *Columbia Revolt* (1968), which focused on the Columbia University student strike, and the compendious *Summer of '68* (1969).

With its name, the organization revived traditions of leftist film-making from the 1930s, when the Workers Film and Photo League had made newsreels with similar aims: to supplement the mainstream press in its coverage of the left and its constituencies and to use film for propaganda, organizing, and consciousness-raising. At the same time, the droll simplicity of the group's name—a wry choice, given the timing of the group's founding[52]—indicated the group's affiliation with the American practitioners of an experimental "pure cinema" in the 1960s, who sought, in their own way, to reduce cinema to its material essence.[53] By adopting the name Newsreel, members of the organization were pledging themselves to contradiction, in the same spirit that Soviet documentary pioneer Dziga Vertov claimed, on behalf of the "Kino-Eye" documentary movement he championed in an early manifesto, "WE affirm the future of cinema art by denying its present."[54] Just as Vertov could speak of the revolutionary newsreel as "an assault on our reality by the cameras,"[55] confrontation defined the realities that Newsreel sought to depict: in Robert Kramer's words, "disgust/ violent disagreement/painful recognition/jolts."[56] Forty years after Vertov wrote that "the movie camera was invented in order to penetrate deeper into the visible world, to explore and record visual phenomena, so that we do not forget what happens and what the future must take into account,"[57] the reasons given by Newsreel for the necessity of a radical form of documentary remain more or less the same:

> We began by trying to bridge the gap between the states of mind and ways of working that we were accustomed to as film-makers, and the engagement/daily involvement/commitments of our political analysis and political activity—not only for our film-making, but for interpretations of what, as film-makers, as people engaged in a struggle against established forms of power and control, against established media of all forces, we had to do *with* or *without* cameras.[58]

Fidelity to the radical cause would consist of broadcasting the revolutionary message without diminishing its explosive charge. "The established media have done the job of popularizing" the radical politics espoused by the New Left, remarked Robert Kramer: "now we must specify and make immediate; convert our audience or neutralize them; threaten."[59]

Newsreel's early films work out a politics of representation at the level of form. The tones of reproach and incitement heard in their sound-tracks matched the singing, screaming, and chanting voices of their subjects. For example, the widely-viewed 1968 agitprop short *Black Panther* (a.k.a. *Off the Pig!*), a product of the San Francisco branch, begins with an image of the bullet-riddled windows of the Black Panthers' Oakland headquarters, in which hung a number of posters of the jailed Panther minister of defense, Huey P. Newton.[60] This sequence, and in particular the shot in which we see that a bullet hole replaces Newton's mouth, said two things. First, it bore witness to the police hostility to the Panthers' publicity. The shattered images of Newton's mouth and other Panther names and images warned that if the Panthers were too successful in spreading their message, the police would destroy the Panthers' ability to speak (see figure 3.7). But second, this image was also capable of suggesting, simply because it had been documented, that an apparatus like Newsreel could provide other radical groups with a mouthpiece, making it possible for them to extend their reach and circumvent repression. In response to this repressive violence, the film presents a scene of Black Panthers and Panther supporters in front of the Alameda County courthouse, giving a militant musical performance that became an emblem of the moment (see figure 3.8). Clapping and marching, the group sings, "No more brothers in jail / Off the pig! / Pigs are gonna catch hell / Off the pig!" The fifteen-minute film concludes with the voice of Black Panther chairman Bobby Seale reading the Panthers' Ten-Point Program over a series of shots from a depressed Oakland neighborhood.

San Francisco State: On Strike (1969), a twenty-minute film explaining the causes and effects of a four-month student protest at San Francisco State University, is narrated in an equally exclamatory style, making no effort to hide the filmmakers' sympathy for the students' cause. The clearly inexperienced narrator is frequently interrupted on the sound-track by an off-key protest singer. (This may or may not be the same singer with the acoustic guitar who appears in a number of nonsynchronous shots of picket lines and confrontations between the students and police.) The singer's words link the action on the SFSU campus to the Panthers' struggle: "They're gonna fall / they're gonna fall / the will of the people is greater than the technology of the Man / Huey

Figures 3.7–3.8. *Black Panther* [a.k.a. *Off the Pig!*] ([San Francisco] Newsreel, 1968). Still captures from VHS.

Newton said that! / Huey Newton said that! / 'bout you and me / sons of liberty." His wailing voice and energetic but tuneless guitar playing are well suited to the strident tone of the Newsreel shorts, which studiously avoided the polish of mainstream media production. But this seemingly haphazard style was intentional: it asserted that a news organization that had time to rehearse and polish its delivery could not provide "news that we feel is significant."[61]

Like the vocal performances recorded in *Black Panther* and *San Francisco State: On Strike,* the films of the Newsreel group were meant not only to stir audiences to action but also, by their very rhetorical audacity, to challenge the codes of public discourse. If the use of raw image and sound materials was one element of this challenge, however, Newsreel filmmakers resisted the spectacular substitution of their films for events. As Michael Renov argues, Newsreel works were often structured so as to undercut identification with the profilmic and to "underscore the primacy of analysis, that is, to narrate ideas."[62] The pattern of this critique is established in *No Game,* the group's account of the Washington antiwar protest in October 1967, and the film generally regarded as the first Newsreel work.[63] Against a piecemeal assemblage of shots, consisting largely of nonsynchronous, hand-held images of protesters and military police at the Lincoln Memorial and the Pentagon, the film arranges a diverse set of voices, often more than one at a time, creating a polyphonous and temporally layered oral history of the event. The soundtrack thus ostensibly bears the same commentative relation to the images that classic voice-over does, but with neither the directness of address nor the omniscience of those singular and stentorian narrators. Because of the frequent shifts from one kind of recorded sound to another, it is always clear that the viewer of *No Game* can adopt the position of the crowds listening to the amplified voices of Benjamin Spock or Peter, Paul, and Mary at the Lincoln Memorial, or to clashes between protesters and police at the Pentagon, only through the mediation of the filmmakers and their recording devices.

The impassioned rhetoric of the voices heard on the film's soundtrack serves as counterpoint to these structures of indirection. Unlike the encompassing speech that governs conventional liberal documentary, Newsreel employed voices that were clearly partial, in both senses. Apart from two sequences that make use of atonal classical music to accompany footage of bombing runs and air battles in Vietnam, the film's soundtrack is a pastiche of voices, never identified individually and sometimes mixed so that it is difficult to separate one from another. Some voices are also presented out of temporal sequence, relative to the images, as when a voice (apparently that of Fugs' leader Ed Sanders) is heard making the promise that "for the first time in the history of the Pentagon, there will be a grope-in within a hundred feet of this place" over images of both the crowds at the Lincoln Memorial and the protests at the Pentagon.[64] Perhaps the best example in the film of Newsreel's remaking of voice-over is a striking section in the middle that moves from reportage to expressionism. The sequence is separated from the rest of the film by the use of prerecorded music and stock footage of bombs, fighter jets, and an undefined landscape we take to be Vietnam. Addressing the soldiers we have seen in earlier images, the voice (that of Marvin Fishman, one of the filmmakers) appeals to their senses of conscience and fear:

> Don't you understand? These people out here, these hundred thousand people that you are trying to put down, are out here protesting to save your life. . . . When the troops over in Vietnam are shot up, more and more of them, you're going to be going over there. You understand what I'm saying? We are protesting against the action of the government that's going to cause your death. How many of you are in combat? How many of you have been the target of napalm? How many of you have sat still in absolute fright while four hundred screaming maniac soldiers come charging at you with blood in their eyes and hate in their voices and you can't see them, all you can do is sit in your jungle hole and listen to them crawl up closer and closer . . . and all you have at that moment is your little gun, and that's the time when you say, oh, my God, somebody help me, but baby the time to be helped is *now.*

Fishman's apostrophe, recorded in a studio after the march, is the antithesis not only of the steadfast voice of conventional newsreel but also of the partisan speech of American war propaganda. Addressing the soldiers with hectoring concern, it retools the voice of motherly love spoken by Jane Darwell on the soundtrack of John Ford's World War II newsreel, *The Battle of Midway* (1942).[65]

Figure 3.9. *No Game* ([New York] Newsreel, 1968). Still capture from VHS.

But if Fishman's voice seems to come from inside the soldiers' heads, it is also clearly identified with the cause and the bodies of the protesters whom we see, elsewhere in the film, clashing with soldiers in front of the Pentagon (see figure 3.9). Such a rhetorical strategy—marked, in Fishman's address, by the shift from "These people out here . . ." to "We are protesting . . ."—was in keeping with the desire of the group's founder to use filmmaking as a means to political ends, blurring the line between documenting and acting, or, rather, as an attempt to prepare the ground for a political discourse that was impossible in the fractious national debate over Vietnam. In this way, the scrupulous inclusion of the voices of right-wing counterprotesters can be understood as something more complex than mere opposition. Instead, it models a public of political speech. The film establishes the position of the audience as the ideal meeting point of all of these different enunciations: speeches and songs from the podium; antiwar and antigovernment chants; interviews with participants; and overheard sounds of battle. The film's final lines, from an interview with a participant in the protest, capture this sense of an ideal resolution of political differences. While the camera passes over the well-known still image of a Vietnamese woman holding out a dead child, the diegetic voice-over describes an inexplicable return of optimism in the Movement. "We couldn't really do anything," the voice says, "Nothing we did has any effect. . . . I realized nothing has changed. But somehow, I don't feel that there is no hope anymore. I feel that something may happen, whether it be violent or nonviolent. There's more of a chance now." Given that "nothing has changed," the viewer may wonder what motivates this transition from despair to wishful thinking, other than the dual status of this statement as both utterance and recorded speech, and its placement at the end of a film meant to be experienced collectively, as a field of dialogue encompassing diverse points of view.

In other words, the disputatious speech that makes up the soundtrack of *No Game* is modeled on the Enlightenment concept of the public sphere of rational discourse, the idea that the public was not found in a place or a particular manifestation of popular opinion so much as in a mode of "behavior."[66] The Movement often expressed the view that the ideal of the public sphere was theoretically and politically flawed because of the way that access to the sphere of rational debate had historically been limited to the white male bourgeoisie. The Newsreel films did not dispute that debate could and should take place. In their rancorous opposition to the classes and institutions that dominated official and quasi-official manifestations of the public sphere, and in their irreverent flouting of the rules of conduct of these conversations, they were simply calling into question the conditions under which they were supposed to take place and foregrounding the role that cinema itself could play in constructing alternative publics. The Newsreel filmmakers refused to separate the content of their films from the material concerns of form: in a rebuke to establishment documentary producers, Robert Kramer said "you cannot encompass our 'content' with those legislated and approved senses."[67] They demanded that audiences comprehend the process of rationalization that had allowed the commercial news media to present the war and other crises as mere "issues." "We want a form of propaganda," wrote Kramer, "that polarizes, angers, excites, for the purpose of discussion—a way of getting at people, not by making concessions to where they are, but by showing them where you are and then forcing them to deal with that, bringing out all their assumptions, their prejudices, their imperfect perceptions."[68]

But for all its rhetorical violence, this argument is more or less in line with the classic conception of the public sphere. In Newsreel's application of this argument, cinema would force middle-class individuals to give up the specific assumptions and prejudices through which they knew themselves *as* individuals and engage instead in public discourse. After all, Newsreel thought of itself as a news service, and it still intended to cover events. In their earliest formulations of the organization's goals, the founders of Newsreel didn't hesitate to describe their methods in conventionally journalistic terms: they still intended to "cover," to "show," and to "provide information."[69] The goal of broadcasting still oriented this conception of documentary. Forced by limited means and an ambitious production schedule to work simply, early Newsreel productions make the *absence* of polish and sophistication into a formal and political strategy. They sought to exploit textually this rushed and impoverished form of production, making the material costs of the medium part of the message.[70]

A film like Newsreel's *People's War* (1969), then, was not only an opportunity to show viewers outside North Vietnam a sympathetic picture of popular resistance to the American invasion. It was also a way to bring the war home, as SDS militants liked to say. ("Our films remind some people of battle footage," remarked Robert Kramer, "grainy, camera weaving around trying to get the material, and still not get beaten/ trapped. Well, we, and many others, are at war. We not only document that war, but try to find ways to bring that war to places which have managed so far to buy themselves isolation from it.")[71] The film combines hand-held images shot by Newsreel cameramen inside North Vietnam and footage supplied by the North Vietnamese Army and the National Liberation Front in a rapid, patchwork montage. By incorporating images produced on the other side of the conflict, some of which are accompanied by commentary, songs, or synch-sound dialogue in Vietnamese that the filmmakers leave untranslated, the filmmakers reinforce the point they make in the visual montage: there was no such thing as an objective position on the war from which it might be viewed simply as an international "crisis." To represent the war in the comprehensive, authoritative manner of the establishment news media was to presume that communications technologies and networks could still be ideologically neutral. For the radical left, this was obviously an impossible position. Both the technology and the public of mass communications were discredited in the eyes of the radical left by their role in the military-industrial complex. The media had been used, as David

James contends, to "present the war as non-ideological, as an apoliti-cal, humane response to ideologically motivated aggression," and, at the same time, to give humanity an American stamp by emphasizing the moral questions of war only where American lives or ways of life were concerned.[72] By contrast, Newsreel sought to provide an account of the war as seen and experienced by the enemy.

The fragmentary, sometimes incomprehensible portrait of North Vietnam presented in *People's War* contributes to this oppositional perspective. The viewer is never allowed to overlook the mechanical process by which the representation is created. The patterns of mon-tage relate the social transformations taking place before the camera in Vietnamese society to the shocks experienced by the viewer, who must adjust his or her perception merely to keep up with the rapid pre-sentation of images. And at the center of this relation is the camera itself, documenting every aspect of national life, from the home to the marketplace and the factory to the battlefield. At one point, the viewer is told about the logs in which detailed records of a village's part in the fighting are kept and the "houses of tradition" in which artifacts of their success—photographs, medals, an American pilot's helmet, a few pieces of fuselage—are displayed. The cameras cataloguing the mi-nutiae of daily life during the war are clearly also meant to be part of this monumental practice, poised between tradition and modernity. Because it is not clear which pieces of footage in the wide-ranging as-semblage come from North Vietnamese sources and which were shot by the Newsreel group who traveled to North Vietnam (only the final credits say anything about the provenance of the images), the montage and the foreign sounds on the soundtrack force viewers to engage with the film as a problem that is at once material, perceptual, and intellec-tual. We are continually made aware, that is to say, that the meaning of revolutionary subjectivity is a construction, one that takes place at the level of the productive process as much as at the level of the subject.

One short section of the film demonstrates this lesson effectively. The section begins with scenes from a simple military training site in Hanoi, not much more than a group of young men and women in street clothes and pith helmets being trained in antiaircraft fire with old ri-fles in what looks like a city park. In translation, we hear voice-over of a young woman, one of the instructors, explain how she was trained to fight and has now returned to Hanoi to train others. The young men and women are enjoying the lesson and appear to be amused by a charmingly simple prop the instructors use to help them practice their aim, a small model of an airplane at the end of a very long pole held up against the sky (see figures 3.10 and 3.11). The voice-over then takes us to other locations essential to the national effort, a textile factory and the polytechnic. Both, we learn, are part of the struggle for modernization and against American imperialism. Then the montage shifts into a choppy sequence of battle footage, apparently composed of images taken from many different sources and battles. Most of the military activity we see in this short sequence is of antiaircraft fire. Recalling the demonstration of only a few minutes earlier, where we saw how a primitive mimetic device can be used to simulate an attack by enemy jets, it is hard not to recognize the analogy being constructed between the two different sequences. In both cases, the materials used to represent an attack by enemy planes—in the first case, a model plane on a stick, in the second, the newsreel footage from which the "real" attack is constructed—are hardly hidden from their respective audiences, the young trainees and the audience of *People's War.*

Since the training we see the young men and women receiving leads to the defense mounted by North Vietnamese soldiers in the battle footage, the simplest reading of this progression—the denotative one—is that despite the primitive nature of the North Vietnamese training and equipment, an effective defense can still be mounted against a technologically sophisticated enemy. But there is also a reflexive lesson to be gleaned about cinema itself as a weapon in the struggle against imperialism. The connotative meaning of this series of sequences is that if we learn to see documentary cinema as a material practice by which meanings are constructed, rather than simply discovered in the world, we will be better able to identify with the Vietnamese people in their struggle. As the intervening images of the textile factory and the polytechnic suggest, this is a struggle carried out on the terrain of industrial and intellectual production, as well as in battle (see figure 3.12). American viewers who take this lesson to heart will be better equipped to do battle on their home turf with the forces of illusion and spectacle (if, as Debord maintained, spectacle is "that which escapes the activity of men, that which escapes reconsideration and correction by their work").[73] The for-

Figures 3.10–3.11. *People's War* ([New York] Newsreel, 1969). Still captures from VHS.

Figure 3.12. *People's War* ([New York] Newsreel, 1969). Still capture from VHS.

mation of popular movements and national liberation struggles was in this way linked to the struggle for a truly popular cinema.

The argument for a dual strategy is made clear by the final sequence of the film, in which a group of men using primitive two-person saws cut apart a huge tree trunk while, around them, other men and women chop smaller pieces of wood with chisels and hatchets (see figure 3.13). After a while, an American voice-over quotes Ho Chi Minh, by way of explanation of the significance of the scene: "My ultimate wish is that our whole party and people, united in struggle, build a peaceful, united, independent, democratic, and prosperous Vietnam and make a worthy contribution to the world revolution." Because it is not immediately clear what the men are building, the activity of work is abstracted into a metaphor of building—of the nation and the revolution. The filmmakers allow the noises of sawing and chopping to go on for a minute and a half before the voice-over interrupts them, and their hypnotic sounds contribute to this abstraction. When the screen goes dark, the sounds continue; it is only after the appearance of a title card, which

Figure 3.13. *People's War* ([New York] Newsreel, 1969). Still capture from VHS.

lists Newsreel as the producer of the film and gives the North and South Vietnamese sources of some of the footage, that the sounds fade. The audio-visual sign of work is thus further abstracted and then recomposed. Carrying the rhythmic sounds of manual labor out of their natural visual context and into a purely discursive image—the list of footage sources, which attests to the collaboration between different sorts of popular resistance movements from different countries—this final construction of sound and image asserts that like the work represented, cinematic representation is merely an instrument of a larger project, the "reconsideration" and "correction" of the image of the Vietnamese people in the Western media and in Western ideology. By its use of sounds that had no immediately apparent meaning, and by imposing a partisan voice-over on images, the Newsreel filmmakers were resisting the technological naturalism that had become commonplace in documentary filmmaking earlier in the decade, the idea that documentary filmmaking was merely a device for observation and recording, whose perfection would make possible social transparency.[74]

SOUNDING THE DEPTHS:
INTERVIEWS WITH MY LAI VETERANS AND *WINTER SOLDIER*

A number of filmmakers took their oppositional politics in a different direction from the vanguardist aesthetics of the early Newsreel films, turning instead toward the method of oral history to challenge the idea of the present. In some works of leftist documentary that followed, the interview became a way for these films to contest the self-evidence of the documentary image. A leading proponent of this new use of testimony was Emile de Antonio. Commenting on the work of de Antonio, Thomas Waugh describes a rhythm of alternation between "the document, a fragment of a past event, and the interview, a living segment of a present reflecting upon and analyzing that fragment."[75] Refined in such films as *Point of Order* (1963), *Rush to Judgment* (1966), *In the Year of the Pig* (1968) and *Millhouse: A White Comedy* (1971), de Antonio's method pitted interview subjects against one another and against the commonsense evidence of official history found in newsreels and other mainstream sources of political information. In *Underground* (1976), his film about the fugitive Weathermen, de Antonio borrowed a tactic of films like *Interviews with My Lai Veterans* (1970), a twenty-two minute compilation of interviews with five soldiers who participated in the infamous March 1968 massacre, and *Winter Soldier* (1972), a film of one of the public hearings on military atrocities staged in 1970 and 1971 by Vietnam Veterans Against the War and produced in collaboration with the veterans. In these films, the physical presence of the Vietnam veteran's intact body was betrayed by the shocking and traumatic nature of his testimony.

In de Antonio's previous films, the documentary interview was put to new uses, with at once more depth and less interiority than was conventional. The interview was a form familiar to American viewers from television, where it was used in literally pedestrian ways to provide evidence that a collective man in the street existed. Practitioners of *cinéma vérité* outside the United States had often used interviews to provoke individual reflection and recollection. But in the hands of de Antonio and other partisan filmmakers of the New Documentary, the interview became a tool of historical analysis, one that was all the more effective as a device of critical cinema, Thomas Waugh observed, "because of its flatness."[76]

Filmed testimony puzzled critics because it belied the presentism of the *vérité* image. "The problem with *Winter Soldier*," complained a reviewer in *Cineaste*, was that film made visible "only a portion of" the war crimes eyewitnesses reported.[77] *Winter Soldier* is "not so much a film," the reviewer lamented, "as it is a cinematic transcript of the hearings," a distinction that entailed the presence or absence of "style and artifice" through which the filmmakers might have "heighten[ed] the emotions of the testimony." (This stubborn refusal to view documentary forms through the same aesthetic lenses the magazine applied to Western European art cinema was in evidence elsewhere in the same issue, which was devoted to radical American cinema. A questionnaire on the state of radical cinema asked impatiently why "most radical American films are documentary in technique. . . . Can the Left not dream?").[78] To *Cineaste*, *Winter Soldier* was merely a reminder of the antiwar movement's failure, and the veterans who appeared in the film, just tokens of the movement's mainstreaming. It took liberal reviewers like Amos Vogel, writing in the *Village Voice*, and *New York Times* critic Vincent Canby to notice that the film was replete with telling silences. "What is obviously missing," Canby noted, "is some explanation as to how we could have managed to raise a couple of generations of people who could participate in the conduct described without experiencing the kind of sorrow that activates consciousness."[79] The moral effect of these films, in other words, came from their ability to leave room for the viewer's projection.

Winter Soldier documents the hearings held in Detroit at the end of January 1971 by Vietnam Veterans Against the War, an event organized to generate national publicity for VVAW's campaign to make public veterans' eyewitness accounts of military atrocities. The campaign was a response to the Senate Foreign Relations Committee, which began hearings on the war in 1967 and had not, in that time, invited veterans to testify before Congress. When the March 1968 atrocities at My Lai were made public in the fall of 1969, VVAW decided to hold its own hearings with the aim of demonstrating that the torture and killing of prisoners and civilians and the wanton destruction of property were hardly aberrations. Indeed, it turned out that criminal acts were committed with the sanction of military commanders and were so well known that they were effectively a tacit military policy or, at the very least, an accepted means of carrying out policy. By staging public hearings, VVAW hoped to bring pressure to bear, through the press, on the official proceedings in Washington. Throughout 1970, hearings were held in cities throughout the Northeast and Midwest, but they only attracted the attention of the local press. Even the Detroit hearings, which were directed at a national audience, were more or less ignored by the national media: the *New York Times* devoted very little space to its coverage, and of the national network news broadcasts, only CBS sent cameras to Detroit, then declined to use the footage they shot.[80] The veterans' collaboration with the Winterfilm collective, a group of leftist filmmakers based in New York City, was intended to spread the veterans' testimony even further, following the path laid by *Interviews with My Lai Veterans,* a short documentary on the same theme from the previous year.

While the Winter Soldier campaign was in the works, *Interviews* had been showing in commercial theaters. But *Interviews's* various successes, including a 1971 Oscar for Documentary Short Subject, could be regarded as something of a fluke, an effect of clever distribution and exhibition. Directed by Hollywood producer Joseph Strick, the film was programmed with other sensations of radical cinema, like Solanas and Gettino's *Hour of the Furnaces* (1968) and de Antonio's *In the Year of the Pig* (see figure 3.14). And, at least in the larger and more permissive cities, the context of its exhibition included another genre of secret knowledge, hard-core pornography, soon to become (with the summer 1972 release of *Deep Throat*) the object of official scorn and popular fascination.

The military-atrocity film shared with pornography the lure of the obscene. Both genres promised to open private and perverse realms of knowledge to public scrutiny. By the time of the Watergate investigation, *Deep Throat* had become a cultural commonplace to the extent that *Washington Post* reporters Bob Woodward and Carl Bernstein could use it to name their source for first-person evidence about the secret government inside the Nixon White House. As with its fictional namesake, this political scandal served to betray the surfaces of public bodies, revealing private desires and languages underneath. As Nixon demonstrated, recording was an unreliable index of this secret truth:

Figure 3.14. Movie advertisements in the *New York Times*, March 1971.

it could always be edited or erased. By 1971, however, this paradox was already familiar to audiences of testimonial documentaries like *Interviews* and *Winter Soldier*. In harrowing eyewitness accounts, the soldiers interviewed in these films describe the interiority of bodies penetrated by bombs, bullets, knives, and sexual violence (see figures 3.15–3.17). In doing so, they establish the metaphorical depths of their own characters, suggesting sensibilities scarred by what they have seen and remembered. Purveyor of secrets just as obscene as the hard-core pornography which would soon follow them into the public sphere, it was perhaps no accident that these films used the same body parts, the throat and the face, as the vessels of another transgressive orality, the filmed testimony of military witnesses to American war crimes.

Figures 3.15-3.16. *Interviews with My Lai Veterans* (Joseph Strick, 1970). Still captures from DVD.

Figure 3.17. *Interviews with My Lai Veterans* (Joseph Strick, 1970). Still capture from DVD.

Neither *Interviews with My Lai Veterans* nor *Winter Soldier* presented much in the way of new information about the atrocities committed by American troops in Vietnam. By the time *Interviews* was released, in the spring of 1970, the story of the March 1968 mass killing of more than 500 civilians at My Lai 4, a hamlet in a group of villages known as Songmy, had been front-page news in the United States for several months. Seymour Hersh, a freelance reporter, broke the story in November 1969, after individual soldiers began telling Army investigators about the atrocities at My Lai that they had witnessed. Congressional hearings on My Lai and other large-scale war crimes began in the fall of 1969 and continued for months. The presentation of testimony in cinematic form in *Interviews* and *Winter Soldier* added two dynamic qualities to the existing wealth of first-hand knowledge about these atrocities, circulation and performance. Recording testimony on film and audiotape made possible its mass distribution, and the creation of wider audiences for it than such testimony would receive as a live

Figure 3.18. *Winter Soldier* (Winterfilm Collective, 1972). Still capture from DVD.

event, whether conducted as a government inquiry, a judicial or military proceeding, or a civic gathering. This distributive character was counterbalanced by the performative displays of anger, shame and remorse these films captured.

That the veterans' confessions and accusations took place in the civic sphere raised the question of how the public expression of their military intelligence and its affective dimension could have legal or political effect. Especially when grouped together in the panel format of the Winter Soldier hearings, this testimony acquired the aspect of performance that Thomas Waugh describes, in his history of gay and lesbian documentary in the 1970s, as "collaborative self-expressivity of a theatrical order" (see figures 3.18–3.20).[81] Because they were staged in a way that resembled a state or legal tribunal, but without the official power of those settings, the theatrics of the hearings cut against another performative aspect of the veterans' speech, its ability (or lack thereof) to institute action. From one perspective, the spare frontality of *Winter Soldier*'s reportage-style shooting exemplifies the aesthetic

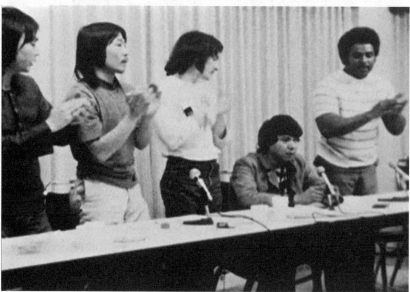

Figures 3.19-3.20. *Winter Soldier* (Winterfilm Collective, 1972). Still captures from DVD.

of *vérité* realism that, according to Waugh, gay and lesbian documentary of the same period explicitly rejected in favor of mannered, highly
self-conscious techniques of mise-en-scène.[82] But when these images of
men sharing their memories and their feelings are considered elements
of a discourse of resistance, one opposed to the official versions of reality, they begin to resemble, in their performativity, scenes of transgressive homosociality in gay and lesbian documentary or scenes of
consciousness-raising in feminist documentary of the period.

As supplements to the slow, remote, and relatively toothless official
investigations being conducted by Congress and the military, the soldiers' melodramatic performances lent immediacy and credibility to
the charges that veterans were making precisely because the official
hearings were opaque and served, in effect, to screen the truth of the
atrocities. Conscience displayed itself on the expressive surfaces of the
faces and voices of the veterans, which became, in effect, surfaces for
projection. This is roughly the point made by Amos Vogel, in his *Village Voice* review of *Winter Soldier,* when he insists that there is "simply no substitute for seeing the faces of the men as they testify, their
strain, tears, hesitations, and artless innocence," all of which serve as
"inexorable guarantors of veracity, none available from a reading of the
testimony."[83] These images of the pain of testimony counterbalance the
color photographs and footage scattered throughout the film in which
American and South Vietnamese soldiers are seen abusing prisoners
and civilians. Some of the visible images that shock Vogel show soldiers
gaily posing with suffering or dead bodies; they are, presumably, snap-
shots made as gruesome prizes, just as American soldiers cut ears from
the dead at My Lai and elsewhere (see figure 3.21). About these images,
Vogel comments that they are of a type so well-known to Americans
by 1972 that they seem like clichés. Nonetheless, Vogel echoes Canby
when he identifies the film's rhetorical power with something that is,
as Canby puts it, "obviously missing" from the film. It is these missing
images that are most shocking: "One feels frightened," Vogel writes, "at
the thought of untold thousand others patiently waiting in television
vaults to be stirred into pitiful life by future researchers, an accusing
army of corpses that we will never surmount."[84] Vogel's horrific archival fantasy follows a structure provided by the film itself, in its scenes
of testimony. Recollected scenes of violence bring their witnesses to

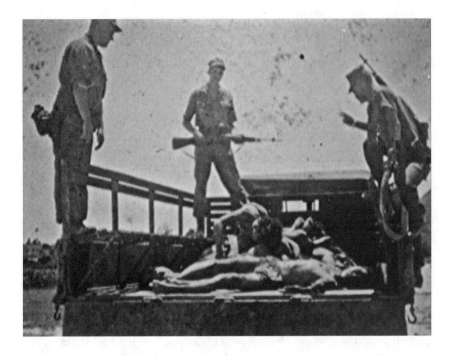

Figure 3.21. *Winter Soldier* (Winterfilm Collective, 1972). Still capture from DVD.

the tears that are, according to Vogel, the "great and ultimate stars of the film."[85]

As documentary discourses, hard-core pornography and filmed testimony both engender a paradoxical limit of visibility. If the "money shot" in early 1970s porn served to extend the visibility of sex by displaying the male climax, it also made women's pleasure invisible by making ejaculation the narrative endpoint of sexual performance (a problem that *Deep Throat* allegorizes by moving its main character's clitoris into her throat).[86] Sound offered a way around this limitation. Groans of female pleasure and other ostensibly spontaneous noises marked out the depths of a desire that could not be shown. The fact that these sounds were often poorly synchronized to the images and quite obviously a product of postproduction techniques hardly affected the illusion of somatic depth they created. One of the last films of this era to work within the structures of the New Left, Emile de Antonio's

1976 *Underground,* exploits this lesson of pornographic aesthetics in order to challenge the liberal premise of individual freedoms of speech. In doing so, it challenged the ontological premise of sound documentary itself.

EXPOSING THE UNDERGROUND

"We grew up and we didn't learn anything about history and we didn't understand very much about how you can't always see on the surface, what you see immediately is not necessarily what's at work and what's happening," says Bernardine Dohrn, one of five fugitive members of the Weather Underground who appear in Emile de Antonio's 1976 documentary about the group, *Underground.* Dohrn's phrasing casts radical consciousness as a problem of vision: the revolutionary sees under the surface of social representation to what another member of the group calls the "massive social situations" that determine the form and meaning of this surface. *Underground* endorses this analysis in its use of nonsynchronous sound and image.

Adopted as a concession to the practical exigencies of the group's precarious situation—its members had been in hiding for nearly six years when de Antonio contacted them—the filmmakers' ethical obligation to obscure the image of their subjects and to separate this image from the sound of their voices serves also to inscribe in the film one of de Antonio's usual concerns, the role that traditional documentary techniques play in the promotion of bourgeois ideology. By defacing the fugitives and detaching their faces from their voices, the filmmakers challenge one of the commonplaces of liberal and left documentary of the period: that marginal subjects must be represented in a way that preserves their integrity, restoring to them a voice and a proper interiority. Offering an illicit peek into the secret lives of outlaws, the film joined both testimonial documentary and pornography in promising to take the viewer behind the facile surfaces of mainstream representation.

In its politics, *Underground* complemented *Winter Soldier.* The object of both films was to bring voices of resistance out of hiding. In the case of *Winter Soldier* and other films based in the testimony of eyewitnesses and victims, the authority of their argument comes in large part from the presence of the speakers and the marks of physical effort and psychic resistance their bodies display as they speak. But as veterans' groups found out, the mere act of speaking in the first person was not enough to guarantee the truth. In a scathing *New York Times* review of Mark Lane's 1970 book about American military misconduct in Vietnam, *Conversations with Americans,* the credibility of the eyewitnesses Lane relied on to make his case was challenged, point by point. In the wake of this review, Vietnam Veterans Against the War was concerned about the presence of "bullshitters" among the Winter Soldier group.[87] VVAW put every veteran who wanted to testify at the hearings through a rigorous process of verifications to fend off similar charges. The images of veterans crying and of conversations and arguments behind the scenes of the hearings provide two different representations of a zone of privacy that film can breach. *Underground,* taking a cue from pornography, took this aesthetics of suspicion one step further. Using the tension between voice and the image of the body, *Underground*— which never shows its principal subjects speaking—suggests the stakes of the act of radical political expression. Indeed, its fidelity to the revolutionary cause of the Weather Underground depended upon a repudiation of the characterological depth of filmed speech. Its suspension of the priority usually given to individual voices in cinema goes hand in hand with the challenge of both the film and its subjects to the bourgeois ideology of the individual.[88]

The film was shot in secret over three days in April 1975 by de Antonio, cinematographer Haskell Wexler, and sound recordist Mary Lampson, who also edited the film. The film took a year to surface, a delay caused in part by a highly public federal effort to seize the footage and suppress the film.[89] (This effort was thwarted, in part by gestures of support for the filmmakers' First Amendment rights by the American Civil Liberties Union and by prominent members of the Hollywood film industry, including Mel Brooks, Shirley MacLaine, Jack Nicholson, and DGA president Robert Wise.) De Antonio became interested in making the film after reading *Prairie Fire: The Politics of Revolutionary Anti-Imperialism,* a 150-page tract that the Weather Underground published in 1974.[90] In *Prairie Fire,* the group accounts for the changes in its tactics and philosophy since its formation in 1969. Placing the

Weather organization in an anti-imperialist context that included the independence movements in Cuba, Vietnam, and Puerto Rico, as well as black and Native American nationalisms and the movement for women's liberation, *Prairie Fire* sought to temper the impression, held by many on the left, that Weather was merely a group of adventurist, middle-class troublemakers, more interested in headlines than political change. *Prairie Fire* sought also to demonstrate the group's sense of history, its own and that of the American left out of which it had grown. The authors reached back to Native American assertions of nationhood and black antislavery resistance, as well as the workers' movements of the nineteenth and twentieth centuries to create a genealogy for the anti-imperialist New Left. The aim of these reflections was neither to disavow nor defend the group's past actions but rather to situate them in the program for broader revolutionary movement. *Prairie Fire* emphasized the organizational work necessary for a protracted battle with the American military-industrial state. The twin embarrassments of Watergate and the defeat of American forces in Vietnam had convinced the group that both imperialism and the state were susceptible. The keys to victory were patience and organization, two qualities new to the group's rhetoric. *Prairie Fire* itself had taken a year to write. That the group agreed to submit to the long, slow process of filmmaking, when previously their preferred modes of publicity had been the broadside, the audiotaped communiqué, and statements ventriloquized by news anchormen, suggested that it had adopted a different perspective on the timetable of social change.

Underground, likewise, seems inspired by the reflective and inclusive mood that Weather displays in *Prairie Fire*. In both its historical perspective and its approach to cinematic narration, the film mirrors the group's new concern with drawing the energies of revolution from many sources. Although de Antonio shares Weather's cynicism about the "monolithic coherence of the System," this bitterness is undercut by the film's distribution of the authority to speak, shared by a variety of voices.[91] The film uses a diverse series of voices in the place where a voice-over might go. In addition to using the members of the Underground who were present at the filming, we hear the voices of Ho Chi Minh, Nuyorican poet Miguel Algarín, and a number of familiar protest singers, each of whom expresses opposition to American imperialism. In the opening minutes, the film provides a history of the group's origins in the guise of personal accounts by each of the members present at the meeting. But these stories are never identified with a member by name. They function to locate the New Left in general and the Weathermen in particular in a variety of overlapping American political genealogies: the industrial working class; the socialist left of the 1930s; McCarthyism; the civil rights movement and the rise of black activism; the student movement; and national liberation movements in the Third World. The use of stock and archival footage further abstracts these introductory testimonies, which serve as a kind of collective autobiography. They scrupulously avoid the confessional disposition we might expect in such reflections. This polyvocality is carried through to the level of the montage, which makes use, in de Antonio's customary fashion, of both original and secondhand materials. So much of the latter is from the work of contemporary political filmmakers, including Cinda Firestone, Chris Marker, and Newsreel, that the film begins to resemble a history of New Left documentary filmmaking, distributing the authority to document radical politics across a network of producers.

If the montage provides one model of collaborative production, another can be seen in the film's unique form of documentary cinematography. The filmmakers employ a number of devices to deface or, as de Antonio put it, "sanitize" the image of the fugitives, including shooting them through a gauzy curtain and silhouetting them (see figures 3.22 and 3.23).[92] One of these setups had Wexler shooting into a mirror, so that all the members of the production were gathered together in a single shot. Such an image inscribes the collective spirit of the production: the Weathermen not only determined the location of filming and the content of the conversations but conducted some man-on-the-street interviews that appear at the end of the film.[93] In one remarkable instance of this reverse-shot of the group interview, while the group is discussing the Greenwich Village townhouse explosion in which three members of the organization were killed, all three of the filmmakers—including Wexler, who can be seen turning away from the camera as it continues to run—look off-screen at Billy Ayers, who speaks from out-

BERNARDINE DOHRN

Figure 3.22. *Underground* (Emile de Antonio with Haskell Wexler and Mary Lampson, 1976). Frame enlargement from 16mm filmstrip. Courtesy of Nancy de Antonio and Anthology Film Archives.

side the frame (see figure 3.24). Watching the faces of the filmmakers as they address the Weathermen, whose backs are to the camera, the viewer experiences a profound disorientation. Despite Wexler's assertion in a subsequent *New York Times* article on the Justice Department's interest in the film that "I make films to be seen, not hidden," this image shows the opposite: that the documentary apparatus can hide by seeing. This and the other images that veil the speakers' identities show how visible evidence can be used to conceal and dissemble.[94]

De Antonio undermined the documentary convention of the omniscient narrator in all of his films, usually dispensing with it in favor of interviews and ironic manipulations of original sound from newsreels and other found materials. The use of the image in *Underground* to delineate the power of invisible sound is a version of this critique. The authority of the interview depends in part on the singularity, silence,

Figure 3.23. *Underground* (Emile de Antonio with Haskell Wexler and Mary Lampson, 1976). Still capture from VHS.

and invisibility of the interviewer. These qualities effect the separation of the scene of production from the knowledge gathered in it and made available through it to the viewer. The difference between filmed subject and filmmaker is blurred in the discussion scenes in *Underground,* as is the hierarchical relationship between knowledge and production in documentary filmmaking. All of the filmmakers of *Underground* ask questions, not just the director, and the subjects are heard complaining about the aggravations of the filmmaking process. This reflexivity is one of a number of methods the filmmakers use to liberate the voice in documentary in an attempt to thwart the liberal rhetoric of democracy as the expression of individual points of view.

Subverting the traditional conception of action in political documentary, *Underground* becomes a film of people listening to one another dilate upon history. Wexler's images and Lampson's editing challenge

Figure 3.24. *Underground* (Emile de Antonio with Haskell Wexler and Mary Lampson, 1976). Frame enlargement from 16mm filmstrip. Courtesy of Nancy de Antonio and Anthology Film Archives.

the audience to notice the resemblance between the discussion on screen and its own act of listening. Furthermore, they encourage us to think of audition as a stage in the process of social change, not merely a preliminary or preparatory activity. When Lampson juxtaposes a silhouetted image of Dohrn, turning her head sharply as if in response to a sound, with an archival image of Jeff Jones, speaking at the Columbia strike in 1968, the effect is of Dohrn listening to a voice that is not only off-screen but calling to her from the past (see figure 3.25). Like so much of Lampson's remarkable work in *Underground*, this cut is felt in different registers at once and lends itself to more than one interpretation. From one perspective, this false match can be read as an emblem of the group's nostalgia for 1968 and the dream of revolution, long after the demise of the New Left. But a different implication of the false

Figure 3.25. *Underground* (Emile de Antonio with Haskell Wexler and Mary Lampson, 1976). Frame enlargement from 16mm filmstrip. Courtesy of Nancy de Antonio and Anthology Film Archives.

match is the one the film allows Dohrn and the other Weathermen to make at great length in their own words: that history can be made "by people." Indeed, this match comes shortly after Dohrn's statement that "the United States government is not invincible. It didn't exist for all time and it's not going to exist for all time," and the film can be seen, here and throughout, attempting to give form to this belief in the discontinuity of history.

Perhaps more than any other American documentary of the period, *Underground* mixes history, theory, and practice. It becomes a formal primer on the strategies of anti-imperialist politics and their incorporation into filmmaking and other intellectual forms. The film is, paradoxically, at its most eloquent when it demonstrates how speech can be separated from and reattached to the filmed body, as when, late in the film, Kathy Boudin reads a poem for the imprisoned black radical Assata Shakur over a completely black screen. In moments like these, *Underground* risks a clumsy translation of experience into cinematic form in order to reiterate the point that many radical films of the period had made: that documentary film was capable of projecting new forms of association, even—or especially—when it was limited in its capacity to make them visible. In the next chapter, I explore the centrality of a particular institution, prison, to the development of this principle in leftist documentary of the time.

4 / DOCUMENTARY COUNTERPUBLICS
Filming Prison

In the previous chapter, I maintained that different versions of the new documentary of the 1960s and 1970s consistently made use of the formal tension between sound and image to express New Left political and social initiatives. By 1971, the movement that such films had helped to establish was losing momentum, handicapped by the murder or exile of many important radical figures and further burdened by squabbles internal to radical filmmaking organizations and within the left in general. While progressives deliberated on the next form of their work, a new horizon of struggle was emerging: the prison. In this chapter, I suggest that the experience of the prisoner became a useful political allegory in the period, after a number of well-publicized instances of violence instigated by state authorities. Serving as the touchstone of a multifaceted popular realism, prison dissidence provided one conception of an oppositional public sphere, what Nancy Fraser has called a subaltern counterpublic.[1] Such formations, like the theory that describes them, are tentative creations. They presume the separation or exclusion of their constituents from the mainstream of society. But at the same time, they address others not similarly "enclaved," with the aim of "expand[ing] discursive space," and rethinking the rules and means by which a public can come into being.[2] The same conditions that make prison a difficult location from which to organize a public or engage in public discourse make it particularly well-suited to test a society's dominant logics of publicness. As activists and progressive artists and intellectuals reexamined their relation to social and political institutions of all kinds, prison became an important site for reflection.

One option for critical intellectuals, faced with the radicalized subaltern, was to reexamine their own privileged position as agents of public consciousness. The September 1971 prisoner revolt at Attica State Correctional Facility in upstate New York, an event that entered nearly immediately into the mythic genealogy of American progressives, played an important role in this reflective analysis, as is evident from the account of the event by one of its primary observers, *New York Times* journalist Tom Wicker. In Wicker's book *A Time to Die* (1975), the events at Attica become a vehicle for a meditation on the public character of intellectual work. Forcing him to reevaluate in personal and historical terms the meaning of liberal subjectivity, the struggle at the prison serves as the backdrop and mirror of Wicker's trials of consciousness.

As a public figure, Wicker is invited to Attica to act as a mediator between the prisoners and the state officials in charge of the prison, but his professional and personal instincts compel him to do more than mediate. His search for the meaning of the Attica disaster leads him to conclude that prison is all around us, a point that Malcolm X had made a decade earlier. His introspective account gives literary form to the process that Michel Foucault—who was at that time involved with prisoners' rights efforts in France and the United States—refers to as *discipline,* the activities of self-surveillance by which the modern individual polices himself and embodies social order. The intersecting stories of *A Time to Die*—the failure of the observers' mission at Attica, the pernicious role of the commercial news media, and the emergence of the public intellectual's guilty conscience—are meant to be read as an allegory of the society that surrounds the prison; "a society," as Foucault writes, "in which the principal elements are no longer the community and public life, but, on the one hand, private individuals and, on the other, the state."[3]

Wicker's story is an example of the professional bildungsroman described by Bruce Robbins, in which vocation is not just the outcome of the story but is itself written *"as literature."*[4] Robbins suggests that for the contemporary intellectual, narratives of professional becoming follow a logic of nostalgia. In such narratives, the profession from within which the intellectual is authorized to comment on and address a public is itself already withdrawing into the past. From this perspective, Wicker's personal history, connected in his mind with the period and administration of the New Deal, functions only as a reminder that he is irreparably separated from the public he tries to serve at Attica in the capacity of observer by the very professional station that makes him desirable to the prisoners. The private obligations and prejudices that eventually doom the observers' group to infighting and ambivalence are anticipated in the book's opening scene, an exclusive gathering of Washington intellectuals:

> The luncheon of the Bill Fay Club . . . was a gregarious affair as usual. The scene of the feast was the executive dining room of the National Geographic Society, in the Society's elegant building. . . . Members met at random for good food and what they assured themselves was "the best talk in Washington." . . . These were erudite men, in everything from art to politics, as Tom Wicker had come to know. He always studied Franc Shor's wine choices with care, and was perennially surprised to find himself able to hold up his end of the conversation, and even on occasion to bring the table to his own point of view. But much of his life had been a surprise to him; and it was not only in the executive dining room of the Geographic that he sometimes had a vivid sense of having come a long, long way.[5]

Wicker's reverie will shortly be interrupted by a call from the prisoners at Attica, and, not long after, he will decide that he is unequal to the task of speaking for them. At the other end of this story he makes a stunned appearance before two groups who stand illegitimately for "the people," bloodthirsty reporters from the electronic media and an equally vengeful mob of working-class racists from neighboring towns who support the deadly assault. This contrasting scene only clinches the point Wicker makes in the opening setting of luxury and privilege: that by the nostalgic logic of the narrative of professionalism, when the professional turns once again to face the public to which he owes his very sense of vocation, "it cannot be public enough."[6]

The private-public structure of the narrative complements Wicker's opinion that the state itself could not be trusted to treat all of its citizens objectively. Having brought "to Attica a belief in the state's ultimate ability to serve its citizens, if properly and persistently prodded by the people,"[7] Wicker comes to see that the standoff replays "the ingrained

American myth of violence . . . the old Puritan notion that 'we' don't commit crimes, only 'they' do. . . . So it is not surprising that it is not 'we' but 'they' who populate the Atticas of America—they, the violent, the lawless, the abnormal, the subhuman."[8] The overtly literary device of writing about himself in the third person, in other words, is meant to call into question the premise upon which Wicker's authority rests and which is the precondition for his presence at the prison: that journalism addresses, serves, and establishes a public sphere.

By displaying the subjectivity of the journalist, Wicker means to demonstrate the gap between the personal and the historical, between the individuated experience of the professional intellectual and the collective experience of the subaltern classes. Though his series of reflections is supposed to close the gap between the two domains, Wicker's literary aspirations serve mainly to reinforce his membership in a professional-intellectual class. This failure is most strikingly demonstrated by the contrast between Wicker's self-conscious attempts to make Attica reflect social and internal dilemmas and a literal instance of reflection that appears early in the account of the siege, when Wicker is asked by the prison administration to tour one of the other cell blocks, to confirm that the prisoners still in their cells are not being mistreated:

As the horrid sound of metal wrenching on metal echoed down the cell tier, Wicker—who happened to be the first of the observer group through the doorway—saw a small mirror pop out the square window of each of the perhaps twenty solid steel doors that lined either side of the long concrete and steel corridor before him. The sight puzzled him. It struck him first that mirrors, being of glass, were potentially dangerous weapons that ought not to be allowed in inmates' hands. Then he saw that the men in the cells had no other way to see who was coming. The small apertures in each of the solid cell doors prevented any one in a cell from looking anywhere but straight across the corridor to the opposite cell with its identical small window. So when shrieking metal signaled the opening of the door to the tier, the only way the men in the cells could see who was approaching them was to look in the mirrors they could hold out through the small openings.

Wicker was literally stopped in his tracks by the spectacle of the mirrors. What he was seeing was not physical brutality, but worse—that a man could not know who was coming unless he had a mirror handy, that he was made to live his life, or a large part of it, behind a blank door with the smallest of openings. With the power of revealed truth, as if a blindfold had been torn from his eyes after years in darkness so that what he first saw would remain as indelibly graven on his brain as if scarred there by light itself, Wicker understood that these men were caged. And he saw in the same instant of blinding truth that to cage a human being was to place the person caged in the condition of a beast in the zoo.[9]

The self-reflection with which Wicker follows and glosses the "spectacle of the mirrors" is redundant, since the image makes Wicker's point clearly enough. In the hands of the prisoners, who lack the means for interiority and individuality, a mirror is not a device for self-reflection but for communication, since it allows the prisoners to temporarily redirect the intense gaze of the institution under which they are normally disciplined.

The true story that Wicker tells from the prison not only causes him to doubt the truth of the story told within his family but compels him to wonder whether professions of art and culture could ever be adequate to the task of representing the unrepresented. For Wicker, the documentary realism of the memoir becomes a way to express a feeling of imprisonment by the conditions of the bourgeois public sphere. As we have seen at other moments in the history of American documentary, the true story and its telling can become a source of pressure on the very identity of the cultural intellectual. This pressure was important to the renewal of intellectual vocation in the 1930s, and its reappearance in a later period would seem to indicate the return of self-consciousness and ambivalence about that vocation and its foundations.

Prison and prisoners came to symbolize one variant of this radical doubt. Gayatri Spivak's trenchant formulation of leftist self-critique—the rhetorical question, "Can the subaltern speak?"—was itself a retort to an exchange between Foucault and Gilles Deleuze on the topic of prisoners and other oppressed groups. In her essay, Spivak refers to the French theorists' position as a disavowal, one that proceeds by a "representationalist realism," and she accuses them of "valoriz[ing] the concrete experience of the oppressed, while being so uncritical about the historical role of the intellectual."[10] Intellectuals who want to act in the interest of society's others should function, Deleuze and Foucault agreed, as relays between them and the publics they wished to address rather than as their figurehead or mouthpiece. Acting in the latter capacity, the intellectual had traditionally functioned as a representative of truth itself: "he was conscience, consciousness, and eloquence," Foucault said, and had primary responsibility for bringing to light what others refused to know, "in the name of those who were forbidden to speak the truth."[11] As in the United States, unrest in French prisons had become a focus of revolutionary thought and organizing, but Foucault and Deleuze agreed that the role of critical intellectuals was simply to "establish conditions where the prisoners themselves would be able to speak," since such masses "know far better" than intellectuals what to say about their situation and how to say it.[12] Foucault and Deleuze used the occasion of recent political activity in and around French prisons to theorize a new kind of intellectual: "no longer a subject, a representing or representative consciousness," the central task of this intellectual was now "to create conditions that permit the prisoners themselves to speak,"[13] as Foucault was doing with the Groupe d'Information sur les Prisons and in the writings (including *I, Pierre Rivière, Having Slaughtered My Mother, My Sister, and My Brother* . . . [1973] and *Discipline and Punish* [1975]) that came out of this relationship with prisoners. To treat prison as another of the realms where knowledge was forbidden was to do the work of the institution, extending its repressive effects out into the public domain. To speak on behalf of prisoners would perpetuate the function of prison as an exclusive and exceptional space, a separation that normalized the society around it.[14] Foucault and Deleuze proposed instead to redefine reality according to "what actually happens in factories, in schools, in barracks, in prisons, in police stations."[15] The problem with this approach, according to Spivak, lay in its understanding of representation, a concept Deleuze was eager to do away with, in favor of something he calls "action." The traditional function of the critical intellectual as one who represents social problems, in the sense of describing them, places in a position of passivity those who are unrepresented, in the sense of being without standing in social and political institutions. Places like factories, schools, and prisons were "beyond" representation, since there the oppressed "speak, act, and know *for themselves.*"[16] But in their conflation of theory and action, or politics, Foucault and Deleuze "represent themselves as transparent," Spivak says, and present "an analogy . . . as proof."[17]

The limits of this analogy can be seen in a quite different popular narrative formed, in the same period, from the Attica prisoners' experience. Based on a real event, Sidney Lumet's 1975 film *Dog Day Afternoon* tells the story of a relatively ordinary crime, the botched robbery of a Brooklyn bank in the summer of 1972. In his well-known reading of the film, Fredric Jameson argues that the film functions as an allegory of class consciousness.[18] Jameson's analysis hinges upon the film's fusion of social materials into a character-driven narrative. To be "accessible to our imaginations," according to Jameson, "the classes have to be able to become in some sense characters in their own right"; class structure is experienced, as Jameson says, "through the tangible medium of daily life."[19] Thus, in the real-life events on which *Dog Day Afternoon* is based, the holdup could be viewed as a stage upon which the social tensions roiling below the surface of the event are unleashed in a dramatic struggle between the underdog heroes (the overworked and underpaid bank employees, the pathetic criminals with their pathologies and personal failures, and the protorevolutionary mass in the street) and their bureaucratic-corporate antagonists, the police, the media, and the parent corporation, pulling the strings behind the friendly local bank.

An allegory is a special kind of narrative, one that calls attention to its capacity to make one set of events refer to another and to the role that the cultural activity of narrative plays in the processes of social integration and social change. Within the Marxist frame of Jameson's analysis, real life is itself merely a medium for another level of reality, that of class and economics. Thus, *Dog Day Afternoon* does not, in this reading, attain the status of an allegory by being about real life but rather because it makes "accessible to our imaginations" the role played in this struggle by mass culture: specifically, mass culture of the sort that Lumet and his collaborators deploy in the service of liberal protest. In other words, if the first phase of the allegorical operation is for the filmmakers to simply notice how the events on which the story is based already speak for the downtrodden, the second is the amplification of these elements of real life by the formal echoes of this ordinary reality. The use of New York locations for shooting, the casual, hand-held style of many of the shots, the languorous movement of the plot, Al Pacino's naturalistic performance: these semidocumentary elements of style amplify the film's claim of social relevance. In one sense, the film is not an allegory unless it makes its audience aware it is (not) just a story and unless it explains how the tension it maintains between mass popular fiction and sociopolitical fact is sutured by "profound formal contradictions to which the public cannot not be sensitive."[20]

Crucial to this interpretation is the presence in the film of figures of the mass itself, the representations of audiences of the crime and its consequences. If the film is properly an allegory, it must show us how our role as an audience is related to that of the audiences that witness and sympathize with Sonny's crime within the story. These include the bank employees being held hostage and the crowd that gathers in the street outside the bank. The relationship between all of these audiences is established through two explicit references to the events at Attica in September 1971, just a year before the events of the story. The first of these is an apparent digression Sonny makes during a conversation with the bank manager about his escape plans, in an office at the rear of the bank. When the manager offers himself as a human shield, Sonny responds: "They'll shoot you, you know. The cops, they don't give a fuck about your bank insurance. You see what they did at Attica? Forty-two people they killed, the innocent with the guilty."

This first invocation of Attica seems to be a matter of conscience or obsession for Sonny, expressed, as it is, in a private conversation, away from the rest of the world. It is followed soon after by a far more public display of the same thought, the scene in which Sonny postures in front of the bank, excoriating the police and inciting the crowd to "remember Attica." (As this performance, or performance within a performance, calls to mind Mick Jagger, the film draws here on recent memories of the rock documentaries discussed in the previous chapter, films like *Monterey Pop* [1968] and *Gimme Shelter* [1970], shot in a *cinéma vérité* style that was intended to recreate the experience of being there.) The direct relationship Sonny establishes with this popular audience is an ironic inversion of the film's indirect and exploitative relationship with *its* audience, which can have no such direct contact with the performers. The difference between the audience *in* the film and the audience *of* the film crystallizes the conflict between the documentary realism to which the film aspires—idealized as an immediate, grassroots form, like Sonny's performance—and the commercial concerns that mark the film as a product of the Hollywood industry.[21] The rest of the film, after this scene, can be read as a farcical repetition of the failed Attica rebellion, with many of the same dramatic elements: hostages, helicopters, live television, duplicitous state officials, a demand of safe passage to Algeria, and the murder of the principals. By the end of the film, the incorporation of Attica as a theme comes to seem less a call to revolution than a symptom of the tension between the public service of popular realist art and the function of the film as mere publicity or mass entertainment.

Even the two examples just presented, Wicker's book and Lumet's film, give a sense of how overdetermined was the signification of prison in the period. That so many significations could be produced from one site, one event, one signifier—Attica—suggests the presence of a powerful, if convoluted, set of countercultural desires and energies. The "overflowing of the signifier by the signified" that seemed to many observers to be taking place in Attica and other American prisons provided a new challenge to leftist documentary, not least because the very meanings and forms of "the left" were themselves under renovation in the period. The rest of this chapter attempts a genealogy of this unstable moment in political culture, for which Attica came to stand as something of an emblem.

FROM REFORM TO REBELLION: CHANGING THE IMAGE OF PRISON

Films that sensationalized the separate, secret world of the cell block and the death chamber had been part of American cinema since at least 1901, when the Edison Manufacturing Company recreated the execution of President McKinley's assassin, Leon Czolgosz, in the short film *Execution of Czolgosz, With Panorama of Auburn Prison*. This preoccupation seemed to renew itself every few decades, changing to suit social and industrial conditions. During the Depression, for instance, the prison film seemed to proliferate in infinite variety, as the extension of the gangster, social-problem, and women's film genres. While serving to diversify the studios' product lines, the topic of prison provided a setting for the exploration of social issues that racked the nation, like class and labor politics, the expansion of government powers, and the changing status of women and children as citizens. In similar fashion, the waning of the Production Code and the exploitation of racial and sexual politics at the beginning of the 1970s produced a spate of racy films with sexy stars like Pam Grier (*The Big Doll House* [1971], *Women in Cages* [1971], *The Big Bird Cage* [1972]). Such films also tapped the Nixonian frenzy of law and order and the rising visibility of the Black Power and women's liberation movements. Less common were the films that attempted to comment in a more direct way on the public or scholarly discourse on prisons or on particular practices of punishment. This category included films like *I Am a Fugitive from a Chain Gang* (1932), Mervyn LeRoy's docudramatic exposé of the hard-labor prison, and Don Siegel's *Riot in Cell Block 11* (1954), a surprisingly sympathetic treatment of rebellious prisoners, made in the wake of the national wave of prison riots of 1952 and 1953.

The People Versus Paul Crump (1962), a documentary film made for television by William Friedkin, falls into the latter category of liberal conscience, while making use of the sensational devices of the former. Best known for thrillers like *The French Connection* (1971) and *The Exorcist* (1973), Friedkin began his career in Chicago television in the early 1960s. In Chicago his social world included leftist intellectuals like Studs Terkel and Nelson Algren. Civil libertarians in the group had taken up the cause of Paul Crump, a black man sentenced to die in 1953 for the murder of a security guard during a robbery in the Chicago stockyards. Crump was the only one of five defendants to receive the death penalty. The others, also black men, received 199-year sentences. Two members of Friedkin's circle, lawyers Donald Moore and Elmer Gertz, were representing Crump in his appeals, and another acquaintance, *Chicago Daily News* reporter John Justin Smith, was writing a series of articles about Crump's rehabilitation in the Cook County Jail, where he had been held since 1954. Looking for a way out of routine public affairs programming at WGN, he pitched rival station WBKB an hour-long film about Crump, who was approaching an execution date.

The resulting film argues that Crump had been framed, and that the Chicago police investigating the case had tortured Crump over

Figure 4.1. *The People Versus Paul Crump* (William Friedkin, 1962). Still capture from VHS.

the course of a two-day interrogation, beating him into a confession he later recanted. Using dramatic re-creations, the film first illustrates the police account of the robbery and then tells the story from Crump's perspective, placing him in businesses and homes on the South Side while the crime was being committed. John Justin Smith speaks on camera with Crump and his mother, who establish this alibi. In interviews with Smith, Crump and his supporters, including the sympathetic warden of the Cook County jail, Jack Johnson, all express their opposition to the death penalty and attest to Crump's rehabilitation, due in part to his compassionate work in the jail's infirmary (see figure 4.1). Although Crump insists he is innocent of the robbery and murder with which he was charged, he isn't bitter. "I've done some things," he says. "They didn't get me for those things, but they got me for this." Crump's fatalism is echoed in the film's final images: a lurid depiction of Crump's nightmares about the electric chair and impressionistic shots in the manner of Rosellini or De Sica of the reporter wandering in a construction site where children are playing. Returning from the jail to the outside world, the ending leaves its subject behind, suspended between life and death. But unlike the ending of *I Want To Live!* (1958), which also follows the crusading reporter back out of the death chamber, the conclusion of Crump's story was not yet known when Friedkin's film ended.

The film was never broadcast by WBKB. The station became nervous about the film's explicit criticism of the methods of the Chicago police and arranged private screenings of the film for people of influence in Chicago politics. These screenings convinced the station's general manager that the film would do more harm than good to its principal subject. (Ironically, some accounts of the film's initial circulation suggest that the governor's decision to commute Crump's sentence was influenced by rumors about the film.) Relegated to film festivals, where it helped establish Friedkin's directing career, the film became a footnote in biographies of Friedkin and Crump.[22]

Until the use of reenactments and interviews was revived by filmmakers of the 1980s and 1990s (notably, Errol Morris, whose own films about prison and punishment, *The Thin Blue Line* [1988] and *Mr. Death: The Rise and Fall of Fred A. Leuchter, Jr.* [1999], make generous use of such techniques), the sensational style of *The People Versus Paul Crump* fell out of fashion among American documentarists. Friedkin's film was forced further into obscurity by *The Chair,* the Robert Drew Associates' 1962 film about Crump and his lawyer. *The People Versus Paul Crump* combines the perspectives of the investigative journalist and the sociologist, placing Crump's story in the context of the culture of Chicago crime and punishment. *The Chair,* on the other hand, employs the method of other Drew productions and of American *cinéma vérité* more generally, restricting itself to recording the unfolding of personal and social crises in the present. *The Chair* was the first program in a series of individual *cinéma vérité* portraits in Drew's syndicated television series, *The Living Camera,* and although the Drew method thrived on complex institutional and political situations, its analysis of social phenomena tended to reduce to psychologistic studies of character. The film focuses on Donald Moore, Crump's principal legal representative, as he struggles to secure high-profile support for clemency, occasionally breaking down in tears under the strain. At the last minute, the celebrity trial lawyer Louis Nizer arrives from New York to help the cause.

This time, the story ends conclusively and happily—"if," as one commentator remarked, "one chooses to regard a man's return to prison for life as an improvement upon electrocution."[23]

Despite their stylistic and ideological differences, these films share a belief in the paradigm of rehabilitation. In their depiction of an exemplary instance of injustice, both films endorse the concept of reform embraced by liberal critics of American prisons for most of the twentieth century. But they also mark the recent shift in focus of these reformist energies, from the institution to the individual. Now it was possible to argue, as Louis Nizer did in Crump's defense, that punishment "brings the hope for a better civilization, a better society."[24] Focused on the themes of responsibility, penitence, and rehabilitation, the story of Crump's time in Warden Johnson's Cook County facility evinces these changes.[25]

The correctional system to which Crump and his defenders attributed his transformation from illiterate beast to novelist and responsible citizen was itself a fairly recent invention. The "miracle of rehabilitation" Crump was said to represent only appeared as a goal of the penal process a decade or so earlier, when the rhetoric of rehabilitation came to the fore in penological discourse.[26] Although the rehabilitative ideal had been around since the nineteenth century, it was only after World War II that a nonpunitive approach became palatable to the public authorities responsible for prison.[27] If inmates at state institutions like San Quentin, Sing Sing, Stateville, and Attica were still housed in stone, cement, and steel tiers by the thousands, the officials responsible for these facilities began to maintain that their prisons were no longer simply human warehouses where criminals would be locked away from the rest of the population until their debt to society had been repaid. They were encouraged in this belief by an increasing number of academic and professional experts in psychological, psychiatric, and sociological approaches to the root causes of criminality. This outward change in philosophy was formalized when the National Prison Association became, in 1952, the American Correctional Association. Instead of merely killing time, residents of correctional institutions would instead be encouraged to make good use of their time away from society, perhaps even making up for time they had lost to unproductive and self-destructive pursuits.

The sentence, in other words, was no longer an abstract quantitative equivalent of the societal debt incurred by the criminal for his crime, a dead unit of time to be paid back directly. Rather, the sentence could now be seen as a flexible schedule for self-improvement, calibrated to the needs of the individual offender. Indeterminate sentencing, an invention of the postwar wave of reforms, was meant to allow prison authorities and parole boards to adjust sentences within a wide range of statutory minimums and maximums, depending on the prisoner's progress toward rehabilitation. In theory, this was meant to provide a humane and economical alternative to arbitrary, court-mandated sentences, and would inculcate in the prisoner a sense of responsibility. Instead of just serving an amount of time, offenders would understand the months or years they spent in prison as an investment in their future, or a reclamation of time they had misspent in the past. Vocational and educational programs, psychological counseling, complex classification systems for identifying and attacking the sources of deviant behavior, new forms of prison architecture and design, and even changes to routines and menus in the dining hall were among the many indices of what Jessica Mitford called this "kind and usual" regime of punishment, intended to better simulate the social world to which the prisoner would one day return.[28] But because these programs tended to be underfunded and understaffed, they had relatively little effect on the problems they were meant to address. Indeterminate sentencing rarely resulted in the shorter sentences its promoters predicted, because the parole boards that applied it tended to have little experience or interest in the question of rehabilitation.[29] The failure of the vaunted reforms and the perception that they were merely hypocritical gestures contributed to the unrest that roiled American prisons in the late 1960s and early 1970s.

Paul Crump, spared execution because he demonstrated remorse and responsibility, remained in prison for another thirty-one years after the governor's reprieve, in part because he had become schizophrenic while incarcerated. The pathos of Crump's situation was, in a way, anticipated in the passive role assigned to him by the intellectuals, artists, and filmmakers who took up his cause. Like the traditional subject of liberal social concern, the languishing prisoner helped the intellectual realize his or her moral vocation, providing a reason to speak out against unchecked power. But changes inside and outside prisons in the later part of the decade produced a different kind of prisoner, a young, radicalized intellectual who spoke in terms of a political "we," not a moral "I." It became the responsibility of traditional liberal intellectuals to transmit and broadcast this voice, to help it find a broader audience. Coinciding with the splintering of the New Left into a variety of social and political movements, the activist prisoner, intending to call the state to account, provoked many on the outside to reflect on their commitments.

The most influential prison activist of the period was George Jackson, a young black man who had been in and out of juvenile detention as a teenager and who was given a one-year-to-life term for his participation in a 1960 gas station holdup. Largely self-educated, Jackson became an articulate revolutionary during his confinement in Soledad and San Quentin prisons, from where he corresponded with prominent San Francisco Bay area militants like Angela Davis and the Black Panther Party. When Jackson and two others were accused of murdering a Soledad guard, his cause spread outside California. But it was the publication of Jackson's collection of correspondence, *Soledad Brother* (1970), a few months later that made Jackson an international figure.

Introduced by Jean Genet, the letters outlined Jackson's coming to political consciousness, his attempt to radicalize his parents and his younger brother (who was later shot to death attempting to spring George from San Quentin), and his debates with other black militants and movement figures, as well as detailing, by description and omission, the repressive environment of maximum security. The barrage of literary publicity that followed the book's release gave Jackson opportunities to establish his credentials as an intellectual and further endeared him to the liberal intelligentsia. In an interview with Jessica Mitford for the *New York Times Book Review,* Jackson explained how he styled himself an "absent-minded bookworm" while serving time in the Youth Authority. A feature on Jackson published several weeks later in the *Times* went into detail about Jackson's "vast literary diet," which consisted of classical economics, American poetry, fiction and letters, and journals like *Ramparts,* in addition to the black militant's usual helpings of Marx, Malcolm X, and Fanon.[30] When Jackson was killed several months later in an escape attempt, his status as a revolutionary martyr was secure; the suspicion that police and prison officials had conspired to assassinate Jackson during the escape merely contributed to his beatitude.

Like the violent events it spurred at Attica, the death of George Jackson led to a furious outpouring of memorial art and culture. One product of this efflorescence was Bob Dylan's ballad "George Jackson," recorded at the beginning of November 1971 and released as a single a week later, spending a month in the *Billboard* top forty.[31] The significance of the song was hotly debated by fans and critics, some of whom regarded it as a sign of Dylan's own resurrection, a return to protest music after several years of introspection and genre experiments like *Nashville Skyline* (1967). *Rolling Stone* described a split between two camps of listeners, "those who see it as the poet's return to social relevance and those who feel that it's a cheap way for Dylan to get a lot of people off his back."[32] The record seemed designed to exacerbate the controversy, since it was the same song in two different settings. On one side was a solo version, with Dylan accompanying himself on acoustic guitar and harmonica. The reverb on his vocal accentuated the sense of isolation expressed in the mournful lyric: "I woke up this morning, / there were tears in my bed / They killed a man I really loved, / they shot him through the head. / Lord, lord, / they cut George Jackson down. / Lord, lord, / they laid him in the ground."[33] Prison crowds the free world by dream and by metaphor, as when Dylan sings, at the end of the song, "sometimes I think this whole world / is one big prison yard / some of us are prisoners, / the rest of us are guards." Dylan's placement of himself in the song as dreamer and thinker encourages the listener to hear it as a reflection on, and of, the demands from his peers and his audience to engage once again with contemporary problems.[34]

The acoustic recording of the song expresses this sense of obligation, and Dylan's anxiety about it. The other side of the record, labeled the "big band" version, brings out the utopian elements of the song, setting the lyrical tribute to Jackson's "power" and "love" in different musical idioms. Relaxing the tempo, this version mixes country music, present in the pedal steel guitar and the walking bass line, and gospel, embodied in the call-and-response structure of the lyrics and the backup singers on the chorus.[35] If the solo version of the song attests to the nearly claustrophobic sense of urgency and proximity with which liberals experienced the highly publicized struggles and deaths of prisoners around 1970, the big band version plays out a vision of coinciding populisms, through the combination of musical styles identified with poor whites and with blacks. Since the cessation of ethnic and racial antagonisms had also been a central theme of the recent Attica uprising, itself set off by Jackson's killing, this version of the song figures prison as a site of social harmony otherwise impossible in American life. In this context, the inconsistency between the record's two sides can be read in two different ways: as a representation of the insoluble opposition between the leftist intellectual and the people and as a kind of tribute to the unlikely coordination of forces the radical prison movement entailed, within and beyond the walls of the institution.

The idea that prison symbolized the violence of social order was repeated frequently in this period, from Malcolm X's statement in a 1963 speech that "America means prison," to Charles Manson's proclamation that "We're all our own prisons, we are each our own wardens, and we do our own time." So strong was the desire, wherever it had become a topic of discourse, to see prison as a "counteraction on the position that I occupy," as Michel Foucault put it, that jailed French intellectual Régis Debray was moved to compare the lives he and other young intellectuals had lived as a kind of imprisonment, their ideas "the daydreams of prisoners."[36] In each of these formulations, the fact of prison is only the pretext for a reflection on the liberal subject and the institutions maintained in its name. In this imaginary form, prison exemplified what Foucault called a "heterotopia," a utopia made real. Like the utopia, the heterotopia is an analogy of society, but with two significant differences. First, the heterotopia is found in a place that already exists within a culture. Second, its difference from the other real sites of the culture is not that it idealizes them, as a utopia does, but that it shows what they are not. The heterotopia is at once a location and a medium, one that can "suspect, neutralize, or invert" the other social institutions or processes to which it is linked.[37]

The paradox of prison as a place, at once inside the state and on the margins of society, meant that it posed a compelling challenge to the representational capacity of social documentary. Prison was not merely another location of social discontent but a site from which to rethink certain paradigms of representation and the place of documentary within them. Given that the most of the documentary films discussed in this chapter are the works of first-time filmmakers, prison might seem to offer a new model of documentary vocation. I now examine in detail three such works. Each of these—Frederick Wiseman's *Titicut Follies* (1967), Christine Choy and Susan Robeson's *Teach Our Children* (1972), and Cinda Firestone's *Attica* (1973)—use a different approach to documentary to challenge the conceptions of state and public constructed in and through the prison.

THE PUBLICS OF PRISON: FREDERICK WISEMAN'S *TITICUT FOLLIES*

Titicut Follies, a *cinéma vérité* film about the Massachusetts Correctional Institution at Bridgewater—a massive facility that was part hospital and part prison, with divisions for criminally insane, drug-addicted, and alcoholic offenders; delinquents suffering from mental retardation; and sexual offenders—was the first documentary work by Frederick Wiseman, a Boston law professor whose previous experience in cinema had included producing Shirley Clarke's film *The Cool World* (1963). Wiseman and his cinematographer, ethnographic filmmaker John Marshall, shot footage at the Bridgewater facility in June of 1966, and Wiseman edited the footage over the next eleven months.[38] The film was shown in public at a few press screenings, film festivals, and a handful of commercial runs in New York in the fall of 1967. By the time the Supreme Judicial Court of Massachusetts handed down a 1969 decision restricting the film's exhibition for the next twenty-two years, *Titicut Follies* had become one of the most controversial works of American documentary cinema.[39]

Well before the case of *Commonwealth v. Wiseman* came to court in the fall of 1967, Bridgewater was already the subject of reform-minded concern. Despite well-publicized troubles at the facility and the attention of various public authorities to the sad state of mental health care in Massachusetts, Bridgewater was decrepit, underfunded, and understaffed. Wiseman had initially received the support of both the superintendent of the facility, Charles Gaughan, and the lieutenant governor of Massachusetts, Elliot Richardson, to make a film that, it was hoped, would both humanize the institution in the eyes of the public and energize efforts to modernize it and similar state facilities. Gaughan and Richardson were understandably concerned that a Massachusetts Correctional Institution facility should be represented sympathetically. Between the time Wiseman and his small crew gathered footage at Bridgewater and the first screenings of the film, public-relations problems at the facility worsened. One inmate was found naked and dead in his cell, and three others, including Albert DeSalvo, the so-called Boston Strangler, escaped, prompting Gaughan to describe MCI Bridgewater as a "chicken coop." Preliminary discussions between Wiseman and his sponsors suggested a traditional liberal work of social documentary. Wiseman had proposed a film that would "give people an understanding of these problems and the alternatives available to the state and its citizens," and he suggested that the film might be broadcast on the new public broadcasting network.[40]

But when the film was released in the fall of 1967 to mixed reviews, Bridgewater administrators and Massachusetts politicians, including Gaughan and Richardson, turned against it. Rather than seeing in the film a description of the institution's troubles, one which would aid them in the pursuit of reforms, the film's former supporters reacted as if its images themselves had escaped from state custody. Almost immediately, the Commonwealth began both legal and political proceedings against the film, in the form of criminal prosecution and a hearing in the state legislature. Legislators and public officials were concerned that *Titicut Follies* would make Massachusetts a laughingstock. Some even accused Wiseman of pursuing a confrontation with the Commonwealth to earn the film a salacious banned-in-Boston reputation. The film also threatened to upstage a legislative study of mental-health treatment commissioned by the governor. Richardson's role in approving the film was, in this light, regarded by Republican opponents in the legislature as an act of betrayal. What did the film's adversaries see in it, and why did this so disturb them?

By contrast with many of the leftist documentary films about prison that followed it, *Titicut Follies* has no overtly political position on the culture of prison. And unlike the flurry of radical documentaries that would come out of the prison activism of the early 1970s, *Titicut Follies* does not take as its starting point a historic instance of conflict between prisoners and the prison. Wiseman is not eager to characterize prisoners as a social class or as the symbols of a political movement. Instead, the film focuses on the banal and continuous forms of repression inside a generic institutional structure. In an analysis of form and structure in Wiseman's early films, Bill Nichols notes that the cross-section of American society these films present is "extremely narrow" because it "fails to examine the larger ensemble circumscribing the boundary between institutions and the public or the characteristics of class struggle found at that boundary."[41] Although this is meant as a criticism of *vérité* style, one might argue that it describes accurately the method of Wiseman's critique. How, we might ask, was it was possible to make a film about prison in the late 1960s that did *not* focus on issues of race and class, and what was Wiseman's intention in doing so? By overlooking the politics of race and class at MCI Bridgewater, Wiseman presents the institution as it sees itself, an objective and fair custodian of the private individuals under its care.

The viewer of *Titicut Follies* experiences a sense of disorientation with respect to the world outside the institution. Inside the institution, things seem to run on their own schedule. The episodic or associative relation of the scenes to one another and the long takes of John Marshall's cinematography foster in the viewer a sense of duration that mirrors the indefinite time of imprisonment. Marshall's camerawork makes frequent use of a zoom or a pan to discover a new source of interest in a scene; this exploratory, improvisational method of shooting gives the impression of an unstructured temporality that subtends the routines of inspection we notice at other moments. Even the more dramatic and confrontational events Wiseman and Marshall record have a kind of pointlessness.

Prison appears in *Titicut Follies* as a cycle of petty humiliations that must simply be endured, treatment that is abusive *because* it is monotonous. Among many painful examples of this, one of the hardest to watch is the sequence with an inmate called Jim, who is chastised by the guards for "dirtying" his barren cell. The guards take Jim down to another level of the building for a wash and a shave, asking him over and over throughout the procedure, "How come your room's so dirty Jim? How's that room, Jim? How's that room going to be tomorrow, Jim?" When they return him, naked, to his cell, Jim makes a protest against this idiotic barrage with the only resources available to

Figure 4.2. *Titicut Follies* (Frederick Wiseman, 1967). Still capture from VHS.

him, stamping on the floor and banging on the window frame. The guards make belittling reference to the musicality of this performance, prompting an exchange about Jim's educational career: Jim lists, in a mutter, the schools from which he graduated: "Fitchburg State Teacher's College, Fitchburg normal school, Fitchburg business college, Fitchburg high school." The list represents a lost history. Or, more precisely, a linear and progressive account of experience that is in stark contrast with the empty time that appears before us, in the image of a naked man in a whitewashed brick cell, part of a sequence of shots that seem to have no logic other than repetition.[42] This exclusion of the historical world makes MCI Bridgewater seem a culture separate from the one in which the viewer exists.

The only respite from this dreary rhythm is the "Follies" from which the film gets its title, an annual variety show featuring members of both the staff and the inmate population (see figure 4.2). Like the rest of the events in the film, the Follies appear without explanation, and it is impossible to tell which performers are inmates and which are guards until they reappear later in the film. But Wiseman staggers the presentation of the Follies so that they appear to merely repeat and enclose the exercises of punishment and observation. Footage from the Follies begins and ends the film. This framing device is one of the film's slight concessions to the viewer's desire for narrative order. Like the shocking sequence in which the force-feeding of an inmate is intercut with the preparation of his corpse for burial, or the droll end titles added to the film by court order,[43] it seems designed to mock the idea that rehabilitation, or progress of any kind, could take place at MCI Bridgewater.

Such gestures employ the tools and precepts of ethnography, by which another culture is studied as a discrete field of practices and meanings, and implicitly or explicitly compared to our own. In a 1969 essay, filmmaker David MacDougall included *Titicut Follies* in a short list of films that could be considered genuinely ethnographic, in the sense that they not only "reveal one society to another," but use film language to *interpret* other cultures.[44] From this perspective, *Titicut Follies* can be seen as a work of reflexive anthropology, posing the question "who is the savage here?" in the manner of *Les Maîtres fous,* Jean Rouch's 1955 film about a West African tribe on the fringes of a society nearing the end of colonial rule. But Wiseman, eschewing any structuring devices in the text beside cutting, effaces the analytical position that Rouch creates to explain the relationship between the West and its other, like the moment in *Les Maîtres fous* when Rouch explains in a voice-over that a certain detail of the Hauka sect's costume is meant to parody the ceremonial garb of the British military. By withholding the interpretive key to the comparison between the society of the inmates and that of their keepers, Wiseman refuses to allow prison to be turned into an obvious metaphor or allegorical figure and thus resists a didactic response to the scenes the film witnesses. In its construction of a self-contained universe that operates under a set of rules immanent to the space it depicts, *Titicut Follies* can be likened to a conventional narrative fiction. But this does not have to mean that the film has no politics. In fact, it is the very sensation that the prison is at once a distant other space and a nearby space accessible to the viewer that allows the film to raise the question of what or where the public is. The film cannot be read apart from the controversy this question produced, and it will be useful to review this infamous history before considering what Nichols calls the "tactless" textual mechanics of its critique of the state.[45]

The outcome of *Commonwealth v. Wiseman* hinged on the issues of privacy and consent. The plaintiffs claimed that Wiseman and his cinematographer John Marshall had photographed both inmates and staff without obtaining proper consent from them and with the intent of commercial exploitation of what the Commonwealth argued were unnecessarily intimate and sensational images, verging on obscenity, of conditions and activities inside the facility. The state also claimed that Wiseman had breached an oral contract with the superintendent of the facility, Gaughan, to give him final approval over the film, an offer Wiseman insisted he never made. Wiseman and his lawyers countered that the issues of privacy and consent were a smoke screen, since the operation of the facility made the violation of these rights a routine occurrence. Some of the men at MCI Bridgewater had been held for decades without ever being charged with a crime, and the state regularly brought groups into the prison to observe the inmates and the operation of the institution, between eight and ten thousand visitors a year.[46] Wiseman's lawyers argued that the public's right to know about the oppressive conditions inside the facility superseded the empty notion of "privacy" the state claimed to uphold on the prisoners' behalf: "it is the privacy of the Commonwealth that is being sought to be protected here, not the privacy of these poor, unfortunate individuals," argued one of the lawyers.[47]

The catalyst of the state's shame was the film's graphic, frontal depiction of a number of inmates. Clearly visible in the disputed scenes were the genitalia of inmates who had been confined naked to their cells and the faces of those who, the Commonwealth argued, had not known to what sort of representation they were consenting, or were simply incompetent to give their consent. (Civil suits later filed by guards asserted that these voyeuristic images had defamed them by sensationalizing and sexualizing their relation to the inmates. None of these lawsuits were successful.) The first decision in the case was that Wiseman had both breached his oral contract with representatives of the Commonwealth and had violated the privacy of the inmates. The court recommended that all prints of the film, its negative, and all sound recordings taken at the prison be destroyed. Wiseman appealed this decision, but the following year, the Massachusetts Supreme Judicial Court upheld the lower court's decision in substance, finding that the film was indeed a "collective, indecent intrusion into the most private aspects of the lives of these unfortunate persons in the Commonwealth's custody."[48] The higher court, however, relaxed the penalty imposed by the lower court, permitting the preservation of unused footage and sound and allowing screenings of the film for audiences of professionals in the fields of law, medicine, or social work, provided that they would attest to their status in those fields in signed affidavits.

For first time in its history, the Massachusetts Supreme Court had defined a right to privacy, deserving of legal protection, that was distinct from property rights. In doing so, the court suggested that the threat of prurient interest in the naked bodies and psyches of the inmates was more urgent than the threat posed by MCI Bridgewater and places like it to patients and prisoners as a class of subjects, or to the public on whose behalf the Commonwealth operated the facility, and more urgent than the threat posed to the democratic ideal of free speech by the suppression of the film and the public discussions that might ensue from its exhibition. In the original decision, the judge had called the film "a piece of abject commercialism, trafficking on the loneliness, on the human misery, degradation and sordidness in the lives of these unfortunate humans," adding that "no amount of rhetoric, no shibboleths of 'free speech' and the 'right of the public to know'" could redeem it.[49] In addition to these legal arguments against the public interest served by the film, Massachusetts legislators, stoked by conservative elements in the Boston press, conducted an inquisition against the film and its makers. The ostensible goal of this investigation was to determine by what failure of oversight the filmmakers had been granted access to the facility. But the legislators sought ultimately to contend that a filmmaker could not represent the general public of the Commonwealth and, moreover, that a film should not be permitted to preempt the properly public processes of investigation and reform. At issue was the legitimacy of competing conceptions of the public.

It is tempting to conclude that the film's politics are displayed in the homology between the profilmic and the filmic, which seems to suggest that what the camera records and discloses at MCI Bridgewater is a kind of separate society, hidden inside the state. Marshall's observational style of shooting gives the viewer the impression of being at once inside and outside this disciplinary space, eyewitness to the follies of the institution but helpless to do anything about them, since they happen in full view and with the apparent sanction of the prison authorities. The montage structure of the film, by creating an all-at-once cross-section of activities at the prison, enhances this impression of panoptical surveillance operated by the institution itself.[50] The film would thus seem to suggest that the viewer is implicated in this incivility by his or her own feckless curiosity. And, by implication, it suggests that the public interest that might be roused by such images is useless against such a state, insofar as it is compromised by it. By indulging in an apparently uninhibited voyeurism, *Titicut Follies* seems determined to make the viewer uncomfortable with the relation between viewing and knowing, as if to say that public display of the terrible conditions at MCI Bridgewater can do nothing but add to the problem.[51]

From one perspective, the argument of *Titicut Follies* appears to be that it reveals an aspect of our society of which we are unconscious, the true, irrational nature of the state.[52] This certainly seems to be the function of the film's interest in one particular prisoner, Vladimir, who is introduced in a long dialogue with the staff psychiatrist, Dr. Ross, where Vladimir maintains that the prison and the medications forced on him are making him crazy. He argues this point forcefully and pleads to be returned to the regular prison. Given what viewers have seen of MCI Bridgewater up to this point in the film, Vladimir's claims about the prison seem reasonable. Furthermore, there seems to be nothing wrong with Vladimir's capacity to reason or to express himself clearly and civilly, especially compared with Dr. Ross, who tells Vladimir that if he should be wrong in predicting that Vladimir is not ready to be returned to a regular prison, "you can spit on my face." When Vladimir appears before a panel of psychologists and social workers to plead his case, the superciliousness with which his complaints are dismissed seems to reinforce the impression that the prison is a world turned upside down and that no one in the institution is to be trusted but the inmates themselves. "He argues in a perfect paranoid pattern," remarks one of the experts reviewing Vladimir's case; "If you accept his basic premise the rest of it is logical, but the basic premise is untrue," a statement that might easily be applied to the film itself. Under such conditions, the film seems to argue, there can be no objective judgment or common sense. Sensing that the facility's experts are wrong about Vladimir, the viewer is put in an antagonistic relation to the scientific and public authorities to whose care patients like Vladimir have been entrusted. As in an imaginative fiction, the world depicted by *Titicut Follies* is both governed by internally consistent rules and unrecognizable. It seems to obey a different logic than the logic of our own world. A schizophrenic logic, but a logic nonetheless.

Perhaps it is more accurate to say that the film reveals to us aspects of our culture of which we would *like* to be unconscious. The film's political position follows from this heterotopic structure. But it is difficult to decide where the film itself comes down on the liberal politics of reform. After all, doesn't it describe a place where reason fails, or, rather, where the instrumental application of reason leads to suffering and injustice? Doesn't the film describe a space of antagonism between civil society and the state, where all of the principles of society are misapplied and turned against us?

Such a conclusion is thwarted by the film's emulation, in its technique, of the very culture it observes. Over and over, Wiseman plants suggestions in the film that the prison's disciplinary mechanism—the "eyes that must see without being seen," in Foucault's poignant phrase—overlaps in an uncomfortably precise way with the methods of documentary cinema. This discomfort is present from the opening shot of the film, which puts the viewer in the position of the audience at the Follies. In none of the subsequent images of the Follies do we ever see any other audience members, despite indications from the performers on stage that they are playing to a crowd and delighting in doing so. The feeling that the performance is exclusively for us is increased by the continually changing frame, as Marshall searches the scene for its most telling detail, mobilizing the frame with zoom, focus, and pan. Such devices were conventional elements in the *cinéma vérité* rhetoric of observation, but as Barry Keith Grant suggests, their use here threatens "the comfortable invisibility of the unacknowledged" viewer, the voyeur or scientific "observer."[53] Our enjoyment of the Follies becomes, in retrospect, a source of anxiety when we realize that this same searching, intense gaze resembles quite strongly the invasive, prying gaze that is directed at the inmates by every level of the prison administration, from the guards to the medical authorities. And it does not help that some of the humiliating performances the inmates are forced to give are clearly for the benefit of the camera. From this point on, the viewer cannot fail to notice how much of what goes on at the prison seems to involve relations of looking and listening: not just surveillance and examination but exhibition, too. For every invasive physical or mental inspection, there seems to be an instance of acting-out by inmates who give noisy speeches, play musical instruments, recite poetry, or sing for anyone in earshot.

The film abounds with examples, but a sequence of a new arrival being admitted, examined, and led naked to a cell is one of the most striking, since it is linked, in an associative series, to the opening act of the Follies. From the end of the first Follies sequence, a close-up of the master of ceremonies, guard Eddie Pacheco, telling a joke, Wiseman cuts to a shot of a new inmate disrobing in a large, noisy intake area. Pacheco, now dressed in his guard uniform, walks into and through the shot, his mouth twitching the same way it did while he told his joke (see figures 4.3 and 4.4). After a number of shots of men undressing and changing into prison uniforms, Wiseman cuts to another scene, a young man being interviewed by Dr. Ross. The faces of the young man and the doctor are squeezed into tight close-ups, a framing that matches the uncomfortably blunt nature of the examination ("How often you masturbate a day? . . . Why you do this when you have a good wife and she is attractive lady? . . . What you are interested in, big breast or small breast?") (see figure 4.5). The film crosscuts between this conversation and the intake room. After the doctor recites the young man's litany of offenses and asks him whether he thinks he is a "normal man," the young man glumly acknowledges that "I need help, but I don't know where I can get it." With as little enthusiasm, Dr. Ross remarks "Well, you get it here, I guess." The young man is then led away by two guards. In a series of very long hand-held takes (see figures 4.6–4.9), we accompany him as he is walked through a hallway, led up a flight of stairs to a guards' station, stripped, and then walked naked down another hall to his cell, passing at the last moment under a

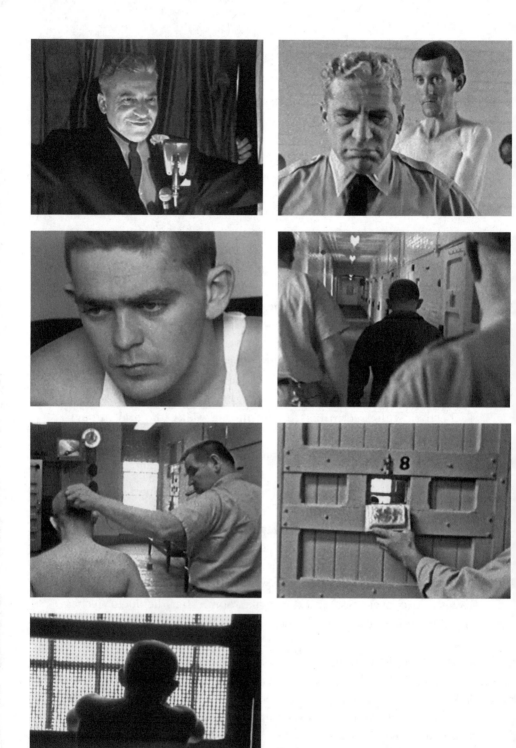

Figures 4.3-4.9. *Titicut Follies* (Frederick Wiseman, 1967). Still captures from VHS.

television monitor broadcasting closed-circuit images from elsewhere in the facility. The camera lingers on the television set, as if momentarily distracted by the sight of a competing apparatus of vision, and zooms in slightly on the screen, where we see a body being wheeled on a gurney. The camera pans to the closing cell door, and then a hand reaches up, from out of the frame, to open a small window in the door. This overt invitation is reinforced by the guard who leans into the frame to look in through the window. The camera approaches the window and zooms in to a medium close-up of the head and shoulders of the young man, who is leaning on a window sill at the opposite end of the cell. His silhouetted figure is pinned between the bars in the foreground of the shot and the wire grid that covers the window. At every step, he is hemmed in by screens and frames.

This sequence can be interpreted in two different ways. On the one hand, it seems to encourage the viewer's identification with the forces that subject the young man to relentless looking. Through the use of the zoom lens to enter the space of the cell, the film seems to suggest that the viewer is on the side of those who scrutinize the prisoners. On the other hand, the narrative of the young man's induction into the prison and the zoom that concludes it inscribe desire in the cell, so that we are invited to read the sequence as if it applied to us, that is, as if the scopic drive in which we have been forced to indulge since the first shot of the film led inexorably to prison.

Can we say which is the film's real moral, or which represents its critical position? Clearly its sympathies lie with the hapless inmates, but it is impossible to overlook the numerous suggestions that in order to take the side of the prisoners, the viewer has to engage in invasive surveillance of them. And it is not only the prisoners but the guards and administrators, too, who are subject to this relentless gaze. Every level of the institution is vulnerable to this inquisitive probing in the name of social reform.

Once we think of power as the production, rather than the suppression, of knowledge, it becomes possible to notice a disquieting resemblance between the documentary apparatus of observation and the disciplinary institution itself. The position of the viewer is sutured uncomfortably into the institution itself: all-seeing and, by comparison with the prisoners, free; at the same time, the passive object of the camera's intrusive gaze, forced to watch.[54] Comparing the power of the documentarist and the power of the prison, the viewer of *Titicut Follies* practices what Foucault would later call the governmentalization of the state, the enactment in the civil sphere of the disciplinary regimen once the province of the state alone.

The film thus parallels, in structure, Foucault's description of the panopticon: "in appearance, it is merely the solution of a technical problem; but, through it, a whole type of society emerges."[55] (As it did for Foucault, the study of the prison inaugurated a whole series of institutional studies for Wiseman, whose subsequent films dealt with a school, a hospital, a police force, a welfare agency, the army, and so on.) In this way, the film discovers itself in the prison: its manner of observation is replicated in its ostensible object. This textual paradox, in which the film's object defines the positions of its enunciator and its reader, threatens the distinction between the public on whose behalf the film enters the prison and the public in whose name the prison is maintained.

As I have already suggested, it may be posing the problem too narrowly to say that the political stance of the film can be determined by a reading of it—in part because *Titicut Follies* was not intended simply as an abstract diagram of disciplinary society but as a work of commercial cinema, a commodity intended to circulate in the mass public sphere. The misreadings of the film and the rumors and hearsay about the film's contents that circulated in public hearings and in the press help it define and address a public that is distinct from both the mass audiences of commercial cinema and the collectivity of citizens. Perhaps it is more accurate to say that the film's textual politics are incomplete without its circulation, actual, imagined, or repressed. Whether affirmative or corrosive, this publicity shapes the film as a text and conditions its availability for interpretation. Thus, the film and its career show how, in the realm of documentary cinema, public and private are not simply static terms in an idealized opposition to each other but rather relative conditions, effects of the film's address. If this means that they are subject to abuse and contradiction—and Wiseman's film is both composed of examples of such and perpetuates them—it also means that what we mean when we speak of the public is open to debate. So is the question, the film argues, of who may speak of, and in, the place of the public.

What are the consequences of this method for the critical function of documentary? As we have seen, the controversy over Wiseman's methods and objectives produced a confusing array of uses of the term "public" when applied to the audiences, the producers, or the subjects of documentary.[56] It is less fruitful to look for the subjective source of this confusion, as if it was simply the result of Wiseman's stubborn reluctance to take a position on the problems he discovers at MCI Bridgewater, than to situate Wiseman's method and all of its ethical and political ambiguities in its moment. Placed in the context of debates about prison and other public institutions in the late 1960s, *Titicut Follies* looks less like the perverse indulgence of a "middle-class authoritarian who demands artistic freedom to create bourgeois art," as one of Wiseman's critics puts it, than an attempt to articulate some of the same questions about the nature of prison and other public institutions that were being posed everywhere at the time.[57]

In what sense is the interior of a state facility a public place, if it houses men who have been, or may be, legally deprived of some of their rights as citizens? Can public opinion protect these subjects from a state which has arrogated the public interest? Or, as the state argued in *Commonwealth v. Wiseman,* are they protected *by* their seclusion from the spectacular realm of the general public, such as might compose an audience of a film screening or a television broadcast? By posing these questions, *Titicut Follies* put into practice the critique of liberal democracy and its public spheres that was being framed by postwar American social theorists like C. Wright Mills, Hannah Arendt, and Richard Sennett, and revised by European critics like Jürgen Habermas. Habermas's influential analysis of the rise and decline of the bourgeois public sphere brought together Arendt's classical critique of modern individualism with a social-scientific perspective on contemporary publicity that he adapted from American sociology and the Frankfurt School analyses of totalitarianism and mass culture.[58] This analysis allowed Habermas to "pinpoint the weak spots of Western democracy from the inside," according to Peter Uwe Hohendahl, "using its institutional frame as his point of departure."[59]

As it does in Habermas, the expression of critique "from the inside" of the public spheres of liberal society often seems to contradict itself in Wiseman's films. The very existence of the films embodies an ideal of publicness that viewers observe being quashed in the particular institutions the films document. The institutions and organizations of liberal society themselves begin to seem a kind of prison in these films, just as for Habermas public opinion becomes, in the twentieth century, a way to consolidate state power rather than a way to challenge it.

From this perspective, the failure of *Titicut Follies* to circulate and speak on behalf of its subjects—or worse, its role in reducing them to objects without agency—appears a kind of anti-ethnography. Repeating the anonymizing rituals of the institution, Wiseman and Marshall demonstrate how American public institutions may actually inhibit the ability of their subjects to define themselves as citizens or to form meaningful social groupings. Prison appears as the primary instance of this anticulture, and in the 1960s there appeared to be no shortage of examples of this phenomenon.[60]

For a number of reasons, the symbolic function of the prison was temporarily displaced at the beginning of the 1970s. The rise of a prisoners' rights movement on both the inside and outside, brought to the attention of the general public by the spectacular rebellions and reprisals that grew out of it, changed the social meaning of prison. The purely exclusionary function of prison, as the negative space that allows the larger society to function, was now opposed by a different image, that of prison as a space of culture and of genuine public discourse. Theorists, activists, and prisoners alike began to speak of prison in terms that one critic called "a populism with its symbols reversed."[61] Although this description was meant as a rebuke to intellectuals like Foucault who were seen to sentimentalize the conditions of social exclusion, it accurately expressed the pressure that the revolutionary discourse in and around prison in the early 1970s placed on other forms of culture. In the next part of the chapter, I focus on a single instance of the public sphere of prison: the prison revolt at the Attica Correctional Facility in upstate New York in September 1971. More than any other single incident of this period of unrest in American prisons, the events at Attica galvanized left intellectuals and artists from a variety of disciplines, uniting them in a mood of despair and suspicion that was nonetheless a font of creativity.

COUNTERPUBLICITY: CINDA FIRESTONE'S *ATTICA*

Like *Titicut Follies,* the films that came out of Attica and other dissident sites focused on the rituals and structures that would make the prison appear as a distinct culture. But where Wiseman's film is content to let the viewer make the connections between these practices and the larger social or political context, leaving them at the level of ethnographic analogy, films by and about activist prisoners and prison activists drew attention to these connections. They were more sensitive than Wiseman's film to the cultural and subcultural differences among prisoners as a class and to the efforts of prisoners in this revolutionary period to set these differences aside. This sensitivity to the complexity of prison society was a reflection, in part, of the divisive struggles within radical media organizations over the status of women and ethnic minorities within such organizations.

For instance, *3000 Years Plus Life* (Randall Conrad and Stephen Ujlaki, 1974), a documentary about a prison in Walpole, Massachusetts, presents a detailed account of the attempt by a prisoners' organization, the National Prisoners' Reform Association, to gain basic civil rights. During an eleven-week walkout by guards in response to the NPRA, the group effectively took over operation of the prison and began instituting a series of reforms, including an antiracist initiative. NPRA members are shown holding racially integrated council meetings; in an interview, an NPRA leader reasons that "if we're all dirt, we want to be dirt together."[62] In another interview, a different member explains that the organization aims to spread its reforms well beyond Walpole, to local and county jails, other state facilities, and federal prisons. The role of the film itself is evidently to help legitimate and disseminate this progressive program and to counteract sensational accounts of violence at the prison, spread by the guards and the local press. Footage of citizens protesting in support of prisoners at other New England facilities underscores the connection between political events inside and outside the prison. Such images and interviews gave form to what Angela Davis called the "new and arduously wrought collective life" of American prisons, a world that was "organically bound up with the dynamics of the liberation struggle in America and across the globe."[63]

Like many activists, Davis regarded the Attica uprising of 1971 as a crucial expression of this familiar collective formation. "In a figurative sense," Davis wrote, "it evoked visions of the Paris Communes, the liberated areas of pre-revolutionary Cuba, free territories of Mozambique."[64] The power of this "figurative sense" can be understood by studying Cinda Firestone's 1973 documentary *Attica,* a film that evokes the mythic dimensions of the uprising while documenting it in ways that counteracted the state's tactics of communication and publicity.

At the center of the film is the September 1971 insurrection at the Attica Correctional Facility. After a four-day standoff, state troopers, correctional officers, and other police forces retook the prison yard, where the rebellious prisoners had set up a highly organized camp. In the attack, twenty-nine prisoners and ten of their hostages received fatal injuries. All but three died from wounds inflicted by police or correctional officers' bullets. A committee of citizens was established by the New York state legislature to determine the facts of the uprising and the events leading up to it. One reason for the establishment of the committee was to offset the effects of sensational stories that had appeared in the New York and national media, stories that parroted the reports by prison officials, soon found to be baseless, that hostages had been brutalized and killed by their captors.

Referred to as the McKay Commission for Robert McKay, the New York University law school dean who chaired it, the committee took a view of the rebellion and the violent confrontation that followed that was very different from the simultaneous investigation by the state attorney general's office. After several months of interviews with every group connected in some way to the facility, from prisoners and the staff to members of the press and residents of the town of Attica, the McKay Commission came to conclusions that contradicted those of the deputy attorney general's investigation, which had resulted in grand jury indictments against dozens of inmates but against not a single prison or police officer or official. While conceding that the breakdown of the negotiations with the armed inmates "left the state with no alternative but to retake the prison by force," the commission found that this force had been irresponsibly managed and employed in a reckless and excessive way during and after the assault.[65] And beyond its criticism of prison and state officials' handling of the uprising, the commission found fault with the state's management of the entire corrections system. Vast reforms were necessary. The prison system needed to be restructured and the premises behind incarceration needed to be rethought. The commission decided that the uprising and its aftermath had demonstrated that "our Atticas are failures."[66]

The McKay Commission's description of the short-lived rebel community was, by contrast, a glowing endorsement of convict self-government. The commission was anxious to correct the theories circulating in the mainstream press, and even in the prison itself, about the motivation behind the uprising. It was not, the commissioners emphasized, the result of agitation by a terroristic hard core of fanatics aligned with one or another gang or political faction. Rather, the commission suggested that the causes of the uprising lay in the social conflicts of the 1950s and 1960s and in the political movements that grew out of this unrest. The growing resistance among prisoners to inhumane living and working conditions at Attica and other American prisons, and their willingness to speak out against such conditions, had produced unprecedented solidarity among prisoners. In the wake of the authorities' insensitive responses to a reasonable list of grievances, as well as the reports from other prisons of unchecked acts of violence by guards, including the August shooting of George Jackson at San Quentin, signs began to appear that prisoners from different factions were willing to set aside their differences in order to present a unified front. The commission pointed to a summit meeting in an exercise yard between the normally antagonistic Black Panthers and black Muslims, mediated by members of the Puerto Rican Young Lords, as an example of this collective spirit. Its description of the uprising evokes the classic definition of the liberal public sphere, as the arena of "rational-critical discourse aimed at the resolution of political disputes":[67]

> The highly organized society in D block yard developed spontaneously, after a period of chaos, rather than by prearrangement; in the hours following the initial violence the leaders of political and religious

groups with preexisting structures, and inmates who were politically motivated, well versed in the law, or otherwise respected by their peers, emerged as spokesmen and took the lead in organizing the yard and drafting demands.[68]

It was not surprising, then, that the McKay Commission took the remarkable step of holding its hearings in the studios of the Rochester and New York City public television stations in April 1972, having resolved that the testimony of "live witnesses" to the events and conditions under review was crucial to "constructive debate" about Attica and that staging the hearings in a broadcast setting would make it easier to integrate audio-visual forms of "testimony" into the public proceedings.[69]

Sensitive to the spectacular and ceremonial aspects of its report, the McKay Commission released its findings to the public on September 13, 1972, the one-year anniversary of the massacre. On the same day, it also released a film version of the report, a ninety-minute documentary, produced by the American Bar Association and funded by the Ford Foundation; the film was shown on more than two hundred PBS stations and was followed on many stations by a discussion.[70] The program was "said to be the first ever developed as a visual supplement to a major governmental report," a claim that was, ironically, somewhat misleading. For one thing, there was nothing official about the film, as the ABA noted in the same *New York Times* story that announced the film. And the film could not even be considered the only "visual supplement" to the commission's work. For several months, a Rochester-based video collective called Portable Channel had been working on its own documentation of the legal and political aftermath of the revolt, conducting interviews with former prisoners, official observers, and the legal team defending the prisoners charged with crimes during the revolt. Using the relatively primitive technology of consumer-level video, Portable Channel members filmed conversations about the intricacies of the prisoners' legal defense strategies, gathered first-hand accounts of prison life from former convicts, and gave activists a forum for promoting their rallies and other events (see figure 4.10). Combining intimacy with permanence, small-format video recording could serve as both broadside and archive; the Portable Channel tapes could in this

Figure 4.10. Portable Channel videotape of interview with Herman Schwartz, 1971 or 1972. Still capture from VHS. Courtesy of Visual Studies Workshop.

way be thought of as a supplement to the commission telecasts, both appealing to an ideal of publicity and both calling the state to account by audio-visual transmission.

Firestone's film can be seen, at one level, as an endorsement of the methods and, to a certain extent, the perspective of the McKay Commission (see figure 4.11). It relies heavily on videotape from the hearings for some of its most damning evidence, including the images of prisoners being shot—in both senses of the term—by state troopers.[71] And like the hearings, the film seeks to give voice to alternative accounts of the event and its history. But where the goal of both the commission and Portable Channel in interviewing inmates and observers was primarily to reconstruct a comprehensive account of the uprising and its causes in order to test and correct official and popular versions of events, the film has a somewhat different goal, that of contesting the very notion of the public on which the commission based its use of noncommercial video. This effort depended in part on a filmic challenge to the supposed transparency of video, its effects of real time and

Figure 4.11. *Attica* (Cinda Firestone, 1973). Frame enlargement from 16mm film-strip. Courtesy of Cinda Firestone Fox. From the collection of The New York Public Library, Donnell Media Center.

self-evidence, and the notions of social commonality these qualities are thought to reflect.[72]

Early on, *Attica* establishes the themes of the duplicity of the state officials and the complicity of the journalistic apparatus. Firestone's skillful editing is instrumental in binding these themes to the technologies of mediation, as when she juxtaposes a televised remark by Russell Oswald, the state commissioner of corrections, on the importance of trust in the negotiations with the prisoners with the comment from a prisoner that they knew they could not trust Oswald when they saw him on their televisions misrepresenting their demands to the press assembled outside the prison. The observational mode of filming used for the scenes inside the yard, most of which were shot on 16mm film by Roland Barnes and Jay Lamarche, cameramen from WGR-TV in Buffalo who stayed with the prisoners, and for the interviews in their homes

Figure 4.12. *Attica* (Cinda Firestone, 1973). Frame enlargement from 16mm filmstrip. Courtesy of Cinda Firestone Fox. From the collection of The New York Public Library, Donnell Media Center.

with former prisoners is similarly juxtaposed to the televisual mode of broadcasting.[73]

An axiomatic instance of this opposition comes at one of the most dramatic moments in the film, the moment when negotiations break down and the attack begins. In establishing a rough chronology of events, the film has been building to the confrontation between the prisoners and the forces massing outside the walls of the prison. Crosscutting between footage taken on both sides of the prison walls contrasts the prisoners, some of whom wear a flimsy armor of football helmets and handkerchiefs, with the lines of police in riot gear carrying heavy artillery (see figure 4.12). Anticipating the sacrificial nature of the attack, the film then inscribes one of the uprising's emblematic utterances, Flip Crowley's heroic proclamation that "if we cannot live like people, we will at least try to die like men."[74] We then see footage of he-

Figure 4.13. *Attica* (Cinda Firestone, 1973). Frame enlargement from 16mm film-strip. Courtesy of Cinda Firestone Fox. From the collection of The New York Public Library, Donnell Media Center.

licopters rising over the wall and the teams of police entering the prison (see figure 4.13). At this point, the film abruptly suspends the moment of confrontation and tempers the emotional pitch it is reaching by shifting from the live recordings of the attack to the retrospective account offered by public officials of the decision to invade the yard.

In excerpts from television appearances, Oswald and Governor Nelson Rockefeller are heard speaking of the attack in the past tense. Oswald asserts that to have delayed the attack any longer would have been to risk "the destruction of our free society." Rockefeller seems simultaneously to take and displace responsibility for the massacre, apparently in response to a question about where the order for the attack came from: "At that point the decision was made, there was no alternative but to go in. I supported that decision, and as chief executive officer I am responsible for that decision" (see figure 4.14). Combined with Firestone's

Figure 4.14. *Attica* (Cinda Firestone, 1973). Still capture from DVD. Courtesy of Cinda Firestone Fox.

shrewd placement of the clip, Rockefeller's use of the passive voice creates a disorienting effect, one with ethical and public dimensions. At the moment in the historical narrative when the confrontation between the opposing forces is coming to a head, we are suddenly drawn away from the event itself and made to view it retrospectively, as an event that has already happened and, moreover, for which someone in power must take responsibility. In the narrative logic of the sequence, the expected but missing piece in the cinematic account of the attack appears to cause a crisis of agency, as if the film is asking: Who will take responsibility for the tragic events that we all know will soon take place?

The grammar of this sequence seems to articulate a public demand for accountability; this demand is met with official circumlocution, in which the governor is heard to refer to himself as the passive subject of his office. This construction drew upon a conventional language in the period for accusing public officials of something worse than self-interest or incompetence. In her account of the trial of Adolph Eichmann, Hannah Arendt cites the popular philosophy of a banal immorality: "we have become very much accustomed by modern psychology and sociology, not to speak of modern bureaucracy, to explaining away the responsibility of the doer for his deed in terms of this or that kind of determinism." The film seems, in this passage, to impute to Rockefeller a similarly mindless kind of self-consciousness, which might in fact have been intended to resemble Eichmann's, since the epithets "fascist" and "totalitarian" occur frequently in leftist polemic in the period. When, in the Newsreel film *San Francisco State: On Strike* (1969), an official from the Department of Justice arrives to serve picketing American Federation of Teachers members with a restraining order to prevent them from joining the students' strike, an AFT member responds caustically, "Am I to understand you're only doing your duty? You're only doing your duty, is that correct? Just like Eichmann did his . . . ?" Such charges were just as easily addressed to institutions, as with Angela Davis's claim that "the American prison betrays itself as a system striving toward unmitigated totalitarianism," and Bettina Aptheker's assertion that recent events had helped Americans "see the relationship between the prison system and fascist ideology." At another level of abstraction, they could be addressed to the nation as such, as in Norman Mailer's lament in *The Armies of the Night* (1968) that he "had been going on for years about the diseases of America, its oncoming totalitarianism, its oppressiveness, its smog."[75]

"Smog" described the difficulty of pinpointing the source of the problems posed by American government in its diffusion as "system." Its portmanteau character, bringing together the form and meaning of two existing terms, characterized Firestone's frequent strategy in *Attica* of resetting an image from one medium or context in another, as in her treatment of Rockefeller's canny evasion of responsibility. As the re-presentation on film of an address originally given on television, it is not only the meaning of Rockefeller's statement but also its provenance that is unclear. Since we can't place the clip and there is no way to read the context of the statement anywhere in the image, the fuzzy kinescoped image adds to the sense of its irresponsibility: the traces of transmission and duplication left in the image give the state officials' rhetoric the quality of hearsay. This technical detail not only places the officials' speech under the same suspicion and obscurity to which prisoners and others on the margins of society are regularly subjected; it also casts doubt on the responsibility of television itself, since it was in the forum of television that the state officials appeared to justify the attack and its results. By containing the temporally ambiguous televisual image within the frame of a cinematic sequence, one overtly concerned with the manipulation of time, the image of television is here submitted to the temporal and historical mechanism of cinema. Firestone asks the viewer to at least become aware of the difference between television and cinema not only as media of communication but also as the materials of historical consciousness.

But since the facts sought by the McKay Commission had been made public several months before the film came out,[76] the film's main reasons for sifting the records and memories of the event cannot be purely historiographic. Rather, as its presentation of the crucial moment in the confrontation suggests, its concerns are predominantly logical and ethical ones. *Attica* borrows its editing pattern from the films of Emile de Antonio, like *In The Year of the Pig* (1968), where a dialogue between opposing points of view is fabricated from interviews and archival footage. (Firestone apprenticed as an editor with de Antonio and was editor Mary Lampson's assistant on de Antonio's film *Painters Painting* [1972].) Like de Antonio, Firestone argues against the revelation of truth in the *cinéma vérité* manner, where intense looking leads to discovery. Instead, *Attica* suggests, knowledge originates in conflict. Although the film is by no means objective in its treatment of its subject (it is somewhat vague and even occasionally misleading about certain factual matters),[77] it nonetheless retains a dialectical logic in the debate it constructs between the combatants. The excerpts from the commission hearings obviously serve as a model of the juridical mode the film tries to establish. Through this pedagogical form of montage, the film establishes a position of judgment for the viewer.[78] Encouraged to come to his or her own conclusions not only about the facts but also the politics of communication, the viewer is in a position to do justice to the experiences of those who are ordinarily denied representation: that is, not only to fill out the historical record with their experience but to testify as well to the effects of the gaps in representation.[79]

Figure 4.15. *Attica* (Cinda Firestone, 1973). Still capture from DVD. Courtesy of Cinda Firestone Fox.

By understanding and appreciating these struggles of the oppressed to speak, the film suggests, the experiences of silence, isolation, and loss themselves can be turned to public and democratic ends. *Attica* foregrounds this memorial function in its repeated use of defiant statements by prisoners that they were ready to die for their cause, or of pleas by the hostages, via the journalists admitted to the yard, that the governor not sacrifice them for the sake of a show of strength; more than once, the film applies a freeze-frame to *vérité* footage of the hostages to "kill" them, in order to demonstrate the callousness with which these pleas were regarded by the state (see figure 4.15).[80]

In fact, we might say that it is in attempting to answer the demand of one of the leaders of the rebellion, Roger Champden, that the news media *apologize to the dead* for its exploitative misrepresentation of the uprising that the film finds its vocation.[81] The retrospective modes employed by the film—the recollective interviews, the recycling of file footage and scenes from the McKay Commission, the frozen moments in the *vérité* footage, the montage of totemic statements and images that comes toward the film's end—connect this elegiac function to the grammar of documentary cinema. It is a memory of viewing that the film must effect if it is to redeem the lives wasted by the state. In this appeal to memory, the film tries to carve out a role for the spectator between those of consumer of publicity and participant in the rational public sphere, using the sympathetic, affective appeal to the imaginary of the former in the service of the appeal to reason and the political sentiment of the latter. The film's examples of how memory is a process of construction are the basis of a simple but effective point: one function of the prison is to exclude or forget part of the social body so that the rest of us may recognize ourselves as citizens. It is in Firestone's presentation of interviews with the prisoners still behind bars, including the leaders of the rebellion, that this is most clear and where the film's modeling of a counterpublic sphere is most effective.

As most of the leaders refused to speak to the McKay Commission out of fear that the state might try to prosecute them on the basis of information revealed in their testimony,[82] the inclusion of their voices in the film has two functions: at the same time that the interviews add to the public record of the event, they leave a trace of the incomplete, exclusive nature of that public sphere. That is to say, the film must eventually realize the limits of the sense of the public entailed by the McKay Commission (and the public nature of broadcasting to which it appealed in its address) when it turns to the question of the effect of the uprising on those still in prison. Their situation, within the film and beyond it, demonstrates that certain domains of the public depend on the sanction of the state in a way that inhibits, or calls into question, their democratizing function. The relationship between the voices of the prisoners and the images that accompany them points to the supplementary function taken on by the film.

State regulations limiting the access of the media to its prisons forced Firestone to use still photographs of the prisoners to illustrate the audiotaped interviews with those members of the rebellion still serving sentences.[83] Firestone arranges the photographs in series that partially animate them, keying the expressions on the faces to the rhythms of the prisoners' voices (see figures 4.16–4.24). The disjunction between sound

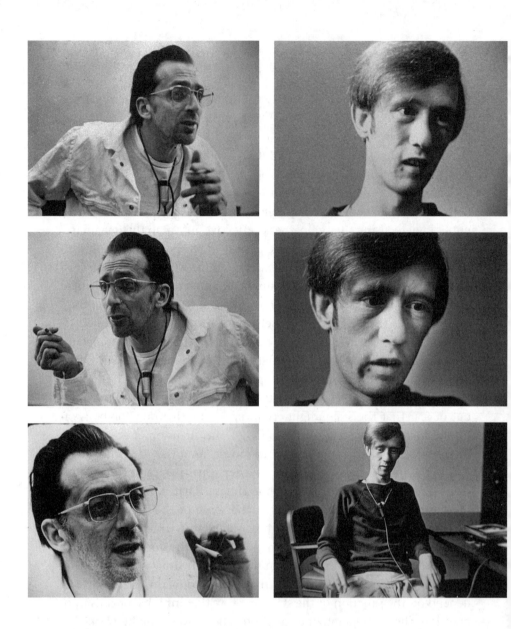

and image that results has the effect of sympathy. The handicapped interviews serve as a cinematic approximation of prison, the mark of an experience of repression the film shares with the prisoners. That is to say, the interviews, beyond their documentary function, become another way for the film to display its desire for an authentic relation to its subject.

This powerful desire is visible in the final sequence, where the film

Figures 4.16-4-26. *Attica* (Cinda Firestone, 1973). Frame enlargements from 16mm filmstrip. Courtesy of Cinda Firestone Fox. From the collection of The New York Public Library, Donnell Media Center.

takes up the prisoners' appeal to move the criticism of the state out of the prison and into the world. Or, one might say, to move from looking back to looking forward, from the service of public memory to the projection of political fantasy. The film returns at this point to interviews with two prisoners we have seen before, James Richie and Frank Smith (see figures 4.25 and 4.26). Their remarks seem to directly address the viewer, urging him or her to honor the dead. Richie's eloquent reflection on the deaths of his fellow prisoners seems, at the same time, to endorse Firestone's method:

> And I think about this, those brothers that didn't make it. They cannot be forgotten, they cannot have died in vain. Their deaths must leave something, they must be known to the people what their deaths meant, you see, what the whole struggle was about. People usually forget, 'cause we're living in a world that's *fast moving,* you know, things are happening every day. Things that happen yesterday today become passé, forgotten about. So I cannot let this die, and I will not let it die, in the minds and hearts of the people. So they can always realize that these things can happen to them.[84]

By slowing down the image of Richie and the other prisoners, the film displays its solidarity with him. In order to do justice to Richie's desire, the film recalls its own moment of origin, and the mythical origin of all cinema, in the relation between still images, as if it were possible to return to a time before the onset of the "fast moving" society of the spectacle, in which the meaningful rituals of art have been replaced by the meaningless ones of capitalism.[85] Can we read the primitive visuals that accompany all of the prisoners' eloquent speeches as a gesture of sacrifice of the film's own faculties? Given that, up to this point in the film, we have seen and heard at length how the modern prison makes ample use of the forms of domination to which Guy Debord gives the name *spectacle,*[86] operations that extract and store the time and labor of the prisoner in the name of the social good, it is understandable that the film seeks some earlier moment when cinema was still capable of changing how we saw life.

We should detect the rhyme here, between the cinematic and political senses of "movement," which the film seems to underscore part of the way through Richie's speech when it leaves behind the staggered images for footage of a memorial march in Harlem for prisoners killed at Attica (see figure 4.27). To Richie's expression of the personal weight of memory, Frank Smith adds a stern call to "the people" to "wake up!" and the combination of sound and moving image makes it appear that his forceful suggestion that the proletarianized masses "deal" with the government, and engage in "petition[ing and] rallies" of just the sort

Figure 4.27. *Attica* (Cinda Firestone, 1973). Frame enlargement from 16mm film-strip. Courtesy of Cinda Firestone Fox. From the collection of The New York Public Library, Donnell Media Center.

the film now shows us. Smith's insistence that we "wake up" echoes a plea heard in other prisoners' interviews that viewers recognize the relation between prison and civilian life; angrily, Smith says to the general viewer, "stop talking 'bout 'were you in jail' and 'you getting three meals a day'": in other words, recognize that prison is not a form of welfare, that prisoners do not have it easy, and that the daily degradation you experience is directly related to what they go through behind the walls. In this final composition, the voices of the prisoners become a kind of voice-over, one whose purely formal character is similar to the use of the voice in classic documentary but whose rhetorical function is altogether different. Richie and Smith's voices appear to inspire the march we see wending its way through the streets, urging it forward: at once floating above this mass movement as its martyred spirit and simultaneously embodying it. The film closes on a gesture of harmony: the voices of the crowd in Harlem, chanting "Attica, Attica," fade up over the image, finally returning fidelity (or synchrony) to the movement. The suggestion the film wishes to leave us with is that the raucous "sound before the fury" of the uprising can be remembered best if it is *displaced by* the harmonious sounds of public pressure on the political sphere.

RADICAL PLAY: THIRD WORLD NEWSREEL'S *TEACH OUR CHILDREN*

The exuberant optimism of *Attica's* final sequence might now seem out of keeping with the anger and sadness that otherwise dominate the film. But hope was one more variety of commemorative response to Attica. One could view the outpouring of art and culture on the subject of the rebellion as a form of celebration in itself. In addition to the fiction and documentary films I have discussed, this flurry of creative activity included collections of poetry and visual art by important contemporary artists, as well as live and recorded works of popular music and jazz.[87] Some of these works were produced in collaboration with artists inside prison, and the authors of many of them donated their earnings to prisoners' defense funds or support groups. But just as significant as the organizational politics of these projects was the formal politics, the startling juxtaposition they could establish between the monotonously linear time and space of prison as a topic and the improvisatory spirit of free verse, modern art, and jazz.

Archie Shepp's concept album *Attica Blues* (1972), to take one example, shifted back and forth between percussive, driving funk and dreamy free jazz, tying the whole together with short bursts of narration by William Kunstler, the radical New York lawyer who had participated in negotiations on behalf of the D yard inmates. There were effective gestures of this sort on a smaller scale in the work of many other artists, like Yoko Ono's song "Born in a Prison" (1972), recorded for the same album as her more topical but considerably less interesting collaboration with John Lennon, "Attica State," a clumsy and literal expression of solidarity with the proletariat, expressed in the refrain: "Attica State, Attica State / we're all mates with Attica State." In "Born in a Prison," by contrast, Ono explores the mobility of the prison metaphor, in a way that anticipates Foucault's list of disciplinary institutions, as when she sings: "born in a prison / raised in a prison / sent to a prison / called school." When Ono sings that "wood becomes a flute when it's loved / razor becomes a mirror when it's broken / look in the mirror and see your shattered fate," she extends this idea: if objects could be transformed by their use, so could institutions. The trick, the song suggests, was to know how to use both love and violence creatively. This was a view of the political applications of fantasy quite close, in certain ways, to the use of fantasy called for by the contemporaneous work of German social theorists Oskar Negt and Alexander Kluge in their response to Habermas, *Public Sphere and Experience* (1972), where they suggest that the logic of the Freudian dream work may be necessary to open the public sphere to the left and to groups in the economic and social minority.

The documentary film closest in spirit to these works is *Teach Our Children* (1972), the first production by a group of filmmakers who broke away from the main New York Newsreel group to form Third World Newsreel in the early 1970s.[88] This group was led by women of color, including the uncredited directors of *Teach Our Children*, Christine Choy and Susan Robeson, granddaughter of Paul Robeson. Politically, *Teach Our Children* shares the counterpropaganda spirit of the early Newsreel films but reflects more strongly the influence of American experimental cinema, in particular the work of such sound-and-image collagists as Bruce Conner. *Teach Our Children* is a patchwork of materials and processes: *vérité* footage, much of it secondhand; photomontage; hand-drawn animation; interviews; handwritten slogans; and recycled news images of the uprisings at Attica and other prisons and of the violence that rocked black city neighborhoods in the middle and late 1960s, including police and rioters in Newark in 1967. This bricolage approach carries over to the soundtrack: in addition to the testimony of unidentified representatives of the domestic Third World about the oppressive conditions of the ghetto or the prison, the soundtrack is composed of citations of popular music, documentary fragments of speech from the Attica rebellion, and sound effects like police sirens and crackling flames.[89]

Teach Our Children was not a film for mass audiences.[90] Its low production values and radical message would have kept it off television, and, at just over thirty minutes, it is an awkward length for commercial theatres. (*Attica* and *Titicut Follies,* by contrast, were widely reviewed in the mainstream press, and *Attica* had a modicum of commercial success in the United States and Europe). It offers neither the dark humor of *Titicut Follies* nor the pathos of mourning that pervades *Attica.* Although, like these two films, it allows prisoners to speak for themselves, it has little interest in the psychology of prison and thus does not allow these portraits to develop into fully fledged characterizations. Compared to even those unpolished productions, the look and sound of *Teach Our Children* is so rough that the viewer often feels as if she could have made this film herself with images and sounds left over from a more polished film.[91]

In its opening construction, *Teach Our Children* proposes an expansive conception of prison. The film begins with a series of shots of the imposing front gate of Attica and the pseudo-medieval towers guarding the entrance. By panning and zooming, the camera operator traces the lines of sight from tower to tower. These movements establish a parallel between the coverage of space made possible by the camera and the administrative power represented by the towers. *Titicut Follies* makes a similar point in its opening, where it stresses the similarity between the scrutiny to which prisoners are subject from the moment they enter the facility and the powers of observation the film, and, by proxy, the viewer, wield. But *Teach Our Children* indicates quickly that it is not only concerned with the contradictory idea of publicness entailed by the state institution; in fact, the point the film makes in these opening shots about surveillance does not figure strongly in the rest of the film, which soon turns its attention to other discourses of social control.

After the towers, the next image is that of two flags, presumably in front of the prison's main gate, the American flag and what appears to be the New York state flag.[92] The camera begins to pan away from the flags, but rather than coming to rest on a guard tower—a trajectory the previous shots have led us to expect—the movement of the frame is interrupted by a cut to a purely graphic image, six lines of white type on a black background that read "DON'T BE SHOCKED WHEN I / SAY I WAS IN PRISON. / YOU'RE STILL IN PRISON. / THAT'S WHAT AMERICA MEANS, / PRISON. / MALCOLM X" (see figure 4.28).[93] In this sudden shift from images to words, the film suggests a change in analytical register. If prison is only the end result of forms of repression

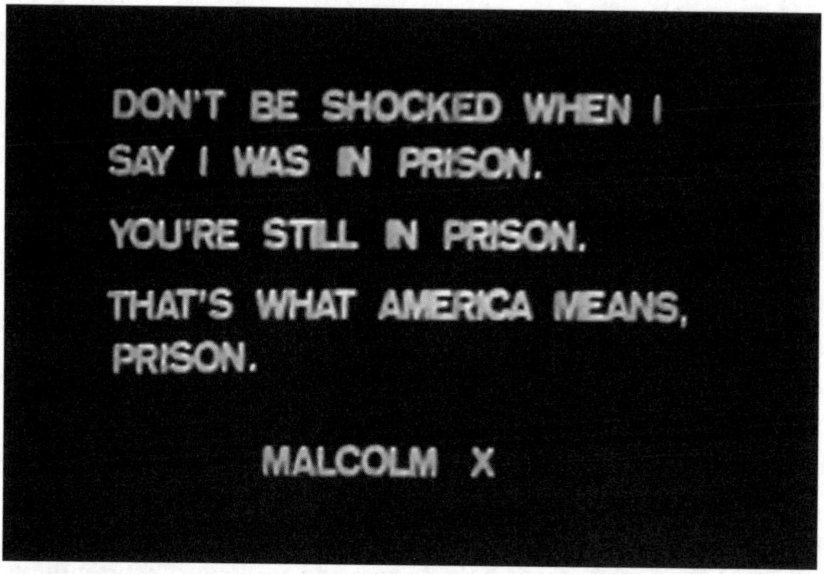

Figure 4.28. *Teach Our Children* (Third World Newsreel [Christine Choy and Susan Robeson], 1972). Still capture from VHS.

inherent in American society, as *Teach Our Children* will argue, then to focus public scrutiny on individual institutions and their reform was short-sighted, literally as well as figuratively. If the nation-state could itself be thought of as a prison, then the conventional tools and weapons of oppositional documentary—the direct recording of the sights and sounds of conflict, and testimonial speech from marginalized subjects—would not by themselves be effective as ways to challenge the state's hegemonic control over the public sphere of social knowledge. If "America means prison," it can no longer be enough for American documentary cinema, a medium hitherto oriented to a national public, to simply depict or speak the truth. Radical documentary would have to sever the relation between the image and the thing that had allowed the image to function as evidence, and had made truth appear to be self-evident. This brief introduction suggested that the vision of a *vérité* documentary cinema that, as Jonas Mekas wished, would "show everything, everything," was no longer politically productive.[94] The idea that class and race violence played a systematic and historical role in structuring American life cut against the premise of fortuitous discovery which had guided political uses of *vérité* filmmaking, since the latter made it seem like violence was something that broke out of the order of American life in a random way, suitable to be captured in the spontaneity of *vérité* film and video.[95] In this light, the pan that moves the viewer's eye from the image of the flag to the image of Malcolm X's words suggests a desire to move out of the imaginary community of the nation entirely, out of the space within which the metaphorics of vision allow the flag to mean America. Political documentary would have to take up instead questions of language. How precisely could one demonstrate, in the language of cinema, that America means prison?

While the monologic concept of nation is being (de)constructed on the level of the image, the soundtrack establishes a dialogic and polyphonic space. After an excerpt from a recording of the demands of the Attica prisoners, which ends abruptly, an instrumental tune with a Latin beat comes up under the images and then shifts shortly into a soul groove.[96] The rhythms signal the filmmakers' intent to turn the issue of prison into an explicitly racial and ethnic one. Accompanying the sounds and following the quotation from Malcolm X are a series of brief documentary images of black and Latino residents of a depressed urban area, many of whom smile, laugh, and move in a playful and unselfconscious way. Among these subjects is a group of children in a vacant lot; we see these children throughout the film. The juxtaposition of these sounds with each other and with the images, in such a way as to draw attention to the procedures of montage, suggests an alternate view of the social. Against the homogenous social body achieved by the segregation of the poor and visible minorities in places like prisons, the viewer can imagine a heterogeneous space of representation.

The rest of the film elaborates the themes presented in the first several shots in this pretitle sequence and goes on to establish the parallel legacies of oppression and revolution: on the one hand, the genealogy of the oppressive conditions at Attica and in American prisons in general, the American class system, and American imperialism going back to the slave trade; on the other hand, an international history of anti-imperialism connecting the Attica rebellion to the emergence of American social movements based on racial and ethnic identity, and anticolonial insurgency in the Third World. Since the film uses no voice-over

Figure 4.29. *Teach Our Children* (Third World Newsreel [Christine Choy and Susan Robeson], 1972). Still capture from VHS.

narration, these connections are implied only by the juxtaposition or intercutting of shots or sequences. At one point, the conflict between the imperialist forces and the various subaltern or oppositional ones is illustrated by a crudely animated photomontage of a hand-drawn scales of justice (showing that the American military, American consumers, and the Statue of Liberty carry more weight than black children, a Vietnamese family, or an African; see figure 4.29).

Underscoring these repeated but only suggestive connections between prisons and what goes on outside them are a number of moments where the film seems to address the viewer directly: for instance, the familiar footage immediately following the film's title in which Elliot (L. D.) Barkley, one of the leaders of the Attica uprising, makes a statement for the press. Barkley ends his presentation with a call to all those watching "to assist us in putting an end to this situation that threatens the lives of not only us but of each and every one of you as well." If it is somewhat ironic that Barkley, who was slain during the siege by state forces, is seen and heard to call for direct action in support of the uprising (and in recognition of its direct relation to social conditions outside the prison) through the highly mediated channel of some well-worn kinescoped news footage, this irony is not lost on the makers of *Teach Our Children*: over and over, the film makes clear that the very fact that we have seen and heard a great deal of the material of which *Teach Our Children* is composed gives the argument that America is another name for prison its resonance in the domain of subjectivity.

If capitalist manufacture and consumption is the substructure of global social and political oppression, then one of the important sites for struggle against state power is the place where images themselves are manufactured. The kinds of firsthand accounts of prison existence on which *Attica* and *Titicut Follies* rely are in short supply in *Teach Our Children*. The apparent poverty of documentary resources available to Choy and Robeson ends up working to the filmmakers' advantage in a number of ways. Its recirculation of materials links the film methodologically to the informal national network of radical prisoners' organizations, which shared the language and in some cases the text of various manifestos through a clandestine distribution system.[97] Furthermore, the fact that audiences might have seen the images of street marches in support of the prisoners many times before and that such repetition might diminish their emotional impact (for example, as an elegiac sign at the end of *Attica*) allows these images to function as reminders to the viewer that the meaning of public events, including their value for memory, is necessarily fabricated or manufactured— and, moreover, that their artifice need not diminish their value in the fight for social justice. The viewer of *Teach Our Children* becomes increasingly sensitive to this point, since the film makes emphatic use of the direct-address methods of advertising. The popular songs on its soundtrack, in particular, seem to speak directly to the viewer about the concepts spelled out in the film's rebus-like collections of images. "Are you sure there's nothing you can do?" the Staple Singers ask on the soundtrack, while cut-and-paste images of Nixon and Rockefeller cover a map marked "Africa," "South East Asia," and "South America." "Keep on keeping on," Curtis Mayfield urges, behind scenes of a street memorial for Attica inmates, while the crowd gives closed-fist salutes to coffins being loaded into hearses. And the massed Voices of East Harlem exhort viewers to "sing a song of freedom" and to "let it fill the air, tell the people everywhere" during the optimistic final section, which compares prisoners building their muscles to revolutionary struggles in the Third World.

In this final sequence of images, which follows an interview recounting the defeat of the rebellion and the reprisals by guards, the film applies its tactics of displacement and reinscription to itself: specifically, to the series of images of black children playing in a vacant lot. The images of these children first appear in the pretitle sequence of the film, and then again a little later, where they illustrate an interviewee's suggestion that living conditions in the inner city are tantamount to genocide, which she defines as poverty, overcrowding, and "keeping people from knowing who they are, what they are, and what they should be about." When these children return again in the context of the final sequence, following scenes of Marxist insurgents in Africa, Southeast Asia, and Latin America and of prisoners working out in the weight room at San Quentin, they appear as images of creative and recreative activity. If the film seems at first to argue that the suppression of dissent inside its institutions is related to the state's genocidal policies at home and abroad, this sweeping claim is at the end of the film viewed with suspicion. This claim is reexamined in such a way that the poverty of the initial construction (using images of children playing in a vacant lot to serve as the documentary evidence of a genocidal state) lays the ground for an expression of self-determination at the end of the film. Like the children playing with left-over construction materials, the prisoners building their strength with the prison's dumbbells, or the rebels in the jungle cobbling together a national resistance movement, the filmmakers face a shortage of resources. By placing these scenes side by side, they turn conditions of physical lack—the children's, as well as their own—into an opportunity for culture, and for the cultivation of a language of resistance.

The documentary function is itself transformed here. The hopeful final images function not as evidence of any sort of victory against the state (indeed, the film has already presented much evidence to the contrary) so much as a celebration of the filmmakers' own wit and creativity. Against the metaphysics of vision to which it refers with its opening images of Attica's front gate, the "phony fortress *a là* Disneyland" by which the difference between the inside and the outside of

Figure 4.30. *Teach Our Children* (Third World Newsreel [Christine Choy and Susan Robeson], 1972). Still capture from VHS.

the prison is maintained,[98] the film proposes a visual semiotics that allows popularly available signs to be translated into other slogans and meanings. The film concludes with a shot of one boy intently lecturing two others, which at first seems like a contradiction of the title, as the film leaves us with the impression of the children teaching themselves (see figure 4.30). This image can be also be understood allegorically, as an image of a new generation of documentary filmmakers freeing themselves from the tutelage of the paternal state, as well as the legacy of the 1930s left, and the white, male, college-educated leadership of the New Left, turning documentary into a revolutionary tool so simple that it could be operated by a child.

In *Teach Our Children,* the theme of representation becomes so prominent that it threatens to overwhelm the text's ability to make sense, to the point where it is difficult to say whether this film is about Attica or prison at all. Through a rather crude application of associative montage, using silent amateur and stock footage and hand-made graphics, the film establishes an extensive set of comparisons: between prisoners struggling for their rights in various American locations; between Americans protesting the government on both sides of the prison walls; between struggling prisoners and political insurgents in the Third World; between prisoners and the poor; between prisoners and people of color; between high-rise housing projects and slave ships; between slaves and poor people of color; between prisoners and the "real" criminals who run the state (Nixon, Rockefeller); and between child's play and revolutionary cinema. In the construction of this long metonymic chain *Teach Our Children* seems to suspend the question of representation that tends to preoccupy the makers and viewers of films about prison, the issue of whether it is ethical or even possible for those on the outside to relate to those inside the prison.

It is in fact by daring to misrepresent experience that *Teach Our Children* is uniquely effective. Its constitution of the neoimperialist empire of signs that transects the prison defines the field of political struggle in postmodernity better than its obligatory citation of revolutionary figures and movements. The hopscotch of comparisons by which child = slave = prisoner = Third World revolutionary creates a situation of metonymy where "each recalls but does not replace the other."[99] This stretching of meaning across the distance of the metonymic pairs keeps returning us to the central political problems of prisoners. The very tenuousness of the transnational and transhistorical connections the film makes between oppressed or subaltern groups reminds us of the immobility of prisoners. Likewise, the borrowed and found materials of the film itself (well-worn stock footage, hand-crafted graphics, copyrighted music used without permission) return us by an exchange or substitution to the issue of the economics of prison, within which the labor of the prisoner is either an appropriation of values to be recirculated elsewhere, in the case of legitimate prison shops, or the sheer production of waste, as with sentences of hard and useless labor. Qualities of the film that one is tempted to see in aesthetic terms, as sloppiness or creativity, can also be viewed as a political decision by the members of the Third World Collective that produced the film: rather than adopting the conventional disposition of the social documentarist to the truth, where the vanguard filmmaker searches for the truth of the social world, hoping to communicate it to a mass audience otherwise bedazzled by spectacle, the makers of *Teach Our Children* hardly seem concerned with truth at all. Rather, they appear preoccupied with the question of what can be made of the various fantasies and desires that prison gives rise to, both radical and reactionary.

Discussing the concept of documentary indexicality, the material capacity of a documentary image or sound to act as a "fragment of reality," Philip Rosen suggests that mechanical reproducibility is the basis of the documentary filmmaker's traditional claim to social utility. His or her ability to educate a mass audience about the meaning of the past depends upon the legibility of these indices.[100] Rosen argues that this purely mechanical connection between capturing the truth of past events and distributing these truths en masse is at the heart of the liberal tradition in documentary identified with John Grierson. The political vision of this movement depends upon a "national projection" of audiences all over the country literally seeing the same view of the past, undiminished in its authenticity by the process of reproduction. "For Griersonian liberalism," Rosen contends, "intellectuals stand, in the classic ideological manner, for the ultimate coherence of the social system and the interest of the universal."[101] *Titicut Follies* and *Attica* represent two attempts to call into question these universal values and the relations of power through which they have been placed in the care of a specialized class of intelligence workers. At the same time, they attempt to indicate the place of documentary representation in this social hierarchy, with the aim of reforming the documentary vocation. Both films are still, after all, oriented to a mass audience they hope to teach a lesson about the state: that it dominates by pathologizing and "individuating" us (*Titicut Follies*); that its force can be overcome by collectivity (*Attica*). By contrast, *Teach Our Children,* in its all-consuming focus on the matter of representability, verges on abandoning the social vocation in which the documentary filmmaker educates the masses about their manipulation by the institutions of the media.

Passing from the realm of representation into the realm of simulation, *Teach Our Children* orients this tradition toward the future in a number of ways. The first is in respect to the historical logic of documentary rhetoric—the rhetoric, specifically, of indexicality. The role of the social advocate in the liberal model of documentary is necessarily oriented toward the past as the site of authenticity. The fact that the object of filming existed before and during shooting separates this object from the audience, which is, in turn, waiting to be moved by it to some form of social intervention. The filmmaker distributes this image-fact to a widespread audience whose collectivity depends upon their recognizing together that this fact is indeed a problem. Of course, this recognition would be either ironic or cynical if it were not accompanied by the belief that ordinary people can be agents of social change, and so it also constitutes a kind of interpellation, an accepted invitation to membership in a democratic society. But what appears significant to the producers of *Teach Our Children* about the images of children that appear throughout the film is less that they prove a fact (black children are playing with garbage in a vacant lot) that represents a problem (racism, poverty, the failure of government to secure the welfare of all) that must be solved than that they demonstrate the mutability of this fact. If the meaning of an image can be changed by its placement in a series, then it is at least open to debate whether or not black people are inevitably a subaltern American class, and games of language and image become important in the construction of alternate futures for the disempowered. Indeed, the film's final image implies that the generational direction of knowledge is interrupted and reversed: it is the children who will teach one another, and we will learn from them.

In this sense, we can say that *Teach Our Children* was ahead of its time. If the places of *Titicut Follies* and *Attica* and the styles of documentary they represent are better established in film history, *Teach Our Children* seems to project with more prescience the anxiety about actuality that documentary evinces today. The ambivalence with which one must approach the analysis of this odd little film today is not unfamiliar to the viewer of the postmodern documentary, for which sarcasm is the condition of truth.[102] Refusing—or, rather, abusing—the linear logics of both narrative form and progressive thought, *Teach Our Children* joins other counterpublic documentaries of its period in proposing alternatives to the despair the left was mired in at the beginning of the 1970s. The recent history of American prison seemed, for cultural critics like Tom Wicker and Bob Dylan, to provide an opportunity to lament the decline of both the public sphere and the vocation of the liberal intellectual who engages with the history of the present. Their work seemed to confirm the conclusion Fredric Jameson reaches at the end of his analysis of *Dog Day Afternoon*, the conventional cultural-Marxist position that "if we can give experience the form of a story that can be told, then it is no longer true." The work of Choy and Robeson, Firestone, and Wiseman proposes that documentary form could be used to undo this bind of capitalist culture: if experience cannot be reduced to a linear narrative, it is no longer false. In this way, their films proposed an alternative to the gloomy prognosis of postmodernity and opened new avenues for counterhistory.

PART III

The Public Sphere of Suspicion

Documentary in the New Obscurity

5 / THE VISION THING

Documentary, Television, and the
Accidental Power of the President

Nobody filmed Jack Kennedy until almost 1959. He was just another senator and not a very distinguished one at that. He was just a good-looking young senator.
—EMILE DE ANTONIO, interviewed by Cinda Firestone in 1972

The use of techniques of publicity borrowed from advertising and commercial entertainment is widely regarded as a primary cause of two complementary problems in American society: the disengagement of the general population from political issues and the democratic process and voters' apparent fascination with political candidates whose charisma, celebrity, or good looks stand in for their qualifications for office.[1] The special recall election to replace Governor Gray Davis of California in 2003 illustrated the populist variant of this thesis. The election allowed a number of publicity seekers to nominate themselves as gubernatorial candidates, some of whom owed their relative fame and fortune to reality-based entertainment in one form or another, including has-been child actor Gary Coleman; adult-film actress Mary "Mary Carey" Cook; L.A. lifestyle artist Angelyne, best known for a series of billboards advertising herself; and Todd Richard Lewis, the on-camera host of the exploitation videotape series *Bumfights,* which features homeless men beating one another with their fists and other weapons. (Lewis pledged to "help the homeless" with his campaign; he finished last.) The eventual winner, action-film star Arnold Schwarzenegger, had himself become famous a quarter-century earlier through his appearance in a documentary film about bodybuilders, *Pumping Iron* (George Butler and Robert Fiore, 1976); in a scene deleted from the release version of the film, Schwarzenegger declared his intention to run for president "when Nixon gets impeached." But given the infusions of corporate, party, and personal wealth required to stage the recall effort and Schwarzenegger's winning campaign, not to mention the acting career on which his name recognition was based, one could just as easily regard the election as a display of populism's relation to authoritarian politics and its cult of the individual. By this logic, blame for the failure of the democratic system lies not with an irresponsible or misguided voting public but with economic and political elites who place their wealth and intelligence in service of a sophisticated campaign of disinformation in which personality is merely one more distraction from the real issues.

To combat these theses of political cynicism, a number of documentary films and television programs of recent years have sought to bring transparency to the electoral process, whether by exposing the workings of the apparatus of publicity now required to even enter any serious political race or, like *Unprecedented: The Story of the 2000 Presidential Elections* (Richard Ray Perez and Joan Sekler, 2002), by revealing corruption and misconduct in the selection and election of public officials. *Unprecedented*, a film that was initially distributed on videotape and DVD with the help of the liberal political organization MoveOn .org, alleges that through cronyism and intimidation the Republican side was able to manipulate the democratic process in Florida at the most elementary levels, through the creation of voter registries and the misrecording and miscounting of votes, stealing the election from the Democrats. Near its conclusion, the film turns toward efforts by citizens' groups to prevent a similar outcome in subsequent elections. The optimistic tone of this conclusion, however, hardly compensates for the prevailing gloom established by the rest of the film, which relies on the analysis of weary experts—journalists, Democratic political operatives, and academics—to suggest that the evils of nepotism, money, and the law have made the political process inaccessible and incomprehensible to ordinary citizens.

For all the expertise it brings to bear on the mechanics of the Florida debacle, however, *Unprecedented* never wonders why the election was so close to begin with: why, in other words, it seemed impossible to tell the two candidates and their parties apart. Thus it cannot consider the question that Max Weber considered essential to understanding the modern state: "when and why do men obey?"[2] What Weber called the vocation of politics needed to be grasped through the phenomenon of charisma. "If the state is to exist," Weber argued, "the dominated must obey the authority claimed by the powers that be."[3] Among a number of "legitimations of domination," the most important was charisma, the devotion and confidence inspired in the person who held high public office by his "qualities of individual leadership."[4] Charisma was a more significant motivation for obedience than ancient traditions or modern laws not only because it bridged the ancient and modern ages but also because it created a bond of identification between leader and governed. The "calling" that inspires the leader's apparent devotion to the work of leadership echoes in his followers, who take the leader's "gift of grace" as proof that their individuality matters.[5]

In the age of television, political vocation is exercised not only through the voice and words of the leader but in an intimate encounter with his or her image as well. Such images need not be appealing in the conventional sense. Although common sense tells us that the appeal of the Kennedys and the first "television presidency" was a direct effect of their beauty, which made them natural subjects of lavish photo spreads and close-up television portraits, the role of ugly, embarrassing, or merely ordinary images in the massively popular administrations of Presidents Nixon, Reagan, and Clinton suggests that traditional standards of beauty are inadequate to the task of explaining presidential iconicity, at least in the age of television. By noting the use documentary film and video have made of such images, we can explain the role documentary has played in testing and reviving authenticity in politics, even while it is assumed that such a quality is obsolete.[6]

THE PARASITE OF TELEVISION

Anxiety about the effects of mass communication on democracy have been a commonplace of American political commentary since at least the 1920s, when Walter Lippmann described the rise of a parapolitical sphere engineered by pollsters, image consultants, speech writers, and other experts in the field of public relations. With frequent reference to the impact of communication technologies like the telegraph and the radio on the conduct and the reporting of the world war, Lippmann described "a world-wide spectacle of men acting on their environment, moved by stimuli from their pseudo-environments."[7] Lippmann's analysis focused on the speed and power these technologies gained as tools of politics and on their capacity to respond to and shape reality. His examples of military and diplomatic gaffes caused by the high-speed and widespread circulation of unsubstantiated rumors cautioned against the technological illusion of immediacy.

Lippmann's analysis could only anticipate, however, the character and depth of the crisis attributed to the use of television as a medium of social experience and political knowledge. The crisis is twofold and paradoxical. On the one hand, while the broadcast nature of television "greatly increases our sense of belonging to a particular population," as Craig Calhoun observes, "it does not give us direct or individually recognizable relationships with the members of that population."[8] Offsetting this broad and abstract sense of publicness, television's intimate image fosters trust in those personalities who best serve its formats of consumption and exhibition: actors and performers, news readers, and national political figures. In the flow of television, where boundaries between forms of programming become fluid, it is easy for viewers to misrecognize the cues of sincerity employed in narrative fictions for integrity on the part of politicians and the journalists who report their activities in the domain of news and public-affairs programming. When the codes of character are freely shared between genres in this way, "bland television-like personalities become the norm," Douglas Kellner warns, "and television images arbitrate what the audience will accept and vote for."[9] Critics like Kellner worry that this emphasis on image and style has driven some voters out of the political process and induced in the rest a kind of affective confusion about politics. The supposition behind such criticism is that voting and television viewing are fundamentally rational activities and that voters and viewers make choices in candidates and programming in line with their interests. But just as we often find ourselves inexplicably watching television programs or personalities we dislike, the insinuation of televisual style into political practice may lead us to political decisions that cut across our self-interest. When voters feel that it is important to "'know' the candidates personally," argues Joshua Meyrowitz, "it is quite possible that many people will vote for candidates with whom they largely disagree, or vote against candidates who share their political philosophy."[10]

What rationalist analyses of this puzzle overlook is that voting, especially once it becomes a form of iconic consumption, need not obey the same self-actualizing logic that liberal political scientists and economists impute to democracies and capitalist markets. Such analyses fundamentally misunderstand the intimate nature of television. In a 1963 essay titled "Learning from Television," John Grierson named this quality its "parasite" effect.[11] Although Grierson gives television this name out of contempt, it nonetheless captures the powerful effects of televisual pathos, effects that came, in 1963, to characterize the presidency in new ways.

Initially, Grierson means only to characterize television as a derivative medium, a "debase[ment] of the original tradition."[12] Televisual form is often defined in negative relation to other aesthetic traditions or genres, as the poor cousin of literature, theater, or cinema. In this respect, television is the parasitical medium par excellence, having even adopted formal conventions to compensate for its use of the same material over and over. (What is the function of the sitcom laugh-track if not to blunt the realization that we have heard these jokes before?) But what concerns Grierson even more is that television "invade[s] privacy . . . exploiting personal emotions and human weaknesses."[13] This second sense of parasitism underscores the relation between aesthetics, technology, and television's social form, its connection between space and feeling. Television is a machine that breaches the division between the home and the world by generating emotions.

Grierson deliberately avoids using the term "public" to describe this sympathetic relationship. His reluctance to do so anticipates the position of media critics like Douglas Kellner, who claims that "the media, especially television, have subverted the very foundations of democracy." Not only has television "failed in recent years to carry out the democratic functions of providing the information necessary to produce an informed citizenry," argues Kellner, but it has also "promoted the growth of excessive corporate and state power."[14] Although convincing in a commonsensical way, this argument contains a contradiction. On the one hand, voters are programmed by the media and the politicians

who control "it"; on the other hand, citizens do not believe or participate in politics anymore because they know that politics is nothing *but*
the media. How is it possible that citizens can be both cynically disaffected and naively engaged by publicity, both know and not know?
This is precisely the parasitical position—an existence in two bodies at
once, one feeding the other—that television makes available.

Taking advantage of the coincidence between the biological sense of
the term and the French word for static interference, *"le parasite,"* Samuel Weber suggests a phenomenological extension of the technological
concept. Television, writes Weber, "entails not merely a heightening
of the naturally limited powers of sight with respect to certain distant
objects; it involves a transmission or transposition of vision itself. The
televisual spectator can see things from places . . . where his or her
body is not (and often never can be) situated."[15] Indeed, it is not clear
how we would distinguish the spaces of television in the first place,
each of which is a field of reception: do we mean the geographical and
geopolitical spaces, terrestrial and extraterrestrial, local, regional, national and transnational, covered *by* television broadcasting? Or the
psychic, social, and physical environments of spectation? Or the layer-
ing of representation *within* programs, where TV acts simply as a kind
of channel for other media of recording?[16] The essence of television,
according to Weber, is that it "differs from itself," insofar as the qualities that are commonly used to define it are in fact derived from three
very different domains: production, transmission, and reception.[17] It is
this essential nonidentity of television that leaves room for a challenge
to the liberal critique of the media as the symptom, or the cause, of
democracy's demise.

It might be said that the sense of community fostered in television
spectators has more to do with disavowal than it does with identification. The television spectator is frequently given the opportunity to
think of *other* spectators and to think of them, moreover, as idiots. Flip-
ping channels late at night, we linger over an inane game show or a
miracle-knife demonstration and ask, who besides me is up at this hour
watching this nonsense? What kind of fool believes this claim?[18] Stanley Cavell names the kind of disaffected attention we pay to television
after the screen itself. Where the film spectator views, the television
viewer *monitors*.[19] With this pun, Cavell restates the awesome inter-

subjectivity Grierson derided as the parasite of television in somewhat more affirmative tones. The American president, I will suggest, has become a form of this intersubjective "monitoring," providing a figure for the fears and fantasies of power to which the imbrication of television and politics give rise.

EGOCRACY

Understood as a critical response to mass politics, ambivalence about the presidency has deep roots in American life, as Alexis De Tocqueville observed on his visit to America in 1831:

> It cannot be denied that democratic institutions have a very strong tendency to promote the feeling of envy in the human heart; not so much because they afford to every one the means of rising to the level of any of his fellow-citizens, as because those means perpetually disappoint the persons who employ them. Democratic institutions awaken and foster a passion for equality which they can never entirely satisfy. . . . The lower orders are agitated by the chance of success, they are irritated by its uncertainty; and they pass from the enthusiasm of the pursuit to the exhaustion of ill-success, and lastly to the acrimony of disappointment. Whatever transcends their own limits appears to be an obstacle to their desires, and there is no kind of superiority, however legitimate it may be, which is not irksome in their sight.[20]

Tocqueville concluded that Americans elect a popular representative who embodies this alienation in order to better evaluate and resist it.

Perhaps this was the reason that, in the days after the death of former president Gerald Ford in December 2006, the term heard most constantly in public remembrances of the so-called accidental president was "decency." Its use was so frequent that one could imagine that it had been established by prior agreement. Asked by CNN interviewer Larry King what she remembered about Ford, former first lady Nancy Reagan remarked, "Well, everybody says this, but I guess it bears repeating, he was a very decent man, a good man, an honest man, all those qualities, he had, which are nice qualities to have." On the same program, former senator Bob Dole told King that Ford's profile was one of "integrity, honesty and decency,"[21] a sentiment echoed in statements by former president George H. W. Bush, who called Ford "one of the most decent and capable men I ever met," and his former chiefs of staff Dick Cheney, who praised Ford's "decency, integrity and devotion to duty,"[22] and Donald Rumsfeld, who called Ford "a man of great decency and towering integrity."[23] Even those outside Republican presidential circles of power found occasion to use the term: the CBS News correspondent Bob Schieffer said Ford was "'the nicest and most decent' public figure he had ever covered"; and *New York Times* television columnist Alessandra Stanley called "Mr. Ford's retirement . . . dignified and decent."[24] Stanley noted the good taste that television programs had shown in suppressing, at least for the first several hours after the announcement of Ford's death, the famously undignified images of Ford stumbling in public and the equally famous parodies of these accidents performed by comedian Chevy Chase on *Saturday Night Live* in the mid-1970s. Following the script, *SNL* producer Lorne Michaels told the *Times* that Ford "was just so incredibly decent and good-natured about the skit."[25]

In part because decency is not a term one expects to hear in connection with high politics—it could only bring to mind Joseph Welch's famous rebuke to Joe McCarthy during the Army-McCarthy hearings of 1954, "Have you no sense of decency, sir? Have you, at long last, left no sense of decency?"—the choice of such a mild and unpresidential quality to characterize Ford made one wonder whether some peccadillo or corruption was being masked by its repetition. The obvious source of this suspicion was, of course, the presidential pardon Ford granted Nixon in 1974. It hardly mattered whether this pardon had really been part of a rumored "deal" that Nixon and his staff offered Ford when they proposed him as Vice President Agnew's replacement, since Ford's function was not to restore dignity to the office but to endow it with the capacity for shame and humiliation—which, in his accidents and his ordinariness, Ford embodied.

Ford did not so much replace Nixon as mute the contradiction between the two ages of power that Nixon occupied. Nixon justified his transgressions in office by reference not only to national exigency but also to historical precedent, claiming, as if he was a premodern monarch, that "when the President does it, that means that it is not illegal."[26] And during the same interview in which he makes this argument of royal prerogative, Nixon invokes a special kind of mortality, that of the martyr, when he refers to himself as the "last casualty" of Vietnam because of his efforts to "win an honorable peace." Nixon's "self-inflicted political assassination"[27] may have evoked historical and mythical precedents, but his remarkable ability to rise from the dead over and over in his political career was the product of a more recent and banal source of immortality: television. Beginning with the spectacular masochism Nixon displayed in the infamous "Checkers" speech of 1952, in which he peevishly recounted his credentials as a member of the middle class, Nixon's career could practically be charted by his self-pitying and exculpatory television appearances. In this respect, Nixon was also symptomatic of the late-modern political phenomenon Claude Lefort called the "egocrat," the type of modern leader who claims to represent the state with his person, in the style of the monarch, but who does so only through the authority of a hyperbolic self-referentiality. Like other iconic brand names, the egocratic leader has a kind of tautological popularity: he seems to represent us because we see him everywhere. The egocrat's main attribute is his recognizability. This is a form of power that is operated through acts of disavowal: the appeal of the egocratic leader is that he "is who he is." The retrospective evocation of Ford's "decency" seemed to legitimate this strategy, even as it appeared to pay tribute to Ford the individual, and to his humility.

When it has addressed the mass-mediated political personality, a problem with which it has been preoccupied since the time of Grierson's critique of television, American documentary takes up and extends the paradox of mass democracy that made Ford seem the solution to the problem represented by Nixon. In their critique of the apparent disjunction between politicians and their publicity images, films on this model provide the concept of political representation with a touchstone. Intimate documentary accounts of electoral politics can restore a measure of characterological authenticity to politics, what at other times was called virtue. But as documentary revived the concept of virtue, inscribing "ordinariness where greatness should be," it can also provide mass politics with an egogratic alibi.[28]

A case in point of this problem is Alexandra Pelosi's self-proclaimed "home movie" of George W. Bush's 2000 presidential campaign, *Journeys with George* (2002), which documents the year the filmmaker spent around Bush, covering his first presidential campaign as a producer for the network news program *Dateline NBC*. Shot with the consumer-level Sony TRV-900 mini-DV camera and edited on a personal computer, the film adopts a casual, irreverent attitude to the topic of American presidential politics. Weighing less than two pounds, the TRV-900 allows Pelosi, who shot most of the footage herself, to achieve a remarkable intimacy with her subjects. In addition to the speeches, rallies, and press conferences that constitute the serious side of the campaign, Pelosi shows us its empathic dimension: the diet of bland sandwiches, the disorienting sameness of endless airports and motel rooms, and the personal relationships, from crushes to jealous feuds, that develop among the journalists. In the seemingly impromptu interviews she conducts with Bush, his staff, and her fellow journalists, Pelosi elicits a range of reactions to the grinding work of electoral politics. Her fellow journalists are candid with her in their cynicism about the election, which they unanimously view as an assembly line of photo-ops and sound bites. Few hold this against Bush himself, whom they treat like a wise-cracking classmate. When Bush is not being kept away from the press by his handlers, he cultivates a genial presence before the camera, offering Pelosi fashion advice and romantic counseling, smoothing relations between her and the press corps after she makes an embarrassing mistake, and happily sparring with her about his status in the polls and the primaries. In another context, the film's haphazard cinematography and muddy sound recording would serve as evidence of the amateur's technical incompetence; here, they function as formal signifiers of the outsider status both she and Bush claim.

Pelosi's claim is just as dubious as Bush's, since she is the granddaughter of a Democratic congressman and the daughter of Nancy Pelosi, then the Democratic House minority leader. Furthermore, the costs of her film were underwritten by two major television networks, NBC and HBO. The film's personal (that is to say, nonprofessional) aesthetic is thus a kind of promise that, notwithstanding the considerable access to power represented by the film's two main characters, the medium, like the political process it documents, is still capable of moments of authenticity and truth. Like *Young Mr. Lincoln* (John Ford, 1939), and told in the same anticipatory past tense, *Journeys with George* concerns the molding of presidential character from crude materials: where Ford's film uses folk tunes and Henry Fonda's relaxed performance of episodes in the log-cabin mythology to signify Lincoln's authenticity, Pelosi's film uses the resources of documentary to explain—or, one might argue, advance—the peculiar credibility of her subject. The appeal of this sort of film comes, to put it another way, from the possibility that it will show us something unexpected about the world of politics. The ample footage of Bush "unplugged," as Pelosi says—chewing with his mouth open, stumbling through his speeches, cutting up with the press corps, proudly modeling his Western attire—serves to establish this reality effect.

Equipped with a short zoom lens capable of focusing on objects less than an inch away, a common feature of consumer-level cameras of this sort, the camera often seems an extension of its operator's body. All manner of objects, from morsels of snack food to the mouth of one of Pelosi's fellow reporters, end up pressed against the lens in extreme, distorted close-up, as if the distinction between the objects she records and the means of recording had eroded. Bush himself appears irresistibly drawn to Pelosi's camera (see figures 5.1 and 5.2), and the film includes a number of images of Bush's eyes, nose, or mouth pressed against the lens, as if it were a baby and he were an old-fashioned campaigner obligated to kiss it. Or, perhaps, as if *he* were a curious child, and the camera, a toy to be pressed into a sensory opening. It is tempting to interpret this reciprocal pair of images as a symptom of the Oedipal problem that would haunt Bush throughout his terms in office. But the easily available Freudian reading is only a first step in understanding how these excessively intimate images are extensions of a social and cultural apparatus, one that is merely signified by the literal, palpable apparatus of the miniature camera.

Placing homely images where public ones should be, *Journeys with George* inverts a particular model of social documentary, one established, according to John Hartley, by *Housing Problems* (Edgar Anstey and Arthur Elton, 1935), the landmark sponsored documentary from Britain about slum clearance. *Housing Problems* demonstrates, writes Hartley, the documentary protocol of "bringing public semiosis to the

Figures 5.1–5.2. *Journeys with George* (Alexandra Pelosi and Aaron Lubarsky, 2002). Still captures from DVD.

aid of private distress,"[29] and it does so according to a televisual logic. Like television, which was in its experimental infancy in 1935, *Housing Problems* seeks to connect the interior spaces of the home to the public spaces of the film's cinematic presentation by its argument that slum clearance serves a nationwide benefit. And because it invites private people to come together in public in order to think about domestic spaces, ones in which problems and privations are revealed with an apparently spontaneous immediacy, the film lays the groundwork, Hartley argues, for the combination of "intimacy and involvement" that television claims (or that is claimed for television by its theorists) as its defining feature.[30]

Journeys with George represents an inversion of this model, insofar as it is difficult to say whether this is a "personal" or a "political" film: with barriers between public and private space increasingly eroded and interiority on constant display, documentary loses the need to serve as an incisive, revelatory aesthetics. In this context, the paradoxical concept of the personal documentary becomes one more manifestation of a general social transformation in which, according to Jean Baudrillard, private and public lose their complementary exclusivity. Under these conditions—exemplified, for Baudrillard, by the television documentary *An American Family* (1973)—a new definition of obscenity is called for: against the "traditional obscenity of what is hidden, repressed, forbidden, or obscure," we now contend with an obscenity of "the visible, of the all-too-visible, . . . the obscenity of what no longer has any secret."[31] From this perspective, the uninhibited display of Bush's body in *Journeys with George* as a private body that we see, and see inside of, in ways inhibited in other public contexts, is less obscene than the very application of a "personal documentary" strategy to this context, since this strategy advances the erosion of the public sphere and its professional categories of representation. For this reason, one cannot simply write off *Journeys with George* as one more personal impression of the social world, an example of what Baudrillard calls the "telematics" of the communication age, wherein "each person sees himself at the controls of a hypothetical machine, isolated in a position of perfect and remote sovereignty," since even (or especially) by this atomization of feeling and expression, leveraged and managed by the most powerful media outlets and industries, the film reflects the new form of advertising, the "omnipresent visibility of enterprises, brands, social interlocutors, and social virtues of communication" that "monopolizes public life in its exhibition."[32] Thus, even as it is meant to educate viewers and citizens about the media strategy of egocracy, Pelosi's approach thus seems to complement this strategy. To understand how American documentary became involved in this problematic, it is necessary to return to the semiotic opposition between the images of Richard Nixon and John F. Kennedy in 1960, an opposition that documentary itself helped establish.

TELEVISION AND THE PRESIDENT'S TWO BODIES

Although Kennedy's defeat of Nixon in 1960 is often attributed to his composure during their televised debates, compared to Nixon's evident discomfort before the cameras, their pairing can also be seen as crucial to the resolution of Kennedy's presidential character. In an influential challenge to prevailing explanations of Kennedy's appeal, Marshall McLuhan contrasted Nixon's television image to Kennedy's. The televised debates of the 1960 contest between the two had been a disaster for Nixon, McLuhan wrote, because he projected a "sharp intense image" that was poorly suited to the "cool," interactive medium of television. Kennedy, by contrast, had a "blurry, shaggy texture."[33] Like television itself, McLuhan argued, Kennedy engaged the viewer precisely because he was ill defined. Although McLuhan's sweeping distinctions idealize the media he describes, dislocating them from history, his observation that Kennedy went beyond a "merely elective presidency" when he appeared on television, approaching the condition of a monarch, points to a shift in the discourse of American politics around 1960. McLuhan's analysis illuminates the historical coincidence of the Kennedy presidency and the style of American documentary known variously as "direct cinema" or "cinéma vérité" which coalesced as an aesthetic at about this time.[34]

   This was also the period of documentary cinema's greatest penetration into the television networks' prime-time schedules, a cultural event that both shaped the Kennedy administration and was shaped by it. When he became president, Kennedy "found it natural to involve the nation in the office of the Presidency," McLuhan reasoned, "both as an operation and as an image."[35] In the hands of producers like Robert Drew, who had developed his craft as a journalist in the Time-Life organization, *cinéma vérité*, an observational style that brought ethnographic and home-movie techniques into the arena of professional journalism, became a kind of scrapbook of intimate impressions of the inner lives of public figures. In its simulation of an eyewitness point of view of such charged social and cultural events as political campaigns and diplomatic crises, instances of social conflict, and rock concerts, *cinéma vérité* allowed viewers to experience subjectivity, the feeling of being present in the scene as an observer, as objectivity, the sense that the representation viewers were watching was free of bias. Through this liberal phenomenology, the producers and corporate sponsors of *cinéma vérité* endorsed the free-market ideology of the Kennedy presidency and helped promote it, at home and abroad, as an aesthetic experience. This conflation of the scene and the process of political representation was, for McLuhan, the defining feature of all of Kennedy's televisual guises and, by the same token, of television as a political apparatus.

Nixon was famously considered the antithesis of the photogenic Kennedys, particularly when viewers were given the chance to compare their images side by side, as they did during Nixon's disastrous first television debate with John F. Kennedy in 1960. By contrast with Kennedy, who looked tanned and fit, Nixon, who was recovering from an extended stay in hospital and a bracing encounter with an unreceptive union audience earlier in the day, looked wan and nervous. Nixon was already uncomfortable with television, and he had a tendency to sweat under the lights, a problem that was accentuated by a warm studio, badly applied makeup (the Nixon staff had refused the services of a CBS makeup artist), and his notorious five o'clock shadow. The tight close-ups of his face that director Don Hewitt used frequently as reaction shots to Kennedy's statements—a stylistic choice that was fiercely contested by both campaigns, during and after the broadcast—only strengthened the impression that Nixon had something to hide. To make matters worse, Nixon's light gray suit blended into the set, so that, next to Kennedy, Nixon appeared to be fading.[36] In a contest focusing on national security, the impression that one of the candidates was a suspicious character, leaking and slipping in and out of sight, was decisive.

Perhaps no one in politics deployed televisual style better than the Kennedys. A key example is their popular television documentary, *A Tour of the White House with Mrs. John F. Kennedy*, first broadcast on CBS and NBC on Valentine's Day in 1962, to the highest ratings of the year in any genre of programming, and subsequently seen internationally by several hundred million viewers.[37] Besides its remarkable number of viewers, among the largest audience for any work of documentary, there is nothing extraordinary about this program. It follows the formal and rhetorical conventions of network documentary of the period quite closely. Indeed, I linger over it only because it demonstrates how the power of high political intimacy was a conventional element of popular political discourse in the 1960s. That the program presents the domestic interior of politics as an open secret helps us understand, by comparison, how the rhetoric of *cinéma vérité* was that of a covert operation, an unveiling of private spaces made possible by technology. The Kennedys' *Tour of the White House* suggests that this revealing gaze was already part of the self-presentation of the state on television.

Hosted by CBS reporter Charles Collingwood but narrated by the first lady, the focus of the program is the design and redecoration of the president's residence. In her narration, Mrs. Kennedy takes great pains to show how the White House furnishings link the Kennedys to past residents and, at the same time, to the present-day Americans who lent furniture or objects. She frequently pauses in her tour to express her gratitude to these private individuals: Mrs. Edith McGinniss of Falls Church, the source of chairs from Lincoln's time; Mrs. Maurice Noun from Des Moines, Iowa, who donated an antique desk; and so on. These acknowledgments counterpoint the gestures of filiation to previous administrations: where the latter place the Kennedys in a line of descent from the founders, from whom they derive their sense of historical importance, the invocation of individual Americans identifies the Kennedys with the body politic, to whom they owe their care and comfort.

An individual named by a president's wife is no ordinary individual, and the national significance of these nominations is redoubled by the fact that she uses the medium of television to deliver them. The complicated role of television in both extending the power of the presidency and keeping it in check is signified by Mrs. Kennedy's voice. As the program's narrator, she gains an unaccustomed authority, one that women rarely had in documentary. At the same time, her ostensibly unrehearsed responses to the CBS reporter's questions are punctuated by pauses, slips, and intakes of breath that distinguish her from professional public speakers like the reporter and her husband, who shows up at the end of the program to deliver some talking-head declarations of his own, summarizing the program, inviting Americans to come visit, and thanking his wife for "bringing us much more intimately in contact with all the men who lived here." Living with the personal effects of previous occupants of the White House, the president explains, "makes these men much more alive." He implores Americans to visit the White House and to come in contact with this living history.

Of course, no ordinary visitor to the White House will have the kind of audience with the first family that CBS has given them, and the subtle implication, here and throughout the program, is that television has an important, if ambivalent, role to play in bringing political history to life. Earlier in the program, Mrs. Kennedy pauses over a portrait of George Washington painted by George Stuart to remark on the "interesting precedent" that the government set by commissioning it: "They commissioned the finest living artist of the day to paint the president and they gave it as a gift to the White House. I often wish they'd followed that because so many pictures of later presidents are by really inferior artists." It cannot escape our notice that she expresses this regret while framed by the camera in a formally composed head-and-shoulders close-up, the television equivalent of the painted portrait (see figure 5.3). Which is *this* that we are now seeing, we wonder, an inferior modern representation or a revival of great art? The irony of Mrs. Kennedy's wish would be amplified a short time later, when the prosaic work of "inferior artists"—press photographers and amateur cinematographers—would result in the most enduring images of the Kennedys, the pictures of the president's assassination and its aftermath. In retrospect, the insistent concern in A Tour of the White House with living history underscores the vital power of television and other moving-image media, not only to bring history to life but to withdraw life as well. In the early 1960s, this power was closely identified with the presidency.

As the 1960 election campaign had demonstrated, these media had the ability to make a politician seem lifeless. On many occasions

Figure 5.3. *A Tour of the White House with Mrs. John F. Kennedy* (Franklin J. Schaffner, 1962). Still capture from VHS.

thereafter, documentary film and television would demonstrate how the same moving image that was vital to the president's political life could also be the president's unmaking. This fading is at once corporeal, as when Kennedy was captured on film, fading from life, and symbolic, a failure to live up to the mantle of greatness, as was the case with Nixon in so many television appearances over the years. In both cases, documentary media help us see a body unbecoming the president. If Nixon and Kennedy appear to represent the two extreme tendencies of presidential iconicity, the shameful and the ethereal, these are just two facets of the same egocratic regime.

THE AESTHETICS OF PARANOIA

In "The Paranoid Style in American Politics," first delivered as a lecture at Oxford within days of Kennedy's assassination, Richard Hofstadter presents the idea of paranoia as a pattern in American social organization. Hofstadter borrows the term paranoia from clinical discourse to describe an "unselfish and patriotic" political sentiment.[38] The clinical paranoiac imagines the world to be organized in a pattern of conspiracy, directed against him in particular, whereas "the spokesman of the paranoid style finds it directed against a nation, a culture, a way of life whose fate affects not himself alone but millions of others. Insofar as he does not usually see himself singled out as the individual victim of a personal conspiracy, he is somewhat more rational and much more disinterested."[39] Hofstadter is careful to distinguish between the content of paranoid hypotheses and the "accents" in which they are delivered. The hysterical tones of the conspiracy theories Hofstadter traces back two centuries in American life (gold speculators, Papist spies) always posit a secret explanation of American life. What Hofstadter calls the *style* of paranoia is precisely the social structure of these fantasies, their capacity to circulate despite—or because of—their improbability. The problem with these theories is not simply that they are wrong but that they form a kind of common sense: the political paranoiac "does not usually see himself singled out as the individual victim of a personal conspiracy [but] is somewhat more disinterested. His sense that his political passions are unselfish and patriotic, in fact, goes far to intensify his feeling of righteousness and moral indignation."[40] The conspiracy theorist may be stupid, in other words, but he is not cynical. The adherent of the paranoid style takes for granted that the state will attempt to deceive him, but he is still capable of imagining a community of like-minded individuals linked by the desire to know and share the truth. Indeed, the political paranoiac desires simply to be able to read the state: beneath the fantasy that Jews or communists run everything is the wish that the principle by which government operates could be discovered.

If the patriotic undertones of much political paranoia point to an imaginary national community behind the rumors, the epistemology on which conspiracy theories depend prevents paranoiacs from forming a properly public sphere of discourse. The evidence that proves their theories is always said to be elsewhere, or in the hands of others who cannot be identified, often because, it is said, their theories are unpalatable to the powers that be in the government and the liberal media. In this way, paranoia can be compared to gossip and distinguished from scandal. Although all three are corrosive discourses, gossip and conspiracy make use of a closed network of speakers, those who know the real story and can keep it a secret. Neither gossip nor paranoia can make use of official or mainstream circuits of information to spread itself, since it must be prevented from falling into the wrong hands. And although all three posit a truth that diverges from and undercuts official truths, gossip and conspiracy are, by definition, unable to produce material evidence.[41] Richard Nixon's reference, in a November 1969 address on the Vietnam war, to a "silent majority" who supported his views exploited the pragmatic similarities between a national television audience and the constituents of a conspiracy theory, converting an absence of opinion into a constituency. Nixon cleverly suggested that the impediments to the group's self-expression were what made it a group worthy of representation.

Even though scandals appear to cause an erosion of trust in officialdom and official sources of information, they do so by mobilizing a manifestly different sense of truth and evidence and thus a different kind of political public. As Laura Kipnis notes, political scandal reassures us that there is still something authentic about politics and trustworthy about the public sphere through which we consume it. Hinging on the (belated) revelation of facts through mainstream and generally respected channels of information, presidential scandal not only affirms our faith in these channels but establishes our (prior) commitment to the office, even on the part of those who do not support the officeholder. Kipnis cites a bumper sticker from the time of the Clinton sex scandal—"First Hillary, then Gennifer, now us"—that expresses the radiating social effects of scandal, the injury mixed with pleasure that scandal spreads from the personal outward to the social.[42]

The assassination of John F. Kennedy may seem, in retrospect, to have been a watershed in the cultural history of American political scandal, a moment when the aesthetic register of scandal shifted from the verbal to the visible. The Kennedy assassination, we might say, made the visual itself into a scandal. The assassination was only one in a series of documentary events involving the presidency in the 1960s; its power can be properly understood only in the context of the documentary culture that enveloped it. The crisis and its collective experience were effected by the obscene visibility of the president's suffering body, a body that had already been on view in various states of intimacy for a number of years. As high politics was increasingly experienced in terms of the visual logic of television, scenes in which the political body failed to contain itself helped to define the new, egocratic power of high office. Nixon's infamous early encounters with television, including his pathetic "Checkers" address of 1952 and his sweaty performance during the 1960 debate with Kennedy, were in this sense just as important as Kennedy's sublime appearances. These images of Nixon set the stage for the national signification of Kennedy's death, which, in turn, laid the ground for Nixon's resurrection.

Since moving images of the assassination could not be shown to a national audience for many years, the traces of the footage that were displayed in public shortly after the event only underscored a different kind of representational failure, the failure of television, a competing medium of record, to fulfill its promise as a national public sphere. In his analysis of the television networks' handling of the assassination and its aftermath, Philip Rosen shows how the four-day national interruption of regular programming that ensued began with a nearly total absence of eyewitness images of the events. But by a paradox that distinguishes broadcast media like television from indexical media like film, this emergency provided television, through its on-air personae, with a way to demonstrate the medium's particular mode of authenticity, what is frequently referred to as "liveness." Because the assassination occurred in a time before the use of portable video cameras for electronic news gathering, television news departments had to wait hours for film footage of the events. The sights and sounds of reporters in national and local newsrooms scrambling to fill the air time with breathless, often emotional descriptions and speculations only served to support the impression that television had a special connection to the real. Indeed, such interruptions in the normal flow of programming are essential to the identity of television, insofar as such crises help spread the "rumor" of instantaneity.[43] Theatrical demonstrations of shock and surprise, like the cracking of Walter Cronkite's voice as he reported the death of the president or the torn sheets of telex paper that newsroom personnel held as they read their contents directly into the camera, contribute to this sense that the medium of television captures the real, even when its professionals falter.[44]

That this struggle for priority amongst documentary media should have been played out over the body of the president was no coincidence, given the role of Kennedy and his administration in the promotion and development of documentary television in general, and the *cinéma vérité* style in particular. The Kennedys themselves were among the most important icons of this style, appearing in a number of significant independent and network-television films, including the Robert Drew Associates' film *Primary,* made for the small television division of Time-Life, and *Crisis: Behind a Presidential Commitment* (1963), made for ABC. If the insouciant charm of the Kennedys offered new reasons to figure out how to use documentary to register character up close, this was only one weapon in a broader strategy that the networks shared with the state to advance the American cause of liberalism at home and abroad.[45]

One consequence of the hysteria caused by the launch of the Russian communications satellite *Sputnik I* in 1957 was increased attention at the level of U.S. national policy to communications technologies in general, and television in particular. As a form of programming that promoted an attitude of rational civic engagement over one of mindless enjoyment, television documentary supported the New Frontier ideologies of participatory citizenship and technological innovation. Current-affairs documentary, a format largely ignored by the networks until the end of the 1950s but for a few programs built around star journalists like Edward R. Murrow, offered opportunities to exploit the ideological and commercial priorities of the Kennedy administration's domestic and foreign policy, as well as to regain the trust of the viewing public and public officials after the quiz-show scandals of the late 1950s. Documentary served the moral function of "ask[ing] viewers to believe what they saw on television once again," as Michael Curtin says. As currency of this trust, the state offered "vital information that was presented as the product of untainted expertise."[46] Viewers trained to take television seriously, especially the young, educated, and affluent audiences that public-affairs programming was thought to attract, were attractive to advertisers. Such programming was also of keen interest to the administration. Domestically, it could help state officials make a case for its foreign policy. Overseas, it could serve as a form of propaganda for American strategic and business interests. In turn, this corporate contribution to the fight against communism helped keep the networks in the forefront of the campaign to exploit new international markets in Latin America and elsewhere.[47]

One can agree with Curtin that the importance of *cinéma vérité* in the overall picture of television documentary in this period has been exaggerated without denying its historical significance as a symptom of the period's political climate. An exemplary case of what Curtin calls "our fascination with seemingly autonomous innovators"[48] in film history and in American life is the Robert Drew Associates' film *Primary*, which converts the antinomies of Cold War liberalism and American exceptionalism to affective cinematic and televisual codes. The first of a number of films produced by Drew for the television division of Time, Inc., *Primary* attempts to counteract political publicity with a pedagogical use of cinema by showing its viewers how charismatic images are constructed and circulated.

Combining the documentary photographic aesthetic of *Life* magazine and the loose journalistic style of *Time,* the film follows the Wisconsin Democratic primary contest between Senator Kennedy and Senator Hubert Humphrey of Minnesota. As is well known, the filmmakers improvised a synchronous-sound rig from a lightweight Auricon 16mm camera, a one-quarter-inch tape recorder, and a Bulova quartz watch, allowing them to record picture and location sound independent of each other in a way somewhat unprecedented in the history of documentary filmmaking. Because the resulting audio-visual reconstructions closely approximated an eyewitness position on events, they allowed the filmmakers to occasionally suspend the use of voice-over commentary, giving the impression that documentary subjects could speak for themselves. For this reason, *Primary* is frequently described as the first successful example of American *cinéma vérité*, although the most cursory examination of even the film's most naturalistic sequences makes clear that reality could "speak" only under certain conditions, including situations of social and psychological distress.

The signature movement of the *cinéma vérité* image was and is the close-up or zoom-in to a tell-tale expressive feature, the twitch or fidget that betrays the subject's discomfort, by which the viewer's gaze is trained on the everyday psychopathology of the camera's subjects. This intimate, penetrating gaze was perfectly suited to American commercial television. Since the early days of the medium, intimacy had been a watchword in the industries of television: television manufacturers, producers, and advertisers alike maintained that, because of its location in the home, its size, and its integration into social ritual, television was a medium of close quarters.[49] Gilbert Seldes, a critic and former television executive, identified these different valences of intimacy when he characterized the TV camera as an "x-ray, penetrating to the reality behind appearance, showing up whatever is exaggerated and falsified."[50] In line with this credo, *Primary* promises the viewer "an intimate view of the candidates themselves" in its opening narration, over a shot from the back seat of a car in which Kennedy is being driven to another Wisconsin rally. In adopting this forensic perspective, *Primary* attempts to teach its audience about how popular images are constructed and how they function in the democratic process; in doing so, it tries to forestall the slide from mass democracy into mass consumption.

The argument of *Primary* consists largely of this critique of image. Against the various manifestations of technologically enhanced charisma, the film posits the ability of cinema to present a true picture of the man behind the image.[51] At the same time, the constant presence of crowds, in the image and on the soundtrack, is meant to confront the viewer with the kind of audience that television is replacing, the chaotic, claustrophobic, and authentically physical audience of the old-fashioned political campaign rally. Pitting these two quite different images of audience against each other, each depiction of the campaigns' public relations machines in operation is an opportunity for the film to posit a spectator more knowledgeable than the mere consumers of the candidates' personal appeal. In addition to a number of noisy political rallies, the film accompanies the candidates to photo sessions, radio interviews, and television appearances (see figure 5.4). In each case, the film's aim is to go behind the scenes of the process of crafting a public persona. A sequence that follows Humphrey through a radio interview purports to show us what the radio itself cannot: that the interviewer prompts Humphrey, off-air, to flatter the listeners of the station. An interview with the radio announcer, apparently conducted after Humphrey has left the building, is edited to suggest that the announcer himself is a poor judge of political character and possibly a liar. Another sequence has Humphrey denouncing the journalistic cult

Figure 5.4. *Primary* (Robert Drew, 1960). Still capture from DVD.

of personality characterized by *Life* magazine while promoting himself to a group of farmers in a school gym as the candidate from the country. Whenever possible, the film demonstrates how these characterological details elude or are hidden by forms of the popular media that place a premium on immediacy. *Primary* argues that for all their efficiency at bringing the candidate to the people in the way that personal appearances once did, the electronic media only perpetuate the deceptive practices of advertising and Hollywood. By contrast, the film asks to be read as an attempt to rescue intimacy from the quality into which it has been collapsed, immediacy.

The commonplace about technological publicity is that it conflates the intimacy of the portrayal with the immediacy of its reception. This is the essence of John Grierson's contemporaneous objection to the parasite of television, which both invades private emotional spaces and extends them unreasonably, making us care about people we will never meet. *Primary,* on the other hand, asserts that in the national space imagined by television, documentary cinema can hold intimacy and immediacy apart, that it can, in fact, restore to publicity the correspondence between the individual and the political.[52] But *Primary* fails in its attempt to separate out an intimacy of representation from the technological character of immediacy because such a separation is impossible.

In order to expose the failure of these immediate media to give a full picture of the candidate, *Primary* has to be constructed, for the most part, along lines not so different from those of classical continuity editing. In its classic form, realism privileges an individuated perception, putting the spectator in a position where he or she takes in a scene from the best possible vantage point, seeing and hearing better than any of the characters "in" the scene. Likewise, though the rhetorical premise of *Primary* is that the behavior of the mass is just the programmed outcome of suggestive images, the film achieves the reeducation of the individual spectator only through carefully constructed narrative and montage sequences that reveal the excesses of the news media or the contradictions in the candidates' own words. If the revolutionary innovation of *cinéma vérité* was supposed to be its immediacy, *Primary* was an unlikely starting point, since its method of "recording life as it exists" depends on a thorough management of the spectator's senses.[53]

The purist aesthetic of American *cinéma vérité* was riddled with inconsistencies. Although its practitioners claimed that the ultimate purpose of their technological and stylistic innovations was to let the social tell its own story, and thus to allow the viewer to make up his or her own mind about the social problems each film depicted, the films themselves are considerably more argumentative and directive than these claims could admit. Critical debate about the films centered on the question of whether the viewer really had, as the Drew Associates claimed, simply been allowed to observe: whether, in other words, the objectivity that was presumed to inhere in mechanical recording devices and an uncontrolled cinematographic style was transferred directly to the viewer's consciousness, where it would, mutatis mutandis, become the basis of the viewer's subjective perspective on the topic of the program. The frequent criticism that the films had already become subjective in the editing process, where the footage was forced to espouse an argument, only further reified the technology of recording because it presumed that, under ideal conditions, a pure cinematic document, one that allowed viewers to simply experience the truth, could be made. (These debates tended to ignore the phases of program development and preproduction, during which ideologically and politically driven choices were made about documentary practice and content. They also overlooked the context of exhibition, including the important issue of sponsorship.) It was more or less taken for granted in these debates that the camera does not lie. In fact, the argument that technology was the key to the mutual liberation of the filmmaker and the viewer was consistent with the ideology of Cold War liberalism, which maintained that free societies had nothing to hide. Or, rather, that citizens of a free society had something to gain by scrutinizing themselves and their institutions; as one of the most important cinematographers of the movement put it, the point of *cinéma vérité* was "to find out some important aspect of our society by watching our society, by *watching how things really happen* as opposed to the social image that people hold about the way things are *supposed* to happen."[54] Social space might contain unconscious or invisible truths, but you could reveal them if you just knew where to point your camera. And once you saw the ways things "really happen," you were free to change the institutions that produced their "social image." And what better proof of this ideology could there be than a president who was willing to open himself and his home to the eyes of the nation?

The value of this ideology was obvious to the advertisers that the networks signed up for their brief experiment with direct cinema. Programming that allowed viewers to make up their own minds appealed to sponsors not only because it aligned them with the anticommunist doctrine of freedom of expression and belief. Documentary was also thought to make viewers better vessels for the advertiser's message. One of the most important sponsors of *cinéma vérité* programming was Bell and Howell, which underwrote ABC's *Bell and Howell Close-Up!* from 1960 to 1963, a program that featured many films produced by Robert Drew Associates. The message that technology was conducive to freedom was particularly appealing to this manufacturer of cameras and projectors, and the national broadcast of films in this style helped popularize the notion that every situation was worth filming. Perhaps the strongest case for this argument was made by an event no sponsor would have wanted to be associated with, the assassination of John F. Kennedy; the most controversial record of this event was made by an amateur cinematographer with a Bell and Howell 8mm camera.

Because few moving pictures of the event were made and because those that did exist—notably, the twenty-six seconds of 8mm footage shot by Abraham Zapruder—were of poor quality, any image of the event had an air of conspiracy. Leaked to the public in an incremental series of fragments, including black-and-white and color frame enlargements published in *Life* (which owned the original footage) in 1963 and 1966 and by the Warren Commission in 1964, the Zapruder "film"—actually, a growing number of copies of Zapruder's film, of notoriously variable quality—took years to be shown as a projected moving picture. In 1969, the footage was shown by prosecutor Jim Garrison in a New Orleans courtroom during the trial of Clay Shaw, an erstwhile conspiracy suspect. Pirated copies began to appear on college campuses and at conventions of conspiracy theorists and assassination buffs over the next several years. In March 1975, it finally received a national television broadcast on two different episodes of *Good Night, America,* a late-night talk show hosted by Geraldo Rivera. (Rivera's analysis of the footage: "Uh, God, that's awful.")[55]

The Zapruder film was difficult to see. For nearly a decade, it was rarely exhibited in public, and even when it was, the poor quality of the craft and technology that produced it made its images at best a suggestion of how the president had been killed. At the same time, the very reasons for its visual obscurity enhanced its value as a document of the event. One way to define documentary cinema in general, and *cinéma vérité* in particular, is as a kind of "uncontrolled" filmmaking. On this premise, the filmmaker finds his or her subjects in the world and thus exercises less control over them than a fiction filmmaker would. By this logic, documentary retains and displays traces of its encounter with the real. This indexicality can take many forms, including the jerky motion of the frame in images shot with a hand-held camera. This effect has entered the repertoire of realist techniques in fiction filmmaking and advertising, but in the early 1960s, when advances in camera technology first made it feasible for documentary filmmakers to carry 16mm cameras on their shoulders, hand-held cinematography lent the work of *cinéma vérité* filmmakers an air of urgent authenticity and engagement: of the filmmaker with the subject and with the act of filming. By the same token, the Zapruder footage was taken to be a reliable account of the shooting of the president in part *because* it was unprofessional and because one could sense in it the visceral effect of a human operator. The images were obscured further by various covert and official distortions, including the optical enhancement of some images in bootleg copies of the film and the misprinting of some frame enlargements in the Warren Report.[56] Such reinscriptions only added to its fantasmatic authority, and the pursuit of a definitive reading of Zapruder's twenty-six seconds became one of the assassination's emblems.

The little strip of film became an instance of the national imaginary not solely because of these crises of authenticity, of course, since the same problems are endemic to documentary discourse. The indexicality of documentary images, their capacity to materialize the unique time and place of their origin, is fraught with national-historical significance in the Kennedy assassination, and by other factors as well. The Zapruder footage featured the destruction of the presidential body, or the reduction of the president's "two bodies" to one corporeal body. In capturing Kennedy's passing, Zapruder's Bell and Howell camera inscribed a sudden failure of the democratic metaphor of representation, a demonstration of the *merely* corporeal nature of the president's body and the collapse of the body politic.

FOUR MORE YEARS

If Nixon's nervous performance in the 1960 debates had seemed to mark his immaturity as a national politician, the Kennedys' embrace of and by documentary routinized the visual scrutiny of the presidential body and residence. But John F. Kennedy's filmed death in 1963 and the paranoia created by its gradual dissemination could, in turn, be seen as the redemption of Nixon's earlier, stumbling performances. And a few years later, Nixon exploited the lessons of *cinéma vérité* to displace the cool image of the Kennedys that television documentary had helped to establish.[57] Whether its evidence was sweat, blood, or slips of the tongue, the principle of *cinéma vérité* was that the real would eventually display itself, so long as you looked directly at it and kept recording. The intimacy of television lent itself to such simulations of depth. The sounds and images of truths leaking from secret places would come to signify presidential virtue in the Nixon-Kennedy era, and they helped establish television documentary as an apparatus of a national-security state. In this way, the opposition of Nixon and Kennedy was key to the definition of television as an instrument of truth. Independent and radical documentarists responded to these developments in the image of the president by abandoning the pursuit of its depth and truth.

Years before the term "Teflon presidency" was applied to Ronald Reagan, Emile de Antonio noticed that Nixon's awkwardness before the camera only added to his appeal. In *Millhouse: A White Comedy* (1971), de Antonio explored the filmic evidence of this perverse power, beginning with the infamous "Checkers" speech of 1952, a nationally televised act of self-abasement that laid the groundwork for the Kennedys' exploitation of visual intimacy. Where Marshall McLuhan considered Nixon too intense for television, de Antonio concluded that Nixon's power lay precisely in his "jerky compulsive nervous" mien. He was a "brilliant politician," de Antonio told Cinda Firestone, "because he's so unlikeable."[58] The left understood that it could not condescend to or ignore this contradictory phenomenon or the role that television played in it. If "Nixon's presence on television had inspired emotions close to nausea," as Norman Mailer wrote, this effect nonetheless "offered every clue of schizophrenia in the American public if they failed to recognize the void within the presentation."[59]

By 1968, when Nixon made his political comeback, he had figured out how to convert this displeasure into a tactical weapon. The staff of his 1968 campaign used McLuhan's media theory to refashion Nixon's image. Adopting McLuhan's distinction between high- and low-definition—hot and cool—media, they worked on an image of Nixon that would be, like the *cinéma vérité* image of the Kennedys, "non-calculated, incomplete."[60] If Nixon could not compete with the Kennedys in sheerly physical terms (what a Nixon speech-writer called the "bobby phenomenon," his erotic appeal to "thousands of little girls who want him to be their president so they can have him on the tv screen and run their fingers through the image of his hair"),[61] he would attempt to produce a similar spectatorial engagement with the image through other means. The Nixon campaign recognized that images were signifiers: an image meant something only in relation to another image. Using innovative forms of television advertising, their strategy was to sow distrust in the image. If the appeal of Robert Kennedy was based, as a campaign memo explained, on "the promise . . . that things can be solved without logic, but just with 'love,'" a promise embodied in "image saturation," Nixon could respond by presenting an awkward, confrontational image.[62] Where *cinéma vérité* encouraged viewers to engage the image in depth, to project themselves into it—in other words, to *love* the image—Nixon's self-presentation constantly drew attention to the shallow and duplicitous character of the television image. The successful television politician of 1968 "should express distaste for television," Joe McGinniss wrote: he should maintain that "there is something 'phony' about it."[63] The Nixon campaign's television strategy was to exploit the candidate's natural discomfort with television, to turn what John Grierson called the "faults and failures, superficialities and vulgarities" of the medium into opportunities to demonstrate that the candidate was authentic and trustworthy.[64]

In contrast to the New Frontier documentaries, which had promoted the role of 16mm documentary cinema in making political processes seem real to ordinary citizens, and thereby increasing popular involvement in government, independent filmmakers of the late 1960s and early 1970s took advantage of increasing cynicism about the state, and distrust of Nixon himself, to invent new approaches and techniques of documentary. Although both the liberal documentary of the early 1960s and the radical forms of the Nixon period sought to expose the role of the mass media in the construction of the political public sphere, they did so on different ontological and epistemological premises. When *Primary* turned its cameras on the machinery of spectacle, it did so in order to prove and preserve the truthfulness of the cinematic image—in particular, the image created by producers working at arm's length from the networks—against the account of politics one would find in other media. When portable video became possible, not only was the primacy and originality of the cinematic image no longer taken for granted, but authenticity itself diminished in value. While critical analyses of video aesthetics frequently emphasize the medium's feeling of immediacy, some works of radical video sought to call this technological-ontological premise into question.

In 1967, Sony introduced a lightweight video camera/recorder combination known as the Portapak. Because the Portapak sold for around $1,500, and because it used one-half-inch tape rather than the larger professional formats, ran under battery power, and weighed less than twenty pounds, the Portapak helped make video available to nonindustrial and nonprofessional applications. Some of the earliest users were artists and activists experimenting with the medium in the representation of politics, as a way of competing with the commercial news organizations. One of the first of these experiments was a pair of hour-long programs about the Democratic and Republican national conventions of 1972 produced by Top Value Television, a collaboration between a number of grassroots video-production organizations, including Raindance Corporation, a New York–based group whose name spoofed the RAND Corporation; Ant Farm, a San Francisco art collective; and the Videofreex, who got their start making public-service tapes before producing a calamitous experimental video program at CBS called *Subject to Change*. As its acronym suggested, TVTV aimed to cover the conventions in a way that would mirror the commercial networks' coverage. In doing so, it would draw attention to the excesses and redundancies of media spectacle. At the same time, the rough, loose style of the TVTV tapes would make an argument for decentralized, independent electronic journalism as a tool for radical politics, one that might replace film as a medium of social change.

In *Guerrilla Television,* his seminal handbook of the independent video movement, Michael Shamberg, a central figure in TVTV and one of the founders of Raindance, called film an "evolutionary link between print and videotape."[65] Film was too much like print to survive the accelerated pace of media evolution, Shamberg argued. The expense and difficulty of its use had prevented it from truly democratizing communication; furthermore, the technical and textual nature of commercial cinema made it an effectively solitary experience for the viewer. While cinema would continue to coexist with print and video, Shamberg predicted, it would survive as a fetishist's medium, a storehouse of spectacles and memories with cult value. Although cinema had revolutionized the mass experience of reality, like print and other established technological media, its effects had been naturalized. This linear historical progression might be interrupted by television, which brought print, visual, and auditory media together in one environment. The diversity of forms that was conventional in television could become something more than an aesthetic feature of the medium, Shamberg argued, if video was properly exploited as a mode of television. The speed and portability of the image-making process in video would also diversify the address of television by making possible active and engaged spectatorship of a sort impossible in other media. Democracies, Shamberg wrote, are "two-way information channels which have many sources."[66] The term "feedback," a reference to the technical capacity of video to produce an image at the same time that the image was being recorded, symbolized this democratic potential.

The redistribution of media power that Shamberg had in mind looked very different from the media strategies of TVTV's predecessors in radical documentary. Distancing himself from groups like Newsreel, which espoused and supported violent oppositionality, Shamberg expressed his impatience with direct action, such as the street protests that had roiled the country in 1968. The counterculture's emphasis on spectacular displays of disorder and incivility (what Shamberg dismissed as "demonstrations and combat, staying up all night listening to music and smoking dope")[67] was starting to look like a tactical mistake. Shamberg's media politics derived from the McLuhanite principle that older media become the content of the ones that succeed them: when protesters relied on primitive forms of collectivity, they merely provided electronic journalism with content. Such actions had little chance of influencing the audiences of these media spectacles, since television viewers identified not with the image on screen but with the screen itself, as a receiver of information. The practitioners of guerrilla television aimed primarily to demystify the process of television production. In this way, they aimed not only to diminish the authority of the national-commercial media but, also, to subtly undermine the analogy between spectatorship and citizenship on which contemporary national politics depends.

The title of TVTV's videotape on the Democratic convention of 1972, *The World's Largest TV Studio* (1972), was an explicit reference to a remark by Norman Mailer in his account of the 1968 conventions, *Miami and the Siege of Chicago* (1968). Both *World's Largest* and *Four More Years* (1972), about the Republican convention, drew inspiration from Mailer's sardonic analysis. Telecommunication became, for Mailer, the motif of such conventions and of the differences between the two parties as representative bodies. The Democrats had failed to harness the widespread resistance to the Vietnam war symbolized by the candidacies of Eugene McCarthy and Robert Kennedy. This failure of the party mechanism saturated the nominating process, right down to the operation of the convention hotel itself. By this logic, it seemed no accident that one had trouble finding a phone in the hotel that worked: "communications in the headquarters of the largest party in the nation most renowned for the technology of its communications was breaking apart under strikes, pressure, sabotage, security, security over-check, overdevelopment and insufficient testing of advanced technical devices."[68] In the face of "the combined onslaught of pressure and street war," the Democrats had turned inward, Mailer suggested; his description of Hubert Humphrey, moments after winning the Democratic nomination in the 1968 presidential campaign, encapsulates his profound dismay at this insular strategy. Watching the proceedings from his hotel suite, Humphrey "rushed to the television screen and kissed the image of his own wife, which was then appearing on the tube."[69] Humphrey's confusion, mistaking television for the world, is the reflection of the image Mailer creates a few pages earlier, when he joins others, "innocent until now of the intimate working of social force," watching from windows high above the street as police beat demonstrators. There was "no metaphor large enough to suffice" for the collapse of this "great liberal party," Mailer lamented, but his description of the scene turns the Hilton into a giant television set, aestheticizing the violence of the world below.[70]

When TVTV went to Miami for the 1972 conventions with their Portapaks, they found an equally narcissistic and insular process in both camps. With a small amount of funding from a number of cable systems and a loose commitment from these systems to broadcast their tapes, TVTV managed to secure one of the nonnetwork press passes to the convention floors.[71] Their appearance and their equipment set them apart from the network crews, alternately drawing suspicious and admiring glances. (In *Four More Years,* Nixon daughters Tricia and Julie pause in their movement along a receiving line to exclaim "Cute!" and "Incredible!" when they see one of the TVTV cameras.) With twenty-eight members and several cameras, TVTV was a large operation by the standards of independent documentary, although it was dwarfed by the several-hundred-person armies of the network organizations.

Governed neither by a prime-time broadcast slot nor by professional codes of craft, TVTV was free to capture impressions that had been "neglected, rejected and missing from media coverage to date," and to do so in ways that drew attention to the expense, hierarchical division of labor, and false sense of urgency that determined the look and pace of network news coverage.[72] This meant that *World's Largest* could feature jokey segments on the construction of the sets for the network broadcast operations and on a *Newsweek* interview with Shamberg on the merits of cable television ("in place of the mass media, we gotta be a special purpose medium"), before shifting abruptly in tone and focus, to follow in detail the challenges by minority delegates to the party platform and convention program. In line with the axiom of feedback, each of these events was equally important, and it was just as important to ask the minority delegates how it had felt to be filmed and what it felt like to watch themselves on a monitor.

Nixon's incumbency meant that the Republican convention provided less dramatic intrigue. Indeed, Nixon barely appears in *Four More Years*, showing up in only two brief shots. Instead, TVTV searches for figures of the "silent majority," the phantom constituency Nixon claimed to represent. Even if the silent majority was, as Jean Baudrillard put it, "an imaginary referent," signs of its existence still had to be produced.[73] *Four More Years* attempts to intervene in this conspiracy by identifying its sites of production. Not all of these sites appear in the profilmic space of the political event. TVTV is careful to point to the role of television itself in masking the emptiness of the convention as an exercise of public opinion.

The easiest targets are the Nixon youth groups, Young Voters for the President and the Nixonettes, who we see being coached in displays of spontaneous enthusiasm (see figure 5.5). During preparations for a Nixonette event, one of the organizers tells the young women that the event had been designed to maximize their enjoyment; she assures them that "the decorations alone will give us the fun we need." Merely reproducing such outrageous statements is enough to ironize them, even when they take on a totalitarian cast (as when a panicked delegate calls for "something akin to Kent State, but on a larger scale" to deal with unruly protesters). The point of these moments first seems just another way to poke fun at the squares for being uptight. As the tape

Figure 5.5. *Four More Years* (Top Value Television, 1972). Still capture from VHS.

proceeds, however, it becomes clear that these are not mere slips of the tongue but rather characteristic expressions of the Republican zeal for order and civility. This rigor extends to the nominating process, which is so carefully orchestrated that it leaves the network correspondents assigned to the convention floor with little to do.[74] When NBC reporter Cassie Mackin complains to TVTV member Skip Blumberg that "it's a very packaged, plastic kind of thing, with very little spontaneity," we understand that the tables have been turned and that it is now the network personnel who are being ironized. CBS correspondent Mike Wallace echoes this complaint, joking that he'd rather be at home, watching the proceedings on television. But when Blumberg asks him whether he thinks a less regimented convention might improve the process, he simply espouses the professional credo of objectivity: "we're here to cover an event and that event is the Republican National Convention." Wallace is echoed by Walter Cronkite, who insists that worrying about the effect of their reporting on its subjects is bad for professional journalists (see figures 5.6 and 5.7).

Figures 5.6-5.7. *Four More Years* (Top Value Television, 1972). Still captures from VHS.

But the Nixon supporters, natural enemies of the long-haired liberals of TVTV, warmed up to the Portapaks precisely because TVTV offered to show them what they looked like on camera and to let them shape their representation. These resolutely unprofessional methods helped the group acquire more revealing material than the networks.[75] It is clear, from their use of montage, that TVTV was far from objective and identified most of all with the antiwar protesters whose cause dominates the last half of *Four More Years*.[76] The tape nonetheless resists treating its nominal subject with scorn, as de Antonio did in his own Nixon documentary. Instead, it consistently returns the viewer to the question of how the documentary form supports or challenges the journalistic doctrine of objectivity. In its use of low-resolution, half-inch video, long takes, and jarring editorial juxtapositions, the tape offers a subtle, equivocal response to Walter Cronkite's suggestion that democracy was sustained by the consumption of many different news sources and that the task of the professional journalist, in a crowded marketplace of information, was to provide a clear picture of events. The blurry pictures recorded by the Portapak only underscored the necessity of interpreting the documentary image. Although the TVTV tapes share with *Primary*, their *cinéma vérité* ancestor, a fascination with the improvisatory possibility of portable recording technologies, they are at pains to point out that the documentary camera was not a window of truth.

This point is made consistently in the last part of the tape, as the antagonism between the protesters and the Republican delegates moves to the foreground. On the last night of the convention, a large crowd of protesters from Vietnam Veterans Against the War threatened to force their way into the convention to disrupt Nixon's nomination and keep Nixon off of prime-time television. Making use of footage captured by TVTV's roving crews, *Four More Years* alternates between inside and outside the convention. As police gas the protesters off-screen, teary delegates and flag-bearing Boy and Girl Scouts are hustled into the hall. Cutting moves the viewer between two versions of "The Star-Spangled Banner": the dissonant version being played outside the hall by a "People's Band" of radicals on trumpet and kazoos who are pinned behind a fence and a cordon of riot police, journalists, and onlookers; and the version sung by the massed voices inside the hall, led by a group of

Figure 5.8. *Four More Years* (Top Value Television, 1972). Still capture from VHS.

smiling performers and a live orchestra (see figure 5.8). When the TVTV cameraperson pans from the fuzzy, faraway image of the People's Band to the clusters of people listening to them, we sense that their image is distant in time, not just in space. We see that their performance is attended to by all manner of official and unofficial observers: the police; journalists with recording devices and notepads; and bystanders taking souvenir photographs and films (see figure 5.9). Because these observers appear in the foreground of the shot, the sound of the People's Band seems to come to us *after* others have registered it. The performance inside the hall has a force and a presence that the People's Band lacks. The sequence echoes Nora Sayre's despondent description of the convention: "Inside the Hall, there were the realities of the Seventies, which culminated in a warmth-binge: Nixon shaking hands with a rapturous line-up while the lights gleamed on Agnew's forehead. What went on outside was back in the Sixties: a suppressed memory of bad days that were over."[77]

Figure 5.9. *Four More Years* (Top Value Television, 1972). Still capture from VHS.

The tight shots of the smiling performers on stage also echo the cinematography of *Primary*, and they uncomfortably recall the vitality of Kennedy's rallies in that film. Where *Primary* came to signify, even in its title, a sense of present urgency and future possibility, *Four More Years* is, for all its technological innovation, a work of nostalgia, one that dreads four *more* years of Nixon. This self-conscious ambivalence about the group's achievement is summed up in the tape's final image, a long tracking shot that backs out of the convention hall while fixed on an NBC News banner. At the same time that the shot moves forward, it looks backward (see figure 5.10). While this progressive movement has the effect of diminishing the significance of the network news operations and symbolically making room in the frame of documentary television for alternative visions, the tape nonetheless ends oriented toward the imprint of commercial television. Many attempts to document the electoral process in subsequent years retained

Figure 5.10. *Four More Years* (Top Value Television, 1972). Still capture from VHS.

this perspective of nostalgic longing for a moment of democratization that failed.

ACCIDENTS OF POWER

Nixon exploited the discontent generated by the civil rights movement shamelessly in his political campaigns of 1968 and 1972, but he demonstrated an especially canny understanding of the movement's rhetoric of injury when he put himself on display as a suffering subject. The "Checkers" speech is the best loved of these pathetic displays, but he employed them throughout his political career, as evidenced by his claim, after leaving office, that he ought to be counted among the victims of the Vietnam war. Since Nixon, it has been difficult to think respectfully of the presidency, a shift that has in no way diminished its authority. Rather, by taking up the gambit of public suffering—or, we might say, making this strategy safe for straight white men—the presidency has maintained its public power, even as the body politic has withdrawn from participation in electoral politics.[78] Even (or especially) when these sacrificial displays of humility or shame are accidental, they help to secure the illusion that high politics is responsive to popular desire. This affective politics can actually help contain the promiscuous spread of extrapolitical alternatives to problems of citizenship.

The monumental shocks of the Kennedy assassination and Watergate have been replaced by a seemingly regular incidence of lies, accidents, or blunders on the part of the president in full view of the American public. From the banal embarrassments of Gerald Ford's stumbling and George H. W. Bush vomiting at a state dinner in Japan to Bill Clinton beating around the bush about the definition of sex, these occurrences simultaneously confirm the fallibility of the president and the omniscience of the documentary media that witness them. These outbursts help maintain the referential illusion of the presidency, the idea expressed in the American axiom that anyone could grow up to be president, even though no one actually believes this to be true. As Joan Copjec has suggested, the power of the presidency has a great deal to do with these national moments of parapraxis, where it is confirmed that, much to our horror, the president does, indeed, bleed, vomit, lie, and forget just as we do.[79] We nevertheless abhor this figure because he stands for something that seems impossible: consensus formed from the multiplicity of individual wills.

This would seem a perverse version of the concept of charisma that Max Weber considered central to the power of the modern democratic leader. The documentary evidence of our leaders' errors and weaknesses hardly affects our belief in their public function; indeed, we now expect that they subject themselves to such public embarrassments, if only to justify the claims their would-be successors make to restore honor to the office. Copjec diagnoses this blind devotion as a late form of the "reality effect" that Roland Barthes said could be found in nineteenth-century literary realism and in modern historiography. Barthes suggested that this effect is inscribed through an "insignificant notation," a particularly apt notion for considering spectacular demonstrations of presidential corporeality.[80] The president is the president, in other words, because his body is insignificant, in a way it is for no other American.

This is to identify, then, a kind of internal contradiction in American democracy, which applies equally to the presidency and the technological media, both of which act as our liaison to the state: in a popular system of representation, the public representatives of the state, those who speak politics back to the governed, are tolerated because their authority is visibly accidental. It would appear today that this accidental form of power is a consequence of the slippage between technological representation and social representation; that is, as the mass media becomes the dominant institution of civil society, we increasingly adopt an attitude of indifference to the signs that our leaders respond only to the exigencies of publicity. But this indifference does not mean that the real has diminished in value. One has only to reflect on the historic significance of the Zapruder film and Nixon's own tape recordings to recognize that these accidents of recording shore up the testimonial power, as well, of even the simplest documentary devices, in spite of the fact that these recordings were notoriously incomplete. That is to say, the expression of this cynical distrust of public officials and the public media alike—an articulation that is, to be sure, impossible without the technological media—brings into being a paradoxical form of collectivity, the society of those who believe they are being lied to.

We seem faced with a reversal of the scenario depicted by John Grierson in 1963. Now simulation does not threaten the authentic aspects of the social; rather, it determines them. The sphere of the family, for instance: what kinds of activity give substance to this realm of identity? Watching television, for one. Referring to the allegations of sexual and ethical misconduct by President Clinton, Senator Joseph Lieberman told a CNN news program in 1998 that "this episode is sorry, and it is sordid, and it has brought down not only our Government and the head of our Government, but the whole country. . . . I mean, the very fact that I have not been able to automatically let my young daughter sit with me and watch the news anymore tells you what has happened here."[81] One could detect, in the senator's outrage, the suggestion that he and his daughter will be forced to learn about something dirty, something that has no place in the family: the president's desire, or perhaps simply desire itself. It was as if in the senator's home, the television had begun to watch *them*, making it impossible for the Liebermans to regard themselves as a family. Against the background of calls from other members of Congress that the president "pour his heart out" to the American people—that he avail himself of the performative gesture of immediacy that has become his trademark, that he invite us to feel *his* pain as he has felt ours—Senator Lieberman's lament indicated precisely the location of the public sphere that forms around the presidency: television. Publicity is not simply what occurs "on" television but rather what uncannily takes place *through* television, when it visits us where we live and transforms our relationship to ourselves and one another.

This ability to occupy various spaces at once, to be at once public and private, means that television need not respect what Jean Baudrillard called the "moral hypothesis" of classical representation, in which perspectival realism simulates the position of power.[82] As we have seen, *cinéma vérité* follows this aesthetic. Its pursuit of the deep or unspoken meanings of the social depends upon the constant projection of a vanishing point of the real.

The ironic attitude that characterizes American *cinéma vérité* depends upon this conception of space, an attitude that persists long past the point at which it ceases to be politically effective. This is the approach, for instance, of *The War Room* (1993), the film about Bill Clinton's 1992 presidential campaign and the dynamic team of advisors who shaped it. One of the film's directors, D. A. Pennebaker, was a camera operator on *Primary,* and *The War Room* recalls *Primary,* as Clinton recalls Kennedy, in its methods and critical perspective. As with its predecessor, *The War Room* provides a behind-the-scenes analysis of the construction of a candidate for high office. But as the film progresses, the candidate himself appears less and less frequently on screen. Much more attention is given to Clinton's campaign strategists, who are seen conducting lengthy and detailed analyses of campaign strategy and defending their candidate from unfavorable reporting. Although the genealogical relation between *Primary* and *The War Room* is strained by the absence of the candidate from the latter film, *The War Room* retains the traditional optimism of liberal documentary by focusing on the personalities of James Carville and George Stephanopoulos, thereby retrieving some measure of originality and integrity from an increasingly routinized exercise in public relations.

This strategy is exemplified by a moment near the end of the film, in which Stephanopoulos is speaking to President-elect Clinton on a cell phone. A hand-held camera brings us into the midst of a celebration, hovering at Stephanopoulos's side as he banters with Clinton about the victory. Stephanopoulos expresses his congratulations and then advises Clinton that though "this is your night, we want you to say whatever you want," they are cautioning him not to be "programmatic." Here, the president-elect seems unreal in inverse proportion to the presence of the camera. The documentary effect is reduced to the confrontation between the event and the recording devices used to capture it. The naturalistic image and sound testify to the immediacy, and thus to the integrity, of the account. It is this rhetoric of presence that allows the film to pose, by implication, an ironic question: Where is the leader? Has politics distanced him from us? But this doubt is offset by our faith in the documentary image: if, at the very moment of the electoral decision, the people's choice is unrepresentable, this is because he is somewhere else than in the center of the image.

Another documentary account of the same election cycle, *Feed* (1992), takes the opposite approach to this problem. Making use of footage shot in *cinéma vérité* style as well as material taken directly from the candidates' own publicity campaigns, *Feed* focuses on the superficiality of the primary process in the age of television, reveling in the indignities candidates are put through in their pursuit of favorable press coverage. (The film's title refers to the use of satellite transmission in television news and by campaigns to reach remote audiences.) Rather than searching for an essential or authentic subject of politics, *Feed* refuses to distinguish the medium of publicity from its subject. Its critique of political spectacle does not rest, in other words, on peeling back the layers of representation to reveal the true character of the political. Instead, *Feed* makes use of a range of documentary techniques to demonstrate the shrinking and flattening of the official space of the political, even as broadcast technologies promise to extend its territorial reach.

In one instance, *Feed* models this critique with a simple lesson in the architecture of two different audiovisual media, film and television.

In this scene, an exchange between a news anchor and a field correspondent takes place, even though technological difficulties should ruin the illusion of such an exchange. The scene begins with film footage of Democratic candidate Bob Kerrey standing in the cold, waiting to conduct an interview by satellite with a New Hampshire television station. In keeping with the conventions of *cinéma vérité*, time seems to pass as slowly for the viewer as for Kerrey, who is plainly upset by the technical difficulties: he cannot hear the news anchor's questions, and the technician scuttling around his feet cannot fix the problem (see figure 5.11). Finally, the news program's producers attempt to conduct the interview. A cut then transports us from Kerrey's authentic—that is, filmed—location into the composite space of the television broadcast, where Kerrey's image is displayed in an electronic window of the newsroom set wall (see figure 5.12). This cut shifts the viewer of *Feed* from the position of the cinematic spectator to identification with the spectator of television. The anchor conducts a conversation with Kerrey through this window, despite Kerrey's incomprehension of the questions. The reconstructive montage of *Feed*, however, allows viewers of the film to hear both ends of the conversation. The film thus suggests that the documentary insight into telecommunication is *neither here nor there:* even though we know that the conversation should be impossible, it proceeds as if nothing was wrong.

Feed's critique of televisual spectacle does not, then, reach back to a primary vision of politics, nor to some haptic form of *vérité* as a guarantee of authenticity or truth. Rather, it seeks to amplify the viewer's sense of disorientation with a series of images taken directly from satellite "backhaul." These images are the work of media artist Brian Springer, who spent a year recording satellite feeds with two backyard dishes. (Springer's own found-video work, *Spin* [1995], includes much more of this material than appears in *Feed*.) Many of these images consist of little more than a static shot of one of the Democratic or Republican candidates, making small talk with campaign staff or video technicians, primping for a television appearance, or simply waiting silently for a cue to begin speaking. The first of these found images is a long shot of President George H. W. Bush, preparing for an interview or campaign appearance delivered by satellite. While we watch, Bush

Figures 5.11–5.12. *Feed* (Kevin Rafferty and James Ridgeway, 1992). Still captures from VHS.

Figure 5.13. *Feed* (Kevin Rafferty and James Ridgeway, 1992). Still capture from VHS.

chats with the unseen crew, produces a pair of glasses with which to read a script, fidgets, and finally just looks into the camera, without appearing to focus on any particular point (see figure 5.13).

This is a doubly fascinating image: it fascinates, in part because it is itself an image of fascination. Bush seems to be transfixed before the gaze of the camera. As a bored, restless viewer, a *monitor,* he models our own look, both mirroring and anticipating it. It is, in a certain way, an obscene image: it shows us too much. But this is a peculiar kind of display, because what we are seeing is not yet an image. Rather, we witness the moments before an event of spectacle, the technological conditions of its display, but with the awareness that what we see is invisible to the proper audience of the broadcast. Although scopic privilege is inscribed in this image and the others like it by the long frontal take and by the unguarded gestures of self-fashioning, these same marks of spontaneity and authenticity force us to experience these images as the negation, not the affirmation, of our power to see "one true thing" in politics, precisely because, as is the case with pornography, their subjects are explicitly unaware of our attention.[83]

In this scene of the sitting president composing himself to speak as the president, or simply waiting to address a distant audience, we sense the tension between the person and the office that is essential to the idea of the American presidency but not usually made so uncomfortably plain. What is most disconcerting about this long series of deferrals of presence is the feeling that they leave no space for irony, no autonomous position for the spectator from which politics looks shallow. The distance required for irony, a clear separation between the position from which documentary looks and the spectacular image of politics at which it looks—a distance that is traditionally required of social documentary—is missing. (Michael Moore uses similar images to great but quite different effect in the title sequence of *Fahrenheit 9/11*, where they are accompanied by a spare and melancholy musical score plucked on a guitar. Serving as an eerie counterpoint to the otherwise banal images of George W. Bush, Condoleezza Rice, Paul Wolfowitz, and Donald Rumsfeld preparing to meet the press, the sound of music establishes the dominant opposition between the remoteness of the Bush administration and the sympathetic perspective the film offers a popular audience. That one of these images makes Bush, rolling his eyes and mugging for the camera, look like a cartoon character—an effect amplified by the transfer of video to film, which muddies the detail of his eyes—only underscores the implicit argument of Moore's approach to documentary, which is that mass-popular techniques can have critical force.) Instead, we are presented with a kind of pastiche, the coincidence of a number of overlapping fields of reception: a satellite image plucked from space, sent to a videotape recorder, and then transferred to film for inclusion in the rest of the documentary, which is later projected in theaters or transferred to video or digital storage media for private viewing. Where the practice of documentary exemplified by *The War Room* privileges a moment of capture or exposé of the truth, a moment where politicians reveal their superficiality to a public projected as "outside" politics, the satellite images in *Feed* demonstrate the essentially technological nature of the political public sphere. In other words, the conditions that make possible the meaningful self-presentation by the president to a remote mass of viewers are the very same technical conditions that enable viewers to receive the empty, insignificant image of the presidency on which I have been dwelling. By the very nature of satellite broadcasting, the legitimate broadcast carries this parasite within it. It is the accidental vigilance of televisual technology itself that produces these disruptions of what Baudrillard calls the "smooth operational surface of communication."[84]

By demonstrating that televisual politics in fact depends upon this kind of error of generality—broadcasting, in the truest sense of the term—*Feed* and films like it suggest that to arrest the hegemonic politics of spectacle, one need not look elsewhere than television itself. As the erratic career of these images suggests, television offers the continual possibility of moments of obscurity within transmission. Since they threaten the analogy of embodied dialogue by which mass-media reception can be likened to a town meeting, it is conventional to regard these demonstrations of the literal irresponsibility of mass media as threats to democracy. In a dire 1984 address to the Spanish parliament, Jürgen Habermas warned that a "new obscurity" had replaced the Enlightenment principles on which modern states and modernity itself depended. Various threats to the future of society, and to humanity itself, have created blockages of thought and imagination. The resulting bewilderment made it impossible, argued Habermas, for people to know how to act and sapped modern societies of the confidence to invent the future.[85] But precisely because they raise the question of how and where action takes place, and how we know it when it does, obscure images are also instances of possibility. Through their displacement from the publicity stream to the reflexive context of documentary, they become moments at which we can imagine that, "despite the capacity of systems of political representation to absorb and channel energies, things happen; unpredictable resistances occur."[86]

6 / TENSE TIMES

Documentary Aporias; Or, the Public Sphere of Suspicion

*The aide said that guys like me were "in what we call the reality-based
community," which he defined as people who "believe that solutions emerge
from your judicious study of discernible reality." I nodded and murmured
something about enlightenment principles and empiricism. He cut me off.
"That's not the way the world really works anymore," he continued. "We're an
empire now, and when we act, we create our own reality. And while you're studying that reality—judiciously, as you will—we'll act again, creating other new
realities, which you can study too, and that's how things will sort out. We're
history's actors . . . and you, all of you, will be left to just study what we do."*
—RON SUSKIND, "Without a Doubt: What Makes Bush's Presidency So
Radical—Even to Some Republicans—Is His Faith-Infused Certainty in
Uncertain Times," *New York Times,* 17 October 2004

*Under the general demand for slackening and for appeasement, we can hear
the mutterings of the desire for a return of terror, for the realization of the
fantasy to seize reality.*
—JEAN-FRANÇOIS LYOTARD, "Answering the Question:
What Is Postmodernism?"

Throughout this book, I have maintained that documentary is not just
an apparatus for the delivery of facts and information that are merely
registered in it automatically, nor simply a vehicle of ideas formed elsewhere and prior to the cinematic process, but a practice of knowledge
unto itself. In this sense, I have been arguing that documentary represents the kind of social imaginary that Raymond Williams calls a structure of feeling. What Williams means by this paradoxical construction is nearly impossible to think, since we usually oppose feelings to
structures. And this difficulty is precisely his point. Over and against
the forms of experience that are observed and studied as "the social"
or "history," Williams identifies a quality of experience that escapes

"explicit and finished" thought but survives in *thinking*, or what he calls "practical consciousness," an aspect of culture that is "now, alive, active, 'subjective.'"[1] Despite its reliance on machines that record sounds and images, the social documentary aims also to engage imagination and thereby to mediate between actuality and the positions, disciplines, and institutions from which experience can be understood, consumed, or acted upon. When William Stott claimed that "social documentary deals with facts that are alterable," he identified the power of this mediating role; "feeling the fact," Stott suggested, "may move the audience to wish to change it."[2]

Offered in the early 1970s as a reflection on the legacy of Depression-era documentary culture, Stott's definition of documentary as a tentative act, one directed at a reality that may not yet exist, was meant to describe an essential and transhistorical quality of this cultural form. But the idea of the documentary as a form of speculation, imagination, or fabrication rather than a form of certainty has lately taken on a renewed urgency, coinciding with two seemingly independent cultural phenomena: a theoretical and antirealist turn in documentary film studies and, originating outside the university but transecting it, a period of heightened anxiety about what is euphemistically referred to as "national security."

Williams devises the concept of the structure of feeling to explain a portent of change in the conditions of social experience. At these times, Williams says, this sense may consist of nothing more than "an unease, a stress, a displacement, a latency."[3] When the "tension between received interpretation and practical experience" has hardened into a familiar opposition between "official" and "practical" consciousness, its moment of possibility has passed, and Williams cautions that the critical faith in "alternative interpretation," because it depends upon received and dominant interpretations, betrays the force of this tension in the social imaginary. The work of intelligence that early advocates of documentary film had in mind was to operate in a similar space of tension between received ideas of government and politics and their meaning in the daily lives of the governed, and I have tried to show that in each new phase or style of this work, one can find both traces of this tension and signs of its domestication within the familiar opposition.

Compared to the distinct developments I have dealt with in detail (the use of voice and textuality in the mid-1930s; *cinéma vérité;* the radical use of sound in the 1970s; nonprofessional video) or only tangentially (the development of the interview as a documentary method, for instance, and its application to minority history and politics), the distinctive stylistic and political traits of American documentary at present are harder to discern. It is harder to establish the precise character of the present than it is that of the New Deal or Popular Front documentary or oppositional documentary of the Vietnam era. All the same, the difficulty of saying definitively whether and how the present appears in documentaries makes them telling indexes of the tension of the times.

This recent style of documentary takes as its object the abstract, covert, spectral, and imaginary forms of a state that relies increasingly on the paragovernmental operations that Walter Lippmann called intelligence work. Even more than the state's pastoral or physical powers, which were a primary concern of New Deal and New Left documentary, the fields of intelligence itself and the feelings of uncertainty, anxiety, or suspicion they can generate concern this new variation on political documentary.

The suspicion of politics coincides with a current in critical thought, versions of which appear in every discipline of moving-image and visual-culture studies and which holds that the referential capacities of documentary media are themselves now subject to suspicion in the face of sweeping changes to the culture and technology of still and moving images.[4] In some cases, it is the critics themselves who appear to have lost faith in the referential image; in others, criticism speaks for or to a popular mood of skepticism or disaffection with the real.[5] But there seems to be general agreement that the democratization of visual technologies ambivalently anticipated by Walter Benjamin is itself part of the problem, the means of what the Frankfurt School called "mass deception" now having devolved from political and industrial control of the mass media and the professional practices of media production to the technologies of digital imaging and distribution available at the level of individual, nonprofessional consumers.

A number of responses to this crisis are of particular relevance to the study of documentary. With the concept of indexicality, some scholars have returned to the basic technical and phenomenological hinge between documentary representations and their objects, a relationship said to be increasingly unstable and untrustworthy with the advent of digital technologies. (This thinking parallels and in certain ways continues the critique of "liveness" undertaken by scholars of television and video and of virtuality in video gaming and other "interactive" media.) Others have used another concept borrowed from linguistics, the performative, to describe the impulse of some recent works of documentary to point to their own construction and to blend elements of mise-en-scène into the realities they purport to document.[6] Another critical perspective alleges that a number of factors, including sweeping changes in the ownership and consumption of news and entertainment media, have led to a hybrid form of nonfiction, one in which documentary techniques mix freely with effects of comedy, parody, drama, and melodrama.[7] By way of conclusion, I will consider a recent tendency in American documentary akin to these problems of referentiality, a certain preoccupation with issues of action and acting and with the ways in which documentary cinema acts and contains or compels action. The films I discuss in these final pages ask what constitutes political and social action or change now.

Of course, the answer depends in part on what the definition of "now" is. Any serious speculation on the new should both note the emergence of products and ideas and, as Williams suggests, test these manifestations of the cultural present against the official and received narratives of progress and change. The films I am considering here all participate in the cultural perspective called postmodernism and in the "interruption of referentiality" said to afflict both culture and cultural criticism after the Second World War, attributed by many theorists to the massified shocks that state violence caused during and after that conflict.[8] The critical recycling of World War II newsreel and combat footage in *Strange Victory*, Leo Hurwitz's 1948 documentary about the lingering problem of American racism, serves as one very early example of this interruption within documentary practice, and one can find other examples well before documentary theory started looking for the traits of postmodernism. In this respect, the interest of recent films in problems of index and action cannot be called new. At the same time, these films suggest that a more precise historicization than "postmodernity" is necessary when the thesis that images no longer (or never did) index reality is applied to a historical medium, one whose material is actuality.

In reflections published in *Libération* in 1991, at the outset of the Persian Gulf war, Jean Baudrillard suggested that its dependence on various kinds of simulation (theoretical models, "live" television, an enemy created by the United States) made the war impossible to see, despite the proliferation of images that accompanied its buildup and prosecution. Inverting the Clausewitzian axiom that war is politics pursued by other means, this war, Baudrillard argued, would demonstrate *"the absence of politics pursued by other means."*[9] The similarity of this prediction to ones that Baudrillard had been making about the United States for decades underscored the continuity between this particular instance of the fading of politics and its primary agent, the state, and a process that had been underway in the United States since the 1980s, with the decisive abandonment of New Deal principles of government and social welfare. The American welfare state was partly defined by the documentary forms that made it seem necessary. A different documentary ideology accompanies the waning of this political imaginary, and its replacement by one suited to an indefinite war with stateless enemies, conducted after the official "accomplishment" of the state's "mission" and prosecuted through means of dubious legality at secret sites. Within the broad cultural and social outlines of postmodernity, then, a more specific problematic emerges, defined by this spectral form of the state, one that flickers up in shocking images to remind us of the state's last prerogative, what Weber called its monopoly on violence, both physical and symbolic. Eye-opening scenes of both kinds of violence, from the videotapes of police brutality to the macabre images of detainee torture at the Abu Ghraib prison, have found their way into the public domain more or less by accident. The capacity of such images to both excuse acts of violence and to justify the state's sovereign authority over the field in which they occur—among other means, by the announcement of national states of emergency—has confounded the disciplines of moving-image and visual interpretation, which had (as the Society for Cinema Studies nervously admitted in a public statement after the acquittals in the "Rodney King" trial)[10] spent years developing techniques for deconstructing the truth of images. Thus, it is no coincidence that these disciplines have returned to the questions of how images refer to the world, how they perform as evidence of that world, and how they act on the world by referring to it, questions once central to the study of cinema but abandoned in the turn to semiotic and psychoanalytic methods of analysis. From this genealogical perspective, it begins to appear that rather than making documentary obsolete, a particular version of postmodernity is defined by its proliferation. Within this historical and conceptual frame, American political documentary is marked by a variety of aporias that work their way into both form and content of expression.

THE "US" IN QUESTION

Toward the end of *Fahrenheit 9/11* (2004), director and narrator Michael Moore engages in one of the theatrical confrontations with power that established his reputation as a provocateur. On the premise that politicians would not be so eager to support the so-called war on terror on its Middle Eastern front if their own children were in the military, Moore goes to Capitol Hill with a U.S. marine, a stack of enlistment forms, and brochures on different branches of the armed services, hoping to coax congressional representatives into volunteering their children for duty (see figure 6.1). Of course, no representative takes him up on his offer, and Moore is led to pose a series of rhetorical questions over a closing montage of young, smiling American soldiers, movingly and skillfully edited (see figures 6.2–6.4). "Who would want to give up their child? Would you?" Moore asks, and, over an image of George W. Bush and his children, "Would he?" The young men and women shown in the montage expect that they will be sent to war only when it is "absolutely necessary," says Moore. He closes his series with one last question: "Will they ever trust us again?" The montage of official perfidy that follows, in which Bush, Donald Rumsfeld, Condoleezza Rice, and Dick Cheney offer long-discredited justifications for the 2003 invasion of Iraq, implies that the young people depicted in the first

Figures 6.1-6.3. *Fahrenheit 9/11* (Michael Moore, 2004). Still captures from DVD.

Figure 6.4. *Fahrenheit 9/11* (Michael Moore, 2004). Still capture from DVD.

montage would have good reason to be cynical, although the sequence leaves somewhat ambiguous who is identified by "us," the despised state officials, the mass public addressed by Moore, or both. The film's final line plays on this ambiguity in a dialogue that Moore and his editors construct from a piece of footage of the president making one of his iconic public speaking gaffes. On this occasion, Bush mangles the saying "fool me once, shame on you; fool me twice, shame on me," substituting ". . . can't get fooled again," a misremembered Pete Townshend lyric, for the correct ending. "For once," Moore deadpans, "we agreed." Few will miss the sarcasm and irony of this line: by re-presenting and remarking on footage of Bush's embarrassing slip of the tongue, Moore articulates the frustration of all those who disagree with the president but have no platform from which to express it. Underscored by the triumphal sounds of "Rockin' in the Free World," the Neil Young song that kicks in after Moore's last line, a song recorded in 1989 as a protest against the George H. W. Bush administration, the ending of the film suggests that popular frustration can be channeled into the anarchic energies of laughter and resistance.

  This ending leaves no doubt that Moore and the president are on different sides. At the same time, it reminds viewers that "us" and "we" are constructions about which the producers, subjects, and audiences of documentary alike should maintain a vigilant suspicion. Indeed, given the degree to which the film has, by this point, employed techniques of irony and parody, together with Moore's habitual manipulation of historical narrative, the question of "us" can be heard as a reflexive expression of doubt. The distrust Moore attributes to the cheerful young soldiers—or, rather, to the future projected in their images—seems to be directed at all Americans in positions of responsibility and authority, even those critics of power, like liberal documentary filmmakers, who are clearly on the side of the innocent. By concluding in these skeptical and somewhat ambivalent terms, *Fahrenheit 9/11* leaves open the question of whether its own commercial success could be taken to prove that a significant transformation of the cinematic public sphere was taking place.

As I was finishing this book, the trade journal *Variety* announced the end of the commercial boom in feature documentary ushered in by the unprecedented box office revenues of Moore's 2002 film *Bowling For Columbine*, which grossed $21.6 million in domestic ticket sales and $58 million worldwide. The occasion for this announcement was the release of Moore's latest film, *Sicko* (2007); *Variety* wondered whether *Sicko* could revive the flagging theatrical market for nonfiction. Since 2004, the year that *Fahrenheit 9/11* led a cycle of politically themed documentaries into theaters, total domestic box office for documentaries had dropped steadily, from $171 million in 2004 to $116 million the following year, to $55 million in 2006, and only $2 million at the midway point of 2007.[11] (On its opening weekend in wide release, ticket sales for *Sicko* more than doubled the last figure, and after four weeks the film had grossed more than $22 million.) Suggesting that the fortunes of documentary in mainstream theaters in recent years had been a fluke, *Variety* explained the slump of the last eighteen months as a "market correction" and a "return to rationality." The magazine made little attempt to explain the shift in consumption patterns, other than to note that a "fatigue factor" had set in with the movie-going public, owing to the "hard subject matter" of war, suffering, and natural disaster that filmmakers were said to have focused on of late. This explanation overlooked the obvious fact that many of the films of the boom, and those that earned the most money, had been concerned with exactly these themes.

The brief recent window of opportunity for documentary filmmakers in the mainstream was initially seen by many commentators as evidence of a collective embrace of truth, rejection of entertainment, or "hunger for the real" on the part of North American audiences after a series of national debacles: the Clinton impeachment crisis, the election crisis of 2000, the September 11 attacks, the consequent ramping up of national security anxieties, and the increasingly disastrous and unpopular Iraq war.[12] Although the attention of mainstream media outlets was predictably focused on the success of those films that were in wide national release and had the financial backing sufficient to generate national publicity, the more interesting phenomenon was the distribution of documentary themes and dispositions across various levels of the culture, from the capital-intensive preserves of network television and the contemporary art scene to the cottage industries and desktops of nonprofessional filmmaking. Released in the wake of the 9/11 attacks and during the opening of the new American wars in Central Asia and the Middle East, *Bowling For Columbine* and *Fahrenheit 9/11* seemed to initiate a political documentary cycle, a tide of feature-length films concerned directly or indirectly with presidential politics (*Unprecedented: The 2000 Presidential Elections* [Richard Ray Perez and Joan Seckler, 2002], *Bush's Brain* [Joseph Mealey and Michael Shoob, 2004], *Bush Family Fortunes: The Best Democracy Money Can Buy* [Steven Grandison and Greg Palast, 2004], *Going Upriver: The Long War of John Kerry* [George Butler, 2004], and *The Hunting of the President* [Nickolas Perry and Harry Thomason, 2004]); terrorism and national security (*Control Room* [Jehane Noujaim, 2004], *Persons of Interest* [Alison Maclean and Tobias Perse, 2003], *The Power of Nightmares: The Rise of the Politics of Fear* [Adam Curtis, 2004], *Uncovered: The Whole Truth About the Iraq War* [Robert Greenwald, 2004], *WMD: Weapons of Mass Deception* [Danny Schecter, 2004], *Why We Fight* [Eugene Jarecki, 2005]); and the experience of the war in Iraq from the perspective of its planners (*No End in Sight* [Charles Ferguson, 2007]), ordinary soldiers (*Gunner Palace* [Petra Epperlein and Michael Tucker, 2004], *Occupation: Dreamland* [Ian Olds and Garrett Scott, 2005], *The War Tapes* [Deborah Scranton, 2006], *The Ground Truth* [Patricia Foulkrod, 2006]), and civilians (*Iraq in Fragments* [James Longley, 2006], *My Country, My Country* [Laura Poitras, 2006]). These films found audiences in theatrical venues, on the film-festival circuit, on home video, on the Internet, or in art spaces, where the avant-garde was showing renewed interest in documentary strategies.[13] Other filmmakers found support for similar work from cable television networks like HBO and Discovery Times—which produced a documentary miniseries, *Off to War* (Brent Renaud and Craig Renaud, 2005), about the training and deployment of Arkansas national guardsmen— and from the few PBS series that contract with independent producers, such as *Frontline, P.O.V.,* and *Independent Lens.*

Most of these films found ways to suggest, explicitly or implicitly, that traditional news sources had not provided truth about political events, or at least not an effective truth, one on which citizen-viewers could act. This argument was present in the work in ways other than the straightforward statement of it as a premise. In the ABC television miniseries *The Path to 9/11* (2006), the methods of docudrama allowed the producers to suggest that the Clinton administration had failed to act on numerous occasions when it had the chance to eliminate the threat posed to Americans by Muslim terrorists. (The liberties that the series took with its source materials, including the final report of the National Commission on Terrorist Attacks Upon the United States, drew the wrath of former president Clinton himself, who orchestrated a public relations campaign against the broadcast, helping to ensure the series' critical and commercial failure; the network was forced to run the series without advertising, attempting to pass it off as a "public service," and to abandon plans to market it, along with study guides, to schools.)[14] Other films drew heavily on the principles of *cinéma vérité*, including the use of visual or audio-visual evidence of realities too grim or too banal for mainstream news media and the adoption of perspectives more subjective and intimate than commercial journalism could afford and retain its national-public identity. Representative of these tactics were certain films produced by HBO about the second Gulf war, like *Baghdad E.R.* (Jon Alpert and Matthew O'Neill, 2006), or *Ghosts of Abu Ghraib* (Rory Kennedy, 2007), which used *vérité* videography and interviews to expose the ugly physical and psychic consequences of the American military occupation of Iraq (see figure 6.5). Through an intense publicity campaign, the network was able to garner considerable attention for these productions, including an endorsement from the *New York Times* for *Baghdad E.R.*: a columnist called it "required viewing for all but the

Figure 6.5. *Baghdad E.R.* (Jon Alpert and Matthew O'Neill, 2006). Still capture from VHS.

youngest Americans."[15] But the pornographic interest of these films in what ordinary television would not show or speak of—the insides of bodies, the sexual lives and fantasies of soldiers—added little to the available knowledge of the places they visited. Their function could be better understood from their position in the network schedule (the premiere of *Baghdad E.R.*, for instance, led into one of the final episodes of *The Sopranos*) or from their place in the industrial logic of HBO, where they shared production staff with the exploitation documentary series *Real Sex* and *Taxicab Confessions,* than from their sentimental and chauvinistic reduction of the war to its effects on American soldiers, as if they were its only casualties.

More significant alternatives to the mass public sphere were offered by those independent productions that made use of affinity networks created through public-access cable, the Internet, satellite "narrowcast," and other alternatives to broadcast, commercial cable, and theatrical distribution. Notwithstanding the logic of their arguments or the reliability of their sources, which were highly variable, these works could make more legitimate claims than the HBO tagline "It's Not TV" to a position outside the commercial mainstream. Adam Curtis's *The Power of Nightmares: The Rise of the Politics of Fear,* for example, a three-hour-

long telefilm about the historical connections between Muslim funda-
mentalism and American neoconservatism that was rejected for broadcast by HBO and without a commercial distributor in the United States,
was made available to download for free from a number of Web sites,
including Google Video and the Internet Archive. The activist media
organization Deep Dish TV used a network of satellite-dish operators
and public-access cable stations, as well as direct DVD sales and the
Internet Archive, to distribute *Shocking and Awful: A Grassroots Response
to War and Occupation* (2004), an anthology of short works about the
war and Iraqi and American civilian resistance to it. MoveOn.org and
other liberal groups made canny use of house parties to promote and
benefit from screenings of films by Moore and Greenwald, redirecting
the Brownian flows of interest on the Internet into more intimate social forms. A similar constellation grew up around a number of 9/11-
conspiracy films. These films, usually produced in digital video, ven-
tured to explain the state's role in the 9/11 attacks, which they called
an "inside job." The explanations for the attacks offered by films like
Painful Deceptions (Eric Hufschmid, 2003), *Mega Fix: The Dazzling Political Deceit That Led to 9/11* (Jack Cashill, 2004), and *Confronting the
Evidence: A Call to Reopen the 9/11 Investigation* (James Walter, 2005) had
been thoroughly refuted by a variety of experts and professionals in
both official and commercial-public media, but this discouraged neither their makers nor their audiences, since populist epistemology dictated that only such explanations and evidence as had not yet found
their way into centralized information networks could be true. Thus,
expert opinion, whether it was offered under the auspices of the 9/11
Commission or *Popular Mechanics* magazine, was suspect by virtue of
its standing in established institutions and its access to mass-public
means of dissemination. The obsession in the conspiracy community
with proving, using documentary methods, that the U.S. government
was behind the attacks seemed to demonstrate that the decline of
public confidence in reality had been overstated by some documentary
theorists and that the real problem was public confidence in the public itself. Among the more interesting and influential examples of this
mindset was *Loose Change* (Dylan Avery, 2005–2006), a nonprofessional
feature-length documentary by a self-taught filmmaker from rural New
York. Its place in the public sphere of suspicion invoked by Moore at

the end of *Fahrenheit 9/11,* and in relation to the affirmative ideas of publicness outlined in earlier chapters, can be better understood if I describe it as an event within a structure of national feeling, one whose theatrics of community it is occasionally possible to witness in person, as I did on the fifth anniversary of the September 11 attacks.

Wearing black t-shirts that bore phrases like "Investigate 9/11," partisans of the "9/11 Truth" movement assembled at the World Trade Center site on the morning of the fifth anniversary, where a memorial service honoring the victims and their families was being held. Official public ceremonies marking the anniversary, including the reading of victims' names, speeches by state officials, the laying of wreaths, and performances of musical elegies, were taking place in the deep pit referred to as ground zero. At street level around the subterranean block, crowds had gathered to observe the ceremonies, which were broadcast by loudspeakers to the periphery of the site, as well as to more distant publics by electronic means. Some of the marchers handed out paper-jacketed DVDs of *Loose Change,* a ninety-minute film purporting to prove that the U.S. government orchestrated the events of September 11 and then covered its tracks by fabricating evidence that Arab terrorists were the culprits.

On a Web site related to the film, its producers later claimed that nearly ten thousand copies were given out at ground zero on the morning of the memorial ceremony.[16] A number of versions of this wildly popular film were already available for purchase, download, and streaming on the Internet. Although reliable numbers for a film self-distributed in this way are hard to come by, impressive claims have been made about the reach of *Loose Change,* including estimations of some ten million viewings through a variety of Web sites, and sales of more than fifty thousand copies of the DVD.[17] However inflated these numbers might have been, the film and others like it played a role in spreading the 9/11 Truth movement through their unsettling use of familiar images and sounds, their sensational "findings," and the word-of-mouth and hand-to-hand means by which they found many of their viewers. Especially in the last of these tactics, *Loose Change* takes to one extreme the democratic vocation of social documentary film and applies this vocation to a public imagined in equally extremist terms.

Abiding by a selective idealization of popular democracy, one that combines a belief in certain items in the Bill of Rights with an anticorporate interest in decentralized media production and the valorization of common sense over professional and intellectual knowledge, *Loose Change* directs its skepticism against official explanations of events and against the journalistic and scientific establishments. A casual and subjective attitude to public facts is evident from the opening title, which warns viewers that possession of the information in *Loose Change* may be a crime under "Section 802 of the USA PATRIOT act [H.R. 1362]," and punishable by detention "without trial at Guantanamo Bay," even though this section of the act—H.R. 3162, not 1362, which concerns pay equity, not terrorism—merely describes lexical and grammatical changes to the section on terrorism in the United States Code. The film continues in this manner, using desktop-computer production techniques to demonstrate that "eye witnesses, video footage, and a little common sense" can be used to refute the analyses of the National Commission on Terrorist Attacks upon the United States and other investigative agencies (see figures 6.6 and 6.7). Most of *Loose Change*'s claims are built on discredited conspiracy theories, misreadings of images and documents, and coincidences of the type favored by assassination buffs, a hyperactive, stream-of-consciousness approach to history that Richard Hofstadter famously called the "paranoid style."[18] Although the film has been recut a number of times in response to copyright challenges and criticism, the persistence of the most fantastical claims from one version to the next suggests that the filmmakers are as focused on ensuring a wide and expanding audience for their film as on creating reasoned public discourse, notwithstanding the film's closing challenge to its viewers: "Now that this evidence has been presented, what will you do about it? Will you find comfort in the official version of events, or will you go out and investigate for yourselves? Will you share this information, or will you ignore it? Will you be at ground zero on September 11th?"

As is made clear by the rippling American flag that fills the screen during this exhortation, most of these are conventional questions in American political documentary, where an infinitely expansive public address is routinely paired with the critical values of curiosity, contro-

Figures 6.6-6.7. *Loose Change* (Second Edition) (Dylan Avery, 2005–06). Still captures from DVD.

versy, and collectivity in the pursuit of social and political change. By associating the potential circulation and diffusion of their film with its social power as a critique of authority and a call to action, the makers of *Loose Change*—which is not marked with an indication that its makers reserve copyright and begins by exhorting its viewers to duplicate and distribute the video—superimpose the ideal of the public sphere onto new technologies of communication, a relatively conventional idea of how oppositionality is achieved in new media. In *States of Emergency: Documentaries, Wars, Democracies* (2000), one of the few works of documentary theory to take on the problem of documentary publics, Patricia R. Zimmermann contends that commercial-industrial control over the means of cultural production and reception "devastates any democratic public sphere," while emergent media of telecommunication, from the satellite, the Internet, and public-access cable TV to the camcorder, the personal computer, and the cell phone, can be counted on to create "newly imagined public spaces," in which "debate and controversy" are mobilized to oppose the national and international centralization of corporate and state power.[19]

It is tempting to think of *Loose Change,* an essentially homemade film with an international reach, as proof of these claims, until one notices that most of the visual evidence *Loose Change* supplies in support of its arguments is taken from commercial, highly capitalized sources of public information and edited using consumer-grade electronics and software. Nearly every video frame of the work is, in this way, stamped with the subjectivity of consumption. The film's otherwise incongruous title, distinguished from the shrill titles of similar films by its indirection, can be read as a comment on this paradox: loose change, after all, is what's left after you buy something. But the title also marks a different aspect of the film's claim to serve as an alternative to mainstream publicity: its foregrounding of circulation. The medium of a fleetingly ethical encounter with strangers ("spare some change?"), loose change allows us to count ourselves into a public and, at the same time, to evade more significant forms of contact. A potential sociality of this sort is one characteristic of any space of circulation we can properly call a public. This imaginary aspect of the public sphere, one of its strengths as a model of a social organization, is also a source of pressure on its users. A public that does not demonstrate the potential to extend its reach to new members, to strangers, is simply a group. Without the capacity to generalize the concern of the film's audience beyond the activity and the duration of viewing, a documentary film is just another pastime, commodity, or source of unassimilable information.

When *Loose Change* asks its viewers if they will gather at ground zero on September 11, it indicates its makers' doubt and confusion about how publicness inheres in the making and viewing of documentary film. Compared to the millions of viewers it is claimed have seen the film on DVD or online, what would a gathering of several dozen or several hundred in person mean, beyond constituting a topical common space?[20] The announcement of the September 11 assembly expresses the film's anxiety that its methods and questions would not have the sovereign force their makers intended, that of displacing the authority of the state—present in the official ceremonies of memory and in the accompanying display of police and legal power over city space—with the popular power of publicity and publication. Thus, given the makers' manifest faith that new technologies might provide the means to finally discover the true causes and culprits of 9/11, the invitation to gather in full view of one another in a public place was a conflicted and nostalgic gesture. This appeal to the ritual power of an embodied public and to the use of documentary form to galvanize such a public draws on the most venerable traditions of American liberal discourse. But it does so in ways that evince a striking distrust of those traditions and their textual conventions. If it can be taken as proof that the problems I have been tracing persist into the present, Avery's film is also a symptom of doubt and suspicion about that intellectual tradition. That is to say, however limited its authority as a documentary, *Loose Change* documents a contradiction seemingly endemic in American political documentary at present: on the one hand, a reinvestment, on all scales of production, in the democratic and artistic potential of documentary forms and, on the other hand, the profound difficulty of imagining the effect of these forms, beyond the time and space in which they occur.

APORIAS IN ACTION

The foreshortening of the social horizon of documentary replays a theme heard for some time in social thought, the idea that the postmodern present is a period of collective confusion about how to act. Examples include Fredric Jameson's contention that postmodern culture expresses "the failure of the new, the imprisonment in the past," Jean-François Lyotard's characterization of the present as "a period of slackening," and Jürgen Habermas's announcement of a "new obscurity," a development "outlined on the threshold of the twenty-first century" in which citizens in Western societies begin to doubt their "readiness to take action" on modern problems as a result of a "worldwide threat to universal life interests."[21] Such dire predictions did not cease with the end of the superpower conflict (which, as Francis Fukuyama infamously claimed, meant the end of history). Baudrillard echoes them in his many variations on the idea that "the passage to action" today "suffers widespread infamy" because a "deterrence of the real by the virtual . . . governs all our behavior."[22] Baudrillard's paradigms of simulation and hyperreality have served documentary theorists as a critical shorthand for a decisive historical shift from a documentary practice based on the difference between true and false, anchored by the indexical capacities of such technologies as photography, audiotape, and film, to a practice that blurs the boundaries by engaging in more or less overt fabrications of past and present realities.[23] For Linda Williams, the regime of simulation provides the impetus to theorize "a newer, more contingent, relative, postmodern truth." If this development requires filmmakers and viewers alike to rethink their commitment to a singular conception of truth, it hardly threatens the vitality of social documentary. Writing in the midst of an earlier revival of popular and critical interest in documentary, Williams asserts that this postmodern truth—exemplified by Errol Morris's film *The Thin Blue Line* (1988)—"still operates powerfully as the receding horizon of the documentary tradition."[24] Morris's film was effective in changing history, Williams argues, despite constantly making clear that we experience the world through images made of it for our distraction. *The Thin Blue Line* demonstrated, as Williams puts it, that actions completed in the past can be acted upon only by their "reactivat[ion] . . . in images of the present."[25]

Precisely the opposite argument is made for documentary by Philip Rosen, who takes Baudrillard's ideas about indexical media, mass circulation, and the function of the masses for critical intellectuals as a direct challenge to the very concept of documentary, since documentary depends for its epistemological authority and political force on distinctions between thing and sign, subject and object, event and representation—distinctions that are suspended under the regime of simulation. Noting Baudrillard's use of examples from documentary film and television to make this argument, Rosen accuses Baudrillard of a narrow and ahistorical understanding of documentary. Baudrillard's remarks about the *cinéma vérité* television series *An American Family* (Craig Gilbert, 1973) appear to Rosen as another idealist variation on the leftist thesis of popular realism as mass deception, one that gives too little credit to the historiographic complexity of all documentary and places too much faith in the idea of a pure break between referential and postmodern representation. Like Williams, Rosen is bothered by the discrepancy between this view and the evidence, available to anyone who turns on a television or scans the movie listings, of a profusion of documentary forms and indexical images in contemporary media culture, a phenomenon that indicates to both theorists the persistence of the documentary tradition, even though the means of documenting reality may have undergone radical transformation.

But given his conclusion that documentary has retained its value not just as an example of the gullibility of viewers but as a discourse on the role of historiography and its professional intellectuals in the exercise of power, it is interesting that Rosen does not remark on the temporality of Baudrillard's frequent repetition of the simulation theme in a variety of published works, nor on the significance of the necessity of repeating it. As concerned as Rosen is to refute the postmodern thesis that the tenses of history have collapsed and to prove that sequence still matters, he does not seem as concerned as one might expect with the punctuality of Baudrillard's utterances on the problem of referentiality and their relation to their moment. The apparent futility of these utterances—"a stupid gamble," as Baudrillard himself admits at the end of "The Gulf War Will Not Take Place"[26]—can itself be taken as the sign of a problem in the intellectual public sphere that cultural critics like Baudrillard share with the filmmakers and critics this book has covered. Baudrillard has on a number of occasions used documentary as the touchstone of these problems—and not documentary in general but the specific historical form known as *cinéma vérité*, by which he seems to mean the American and not the French version of this style— for instance, in the extended riff on *An American Family* that appears in *Simulations*.[27] In his comments on the Gulf War, Baudrillard compares the impossibility of its representation to the "aporia" of *cinéma vérité*. The latter, according to Baudrillard, seeks to "short-circuit the unreality of the image in order to present us with the truth of the object."[28] These repeated appearances of documentary as a metaphor for a generalized social crisis suggest a different kind of periodization. Perhaps it is not that postmodernity threatens the integrity of documentary per se, but the other way around. By engaging with particular events and conditions, documentary filmmaking provides terms for making sense of the social and epistemological crises named by postmodernity.

The films of Errol Morris have served as touchstones of an aporetic style of truth in documentary, a truth built on the rhetoric of doubt rather than the rhetoric of certainty. Morris's borrowings from narrative fiction are the usual focus of this argument, but his practice of the interview performs its own unique folding of these problems into the form of documentary. In *The Fog of War: Eleven Lessons from the Life of Robert McNamara* (2003), Morris's use of a device he calls the "Interrotron," a kind of two-way mirror that allows the interviewee to see Morris's face as he looks into the camera, establishes a metaphor of ethics within the space of production. The effect of this device is to produce the appearance of a direct confrontation between the interlocutors and, consequently, a more palpable sense of the reversibility of two positions—Morris's and his subject's; the subject's and the viewer's—than is usually possible in the documentary interview. Morris's name for the device splices interrogation to terror, and it is no coincidence that two of the films in which he employs the Interrotron pursue the question of how the law, the state, reason, and humankind confront their other. Morris's point is that the terms whose opposition defines Western civilization are closer together than we know or are prepared to admit.

Morris draws out McNamara on the ethics of war, and although he does not exactly extract the confession or apology that many viewers had hoped to hear from the architect of U.S. military policy in Vietnam, the conversation frequently comes around to the topic of empathy, which McNamara claims to regard as the highest principle of statecraft, citing a lesson learned from Khrushchev during the Cuban missile crisis. At one point, while discussing the American firebombing of Japanese cities during World War II, McNamara is brought to the point of tears—not, as we might expect, from the thought of hundreds of thousands of Japanese civilian deaths but instead from the memory of a discussion between American commanders about a single American flyer killed in the firebombing campaign. McNamara's voice cracks as he recalls Major General Curtis LeMay, a legendarily brutal man, tell-

Figure 6.8. *The Fog of War: Eleven Lessons from the Life of Robert S. McNamara* (Errol Morris, 2003). Still capture from DVD.

ing the dead soldier's commanding officer that "it hurts me as much as it does you." The lesson of the exchange can easily be reduced to the importance of putting oneself in another's shoes; this point would seem to be underscored by the theatrics of the recollection, with McNamara speaking LeMay's words while looking and gesturing directly at his interlocutor and, through him, into the eyes of viewers (see figure 6.8). LeMay's reaction could be a parable of individual moral responsibility, were it not for the last line of the story, LeMay's reported retort to the commanding officer: "You lost one wingman, and we destroyed Tokyo." This blunt statement of moral economy underscores the doubt that runs throughout the film, and a number of Morris's films, about American moral exceptionalism as a justification for war and other forms of state violence, a doubt which is amplified by the audio-visual machinery necessary for the staging of reciprocity—one guise of ethics—in the interview. This dichotomizing moral logic of self and other ties the documentary to other liberal institutions and, indeed, to the idea of national interest that governs the American conception of geopolitics today.[29] One might in fact read the self-congratulatory scenario of *The Fog of War*—two reasonable men solving national problems of justice and history face-to-face—as a sign of ambivalence about the literal responsibility of power.

An auteurist approach would note the continuous braiding of historiography and ethics in Morris's work and the development of his directorial style as they can be observed in the performances of history in the present in front of the camera that have become one of his signatures. But if one thinks of a career itself as a kind of performance, the exemplary auteur of American political documentary is not Morris, but Jill Godmilow, a filmmaker whose career spans and tracks monumental political changes, a New Left counterpart to Leo Hurwitz. Godmilow's first feature documentary, *Antonia: A Portrait of the Woman* (1974), codirected with the singer Judy Collins, was a biography of the first female conductor of a major orchestra and a landmark of feminist documentary, showing the filmmakers at ease and at home with their subject in intimate conversation about the trials of life and art in a male-dominated world. A decade later, Godmilow abruptly discarded the style and philosophy of *Antonia* and her other artist-portraits in *Far From Poland* (1984), a film ostensibly about the Solidarity movement in Poland.[30] After failing to secure visas to travel to Poland, Godmilow decides to make the film anyway, substituting sets in New York City for authentic locations, reenactments and blurry television coverage of the shipyard strikes for *vérité* footage, and bits of personal correspondence, diaries, and dreams for eyewitness testimony or first-person interviews. Although viewers can still glean some understanding of the complexities of the Solidarity movement and of late–Cold War realpolitik from the film, *Far From Poland* is more concerned with political affect and international structures of feeling than with any sense of politics recognizable to makers of American leftist documentary of the time.

Godmilow's 1998 film *What Farocki Taught* takes the irony of *Far From Poland* to a deadpan extreme. A shot-for-shot Kodachrome remake of German filmmaker Harun Farocki's black-and-white *Inextinguishable Fire* (1969), a short Brechtian dramatization of the process by which napalm was produced for the U.S. military by Dow Chemical, *What Farocki Taught* restages the earlier film's didactic lesson about the military-industrial complex (see figures 6.9 and 6.10). Presenting the earlier film as a lesson to documentary filmmakers, Godmilow also revives the earlier film's critique of indexicality and of *cinéma vérité*. Both films occupy the aporetic space identified by Baudrillard, and in slightly different ways. Each presents the viewer with images that are patent fab-

Figure 6.9. *Inextinguishable Fire* (Harun Farocki, 1969), as reproduced in *What Farocki Taught* (Jill Godmilow, 1997). Still capture from DVD.

Figure 6.10. *What Farocki Taught* (Jill Godmilow, 1997). Still capture from DVD.

rications, beginning with Farocki's address to the camera at the beginning of *Inextinguishable Fire,* where he disclaims the power of indexical images of violence as an effective means of critique and then burns himself with a lit cigarette to demonstrate his argument. Germans speaking German play Americans in Farocki's film; redoubling this effect of estrangement, Godmilow's film features Americans speaking English in 1996, playing Germans of 1969 playing Americans. The later film can thus be regarded not only as a rejection of the documentary faith in the revelatory powers of the camera—which can already be said of *Inextinguishable Fire*—but as the demonstration of an utter refusal, or incapacity, to comment on images or to say anything.

One might observe that Godmilow's film was produced midway between the first and second U.S.-Iraq wars, if such a measurement did not deny that war was conducted continuously throughout this period by other means, including a decade of surveillance flights and bombing runs over Iraq by the United States and its coalition partners and a disastrous U.N. program of economic sanctions that had the effect of enhancing Saddam Hussein's dictatorial power while contributing to the deaths of hundreds of thousands of civilians in that period.[31] This structure of disavowal is displayed on the very surface of the film, which is haunted by the irregular appearance of ghost images from Farocki's film, superimposed off-center from Godmilow's own (see figures 6.11 and 6.12). Godmilow apparently regarded her film as part of an ongoing investigation of the personal and national significance of the Vietnam war and as a way to pay tribute to Farocki's work, which was not as well known outside of Europe as that of some of his compatriots in the New German Cinema. In an interview conducted shortly after the film's completion, Godmilow speaks at length about both issues without once mentioning the more recent war. In the same joint interview, Farocki admits that it took him decades to realize that his film doesn't mention Auschwitz, despite the obvious similarities between the Nazi death factories and the American production of the atomic bomb and napalm; "my omission," he says, "made me think that the terrible war the United States waged in Vietnam not only horrified the Germans, but unburdened them as well."[32] In this respect, the film operates less as a self-expressive act—despite its mode of production and its coda, where Godmilow appears as herself to explain her reasons for making

Figures 6.11-6.12. *What Farocki Taught* (Jill Godmilow, 1997). Still captures from DVD.

the film—than an unconscious one. If it recalls political and cinematic history, it does so in a way that testifies to the repressed character of these pasts and also to the repressive character of their memory. A repetition rather than a working-through, the remake has the effect of depriving the filmmaker of the elements of cultural capital most valuable to independent and avant-garde filmmakers: the uniqueness of the artist's signature, and the originality of the work. One might also say that it appears a therapeutic act, since it relieves the filmmaker of this obligation to make new work and to have new ideas.

The term "self-reflexive" is often applied, with approval, to filmmaking so conscious of its materials and expressive means. The art and analysis of so-called postmodern documentary have tended to privilege gestures of skepticism about the idea of a documentary tradition and about the concepts of referentiality and truth upon which every previous step in this tradition is said to depend. The postmodern critical maxims about communication—that transparency is an ideological effect; that nothing is real besides the material of representation—have not quashed entirely the documentary impulse, but they have encouraged, among many filmmakers sensitive to "theory," a retreat into the parochial interiority of the self and the work, in pursuit of a less incorrect (rather than more true) image. Although it participates in this withdrawal, Godmilow's act of remaking can also be seen as the rejection of the state of self-consciousness and the positive value accorded to individuality in the rarified cultural atmosphere where films like What Farocki Taught are produced and circulated: film festivals, art cinemas, galleries, and universities. The film's value lies instead in its stubborn assertion that intelligence does not prevent wars and, moreover, tends nowadays to be their excuse, even when it is false. Thus, the film's most oppositional gestures are not its declared opposition to war, imperialism, or the multinational corporation—for who in its self-selecting audience would support these things?—but its replacement of cleverness and invention, and the independent moral agent these virtues imply, with what Godmilow calls its "obscene gesture of replication."[33] The critical force of this gesture lies in its exposure and display of confusion: the willful confusion of self and other that rationalizes American interventionism and the unwitting confusion about where, exactly, war takes place.[34]

Rather than replacing the false images of the other with true or correct ones of Vietnamese suffering or resistance, as did so many political documentaries of the period, Farocki's film offers another false image, one that makes alterity into a Western quality, estranging his German actors from their bodies and their lines and from the Americans they play. By replicating Farocki's pantomime of American intelligence, Godmilow expands upon this play of blindness and insight, repatriating an image of Americans as seen by others, an image that is thus doubly uncanny. Now Farocki's film signifies a blindness in the present—imperial state violence disguised as scientific progress—and a blindness embedded in history: the ghost images of Farocki's film stand for the systemic oversight by which, according to Godmilow, American activists and filmmakers were deprived for a quarter-century of *Inextinguishable Fire* and its lessons for politics and for craft. As a gesture of homage, Godmilow's film is a deeply conflicted one, since it suggests that ignorance of the existence of a work of avant-garde cinema is comparable to the mass deception that blinded Americans to the role of corporations in the deaths of millions—an audacious suggestion, not least because it implies that there might be no position in culture, or in consciousness, to which the artist could retreat from the history of violence.

Its focus on its own materiality allows us to say that *What Farocki Taught* is both reflexive and deconstructive. Despite evidence to the contrary, I hesitate to call it a *self*-reflexive film, since it labors to show, by its own example, that a film is ultimately made by events and conditions beyond the control of individuals, including histories of which we are unconscious.[35] The film fits the conundrum of documentary postmodernism offered by Michael Renov—"provocative in its refusal of individualist truth, profoundly moral in its call for, and reliance on, individual moral responsibility"[36]—since what Godmilow's film models is the radical suspension of such protocols as originality, self-expression, and the other measures of individuation by which a subject is distinguished from its others. It is perhaps missing the point to ask what the filmmaker is trying to say with this gesture. I take the film's coda, where Godmilow anticipates and answers this question on screen and in the first-person, to be yet another gesture of negation or parody, in the spirit of David Harris's half-hearted psycho-biographical alibi for his crimes near the end of *The Thin Blue Line,* an utterance that the filmmaker includes because it is conventional and expected, only to demonstrate its poverty as an explanation. Along these lines, the use of reenactment in *What Farocki Taught* exemplifies a significant new tactic of American political documentary, one that could be termed *speaking indirectly*, in deference to Jon Jost's great documentary experiment on the geopolitical conditions of the American speech act, *Speaking Directly* (1973).

SPEAKING INDIRECTLY: COUNTERPERFORMATIVITY

Like indexicality, another concept borrowed from the philosophy of language, the idea of performativity has had significant appeal for theorists seeking to describe the limits of documentary under present cultural conditions. While the term "performance" can be applied to various aspects and kinds of documentary cinema, the notion of the performative documentary draws specifically on the linguistic concept of the performative speech act, a kind of utterance that does what it says and does so by marking its constitutive relation to the audience to whom the act of speech is addressed. To speaker and addressee, the speech act can function as a commitment or guarantee. This genre of utterance includes pronouncements like "let there be light," "I now pronounce you husband and wife," and "I sentence you to death," as well as the more quotidian "I bet you . . ." or "I promise that . . ." or "I apologize." Unlike the cinematic function of indexicality, which is said to have been continuous with the documentary tradition and to originate with the mechanical apparatuses of photography and cinema themselves, the performative would appear to be an emergent mode of documentary, and some theorists have claimed that the appearance of the performative mode demands a rethinking of established categories and systems of analysis.[37]

Where the concept of indexicality has been used to theorize the threats posed to documentary signification by the technology of new media, performativity has been applied to a different aspect of the capacity for reference and representation. Uniting the paradigm of simulation and the poststructural sensitivity to embodied and particular practices of knowledge, the analytic of performativity focuses on the rhetoric of documentary truth claims. Documentaries in this mode not only place their own textual and formal constructions front and center but, moreover, emphasize the appeal of these constructions to the viewer or viewers for whom the film's statements are meaningful and true. Performativity, according to Bill Nichols, makes the viewer, and not the historical world, the primary referent of its utterances.[38] Although many reflexive works of documentary, especially those made in the first-person, seem conscious that they are addressing their viewers, performativity is most apt when applied to those examples that indicate that documentary truth is particular to its medium and also that, in "speaking" this truth, it effects a certain discourse community, one that may or may not include every member of a viewing public, depending on their ability to identify with the voice in which the film's perspective is declaimed. For this reason, the performative mode has been associated with identity politics; Marlon Riggs's innovative film about homosexuality and black masculinity, *Tongues Untied* (1989) is one prominent example. The controversy attending public presentations of Riggs's film attests to this rhetorical particularity, especially when its reception is compared to the mainstream success of Jennie Livingston's *Paris Is Burning* (1991), a relatively conventional film about New York drag queens that has become a standard example of the performative documentary.[39]

It is less important, I think, to test or contest these various definitions of the performative than to wonder at the appeal of this abstract concept for documentary theory. Even Nichols, a theorist who did much to give the term credibility for documentary studies, has warned that in "the absence of a specifically political frame within which performative documentary might be received," its practice "will collapse back into the solipsistic terms of a privatized consciousness."[40] In a moment when torture—which poses a question that cannot be answered, a question designed to result in punishment—can be officially justified as a legitimate practice of state intelligence, the timing of this return to an idea of direct and responsible speech is, to say the least, interesting. (*Shut Up and Sing*, Barbara Kopple and Cecilia Peck's 2006 film about the life of an irreverent remark about president Bush made by the lead singer of the Dixie Chicks during a performance is, at one level, a study of this situation and the consequences of speech and inflection in a thoroughly unironic moment of the public sphere of politics. The band discovers what Roland Barthes said every intellectual speaking in public discovers: that because "all speech is on the side of the Law," no accident of speech can be undone, and that clarity is valued above all else.)[41] But questions about the politics of the performative are not limited to the sphere of academic criticism. There is ample evidence of them in documentary work today, from the work of the best-known auteurs to the relative obscurity of the avant-garde. Besides a shared critical interest in the discourses of insecurity and crisis that have come to define national political life since the September 11 attacks, these two kinds of work may not have much in common. Nonetheless, one can discern in both a subtle but concerted aesthetic strategy of resistance to official and quasi-official public spheres of social knowledge, to the state-corporate manufacture of reality, and to the formal acts of performative political speech that Deleuze and Guattari termed the order-word of power and that became a signature of the Bush-Cheney administration: false or betrayed promises, empty threats, lies under oath, sentences without end.[42] These films practice a version of the political unconscious inscribed by *What Farocki Taught* in its superimpositions, repetitions, and reenactments. They document the spaces on which the state has left its imprint through order-words, whether by the announcement of an initiative, a target, or a crisis, or conversely by remaining silent in situations where such a declaration would serve the public interest.

An effective demonstration of this counterperformative approach appears in the final act of *Sicko,* where Moore accompanies an ailing group of 9/11 rescue workers to Cuba to provide them with the medical care they could not find at home. Taking his familiar practice of street theater to the high seas, Moore literally calls out the state by megaphone, asking permission to enter the Guantánamo Bay Naval base and gain for his pathetic charges the same level of care that "Al Qaeda is getting," but eliciting only silence from a guard tower.[43] Since their own government has failed the rescuers, Moore acts instead, getting them the medical and pharmaceutical help that has eluded them in the United States. Physically rebuilt by an enemy state, the rescuers return to the United States mainland, one might say, as counteragents, firsthand witnesses to the good that can be done in a social system condemned by their own government. Taking action in the face of state and corporate intransigence is a convention of Michael Moore's films, and of activist documentary in general. But the more impressive action Moore takes here is the ideological one, acting on the symbol of the 9/11 victims and heroes in whose image and name the state's punitive actions at Guantánamo Bay and elsewhere have been justified as revenge.

Moore was joined on this new documentary front by artists at the other end of the spectrum of capitalization and accessibility, including a number of works by artists whose training, constituency, and support comes mainly from the bicoastal art worlds and the academy. The documentary work of Julia Meltzer and David Thorne (who release their films as The Speculative Archive), for instance, is devoted to a similar critique of state speech and official knowledge. The pair's first film, *It's Not My Memory of It: Three Recollected Documents* (2003) is a study of antiepistemology in American intelligence agencies.[44] The film focuses on three instances of fabricated intelligence, grounding evidentiary effects of image and sound recording in problems of bureaucracy, citizenship, and national identity. In *We Will Live to See These Things, Or, Five Pictures of What May Come to Pass* (2007), the pair reverse the angle of vision of their first film, turning from the false pasts Americans construct for others to those others' national self-projection (see figure 6.13). In five quite distinct parts, *We Will Live to See These Things* documents the feelings of anticipation and anxiety that define everyday life in Syria, a society caught, according to the different voices on the film's soundtrack and screen, between a variety of futures, some governed by cultural tradition, some by histories of geopolitical antagonism, and some by the hope of intellectual and political freedom. Meltzer and Thorne have maintained that their films are documentaries, not "experimental" or "mock" documentaries, but metadocumentary might be an appropriate description, since along with the grain of contemporary history, they also document the ideological premises and political practices that make experience visible or invisible as intelligence. In this sense, their films are works of what Michel Foucault referred to as archaeology, since their object is less what happens before the camera than the very claim that things can be said to have happened and the hegemonic power that makes such claims effective.[45]

Construction according to my plans never begins.

Figure 6.13. *We Will Live to See These Things, Or, Five Pictures of What May Come to Pass* (The Speculative Archive, 2007). Still capture from DVD.

The state's power to judge when an act or event has taken place is the focus of a number of other recent works, each of which take documentary as a format for testing and challenging historical and legal judgment. In his short found-footage film *National Archive V.1* (2001), made while he was a graduate student at California Institute of the Arts, Travis Wilkerson traces this specter of the state from the gun sights of fighter jets in the skies over Vietnam into the repositories of national history. Working with military footage he discovered in the National Archives, where it had rested apparently unseen since being deposited, Wilkerson limits his intervention to reprinting, trimming, and compiling shots, reproducing the minimally descriptive titles that appear in the National Archives database ("Target: Landing Zone"; "Target: Fortified Village"; "Target: VC in trees"; "Target: Water Buffalo") and adding an equally minimal sound track, the steady throb of an acoustic guitar that is eventually replaced by a high-pitched metallic whine. Although political uses of found footage have many American precedents, the functional qualities of the material have usually been set off in such

Figure 6.14. *National Archive V.1* (Travis Wilkerson, 2001). Still capture from VHS.

films by broadly ironic montage or satirical commentary (*The Atomic Café* [Jayne Loader, Kevin Rafferty, Pierce Rafferty, 1982]; *Tribulation 99: Alien Anomalies Under America* [Craig Baldwin, 1991]). And unlike Bruce Conner's *Crossroads* (1976), a film made entirely from footage of the 1946 Bikini Atoll nuclear test found in the National Archives and set to a Terry Riley score, *National Archive V.1* has relatively little aesthetic appeal. By contrast with the sublime mushroom clouds in *Crossroads*, the indistinct images of the Vietnamese countryside, faintly impressed with a jiggling target ring, allow the viewer little distance from their apparently indexical purpose (see figure 6.14). What function can these banal images of violence have had for their original makers and audiences? To prove? To justify? To exculpate? By withholding or simply failing to know the answers to these questions, Wilkerson's film allows them to be posed. In doing so, it opens a space between the "doing" of performative speech that haunts these images and the inert historical "being" of their status as footage or artifact.[46]

The enemy of the state appears in another guise in Paul Chan's *Untitled Video on Lynne Stewart and Her Conviction, the Law, and Poetry* (2006), a fragmentary portrait of the radical human-rights lawyer Lynne Stewart. Chan filmed Stewart while she was awaiting sentencing for the crime of providing material aid to terrorism, which the federal government claimed she had done by transmitting messages from her imprisoned client, Sheikh Omar Abdel Rahman, to Egyptian supporters. *Lynne Stewart* continued Chan's work in a variety of media on the theme of national security, including the video documentaries *Baghdad in No Particular Order* (2003), and *Now Promise Now Threat* (2005). The unlikely pairing of Chan, an avowed postmodernist, and Stewart, who was willing to be jailed for her belief in the Constitution, the least ironic position one can imagine, embodied the principle of the documentary front. The combination of low-production-value documentary techniques with fury and humor in equal measure suggested connections with Moore's work (whose "experimental" qualities Chan extols in a published conversation with Martha Rosler) and with the legacies of the radical American newsreel tradition.[47] In the spirit of the filmic pamphleteering practiced by the Film and Photo League and The Newsreel, Chan's seventeen-minute video presents Stewart with the opportunity to share her views on the three topics listed in the title and to read selections from her favorite political poems. Like the Robert McNamara who appears in *The Fog of War,* Stewart shows herself to be a well-rounded intellectual, an expert in her professional field, and equally knowledgeable about other areas of thought. But her good humor in the face of a long prison sentence projects a very different style of intellectual publicness than the image projected by McNamara. Compared to *The Fog of War,* which allows both Morris and McNamara to display their mastery of a wealth of material, technology, and manpower, *Lynne Stewart* is a work of humility and empathy. Its violations of the basic codes of documentary legibility—soft focus, awkward framing, separating a talking head image from its sound, oversaturating the image with color—can be read in two divergent ways: as the ludic suspension of discipline within a discourse of sobriety, equivalent to Stewart's own tendency to read poetry to juries; and as an index of its subject's state of anticipation or anxiety, awaiting judgment (see figure 6.15).

The difficulty of resolving this contradiction in Chan's work is a mark of its commitment to what Judith Butler has called the precariousness of the other in a new imperial era. Derived from Emmanuel Levinas and retooled to address a climate of xenophobia and national aggression, this ethics assumes the primacy of the other and of its dis-

Figure 6.15. *Untitled Video on Lynne Stewart and Her Conviction, the Law, and Poetry* (Paul Chan, 2006). Still capture from DVD.

concerting demand on us: "what is morally binding," writes Butler, "does not proceed from my autonomy or from my reflexivity. It comes to me from elsewhere, unbidden, unexpected, and unplanned."[48] Where Baudrillard maintains that the primary violence of postmodern war is its effacement of the other ("Americans can only imagine and combat an enemy in their own image"), Butler suggests that aggression is extended, or justified, by the liberal reduction of this other to an evidentiary image of suffering and pain, an image that confirms our moral primacy and agency.[49] What is called for instead is a representation that *fails* to capture what is simply human about the other: not its universal humanity, its likeness to our image, but its particularity, its radical alterity. This quality is something unrepresentable, Butler writes, "that we nevertheless seek to represent."[50]

To maintain a commitment to the documentary impulse under these paradoxical conditions of representation would test the continuity of the American documentary tradition in a serious way. Making visible the invisible elements of American society, it should be recalled, was one of the ways that Walter Lippmann described the role of the paragovernmental intelligence workers he considered crucial to the operations of the state. Lippmann's example was the positive effect that intellectuals studying child welfare had had on infant mortality rates: "statistics," Lippmann concluded, had given this unrepresented element of the population an image, making them "as visible as if the babies had elected an alderman to air their grievances."[51] In its earliest liberal-democratic incarnations, social documentary aimed to integrate individuals into the state through a parallel process of illumination, educating them about the obscure realms of government in which positive changes to their society would be effected. The Gramscian inversion that quickly arose asserted the sovereign authority of collective society against that of the state, contesting the legitimacy and direction of the civilizing process with images of another reality, drawn from popular experience. Both approaches to documentary mediation presumed the positive qualities of the social images they formed—their capacity to index or reference something real but invisible about collective experience—and the capacity of such images to effect something not yet real: belief in the state, on the one hand, or popular hegemony, on the other.

By performing aporias, the kinds of films I have considered in this final chapter remain committed to the idea of documentary while seeking alternatives to the conflict between its "official" and "practical" faculties of social intelligence and illumination. In place of the certain and positive character of scientific, historical, and political statements, this documentary form poses Marx's imperative as a disarming question: Must they be represented? Since these films tend not to state their motives directly (but only speak, as Trinh T. Minh-ha says in *Reassemblage* [1983], "nearby" their topic), it is by juxtaposition with the conventions of documentary representation that this question is posed. Their emphasis on the aesthetic aspect of representation, on formal experimentation, makes it harder to understand just what such works mean to say. To the extent that this commitment to form reduces their transparency and their circulation, one can see their avant-gardism as a rejection of the protocols of communication and mass mediation. But one can say at the same time that this emphasis on film style is also the expression of an intense commitment to the particular occurrence of a given social or political principle, the attempt to create a form most appropriate to the specific instance or subject of a problem.

Among the most poignant recent articulations of this method is Liza Johnson's lyrical documentary *South of Ten* (2006), one of many documentaries made in the aftermath of Hurricane Katrina, but one of the few to look beyond the devastation of New Orleans. Eschewing the forensic and traumatic aesthetics that are conventional in coverage of disaster, *South of Ten,* which uses ruins as its setting but never makes direct reference to the storm, manages to be at once literal and allusive. In this way, the film presents in its form the documentary principle of allegory that I have argued for as a principle of interpretation throughout this book.

Johnson and cinematographer Anne Etheridge returned to the Mississippi Gulf Coast region where both had, several months earlier, volunteered in relief efforts to stage and film a series of small gestures with survivors of the storm, still living in temporary housing amid the ruins. "Ten" thus refers to the area in which the film was shot, the area south of Interstate 10; it refers as well to the ten vignettes that compose the film, and to its ten-minute length. These structural correspondences between subject and form promise a performative film, one that says what it is and does what it says, a conclusion that would be supported by the simple story of the film's genesis: like many, the filmmakers were moved by the pictures and voices that television presented of the storm's effects and by their government's empty promises and inaction, and they decided to act on their own. But the film that Johnson and Etheridge create is quite different from this pragmatic media citizenship. Instead, Johnson directs her "cast" in a series of curious, inconclusive gestures whose conglomeration makes it difficult to call them actions: finding a trombone, lifting a house, playing, waiting (see figures 6.16 and 6.17). The intrigue of these enigmatic performances is enhanced by the performers' mute but not silent activity and by Etheridge's Super16mm color cinematography and the film's sound and editing, which give the brief scenes the look and feel of a fiction film. Some of the people Johnson filmed had already appeared on television, telling their sad stories to reporters; their casting and wordless performances in *South of Ten* thus relieve them of the burden of pa-

Figures 6.16-6.17. *South of Ten* (Liza Johnson, 2006). Still captures from DVD.

thetic self-representation and permit them a moment of self-fashioning
and reinvention.

Unlike Spike Lee's treatment of the natural and political disaster of
Hurricane Katrina in his epic HBO documentary *When the Levees Broke:
A Requiem in Four Acts* (2007), which focuses on New Orleans, *South of
Ten* offers no explanations and makes no explicit charges or demands.
Like Johnson's film, Lee's is indebted in certain ways to television, al-
though the medium's influence on *Levees* is explicit rather than im-
plicit. That government officials learned about the scale of the disaster
from television reports, rather from firsthand observation, is damning

evidence of their contempt and incompetence. And considerable use is made by Lee and his editors of television news coverage of the storm and its aftermath, footage that testifies not only to the awesome power of the storm but also the media power accessed by Lee himself. (Or, if one prefers, to the industrial synergy that gave Lee priceless access, through HBO and its corporate parent, TimeWarner, to the archival resources of CNN, another TimeWarner company.) More to the point, *Levees* abides by a televisual logic of justice: sharply delineated claims and counterclaims, articulated in close-up by charismatic, unselfconscious individuals who range from poor and middle-class private citizens to famous actors, esteemed intellectuals, and high public officials. These grand testimonial performances are made more dramatic by their orientation to the mysteries of the past and the goal of recrimination: Why did the levees fail? What should have been done? Who was responsible? These are, undoubtedly, important and necessary questions. Set against the national and international stages of politics in which the state acts by asserting a forceful presence, as when it prosecutes justice or war, the interest of contemporary documentary practice and theory in performativity has helped us see that questions of this sort are made all the more urgent by the state's absence from the social field, by the disorder left in its wake. But by virtue of its focus on victims whose suffering had already risen to the level of an event, whose suffering had already been made visible and legible by the dominant networks of publicity, *Levees*'s "alternative interpretation" confirms the authority of these quasi-official accounts, reducing the history of the event to a conventional struggle between the state and the people. It cannot ask the fundamental questions *South of Ten* poses in its mise-en-scène alone: What are the conditions of representation of the other whose relation to me is not known in advance? What is the meaning of an action committed on film? And what constitutes an act?

By design, the political effect of *South of Ten* and films like it is, in the ordinary sense of politics, limited. Their circulation is restricted to a nontheatrical domain of festivals, museums, and classrooms. And their preoccupation with form raises what Nichols calls "questions of magnitude" of their "social subjectivity and historical engagement" and their role in "political organization and process."[52] Of course, magnitude is not simply a measure of the numbers of viewers a film can draw or con-

vert to its cause, but nor is it only enacted or performed by films themselves, as a matter of their subjectivity and their aesthetics. Rather, it is a
measure of their capacity to generate a public sphere, or what Raymond
Williams simply called "thinking," which is always an experimental action. By focusing viewers' attention on the "tension," as Nichols puts it,
"between representation and represented," such films can exert pressure on the audio-vision of mass politics, the styles of mass political
discourse that depend upon direct and transparent sounds and images
of the real.[53] This counterpressure comes not only from the overt negation of ordinary, received, or commonsense sounds and images of the
present or the past but also from the sheer enjoyment of practice—in
the sense of a rehearsal, an act of preparation, an incomplete process
or routine—that such works display. They give form to structures of
feeling, those experimental forms of the social that are not, or not yet,
expressible as fact. This practice of underrepresentation keeps alive the
critical tension between social artifact and social imaginary, the very
dynamic indicated by the "-ary" in "documentary." They remind us of
the insecurity that this formation inscribes in the site and moment of
its origin, and they maintain the ambivalence of this ending.

INTRODUCTION: THE INTELLIGENCE WORK OF DOCUMENTARY

1. Paul Rotha, *Documentary Film* (1935; Boston: American Photographic Publishing Co., 1936), pp. 131–33.

2. Charles Taylor, *Modern Social Imaginaries* (Durham, N.C.: Duke University Press, 2004), p. 23.

3. John Grierson, preface to Paul Rotha, *Documentary Film* (1935; Boston: American Photographic Publishing Co., 1936), p. 5; Rotha, *Documentary Film*, p. 16.

4. Many of the works this book deals with originate in video or digital media and not on celluloid. And audiences are increasingly likely to watch them in electronic forms, rather than projected from film prints in theaters. Nonetheless, I will use the term "film" to refer to a discrete moving-image work, keeping in mind the importance of a medium-specific analysis of the means of production, circulation, and reception of individual works, or "films."

5. Rotha, *Documentary Film*, pp. 131, 139, 150–51.

6. Michael Warner, *Publics and Counterpublics* (New York: Zone Books, 2002), p. 106.

7. John Grierson, "Flaherty's Poetic *Moana*," in *The Documentary Tradition: From Nanook to Woodstock*, ed. Lewis Jacobs (New York: Hopkinson and Blake, 1971), p. 25.

8. Grierson, "Flaherty's Poetic *Moana*," p. 26.

9. Grierson, "Flaherty's Poetic *Moana*," p. 25.

10. Luc Boltanski, *Distant Suffering: Morality, Media, and Politics*, trans. Graham Burchell (Cambridge: Cambridge University Press, 1999).

11. Grierson, "Flaherty's Poetic *Moana*," pp. 25, 26. Jane M. Gaines's essay "Political Mimesis" takes the sensuous response of the audience, the same empathy described by Grierson, as the basis of a critical question about how the promises of social movement and social change can be made by documentary. See "Political Mimesis," in *Collecting Visible Evidence*, ed. Jane M. Gaines and Michael Renov (Minneapolis: University of Minnesota Press, 1999), p. 100, and below.

12. Tom Gunning, "Before Documentary: Early Nonfiction Films and the 'View' Aesthetic," in *Uncharted Territory: Essays on Early Nonfiction Film*, ed. Daan Hertogs and Nico De Klerk (Amsterdam: Stichting Nederlands Filmmuseum, 1997), p. 20. I am grateful to Oliver Gaycken for bringing Gunning's essay to my attention and for sharing with me his own work on scientific film.

13. James Clifford, "On Ethnographic Allegory," in *Writing Culture: The Poetics and Politics of Ethnography: The Work of Film in the Age of Video*, ed. James Clifford and George E. Marcus (Berkeley: University of California Press, 1986), p. 101.

14. My use of the term "institution" is somewhat different from the application proposed by Bill Nichols in *Representing Reality: Issues and Concepts in Documentary*, where he has in mind the more conventional understanding of institution as a stable, centralizing, and constraining entity or process. In speaking of documentary as a form of institution, and of Grierson's review as an instituting moment, I am thinking also of the definition offered by Wlad Godzich. An institution is not only a set of rules and conditions for speech, knowledge, or membership in a group; it is also, as Godzich reminds us, "a guiding idea, the idea of some determined goal to be reached for the common weal . . . adopted by a group of individuals who become its public possessors and implementers." Insofar as institutions are, as Godzich puts it, "instruments of reproduction," every institution has a temporality, leading from its founding idea—often forgotten or ignored in the day-to-day life of the institution and its constituents—to a goal or ideal. Nichols, *Representing Reality: Issues and Concepts in Documentary* (Bloomington: Indiana University Press, 1991), pp. 15–18; Wlad Godzich, "Afterword: Religion, the State, and Post(al) Modernism," in Sam Weber, *Institution and Interpretation* (Minneapolis: University of Minnesota Press, 1987), pp. 156–57. In *Projecting Canada: Government Policy and Documentary Film at the National Film Board* (Montreal: McGill-Queen's University Press, 2007), Zoë Druick presents a full-length case study of the liberal institution of documentary, a national example with certain important similarities to and differences to the American case.

15. Walter Lippmann, *Public Opinion* (1922; New York: The Free Press, 1965), p. 19.

16. This impression has been abetted by a critical convention, established in the 1970s, of treating documentary filmmakers as the best interpreters of their own work, a technique that reflected the belief that technology should be used to let events and people speak for themselves and that recordings of authentic speech, in *cinéma vérité* and in the interview-based historical documentary, were not only the most accurate but also the fairest mode of representation an independent filmmaker could use. At a moment when narrative film scholarship had more or less abandoned biographical history in favor of textual analysis, new and significant publication on documentary was focused on the life stories and oral testimony of liberal and leftist filmmakers. Notable examples include G. Roy Levin, *Documentary Explorations: Fifteen Interviews with Film-makers* (New York: Anchor Press, 1971);

Erik Barnouw's venerable *Documentary: A History of the Non-Fiction Film* (New York: Oxford University Press, 1974); Alan Rosenthal's collections of interviews with committed filmmakers, *The New Documentary in Action: A Casebook in Filmmaking* (Berkeley: University of California Press, 1971), and *The Documentary Conscience: A Casebook in Filmmaking* (Berkeley: University of California Press, 1980); and William Alexander, *Film on the Left: American Documentary Film from 1931 to 1942* (Princeton, N.J.: Princeton University Press, 1981), a narrative account based on conversations with veterans of the communist and New Deal documentary organizations of the 1930s. This biographical perspective was symptomatized by Christian Metz's refusal in a 1979 interview even to consider theorizing documentary; remarking on Barbara Kopple's *Harlan County, U.S.A.* (1976), Metz simply declared, "It is unfair in a sense to call a film into question on terms which are not within the film-maker's purpose. She intended to . . . support the strike and she did it" (Metz, "The Cinematic Apparatus as Social Institution—an Interview with Christian Metz," *Discourse* 1 [1979]: 30). The belated introduction of critical and cultural theory to the study of nonfiction film has not necessarily dispelled the notion that documentary filmmaking is closer than other cultural practices to democratic action. Thus, Patricia R. Zimmermann's recent argument, in *States of Emergency: Documentaries, Wars, Democracies* (Minneapolis: University of Minnesota Press, 2000), that documentary can "shift the new world image order into more democratic spaces" when it "shed[s] its older forms of argument and its allegiances to maintaining nation-states" (xv) seems merely to restate in a different political language Rosenthal's hopeful assertion, in his introduction to *The Documentary Conscience*, that a "growing political sophistication as to how the mass media work" has led to an increasing use of documentary by "[p]eople involved in political struggles," in part because "the cost of making films has gone down enormously" (11). I am grateful to Meg Jamieson for pressure on this point about the rhetoric of democracy.

17. A. D. Lindsay, *The Essentials of Democracy* (London: Oxford University Press, 1935), pp. 9–10, 20–50. John Grierson takes up Lindsay's account of the role of discussion in the public sphere in "Propaganda and Education," in *Grierson on Documentary*, ed. Forsyth Hardy (London: Faber and Faber, 1979), pp. 149–50.

18. The claim of Lindsay's influence on Grierson, who was a student in the philosophy department Lindsay chaired at the University of Glasgow between 1922 and 1924, is made most strongly by Peter Morris, in "Re-thinking Grierson: The Ideology of John Grierson," in *Dialogue: Cinéma Canadien et Québécois/Canadian and Quebec Cinema*, ed. Pierre Véronneau, Michael Dorland, and Seth Feldman (Montreal: Mediatexte Publications, 1987), pp. 21–56; and is described by Grierson himself in "Propaganda and Education," which offers an account of the development of the political concept of documentary, as well as by Ian Aitken. See Ian Aitken, *Film and Reform: John Grierson and the Documentary Film Movement* (London: Routledge, 1990), pp. 46–47.

19. Aitken, *Film and Reform*, pp. 49, 53; Jack C. Ellis, "The Young Grierson in America, 1924–1927," *Cinema Journal* 8, no. 1 (Autumn 1968): 12–21.

20. Lippmann, *Public Opinion*, pp. 3, 18.

21. Lippmann, *Public Opinion*, p. 248.

22. Lippmann, *Public Opinion*, p. 250.

23. Lippmann, *Public Opinion*, p. 248.

24. Grierson, "Propaganda and Education," pp. 150–51.

25. Grierson, preface to Rotha, *Documentary Film*, pp. 13–14.

26. John Dewey, *The Public and Its Problems* (1927; Athens: Swallow Press and Ohio University Press, 1954), p. 207.

27. Dewey, *The Public*, p. 207. The shoe-pinching argument is cited by Richard Dyer MacCann in his history of American government filmmaking; see *The People's Films: A Political History of U.S. Government Motion Pictures* (New York: Hastings House, 1973), p. 9 n. 8.

28. A. D. Lindsay, *The Modern Democratic State* (1943; New York: Oxford University Press, 1962), p. 270.

29. Grierson, "Propaganda and Education," p. 150.

30. John Grierson, "Searchlight on Democracy," in *Grierson on Documentary*, ed. Forsyth Hardy (London: Faber and Faber, 1979), pp. 90, 91.

31. John Grierson, "Flaherty," in *Grierson on Documentary*, ed. Forsyth Hardy (London: Faber and Faber, 1979), pp. 30, 33.

32. See Druick, *Projecting Canada*, pp. 90–91.

33. See, for instance, Robert C. Allen and Douglas Gomery, *Film History: Theory and Practice* (New York: McGraw-Hill, 1985), p. 221.

34. A startling example is the use made of such techniques in *The Hunting of the President* (Nickolas Perry and Harry Thomason, 2004), the film about what Hillary Clinton called the "vast right-wing conspiracy" to disable the Clinton administration through dirty tricks and scandal. The filmmakers borrow footage from Joris Ivens's film for the New Deal, *Power and the Land* (1940), to illustrate the concept of subterfuge, turning Bill Parkinson, the Ohio farmer whose home we see being modernized by the Rural Electrification Administration in the original film, into an icon of conspiracy. Since the REA and the film project that Ivens participated in were both pointed to as evidence that the Roosevelt administration had communistic tendencies, Perry and Thomason's choice of historical images, most likely the result of hasty research for footage at the National Archives or elsewhere, is at least ironic.

35. The "snoops" comment was made by James Schlessinger and recounted by D. A. Pennebaker during a plenary presentation at the Film and History League Biennial Conference, Dallas, November 2006.

36. James Agee and Walker Evans, *Let Us Now Praise Famous Men: Three Tenant Families* (1941; Boston: Houghton Mifflin, 1988), p. 7.

37. The critical concept of the public has had greater appeal in studies of television and video, across a wide range of perspectives. See, for instance, Patricia Aufderheide, "Public Television and the Public Sphere," *Critical Studies in Mass Communication* 8 (1991): 168–83; Michael Curtin, *Redeeming the Wasteland: Television Documentary and Cold War Politics* (New Brunswick, N.J.: Rutgers University Press, 1995); Martha Gever, "Pressure Points: Video in the Public Sphere," *Art Journal* 45, no. 3 (Autumn 1985): 238–43; Anna McCarthy, *Ambient Television: Visual Culture and Public Space* (Durham, N.C.: Duke University Press, 2001); Laurie Ouellette, *Viewers Like You? How Public TV Failed The People* (New York: Columbia University Press, 2002); and Barry Dornfeld, "Putting American Public Television Documentary in Its Places," in *Media Worlds: Anthropology on New Terrain*, ed. Faye D. Ginsburg, Lila Abu-Lughod, and Brian Larkin (Berkeley: University of California Press, 2002).

38. "Common fund" is a phrase Waugh takes from André Bazin. See Thomas Waugh, "Introduction: Why Documentary Filmmakers Keep Trying to Change the World, *or* Why People Changing the World Keep Making Documentaries," in *"Show Us Life": Toward a History and Aesthetics of the Committed Documentary*, ed. Waugh (Metuchen, N.J.: Scarecrow Press, 1984), p. xvii.

39. In "The Camera I: Observations on Documentary," Annette Kuhn notes that documentary has generally been exempt from the kind of semiotic analysis then being applied as a matter of course to other kinds of cinema; see "The Camera I: Observations on Documentary," *Screen* 19, no. 2 (1978): 71–83. In "The Production of Outrage: The Iraq War and the Radical Documentary Tradition," *Framework* 48, no. 2 (Fall 2007): 36–55, Jane M. Gaines provides an interesting treatment of this exemption, placing it in the historical context of U.S. military aggression in Vietnam. Bill Nichols's use of semiotic concepts in the chapters of *Ideology and the Image: Social Representation in the Cinema and Other Media* (Bloomington: Indiana University Press, 1981) that deal with documentary marks a relatively early appearance of these concepts in North American documentary criticism. Approaches to documentary that extend the semiotic logic of difference into the historical analysis of American cultural formations include Paula Rabinowitz, *They Must Be Represented: The Politics of Documentary* (London: Verso, 1994); the two chapters on documentary in Thomas Cripps, *Making Movies Black: The Hollywood Message Movie from World War II to the Civil Rights Era* (New York: Oxford University Press, 1993); and the discussion of documentary texts sprinkled throughout Michael Denning, *The Cultural Front: The Laboring of American Culture in the Twentieth Century* (London: Verso, 1998). These texts are complemented by the descriptive essays and interviews in Phyllis R. Klotman and Janet K. Cutler, eds., *Struggles for Representation: African-American Documentary Film and Video* (Bloomington: Indiana University Press, 1999).

40. Waugh, "Introduction," pp. xviii–xix.

41. Zimmermann, *States of Emergency*, p. xix.

42. Alexandra Juhasz, *AIDS TV: Identity, Community, and Alternative Video* (Durham, N.C.: Duke University Press, 1995), p. 9.

43. Juhasz, *AIDS TV*, p. 12.

44. Zimmermann's *States of Emergency* offers a sustained engagement with these problems, as they bear on the definition of a contemporary public sphere in which radical documentary and experimental filmmakers and viewers compete for resources and space with forces of middle-brow and conservative media. Her rich account of the culture wars and economic pressures that compromised the publicness of American public airwaves and institutions in the 1980s and 1990s draws attention in valuable ways to the contexts of funding, distribution, and reception that have tended to be overlooked in studies of documentary and experimental media; her description, for instance, of the role played by intelligence workers like the Heritage Foundation in providing ammunition for the congressional assault on public broadcasting in the mid-1990s is a particularly incisive analysis of the ideological and political uses to which the term public could be put. But Zimmermann tends to avoid the question of how such problems shape the independent filmmaking she champions, other than to provide it with a moral imperative, and she treats politically or formally radical works as a vehicle of ideological content to be read off of the surface of such works, as if those on the correct (i.e., left) side of the struggle were immune to the question of how a text enters, addresses, and animates a public. See *States of Emergency*, pp. 7–10 and passim.

45. MacCann, *The People's Films*, p. 14.

46. MacCann, *The People's Films*, pp. 83, 48–49, 125.

47. See, for example, Julia Lesage, "Feminist Documentary: Aesthetics and Politics," in *"Show Us Life": Toward a History and Aesthetics of the Committed Documentary*, ed. Thomas Waugh (Metuchen, N.J.: Scarecrow Press, 1984), pp. 223–51.

48. MacCann, *The People's Films*, p. 4.

49. Hannah Arendt, *The Human Condition* (Chicago: University of Chicago Press, 1958), p. 55.

50. Arendt, *The Human Condition*, p. 50.

51. Arendt, *The Human Condition*, p. 52.

52. Jürgen Habermas, *The Structural Transformation of the Public Sphere: An Inquiry Into a Category of Bourgeois Society*, trans. Thomas Burger (1962; Cambridge: MIT Press, 1989), p. 37.

53. Michael Warner, *Publics and Counterpublics* (New York: Zone Books, 2002), p. 89.

54. Warner, *Publics and Counterpublics*, pp. 68–69.

55. Benjamin Lee, "Going Public," *Public Culture* 5 (1993): 170.

56. These dominant paradigms included Marxist and psychoanalytic theories of mass culture, wherein the spectator merely consumes or enjoys what she is programmed to, and the equally rigid, if affirmative, accounts offered by historico-

empiricist and cognitive perspectives on participatory spectatorship, in either individual or group terms. See Miriam Hansen, *Babel and Babylon: Spectatorship in American Silent Film* (Cambridge, Mass.: Harvard University Press, 1991), pp. 1–19; Miriam Hansen, "Early Cinema, Late Cinema: Transformations of the Public Sphere," in *Viewing Positions: Ways of Seeing Film*, ed. Linda Williams (New Brunswick, N.J.: Rutgers University Press, 1994), pp. 134–52. An early review of *Structural Transformation* by Dana Polan anticipates the disregard with which the book was met in film and media studies for the next decade and a half. Polan notes a strain in Habermas of a particular theory of "the media," that of commercial media as an invasive presence in ordinary life; one might argue that this meant that Habermas, paradoxically, was already too consistent with a certain populist tendency in American media studies. See Dana Polan, "The Public's Fear, or Media as Monster in Habermas, Negt, and Kluge," *Social Text* 25/26 (1990): 260–66.

57. It is perhaps for this reason that Habermas had more impact in television studies, where narratives of decline—of the immersive or collective experience of public exhibition—simply did not apply.

58. William Rothman, "The Filmmaker as Hunter: Robert Flaherty's *Nanook of the North*," in *Documenting the Documentary: Close Readings of Documentary Film and Video*, ed. Barry Keith Grant and Jeannette Sloniowski (Detroit: Wayne State University Press, 1998), p. 23.

59. See Lee, "Going Public," p.167.

60. See Michael Warner, *The Letters of the Republic: Publication and the Public Sphere in Eighteenth Century America* (Cambridge, Mass.: Harvard University Press, 1990), pp. 103, xii.

61. This point is an extension of, and in some ways a rejoinder to, the interesting concept of "political mimesis" that Jane M. Gaines employs to describe the "sympathetic magic" that connects audiences to scenes of political action in documentary films. See Gaines, "Political Mimesis," in *Collecting Visible Evidence*, ed. Jane M. Gaines and Michael Renov (Minneapolis: University of Minnesota Press, 1999), p. 94.

62. John Tagg, *The Burden of Representation: Essays on Photographies and Histories* (Amherst: University of Massachusetts Press, 1988), p. 27. Tagg's post-Althusserian analysis of the documentary ideology in North Atlantic applications of photography to the nascent welfare state is unsurpassed in its rigorous attention to the North Atlantic welfare-state economy of visual signs, but it is rarely cited by scholars of documentary film, even those concerned with the same periods he studies.

63. This poignancy of this ironic situation is captured in an observation by documentary artist and theorist Martha Rosler, in the afterword to the 2006 edition of her *3 Works*. Reflecting on decades of teaching documentary, Rosler recalls that in the 1980s, her students associated the term "documentary" with objectivity and truth. Today, however, her students view the discourse of documentary with suspicion, even though the same students, when presented with *particular* documentary

images, have no trouble treating them as authentic expressions of social reality. "They *believe*," remarks Rosler, "that they mistrust mediated representations." Martha Rosler, "Afterword: A History," in *3 Works* (Halifax: The Press of the Nova Scotia College of Art and Design, 2006), p. 101.

64. Gaines, "Political Mimesis," p. 89.

65. Gaines, "Political Mimesis," p. 89.

66. Michel Foucault and Paul Rabinow, "Polemics, Politics, and Problematizations: An Interview with Michel Foucault," trans. Lydia Davis, in Michel Foucault, *Ethics: Subjectivity and Truth*, vol. 1 of *The Essential Works of Michel Foucault, 1954–1984*, ed. Paul Rabinow, trans. Robert Hurley et al. (New York: The New Press, 1997), p. 117.

67. Foucault and Rabinow, p. 114; Warner, *Publics and Counterpublics*, p. 157.

68. Charles Wolfe, "Historicizing the 'Voice of God': The Place of Vocal Narration in Classical Documentary," *Film History* 9, no. 2 (1997): 150.

69. The pedagogical theatrics of *An Inconvenient Truth* call to mind the untimely place of the illustrated lecture in the history of cinema, as described by Charles Musser in various publications, including "Historiographic Method in Early Cinema," *Cinema Journal* 44, no. 1 (Fall 2004): 101–7.

70. Al Gore, interview with Charlie Rose on "The Charlie Rose Show," 19 June 2006, http://video.google.com/videoplay?docid=3412657607654281729.

71. In an interview with National Public Radio interviewer Terry Gross, Gore justified the film in terms very similar to the ones that Lippmann and Grierson used, speaking of "the vulnerability of our marketplace of ideas, our public conversation, if you will, to manipulation by the kinds of techniques that were innovated early in the twentieth century and were labeled propaganda" (Al Gore, interview with Terry Gross, on *Fresh Air with Terry Gross*, 30 May 2006, http://www.npr.org/templates/story/story.php?storyId=5439305).

72. John Michael, *Anxious Intellects: Academic Professionals, Public Intellectuals, and Enlightenment Values* (Durham, N.C.: Duke University Press, 2000), pp. 18–19.

73. Michael, *Anxious Intellects*, p. 143.

74. See Hansen, "Early Cinema, Late Cinema," p. 142.

75. It has to be said that the considerable industrial muscle behind *An Inconvenient Truth*, which includes old and new Hollywood elements, made its success more likely. The film's North American theatrical distributor was Paramount, and its producers included former eBay president Jeff Skoll, whose production company, Participant Productions, has generated a number of successful documentary and fiction films on liberal topics and figures. See Anya Kamenetz, "Moving Pictures," *Fast Company* 108 (September 2006): 90.

76. I am adapting here John Michael's observation that his connection to technologies of word and image make Hawking "the typical and emblematic instance of the position and nature, the displacement and denaturing, of the universal intellectual at this time." See Michael, *Anxious Intellects*, p. 143. On the functions

of traditional and organic intellectuals, see Antonio Gramsci, *An Antonio Gramsci Reader: Selected Writings, 1916–1935*, ed. David Forgacs, trans. Quintin Hoare and Geoffrey Nowell-Smith (New York: Schocken, 1988), pp. 307, 304.

77. The essential modern theoretical formulation of this paradox is Louis Althusser's essay "Ideological and Ideological State Apparatuses (Notes Toward an Investigation)," in *Lenin and Philosophy and Other Essays*, trans. Ben Brewster (New York: Monthly Review Press, 1971), an essay whose relevance to the analysis of documentary is less frequently noted than one might expect. There, Althusser remarks: "It is indeed a peculiarity of ideology that it imposes (without appearing to do so, since these are 'obviousnesses') obviousnesses as obviousnesses, which we cannot *fail to recognize* and before which we have the inevitable and natural reaction of crying out (aloud or in the 'still, small voice of conscience'): 'That's obvious! That's right! That's true!'" (p. 172).

78. Fredric Jameson, *The Political Unconscious: Narrative as a Socially Symbolic Act* (Ithaca, N.Y.: Cornell University Press, 1981), p. 283.

79. Stuart Hall et al., *Policing the Crisis: Mugging, the State, and Law and Order* (London: Macmillan, 1978), p. 205.

80. Ernesto Laclau and Chantal Mouffe, *Hegemony and Socialist Strategy: Toward a Radical Democratic Politics* (London: Verso, 1985), pp. 10–11; emphasis in the original.

81. Jürgen Habermas, "The New Obscurity," in *The New Conservatism: Cultural Criticism and the Historians' Debate*, ed. and trans. Shierry Weber Nicholson (Cambridge, Mass.: MIT Press, 1989), pp. 50, 51.

82. G.W.F. Hegel, *Hegel's Philosophy of Right*, trans. T.M. Knox (London: Oxford University Press, 1952), pp. 163–64.

1. NATIONAL FABRIC: AUTHORSHIP, TEXTUALITY, AND THE DOCUMENTARY FRONT

1. Warren I. Susman, "The Thirties," in *The Development of an American Culture*, ed. Stanley Coben and Lorman Ratner (Englewood Cliffs, N.J.: Prentice-Hall, 1970), p. 190 and passim.

2. Raymond Williams, *Marxism and Literature* (Oxford: Oxford University Press, 1977), p. 133.

3. Williams, *Marxism and Literature*, p. 130.

4. Susman, "The Thirties," p. 191.

5. David W. Moore, "Majority of Americans Expect to See Fahrenheit 9/11," Gallup News Service, 20 July 2004, http://brain.gallup.com/content/default.aspx?ci=12379.

6. Michael Moore, *The Official Fahrenheit 9/11 Reader* (New York: Simon & Shuster Paperbacks, 2004), p. xiii. Charles R. Acland conducts a thoughtful analysis of these

numbers and the claims made about them, by Moore and others, in "Moore Than This: *Fahrenheit 9/11*, Screen Numbers, and Political Community," *Environment and Planning D: Society and Space* 22 (2004): 901–6.

7. See for instance the claims in Peter Schweizer's *Do As I Say (Not As I Do): Profiles In Liberal Hypocrisy* (New York: Doubleday, 2005), repeated as hearsay in the Wikipedia entry on Moore and elsewhere on the Internet, including the March 2005 *Vanity Fair* profile of Moore. See http://en.wikipedia.org/wiki/Michael_moore#Controversy_and_criticism; Judy Bachrach, "Moore's War," *Vanity Fair* 535 (March 2005): 240.

8. Like *Michael Moore Hates America*, these films—which include *Michael and Me*; *Fahrenhype 9/11* (a film cowritten by disgraced Clinton advisor Dick Morris), *Celsius 41.11*—benefited from funding and promotion by conservative groups. Some of the former titles were shown at the 2005 Traverse Bay Freedom Film Festival in Moore's second home of Traverse City, Michigan, an event staged by the conservative organization American Film Renaissance as counterprogramming to Moore's own Traverse City Film Festival.

9. On the connection between documentary and scientific empiricism, see Brian Winston, *Claiming the Real: The Griersonian Documentary and its Legitimations* (London: BFI Publishing, 1995), pp. 130–37.

10. A similar terror inspires the series of paintings called *America's Most Wanted*, created by conceptual artists Vitaly Komar and Alexander Melamid, who set up a public opinion poll to determine what elements "most" Americans would like to see in a painting. The resulting "dishwasher-size" painting, stuffed with realistic and iconic elements (George Washington, deer, ordinary people, mountains), is either an elitist jibe at uncultured taste, or a clever analysis of public opinion polling and of the concept of public art, depending on how one looks at it. See JoAnn Wypijewski, ed., *Painting by Numbers: Komar and Melamid's Scientific Guide to Art* (Berkeley: University of California Press, 1997), pp. 6–7 and passim.

11. Spurlock can be thought of as engaging in what Bakhtin called a "hidden polemic" with Moore, who is himself the master of the hidden polemic. The hidden polemic, according to Bakhtin, is a kind of stylization in which "the author's discourse is directed towards its own referential object, as is any other discourse, but at the same time every statement about the object is constructed in such a way that, apart from its referential meaning, a polemical blow is struck at the other's discourse on the same theme, at the other's statement about the same object." Moore's satirical tactic of taking seriously ridiculous promises made by businesses and corporations—like the scene in *Bowling for Columbine* when he takes up a bank's offer of a free gun for new customers—is one form of this satirical device. A more subtle example is his ubiquitous baseball cap, which marks his genuine affiliation with the working class less than his intention to inhabit the stereotypes of class for various purposes. See Mikhail Bakhtin, *Problems of Dostoevsky's Poetics*, ed. and trans. Caryl Emerson (Minneapolis: University of Minnesota Press, 1984), p. 195.

12. Williams, *Marxism and Literature*, p. 132.

13. Williams, *Marxism and Literature*, p. 128.

14. William Stott, *Documentary Expression and Thirties America*, pbk. ed. (1973; New York: Oxford University Press, 1976), p. 123.

15. Dorothea Lange, "Documentary Photography," in *Photographers on Photography*, ed. Nathan Lyons (Englewood Cliffs, N.J., and Rochester, N.Y.: Prentice-Hall and The George Eastman House, 1966), pp. 67–68.

16. Lange, "Documentary Photography," p. 68.

17. Lange, "Documentary Photography," p. 68.

18. See, for instance, Jürgen Habermas, *The Structural Transformation of the Public Sphere: An Inquiry Into a Category of Bourgeois Society*, trans. Thomas Burger (1962; Cambridge: MIT Press, 1989); and Michael Warner, *The Letters of the Republic: Publication and the Public Sphere in Eighteenth-Century America* (Cambridge, Mass.: Harvard University Press, 1990).

19. Warner, *The Letters of the Republic*, pp. 22–24 and passim.

20. Walter Benjamin, "The Author as Producer," in *Reflections: Essays, Aphorisms, Autobiographical Writings*, ed. Peter Demetz, trans. Edmund Jephcott (New York: Schocken, 1986), p. 233.

21. James Agee and Walker Evans, *Let Us Now Praise Famous Men: Three Tenant Families* (1941; Boston: Houghton Mifflin, 1988), pp. 8–9. The inverted commas in which Agee encloses long sections of his "Preamble" to "Book Two" of the book, which I have preserved in my quotations, might also be read as another mark of the text's obsessive reflexivity, and its attempt to demonstrate that authorial subjectivity is an effect of typography, among other textual devices.

22. Stott, *Documentary Expression*, p. 19.

23. Alfred Kazin, *On Native Grounds: An Interpretation of Modern American Prose Literature* (New York: Reynal and Hitchcock, 1942), p. 491.

24. Sherwood Anderson, *Puzzled America* (1935; Mamaroneck, N.Y.: P.P. Appel, 1970), pp. ix–x.

25. The most successful example of this apparatus—no less because it was the most heavily capitalized than because of its suitability for nostalgic populist narration—was John Steinbeck's *The Grapes of Wrath* (1939), which was the culmination of a long process of collaboration between the state, an independent artist, and the culture industry. Steinbeck's novel—made into a successful film by John Ford the following year—originated in a collection of articles on migrant labor originally published in *The San Francisco News* in October 1936, illustrated by photographs taken by Dorothea Lange in her work with Paul Taylor on behalf of the California State Emergency Relief Administration in 1935. Steinbeck had posed as a migrant laborer to collect stories, intelligence work that was made possible by the Farm Security Administration, who subsidized it and helped place Steinbeck in the field. See Carol Shloss, *In Visible Light:*

Photography and the American Writer: 1840–1940 (New York: Oxford University Press, 1987), pp. 215–17.

26. Erskine Caldwell, *Some American People* (New York: Robert M. McBride and Company, 1935).

27. Quoted in Kazin, *On Native Grounds*, p. 493.

28. Antonio Gramsci, *An Antonio Gramsci Reader: Selected Writings, 1916–1935*, ed. David Forgacs, trans. Quintin Hoare and Geoffrey Nowell-Smith (New York: Schocken, 1988), p. 321.

29. Lange recalls being hired as a stenographer, a role supposedly more acceptable to state administrators than photographer. See Shloss, *In Visible Light*, pp. 204–5; Richard K. Doud, "Lange Interview with Richard K. Doud," in *Dorothea Lange: Farm Security Administration Photographs, 1935–1939*, vol. 2, ed. Howard M. Levin and Katherine Northrup (Glencoe, Ill.: The Text/Fiche Press, 1980), p. 62.

30. Shloss calls this Lange's "official identity." See Schloss, *In Visible Light*, pp. 202–6; Linda Gordon and Gary Y. Okihiro, eds., *Impounded: Dorothea Lange and the Censored Images of Japanese American Internment* (New York: W. W. Norton, 2006).

31. Quoted in Shloss, *In Visible Light*, p. 205.

32. Her recollection is, in this sense, a "hidden polemic"—not only with social science, but with herself.

33. As Josephine Herbst recalls in a memoir of the 1930s, *What Is to Be Done?* was ubiquitous on left bookshelves. See Susman, "The Thirties," p. 179.

34. Quoted in Barbara Foley, *Radical Representations: Politics and Form in U.S. Proletarian Fiction, 1929–41* (Durham, N.C.: Duke University Press, 1993), p. 275.

35. See Georg Lukács, "Reportage or Portrayal?" in *Essays on Realism*, ed. Rodney Livingstone, trans. David Fernbach (Cambridge: MIT Press, 1981), pp. 45–75, and the discussions of the reportage approach at the 1935 American Writers' Congress, including Joseph North's "Reportage," where he approvingly cites the examples of radical nonfiction authors like Meridel Le Sueur, Agnes Smedley, and John Spivak, against the bourgeois reporters for whom "the fact is a corpse." Joseph North, "Reportage," in *American Writers' Congress*, ed. Henry Hart (New York: International Publishers, 1935), p. 121.

36. Foley, *Radical Representations*, 275.

37. Meridel Le Sueur, "The Fetish of Being Outside," in *Harvest Song: Collected Essays and Stories*, rev. ed. (Minneapolis: West End Press, 1990), p. 201.

38. Michael Denning, *The Cultural Front: The Laboring of American Culture in the Twentieth Century* (New York: Verso, 1998), p. 119.

39. Erskine Caldwell and Margaret Bourke-White, *Say, Is This the U.S.A.* (New York: Duell, Sloane and Pearce, 1941), pp. 8–14.

40. Muriel Rukeyser, "The Book of the Dead," in *Out of Silence: Selected Poems*, ed. Kate Daniels (Evanston, Ill.: TriQuarterly Books, 1992), p. 10.

41. The poem is saturated with references to visual technologies, but the deictical gestures here suggest another medium important to the development of documentary rhetoric: radio. As William Stott notes, the use of rhetorical phrases like "this is" and "we take you" or "we return you" in radio broadcasts of the period was one form the "documentary bent" took in that medium. See Stott, *Documentary Expression*, p. 84.

42. See Walter Kalaidjian, *American Culture Between the Wars: Revisionary Modernism and Postmodern Critique* (New York: Columbia University Press, 1993), pp. 160–75; Michael Thurston, "Documentary Modernism and Popular Front Poetics: Muriel Rukeyser's 'Book of the Dead,'" *Modern Language Quarterly* 60, no. 1 (March 1999): 59–83.

43. Benjamin, "The Author as Producer," p. 235.

44. See Martin Cherniak, *The Hawk's Nest Incident: America's Worst Industrial Disaster* (New Haven, Conn.: Yale University Press, 1986); Kalaidjian, *American Culture*, pp. 165–72.

45. See Susman, "The Thirties," p. 185.

46. Carl Becker, "Everyman His Own Historian," *American Historical Review* 37, no. 2 (January 1932): 223.

47. Becker, "Everyman," p. 224.

48. The phrase "noble dream" is from a 1935 exchange in *American Historical Review* between Becker and Theodore Clarke Smith, an opponent of the utilitarian history proposed by Becker and others. The image of "heavy tomes" is from a letter to Becker from a sympathetic colleague. See Peter Novick, *That Noble Dream: The "Objectivity Question" and the American Historical Profession* (Cambridge: Cambridge University Press, 1988): pp. 259, 268, 269.

49. Becker, "Everyman," p. 226.

50. "History as Low-Brow," *New York Times*, 10 January 1932.

51. "History as Low-Brow"; Novick, *That Noble Dream*, p. 273.

52. See, for instance, the 1930 review of Grierson's *Drifters* (1929) in *New Masses* by Sam Brody, one of the founding members of the Workers Film and Photo League. Brody compares *Drifters* favorably to the work of Soviet filmmakers and laments that "we have learned to look upon the documentary as an unimportant item in filmmaking while the Russians have, with films like *Shanghai Document* and *Turksib*, raised it to the highest level of cinema achievement." Quoted in Russell Campbell, *Cinema Strikes Back: Radical Filmmaking in the United States, 1930–1942* (Ann Arbor: UMI Research Press, 1982), p.18.

53. Denning, *The Cultural Front*, pp. 118–20.

54. In a study of a later period of American documentary filmmaking, Patricia R. Zimmermann raises a similar objection: documentary has been associated with "a notion of democratizing communications through alternative media as

an evocation of some idealized public sphere." But in asserting that "democracy is no longer a given," and that there is now "not one democracy, but multiple democracies . . . not one form of documentary, but multiple documentary practices," Zimmermann's progressivist approach reinscribes as history the very ideas that Denning challenges: that documentary was ever a coherent form, and that democracy was ever a simple construction. See Patricia R. Zimmermann, *States of Emergency: Documentaries, Wars, Democracies* (Minneapolis: University of Minnesota Press, 2000), p. 23.

55. Harry Alan Potamkin, "Movies and Revolution," in *The Compound Cinema: The Film Writings of Harry Alan Potamkin*, ed. Lewis Jacobs (New York: Teachers College Press, 1977), p. 514.

56. John Tagg, *The Burden of Representation: Essays on Photographies and Histories* (Amherst: University of Massachusetts Press, 1988), p. 8.

57. Leo Hurwitz, "One Man's Voyage: Ideas and Films in the 1930s," *Cinema Journal* 15, no. 1 (Autumn 1975): 12.

58. See Campbell, *Cinema Strikes Back*, pp. 1–28.

59. Hurwitz, "One Man's Voyage," p. 12. In tethering questions of form and practice to ideology, the radical tendency in documentary resembled the Soviet concept of montage of the previous decade, a concept which similarly extended a critical analysis of society to new formal and social structures. Not surprisingly, many of the earliest American filmmakers to speak of their practice as documentary were among the first reviewers and exhibitors of the work of Soviet filmmakers like Eisenstein and Vertov in the United States, under one or another of the cultural auspices of the Communist International, including the Party-affiliated journals *New Masses*, *New Theatre*, and *The Daily Worker*, and the New York branch of the Workers Film and Photo League collective.

60. This is a point that Michael Denning makes frequently in *The Cultural Front*. See, for instance, his discussion of the Kenneth Burke controversy at the 1935 American Writers' Congress, inflamed by Burke's premature but prescient substitution of "people" for "workers"; Denning asserts that "melodramas of orthodoxy and heresy" which pitted Burke against doctrinaire pre–Popular Front communists, fail to recognize how important controversy was to the institutions of the left (Denning, *The Cultural Front*, pp. 439–45).

61. References for the contributions of Dos Passos, Conroy, and Le Sueur are to *American Writers' Congress*, ed. Henry Hart (New York: International Publishers, 1935).

62. See Denning, *The Cultural Front*, pp. xix, 62–63, and passim. As Denning and others have pointed out, even histories of the left told by its partisans are formed by the pressure of these two meanings. For instance, the most detailed documentary histories of the Film and Photo League (whose short-lived organ was called *Filmfront*), Campbell's *Cinema Strikes Back* and William Alexander's *Film on the Left*,

are forced to be inconclusive on certain details of the organization's collective work because the surviving league members remember their ideological and political commitments differently.

63. See note 37.

64. See Gramsci, *Gramsci Reader: Selected Writings*, pp. 349–50.

65. See Campbell, *Cinema Strikes Back*, pp. 115–44.

66. See Campbell, *Cinema Strikes Back*, pp. 145–50.

67. Alexander, *Film on the Left*, p. 30.

68. William Alexander quotes Ben Maddow, who is credited (as "David Wolff") as Caldwell's assistant on the film's commentary, as having "no memory of ever meeting Erskine Caldwell"; Alexander provides evidence to the contrary from an interview with Paul Strand (*Film on the Left*, p. 174, note k).

69. Although the first technical credits that appear name it as a film by "Robert Stebbins" (Sidney Myers) and "Eugene Hill" (Jay Leyda), Jack C. Ellis claims in *The Documentary Idea: A Critical History of English-Language Documentary Film and Video* (Englewood Cliffs, N.J.: Prentice Hall, 1989) that the film was directed by Elia Kazan and photographed by Ralph Steiner (p. 94), a slip that is repeated in Ellis's book with Betsey A. McLane, *A New History of Documentary Film* (New York: Continuum, 2005), p. 94. In fact, Kazan and Steiner were probably only responsible for principal photography; Steiner left the group before the film was released for ideological and professional reasons, and Kazan had theatrical obligations that took him away from the group during later stages of production. Their initial work on the film, deemed inadequate by the rest of the group, had to be supplemented by reshooting in Tennessee. See Alexander, *Film on the Left*, pp. 172–74; Campbell, *Cinema Strikes Back*, pp. 218–20.

70. A particularly cynical view of this turn is offered by an original Workers Film and Photo Leaguer, Sam Brody, who found himself on the opposite side of the group that formed Nykino and, later, Frontier. In an interview from 1977, Brody suggested that the pursuit of "cinema art," rather than staging an unrelenting opposition to Hollywood through the production of "short documentaries born in the heat of the class upheavals of the time," was the cause of the latter organization's collapse. Frontier, Brody argued, "exhausted its energies and resources in the production of films which, by the time they were finished, were obsolete in relation to current events. Even if one were to set aside all other objections to this policy [of feature production], the exhausting and endless quest for funding such films drained the group of most of the creative drive and energy needed to create such long-range projects" (Tony Safford, "Samuel Brody Interview: The Camera as a Weapon in the Class Struggle," *Jump Cut: A Review of Contemporary Media* 14 [1977]: 30).

71. See Campbell, *Cinema Strikes Back*, pp. 222–23.

72. Campbell, *Cinema Strikes Back*, pp. 214–15.

73. Mary Losey, "Joris Ivens's *Power and the Land,*" in *The Documentary Tradition: From Nanook to Woodstock,* ed. Lewis Jacobs (New York: Hopkinson and Blake, 1971), p. 192.

74. In a publicity statement issued prior to the release of *People of the Cumberland,* the group expressed optimism that its "living and purposeful films" could make an impact on the conventions of nonfiction-film production and distribution in the United States: "Our facilities are already at the disposal of responsible agents which cut across the bias of modern life—the trade unions, the cooperative societies, educational institutions, social-welfare groups, peace organizations, public forums, churches of whatever denomination, schools, and the like. We hope to utilize all these channels in the regular distribution of our films. In time we expect to include an even more widely scattered audience in a program of organized road shows which will tour the farming communities and mill towns of the nation" (quoted in Campbell, *Cinema Strikes Back,* p. 150). These ambitious plans were never fully realized. Although *People of the Cumberland* did receive the endorsement of a number of unions and was circulated quite widely through labor and cultural organizations, reaching diverse audiences in a great variety of settings, neither it nor Frontier's other documentaries produced quite as much in the way of sale or rental revenue, especially after 1939, as the group had hoped. In the case of *People of the Cumberland,* this was due in part to agreements with Garrison Films and the Highlander School that limited Frontier's share to a third of gross revenues from ticket and print sales and rentals. See Campbell, *Cinema Strikes Back,* pp. 150–51, 221.

75. Benjamin, "The Author as Producer," p. 231.

76. Steiner and Hurwitz, quoted in Campbell, *Cinema Strikes Back,* p. 134.

77. One could say that it takes the work of Barbara Kopple, with *Harlan County, U.S.A.* (1976), and, in a different way, *American Dream* (1990) to mine the full potential of this problem in laborist documentary. Paula Rabinowitz positions Kopple's work against the masculinist iconography of the old left in "Melodrama/Male Drama: The Sentimental Contract of American Labor Films," in *Black and White and Noir: America's Pulp Modernism* (New York: Columbia University Press, 2002), pp. 141–61. In their own way, Michael Moore's depictions of grieving mothers in *Bowling for Columbine* and *Fahrenheit 9/11* are attempts to give a second life to Lange's iconic images of dust-bowl mothers.

78. Petric, quoted in Campbell, *Cinema Strikes Back,* p. 230.

79. Kenneth Burke, "Revolutionary Symbolism in America," in *American Writers' Congress,* ed. Henry Hart (New York: International Publishers, 1935), pp. 87–94.

80. Campbell quotes a 1934 article by Ralph Steiner in which Steiner argues that documentary should include "events which happen only once, and those of which capitalist society may not be sufficiently proud to want recorded" (Campbell, *Cinema Strikes Back,* p. 230).

81. The phrase is from a response by Paula Rabinowitz to a questionnaire from the editors of *Cineaste* about *Fahrenheit 9/11* and the future of political documentary: "The Political Documentary in America Today," *Cineaste* 30, no. 3 (Summer 2005): 31.

2. VOICE-OVER, ALLEGORY, AND THE PASTORAL
IN NEW DEAL DOCUMENTARY

1. James Scott, *Seeing Like a State: How Certain Schemes to Improve the Human Condition Have Failed* (New Haven, Conn.: Yale University Press, 1998).

2. Wayne H. Darrow, memo to Russell Lord, 18 March 1940, Robert Flaherty Archives, box 35, Columbia University Special Collections.

3. *The Land* premiered at the Museum of Modern Art in April 1942. A 16mm print of the film was subsequently made available by the Department of Agriculture for limited nontheatrical release. The State Department sent a 35mm print to England for use as stock footage; Paul Rotha kept this copy during the war and used material from it in two films. See Paul Rotha, *Robert J. Flaherty: A Biography*, ed. Jay Ruby (Philadelphia: University of Pennsylvania Press, 1983), pp. 222, 342 n. 19; also Wayne H. Darrow, letter to Robert Flaherty, 30 May 1942, Robert Flaherty Archives, box 35, Columbia University Special Collections.

4. Quoted in Kate Lacey, "Radio in the Great Depression: Promotional Culture, Public Service, and Propaganda," in *Radio Reader: Essays in the Cultural History of Radio*, ed. Michele Hilmes and Jason Loviglio (New York: Routledge, 2002), p. 29.

5. Michele Hilmes, *Radio Voices: American Broadcasting, 1922–1952* (Minneapolis: University of Minnesota Press, 1997), pp. 1–21.

6. Siegfried Kracauer, *Theory of Film: The Redemption of Physical Reality* (New York: Oxford University Press, 1960), p. 118.

7. Michel Chion, *Audio-Vision: Sound On Screen*, ed. and trans. Claudia Gorbman (New York: Columbia University Press, 1994), p. 5.

8. Chion, *Audio-Vision*, p. 7; Chion, *The Voice in Cinema*, ed. and trans. Claudia Gorbman (New York: Columbia University Press, 1999), pp. 17–29.

9. Steven Conner, *Dumbstruck: A Cultural History of Ventriloquism* (New York: Oxford University Press, 2000), p. 15.

10. I am drawing on Steven Conner's history of ventriloquism, where he argues that the "eye and ear operate in, and require space. . . . The space of hearing is not ungoverned in comparison with the space of the eye; but it is differently governed" (Conner, *Dumbstruck*, p. 15).

11. Quoted in Conner, *Dumbstruck*, p. 15.

12. Connor, *Dumbstruck*, p. 15.

13. Walter Benjamin, *The Origin of German Tragic Drama*, trans. John Osborne (London: Verso, 1998), p. 175.

14. James Clifford, "On Ethnographic Allegory," in *Writing Culture: The Poetics and Politics of Ethnography: A School of American Research Advanced Seminar*, ed. James Clifford and George E. Marcus (Berkeley: University of California Press, 1986), p. 100.

15. Catherine Russell, *Experimental Ethnography: The Work of Film in the Age of Video* (Durham, N.C.: Duke University Press, 1999), p. 6.

16. Richard Dyer MacCann mentions, briefly and somewhat dismissively, state filmmaking operations within the Department of Agriculture, the Department of the Interior, and other branches of government, from the beginning of the 1910s; see *The People's Films: A Political History of U.S. Government Motion Pictures* (New York: Hastings House, 1973), pp. 43–44. In recent research on government filmmaking of the 1910s, 1920s, and 1930s, Gregory Waller and Jennifer Zwarich have provided much fuller accounts of these operations. In "Free Talking Picture—Every Farmer Is Welcome: Non-theatrical Film and Everyday Life in Rural America During the 1930s," in *Going to the Movies*, ed. Melvyn Stokes, Robert Allen, and Richard Maltby (Exeter, U.K.: University of Exeter Press, forthcoming).Waller describes an extensive network of 16mm and 35mm film distribution and exhibition emanating from the Department of Agriculture and managed by intermediaries like the American Farm Bureau Federation. In a work-in-progress on U.S. government nontheatrical film, Zwarich argues that the persuasive form of rhetoric associated with the later development of the documentary can be found in government filmmaking as early as 1913. I am grateful to Waller and Zwarich for sharing their research with me.

17. Dorothea Lange and Paul Taylor, *American Exodus: A Record of Human Erosion* (New York: Reynal and Hitchcock, 1939), p. 87.

18. Erskine Caldwell and Margaret Bourke-White, *You Have Seen Their Faces* (New York: Modern Age Books, 1937), n.p.

19. Archibald MacLeish, *Land of the Free* (New York: Harcourt, Brace and Company, 1938), pp. 49–50.

20. Gilles Deleuze and Félix Guattari, *A Thousand Plateaus: Capitalism and Schizophrenia*, trans. Brian Massumi (Minneapolis: University of Minnesota Press, 1987), p. 88.

21. John Dewey, *The Public and Its Problems* (1927; Athens, Ohio: Swallow Press and Ohio University Press, 1954), p. 111.

22. James M. Cain, *Our Government* (New York: Alfred A. Knopf, 1930), pp. xi, viii.

23. Cain, *Our Government*, p. 23.

24. Dewey, *The Public*, p. 111.

25. Dewey, *The Public*, p. 149.

26. Dewey, *The Public*, p. 6.

27. For instance: "Regarded as an idea, democracy is not an alternative to other principles of associated life. It is the idea of community life itself. It is an ideal in the only intelligible sense of an ideal: namely, the tendency and movement of some thing which exists carried to its final limit, viewed as completed, perfected. Since things do not attain such fulfillment but are in actuality distracted and interfered with, democracy in this sense is not a fact and never will be. But neither in this sense is there or has there ever been anything which is a community in its full measure, a community unalloyed by alien elements" (Dewey, *The Public*, p. 148).

28. Descriptions of postscreening discussions and their significance in the North American feminist and gay rights movements of the 1970s and 1980s appear in Julia Lesage, "Feminist Documentary: Aesthetics and Politics," in *"Show Us Life": Toward a History and Aesthetics of the Committed Documentary*, ed. Thomas Waugh (Metuchen, N.J.: The Scarecrow Press, 1984): pp. 223–51; Jan Rosenberg, *Women's Reflections: The Feminist Film Movement* (Ann Arbor, Mich.: UMI Research Press, 1983); Thomas Waugh, "Walking on Tippy Toes: Lesbian and Gay Liberation Documentary of the Post-Stonewall Period, 1969–84," in *The Fruit Machine: Twenty Years of Writing on Queer Cinema* (Durham, N.C.: Duke University Press, 2000): pp. 246–71. Charles Acland examines the role of discussion in the film-council and adult-education movements in the United States and Canada before and after World War II in a number of forthcoming articles, including "The Film Council of America and the Ford Foundation: Screen Technology, Mobilization, and Adult Education in the 1950s," and "Classrooms, Clubs. and Community Circuits: Cultural Authority and the Film Council Movement, 1946–1957." Related research by Anna McCarthy has noted the use of film to teach the liberal principles of discussion in the 1950s; see Anna McCarthy, "Mortimer Adler, Thor Heyerdahl, and Stanley Milgram: Experimental Filmmakers of the Cold War," paper presented at the Society for Cinema and Media Studies Annual Convention, Vancouver, March 2006.

29. Bernard Lichtenberg, "Business Backs New York World Fair to Meet the New Deal Propaganda," *The Public Opinion Quarterly* 2, no. 2 (April 1938): 314–20.

30. Bosley Crowther, "Onward March the Documentaries," *New York Times*, 4 February 1940.

31. Richard Griffith, "Films at the Fair," *Films* 1, no. 1 (November 1939): 62.

32. Griffith, "Films at the Fair," p. 63.

33. Charles Wolfe, "Historicizing the 'Voice of God': The Place of Vocal Narration in Classical Documentary," *Film History* 9, no. 2 (1997): 150.

34. An extensive analysis of the musical score in the New Deal documentary appears in Neil William Lerner, "The Classical Documentary Score in American Films of Persuasion: Contexts and Case Studies, 1936–1945" (Ph.D. diss., Duke University, 1997).

35. Keil's analysis of *The City* and other New Deal–era social documentaries builds on, and recasts in historical terms, Bill Nichols's metaphor of "The Voice of

Documentary," by which Nichols means a film's "social point of view." See Charlie Keil, "American Documentary Finds Its Voice: Persuasion and Expression in *The Plow That Broke the Plains* and *The City*," in *Documenting the Documentary: Close Readings of Documentary Film and Video*, ed. Barry Keith Grant and Jeannette Sloniowski (Detroit: Wayne State University Press, 1998), p. 121 and passim; Bill Nichols, "The Voice of Documentary," *Film Quarterly* 36, no. 3 (Spring 1983): 17–30.

36. Lewis Mumford, *The Culture of Cities* (New York: Harcourt, Brace and Company, 1938), p. 8. On the concept of the social imaginary, see Charles Taylor, *Modern Social Imaginaries* (Durham, N.C.: Duke University Press, 2004).

37. See William Alexander, *Film on the Left: American Documentary Film from 1931 to 1942* (Princeton, N.J.: Princeton University Press, 1981), pp. 243–57.

38. Mumford, *Cities*, p. 5.

39. This repertoire of images is rich with historical meaning, and not only in the ways that the narration intimates. The water-powered mill wheel, the loom, and weaving are all named by Marx as crucial to the formation of the antagonism between labor and capital in early modernity; the mechanization of textile production, from shearing and spinning to weaving, is cited a number of times in *Capital* as the example of the "demonic power" of industrial capitalism. The spirit of the revolution Marx describes against this "mechanical monster" is summoned by Soviet filmmakers like Eisenstein and Vertov when they put workers at the center of wheels and spinning machines, as in the workers' hijinks with a crane and a wheel in Eisenstein's *Strike* (1925) or the delirious images of centrifuges in *The General Line* (1929) and Vertov's own utopian city film, *The Man with a Movie Camera* (1929), a film that does for the urban centers of Soviet Russia what *The City* means to do for the Washington Beltway. See Karl Marx, *Capital: A Critique of Political Economy*, trans. Ben Fowkes (New York: Vintage, 1977), vol. 1, pp. 503, 553–58.

40. Wolfe, "Historicizing the 'Voice of God,'" p. 150.

41. Christian Metz, "The Impersonal Enunciation, Or, The Site of Film: In the Margin of Recent Works on Enunciation in Cinema," trans. Beatrice Durand-Sendrail with Kristen Brookes, in *The Film Spectator: From Sign to Mind*, ed. Warren Buckland (Amsterdam: Amsterdam University Press, 1995), p. 146.

42. Ronald Greene's analysis of educational film screenings by civic organizations like the YMCA in the 1920s makes a convincing case that such screenings extended the power of the state. Greene, borrowing from Michel Foucault's thesis of governmentality, argues that the "pastoral power" of such screenings—often accompanied by a speaker who helped the audience interpret the film, in the manner of a pastor—was a way of moderating the force of the liberal state, maintaining a formal distance between the government and the people, while allowing the state to reach into in the lives of individuals through nongovernmental discourses of "guidance." See Ronald Walter Greene, "Y Movies: Film and the Modernization of Pastoral Power," *Communication and Critical/Cultural Studies* 2, no. 1 (March 2005): 29–30 and passim.

43. Greene, "Y Movies," p. 23.

44. Even in such a simple film, one that seems to use only the most perfunctory means of expression, as if meeting its subjects' poverty with its own expressive poverty, connotation is possible. The filmmakers' choice of the smallest syntagmatic unit to depict this man's struggle with his meager piece of land and his inadequate equipment, a single or autonomous shot, underlines the separation between human beings that is the point of this opening sequence. The isolation of this shot is a figure for the isolation of individuals from one another, or of individual social units from one another, that it was the goal of the FERA to overcome. See William Guynn, *A Cinema of Nonfiction* (Cranbury, N.J.: Associated University Presses, 1990), p. 46.

45. Metz, "Enunciation," p. 142.

46. This I take to be the point of Chion's remark about Chris Marker's famous experiment with voice-over and image in *Letter from Siberia* (1957), in which Marker shows the same "innocuous" image three times, each time with commentary from "different political persuasions." Marker's mistake, Chion argues, is to assume that there *could* be some politically neutral way of speaking, about the image or otherwise. Chion might also have pointed out that Marker's experiment presumes that the "pure" image would be such a way of speaking. See Chion, *Audio-Vision*, p. 7.

47. In his analysis of documentary textuality, William Guynn uses the system of an earlier, structuralist phase of Metz's film theory to demonstrate the relation between the rhetorical or ideological strategies of classical documentary and its textual organization. His analysis begins with an enumeration of the various types of "syntagma," or the grammatical conglomeration of shots that compose the documentary text; he finds that the syntagmatic units most common to narrative cinema are typically displaced in the classical documentary text by others, including the "descriptive" syntagma ("any sequence of shots which serves to describe a locale rather than relate an action") and the "bracket" syntagma ("brief scenes lacking in syntagmatic development are linked by montage . . . without suggesting any chronological relationship") that predominate in *The New Frontier*. See Guynn, *A Cinema of Nonfiction*, pp. 45–46, and in general chapters 2 and 3.

48. See Metz, "Enunciation," p. 145.

49. The file on *The New Frontier* at the National Archives indicates that as late as 1935 there were two versions of the film in circulation, a silent version and the sound version to which I refer here. The two-shot digression on sound technology does not appear in the "Final Scenario" for the silent version, in which, of course, the reflexive humor of the commentary would make no sense.

50. Metz, "Enunciation," p. 146. On Metz's attitude to documentary as a critical object, see, for instance, his remarks about *Harlan County, U.S.A.* in "The Cinematic Interview as Social Institution—an Interview with Christian Metz," *Discourse* 1 (1979): 30.

51. Deleuze and Guattari, *A Thousand Plateaus*, p. 76.

52. See Scott, *Seeing Like a State*, p. 2.

53. Quoted in Robert L. Snyder, *Pare Lorentz and the Documentary Film* (Reno: University of Nevada Press, 1994), pp. 202–3.

54. Van Rensselaer Sill, memo on *The Land* (1942) to Wayne Darrow, director, Division of Information, Agricultural Adjustment Administration, Robert Flaherty Archives, box 35, Columbia University Special Collections.

55. Louis Althusser, "Ideology and Ideological State Apparatuses (Notes Towards an Investigation)," in *Lenin and Philosophy, and Other Essays*, trans. Ben Brewster (New York: Monthly Review Press, 1971), p. 174.

56. Quoted in MacCann, *The People's Films*, p. 63.

57. Carl Fleischhauer and Beverly W. Brannan, eds., *Documenting America: 1935–1943* (Berkeley: University of California Press, 1988), p. 2.

58. H. S. Person, *Little Waters: A Study of Headwater Streams and Other Little Waters, Their Use and Relation to the Land* (Washington: Government Printing Office, 1936), p. 3.

59. Film Service officers reported to Congress that in the first nine months of the service's existence, *The River* had been shown over ten thousand times in commercial venues and over five thousand times in educational settings. See U.S. Cong. Senate. Subcommittee of the Committee on Appropriations, *Hearings on H.R. 9007 [Labor-Federal Security Appropriation Bill for 1941]*, 67th Cong., 3rd sess. (Washington: Government Printing Office, 1940), p. 245.

60. Franklin D. Roosevelt, letter to Lowell Mellett, August 13, 1938, quoted in Snyder, *Pare Lorentz*, p. 204.

61. On Crosby, see Thomas Waugh, "Joris Ivens and the Evolution of the Radical Documentary, 1926–1946," Ph.D. diss., Columbia University, 1981, p. 441.

62. Quoted in Waller, "Free Talking Picture," p. 24.

63. Franklin D. Roosevelt, letter to John Studebaker, July 1, 1939, quoted in Snyder, *Lorentz*, p. 209.

64. Lorentz quoted in United States Cong., Senate Subcommittee of the Committee on Appropriations, *Hearings on H.R. 9007 [Labor-Federal Security Appropriation Bill for 1941]*, 67th Cong., 3rd sess. (Washington: GPO, 1940), p. 261.

65. Frank S. Nugent, "The Screen," *New York Times*, 7 March 1940.

66. Guynn, *A Cinema of Nonfiction*, p. 21.

67. Thomas R. Adam, *Motion Pictures in Adult Education* (New York: American Association for Adult Education, 1940), p. 12.

68. Waugh, "Joris Ivens," p. 456.

69. Waugh, "Joris Ivens," p. 434.

70. Quoted in Joris Ivens, *The Camera and I* (New York: International Publishers, 1969), p. 206.

71. Mumford imagined that "scientific method and the machine technique" would put modern man in touch with the concept of the "neutral world," a world

free of subjectivity and its social travails. Mumford imagined that the motion-picture camera would help man assimilate this concept, bringing him closer to realizing the ideal of collective life. *The City* can be read as the cinematic enactment of such a meaningless and technocratic concept of collectivity. See Mumford, *Technics and Civilization* (New York: Harcourt, Brace and Company, 1934), pp. 361, 244; and Casey Nelson Blake, *Beloved Community: The Cultural Criticism of Randolph Bourne, Van Wyck Brooks, Waldo Frank, and Lewis Mumford* (Chapel Hill: University of North Carolina Press, 1990), pp. 283–88.

72. Ivens, *The Camera and I*, p. 133.

73. The analogous functions of electricity as theme and narrative as form are consistent with the structures of New Deal documentary, and with New Deal rhetoric more generally. As Anna Siomopoulos suggests in a perceptive reading of *The River*, New Deal documentary could be seen as promoting a " 'good' consumption done in the name of the family, the nation, and 'the general welfare' " against a " 'bad' consumption done for the purposes of 'individual self interest' and class rise." Consistent with this rhetoric of consumer citizenship, *The River*, like other New Deal documentaries, suggests that a "moral" consumption distinguishes Americans in the present from the immoral excesses of American consumers of the past. In this view, milk is a medium of consumer citizenship in *Power and the Land*, since in its even flow between regions and classes, it is a social good: no one could deny that children of all kinds need milk. See Anna Siomopoulos, "The Flow of Consumer Citizenship: The New Deal, Hollywood Cinema, and Pare Lorentz's *The River*," paper presented at Film and History League Biennial Conference, Dallas, November 2006.

74. In fact, as historians of rural electrification and the TVA have shown, the Roosevelt administration's initiatives in rural electrification helped open the way for increased consumption in rural areas. The administration saw what the electrical industry could not, which was that families without the cash to buy new appliances and to pay for the electricity to run them would be willing to go into debt, either individually or as rural cooperatives, to pay for "modernizing." See Ronald C. Tobey, *Technology as Freedom: The New Deal and the Electrical Modernization of the American Home* (Berkeley: University of California Press, 1996), pp. 92–126.

75. Tobey, *Technology as Freedom*, contends that for Roosevelt, even before the presidency, "social modernization as transformation of the home was a politically defined vision, the domestic microcosm of the national body politic" (p. 95). Tobey connects this political "vision" to the liberalism of the Progressive movement, embodied in David Lilienthal, whom Roosevelt made chairman of the Tennessee Valley Authority. In *TVA: Democracy on the March* (New York: Harper and Brothers, 1944), p. 222, Lilienthal argues that a public works project like rural electrification was ethical simply because the modernization and prosperity it would bring to its beneficiaries gave them the moral agency in their lives: "There are few who fail to

see that modern applied science and the machine are threats to the development of the individual personality, the very purpose of democratic institutions. It is for this reason that the experience of the last ten years in the valley of the Tennessee is heartening. In this one valley (in some ways the world in microcosm) it has been demonstrated that methods can be developed—methods I have described as grass-roots democracy—which do create an opportunity for greater happiness and deeper experience, for freedom, in the very course of technical progress. Indeed this valley, even in the brief span of a decade, supports a conviction that when the use of technology has a moral purpose and when its methods are thoroughly democratic, far from forcing the surrender of individual freedom and the things of the spirit to the machine, the machine can be made to promote those very ends."

76. Deleuze and Guattari, *A Thousand Plateaus*, p. 76.

77. United States Film Service, *Study Guide: "The Plow That Broke The Plains"* U.S. *Documentary Film* (Washington: U.S. Film Service, 1938), pp. 13, 40, 41.

78. Guynn, *A Cinema of Nonfiction*, p. 104.

79. Guynn, *A Cinema of Nonfiction*, p. 104.

80. This playfulness can be read as in line with the belief held by some members of the Roosevelt administration during the so-called Second New Deal that the key to reviving the economy was to stimulate consumption rather than focusing on making production cheaper and more efficient. Against the stark division between the gendered spaces of work and domesticity we see earlier in the film, these moments of play show the Parkinsons, and especially the Parkinson men, learning to enjoy leisure time and to treat tools as toys. At the end of the film, Bill Parkinson is shown with a motor-driven whetstone, enjoying the formerly monotonous task of sharpening his tools. I am grateful to Michelle Lekas for this insight.

81. The "politics of scientific management" is the phrase Casey Nelson Blake uses to describe Lewis Mumford's technocratic idealism in *Technics and Civilization* and *The Culture of Cities*. One can find strong resonances of this attitude in the Service's films, as I have suggested. See Blake, *Beloved Community*, p. 286.

82. Benjamin, *Origin*, p. 178.

3. REVOLUTIONARY SOUNDS

1. Movement filmmakers and their audiences turned the constraints of 16mm film to creative advantage in various ways. For historical accounts of gay and lesbian and feminist documentary in the 1970s, with attention to the kinds of interaction this format motivated between filmmaker and subject, or among filmmaker, film, and audience, see Julia Lesage, "Feminist Documentary: Aesthetics and Politics," in *"Show Us Life": Toward a History and Aesthetics of the Committed Documentary*, ed. Thomas Waugh (Metuchen, N.J.: Scarecrow Press, 1984), pp. 223–51; Jan Rosenberg,

Women's Reflections: The Feminist Film Movement (Ann Arbor: UMI Research Press, 1983); Thomas Waugh, "Walking On Tippy Toes: Lesbian and Gay Liberation Documentary of the Post-Stonewall Period, 1969–1984," in *The Fruit Machine: Twenty Years of Writing on Queer Cinema* (Durham, N.C.: Duke University Press, 2000), pp. 246–71.

2. See, for instance, the debate among the leftist film critics and filmmakers surveyed by *Cineaste* in their 1972 "Radical American Film?" questionnaire. "Radical American Film?: A Questionnaire," *Cineaste* 5, no. 4 (1972): 14–20.

3. D. N. Rodowick, *Reading the Figural; Or, Philosophy After the New Media* (Durham, N.C.: Duke University Press, 2001), p. 172.

4. Paul Arthur, "Jargons of Authenticity (Three American Moments)," in *Theorizing Documentary*, ed. Michael Renov (New York and London: Routledge, 1993), p. 108.

5. Arthur, "Jargons of Authenticity," p. 108.

6. Given that Arthur's study deals only with mainstream films and that it maintains that all such documentaries "quest" for truth, this is perhaps an unsurprising conclusion. Arthur, "Jargons of Authenticity," pp. 131, 133.

7. Arthur, "Jargons of Authenticity," p. 134.

8. Louis Althusser, "Ideology and Ideological State Apparatuses (Notes Towards an Investigation), in *Lenin and Philosophy, and Other Essays*, trans. Ben Brewster (New York: Monthly Review Press, 1971), pp. 160–61.

9. On the complex nomenclature of the Weather organization, see Kirkpatrick Sale, *SDS* (New York: Random House, 1970), p. 579.

10. Any count of SDS membership, especially as the organization grew beyond the capacity of its National Office to keep accurate records, was an estimate. See Sale, *SDS*, 479, 529.

11. Sale, *SDS*, pp. 606–7.

12. Joan W. Scott, "Fantasy Echo: History and the Construction of Identity," *Critical Inquiry* 27, no. 2 (Winter 2001): 292. Scott's article is a counterpart to her earlier essay "The Evidence of Experience," where she explores the force of testimonial history in endowing social categories of difference with the status of incontrovertible truths. Such accounts are often rendered in terms of visual metaphor, described as scenes that readers, listeners, or viewers are invited to "see for themselves." One could say, then, that *The Weather Underground* could be said to resist the evidence of experience when it separates sound from its image, and from the historical period of its images, while embracing it in the use it makes of sound and image in its interviews. See Scott, "The Evidence of Experience," *Critical Inquiry* 17, no. 4 (Summer 1991): 773–97.

13. Christian Metz, "Aural Objects," in *Film Sound: Theory and Practice*, trans. Georgia Gurrieri, ed. Elisabeth Weis and John Belton (New York: Columbia University Press, 1985), p. 159.

14. See Scott, "The Evidence of Experience."

15. Or, as Sale put it, "not only do white middle-class college-educated people have no battles of their own to fight, they have no legitimacy as a stratum or validity as a force" (Sale, *SDS*, p. 563).

16. Walter Benjamin, "Left-Wing Melancholy," in *The Weimar Republic Sourcebook*, ed. Anton Kaes, Martin Jay, Ed Dimendberg (Berkeley: University of California Press, 1994), pp. 304–6.

17. Benjamin, "Left-Wing Melancholy," p. 305. Commenting on Benjamin's short essay, Wendy Brown characterizes the melancholic position as "a certain narcissism with regard to one's past political attachments and identity that exceeds any contemporary investment in political mobilization, alliance, or transformation." The melancholic's "loyalty" to his beloved converts "its truth," Brown comments, "into a thing, indeed, imbues knowledge with a thinglike quality." See Wendy Brown, "Resisting Left Melancholy," *boundary 2* 26, no. 3 (1999): 21.

18. Scott, "Fantasy Echo," p. 287.

19. Kirkpatrick Sale points out that the line to which the Weatherman name referred—"You don't need a weatherman to know which way the wind blows"—had a quite specific meaning in the context of the struggles over leadership of SDS. Not only was the association with the counterculture, in the form of Dylan fandom, meant as a deliberate affront to the Progressive Labor contingent; in addition, the line in question was taken as a jibe at PL, who, according to the Weather faction, dictated to the student troops, rather than taking direction from below (Sale, *SDS*, p. 559).

20. Stephen Mamber, *Cinema Verite in America: Studies in Uncontrolled Documentary* (Cambridge, Mass.: MIT Press, 1974).

21. Arthur, "Jargons of Authenticity," p. 118.

22. Arthur, "Jargons of Authenticity," p. 122.

23. Guy Debord, *Society of the Spectacle* (Detroit: Black and Red, 1983).

24. Pauline Kael, "The Current Cinema," *New Yorker*, 19 December 1970, p. 112.

25. Kael, "Current Cinema," p. 112.

26. Pascal Bonitzer, "The Silences of the Voice (*A Propos* of *Mai 68* by Gudie Lawaetz)," trans. Philip Rosen and Marcia Butzel, in *Narrative, Apparatus, Ideology: A Film Theory Reader*, ed. Philip Rosen (New York: Columbia University Press, 1986), p. 320. Michael Renov's essay on the early films of the Newsreel group, referred to below, deals briefly but acutely with the soundtracks of those films, in a manner consistent with Bonitzer's analysis.

27. For a summary of these debates, see Jeanne Hall, "Realism as a Style in Cinema Verite: A Critical Analysis of *Primary*," *Cinema Journal* 30, no. 4 (Summer 1991).

28. This account of The Film Group comes from Mike Gray, telephone conversation with author, 17 March 2007.

29. The converted Auricon predated the Eclair NPR, whose weight, balance, relatively silent operation, and price made it the camera sought by independent documentarists, by two or three years. Mike Gray, e-mail to author, January 10, 2007.

30. Although press coverage of King's withdrawal describes it as the result of negotiations with Daley and other Chicago officials, it was suspected that this was simply a way of helping King save face after being stonewalled by Daley, who had dragged his feet on guaranteeing the marchers' security. Mike Gray, telephone conversation with author, March 17, 2007.

31. See "Cicero Demonstration Set, with or Without Cops' Help," *Chicago Daily Defender*, 9 August 1966, pp. 1, 3; "Tell Cicero March Plans," *Chicago Tribune*, 26 August 1966; Jacques Nevard, "Housing Pact Set, Dr. King Calls Off Chicago Marches," *New York Times*, 27 August 1966; Arnold Rosenzweig, "WSO Insists Cicero March Is Still On," *Chicago Daily Defender*, 31 August 1966, p. 3; "March Ends in Rock Fight," *Chicago Tribune*, 5 September 1966; "The Big March: 200 Venture Into Cicero," *Chicago Daily Defender*, 6 September 1966, p. 4.

32. "Government on Camera," *New York Times*, 23 October 1966; Jack Gould, "TV: Too Many Cameras," *New York Times*, 22 October 1966. An early film-studies critique of the Drew approach is offered in Henry Breitrose, "On the Search for the Real Nitty-Gritty: Problems and Possibilities in *Cinéma Vérité*," *Film Quarterly* 17, no. 4 (Summer 1964).

33. Herbert Marcuse, *An Essay on Liberation* (Boston: Beacon Press, 1969), p. 35.

34. Roland Barthes, "The Reality Effect," in *The Rustle of Language*, trans. Richard Howard (Berkeley: University of California Press, 1989), p. 148.

35. A similar point was made by some materialist-feminist film theorists of the 1970s, in their rejection both of the stereotypes of women circulated in dominant cinema and of the claims of women's documentary to allow women's voices to be heard clearly, speaking about their oppression. See, for instance, Christine Gledhill, "Image and Voice: Approaches to Marxist-Feminist Film Criticism," in *Multiple Voices in Feminist Film Criticism*, ed. Diana Carson, Linda Dittmar, and Janine R. Welsch (Minneapolis: University of Minnesota Press, 1994); Claire Johnston, "Women's Cinema as Counter-Cinema," in *Feminist Film Theory: A Reader*, ed. Sue Thornham (Edinburgh: Edinburgh University Press, 1999).

36. The effect was intentional. The editor of *Bonnie and Clyde*, Dede Allen, gave the gunshots extra volume to make the film's violence more visceral. See Paul Monaco, *The Sixties: 1960–69*, vol. 8 of *History of the American Cinema*, gen. ed. Charles Harpole (Berkeley: University of California Press, 2001), pp. 106–8. On the allegorical readings of the film's violence, see J. Hoberman, *The Dream Life: Movies, Media, and the Mythology of the Sixties* (New York: New Press, 2003), pp. 177–85.

37. Norman Mailer, *Miami and the Siege of Chicago* (1968; New York: Donald I. Fine Books, 1986), p. 156

38. Simon Frith, "Rock and the Politics of Memory," *The 60s Without Apology*, ed. Sohnya Sayres et al. (Minneapolis: University of Minnesota Press, 1984), p. 66.

39. Stephen MacDonald, "*Woodstock*: One for the Money," in *The Documentary Tradition: From Nanook to Woodstock*, ed. Lewis Jacobs (New York: Hopkinson and Blake, 1971), p. 493.

40. This remark, from David Denby, comes at the end of an article about the early films of Frederick Wiseman: "as long as Wiseman keeps his camera pointed toward the center of our society and not toward hippie communes and rock festivals, his work will be the cause of anger and contention" (David Denby, "Documenting America," in *The Documentary Tradition: From Nanook to Woodstock*, ed. Lewis Jacobs [New York: Hopkinson and Blake, 1971], p. 482). More pointed versions of this charge were leveled by Emile de Antonio ("What is wrong [with *cinéma vérité*] is the space the best known practitioners of cinéma vérité occupy today: publicity films for rock groups") and Thomas Waugh, who argued that "*cinéma vérité* per se had nothing to contribute to the real job that faced the counterculture; it merely reflected and reinforced a mood. . . . As the [Vietnam] war escalated and escalated, the cinéma vérité people were preoccupied with rock concerts and easy targets like police-chief conventions and boot camps." See Thomas Waugh, "Beyond *Vérité*: Emile De Antonio and the New Documentary of the Seventies," in *Movies and Methods: An Anthology*, vol. 2., ed. Bill Nichols (Berkeley: University of California Press, 1985), pp. 235–36; de Antonio is quoted in Waugh, "Beyond *Vérité*," p. 247.

41. See Paul Ramaeker, " 'You Think They Call Us Plastic *Now* . . .': The Monkees and *Head*," in *Soundtrack Available: Essays on Film and Popular Music*, ed. Pamela Robertson Wojcik and Arthur Knight (Durham, N.C.: Duke University Press, 2001), pp. 74–102; and Peter Biskind, *Easy Riders, Raging Bulls: How the Sex-Drugs-and-Rock 'N' Roll Generation Saved Hollywood*, (New York: Simon and Schuster, 1998).

42. Pauline Kael, "The Current Cinema," *New Yorker*, 23 November 1968, p. 202.

43. The other well-known version of this image is the still photograph taken by Associated Press photographer Eddie Adams, for which Adams won a Pulitzer Prize. See Hoberman, *Dream Life*, p. 188 on the contemporary significance of the image.

44. The vicious irony of this sequence is mirrored, several years later, in a short Super-8 film called *Pobre Del Cantor*, the work of the Mexican collective El Taller Experimental de Cine Independiente (or the Experimental Workshop of Independent Film). The "Cantor" of the title is, in this case, Elvis, wearing a white suit that bears a strong resemblance to the white suits the Monkees wear for "Circle Sky." I am grateful to Jesse Lerner for sharing the work of El Taller Experimental with me.

45. From some "half-official announcements" reprinted in Jonas Mekas's *Village Voice* film column, January 25, 1968. Mekas, *Movie Journal*, p. 305.

46. The constitutive force of this tension for the Newsreel approach to political filmmaking is expressed clearly in Norm Fruchter's remarks to *Film Quarterly*: "We're tied to events, and we shouldn't be: Pentagon, Columbia, Chicago, the

Haight. Where should we begin? Most instincts are particular: narrow it down—this group, this action. Follow the officers of the Hanna Company in their jaunts through Brazil? Follow a Peace Corps volunteer? But why document the obvious—none of the people we make films for need *that* bad joke exposed: they've lived with (and often worked within) the reality. . . . New forms? But how much will time, limited energies, finance, and the wearing pressure of events, the race to stay responsible, limit us?" Norm Fruchter, in "Newsreel" [collected statements], *Film Quarterly* 20, no. 2 (Winter 1968–69): 44.

47. Robert Kramer, in "Newsreel" [collected statements], p. 47.

48. Bonitzer, "The Silences of the Voice," p. 319.

49. Marilyn Buck and Karen Ross, in "Newsreel" [collected statements], p. 44.

50. Kramer, in "Newsreel" [collected statements], p. 48.

51. Kramer, in "Newsreel" [collected statements], p. 45.

52. David James, *Allegories of Cinema: Film in the Sixties* (Princeton, N.J.: Princeton University Press, 1989), p. 214, reports that "what was to become New York Newsreel first met on 22 December 1967, the same day that the last of the theatrical newsreels, the Universal Newsreel Service, closed."

53. Michael Renov, "Newsreel Old and New—Towards an Historical Profile," *Film Quarterly* 41, no. 1 (Fall 1987): 22.

54. Dziga Vertov, *Kino-Eye: The Writings of Dziga Vertov*, ed. Annette Michelson, trans. Kevin O'Brien (Berkeley: University of California Press, 1984), p. 7. Renov remarks on the ways in which the Newsreel project resembles Vertov's "kino-eye," comparing their "youthfulness, enthusiasm, and volatility." See Renov, in "Newsreel," [collected statements], pp. 21–22.

55. Vertov, *Kino-Eye*, p. 34.

56. Kramer, in "Newsreel," [collected statements], p. 48.

57. Vertov, *Kino-Eye*, p. 67.

58. Kramer, in "Newsreel," [collected statements], p. 45.

59. Kramer, in "Newsreel," [collected statements], p. 47.

60. The image of the Panthers' headquarters also appears in Agnes Varda's film of the same year, *The Black Panthers: A Report*.

61. Jonas Mekas, *Movie Journal: The Rise of the New American Cinema, 1959–71* (New York: Macmillan, 1972), p. 305.

62. Michael Renov, "Early Newsreel: The Construction of a Political Imaginary for the New Left," in *The Subject of Documentary* (Minneapolis: University of Minnesota Press, 2004), p. 18.

63. Roz Payne, e-mail correspondence with author.

64. Norman Mailer records Sanders's words in his account of the Pentagon march, *The Armies of the Night: History as a Novel, the Novel as History* (New York: New American Library, 1968), p. 141. Roz Payne of Newsreel, however, remembers this as the voice of Allen Ginsberg. Roz Payne, e-mail correspondence with author.

65. On the ideological function of Darwell's voice, and of classical American documentary voice-over in general, see Charles Wolfe, "Historicizing the 'Voice of God': The Place of Vocal Narration in Classical Documentary," *Film History* 9, no. 2 (1997): 149–67.

66. Jürgen Habermas, "The Public Sphere: An Encyclopedia Article," trans. Sara Lennox and Frank Lennox, *New German Critique* 3 (Fall 1974): 49.

67. Kramer, in "Newsreel," [collected statements], p. 48.

68. Kramer, in "Newsreel," [collected statements], p. 46.

69. Mekas, *Movie Journal*, p. 306.

70. On Movement documentary, David James argues, "subject and agency of representation as well as method of filmmaking were all interdetermining. The realization that control of the means of production and distribution of images set the limits to the discourse these images could serve revealed that contestation of the ideological perspectives of the established media necessitated contestation of those media as institutions and as practices. Accurate representation on film demanded adequate representation in cinema—and the construction of new cinemas" (James, *Allegories*, 173).

71. Kramer, in "Newsreel," [collected statements], pp. 47–48.

72. James, *Allegories*, pp. 201–3.

73. Debord, *Spectacle*, p. 18.

74. Mick Eaton, "The Production of Cinematic Reality," in *Anthropology–Reality–Cinema: The Films of Jean Rouch*, ed. Mick Eaton (London: British Film Institute, 1979), pp. 49–50, describes the personalized commentaries in Jean Rouch's ethnographic films in similar terms.

75. Waugh, "Beyond *Vérité*," p. 247.

76. Waugh, "Beyond *Vérité*," p. 247.

77. Lenny Rubenstein, review of *Winter Soldier*, *Cineaste* 5, no. 4 (1972): 48.

78. Editors, "Radical American Film? A Questionnaire," *Cineaste* 5, no. 4 (1972): 16.

79. Vincent Canby, "Vietnam Documentary Opens at the Whitney," *New York Times*, 28 January 1972.

80. Richard Stacewicz, *Winter Soldiers: An Oral History of Vietnam Veterans Against the War* (New York: Twayne, 1997): pp. 234–36, 240.

81. Waugh, "Walking on Tippy Toes," p. 253.

82. Waugh, "Walking on Tippy Toes," p. 254.

83. Amos Vogel, untitled review of *Winter Soldier*, *The Village Voice*, 3 February 1972, p. 73.

84. Vogel, untitled review, p. 73.

85. Vogel, untitled review, p. 73.

86. Linda Williams, *Hard Core: Power, Pleasure, and the "Frenzy of the Visible,"* (Berkeley: University of California Press, 1989), p. 94.

87. See Neil Sheehan, review of *Conversations with Americans*, *New York Times*, 27 December 1970; Stacewicz, *Winter Soldiers*, p. 236.

88. See Mary Ann Doane, "Ideology and the Practice of Sound Editing and Mixing," in *Film Sound: Theory and Practice*, ed. Elisabeth Weis and John Belton (New York: Columbia University Press, 1985).

89. For accounts of F.B.I. harassment of the filmmakers and the abortive federal grand-jury proceedings against the film, see "Subpoenaed Over a Movie on Radicals," *New York Times*, 5 June 1975; Peter Biskind, "Does the U.S. Have the Right to Subpoena a Film in Progress?" *New York Times*, 22 June 1975; John Hess, "Feds Harrass Film Crew," *Jump Cut* 7 (August–September 1975): 23–25. A thorough account of the film's production is provided by Peter Biskind and Marc N. Weiss, "The Weather Underground: Take One," *Rolling Stone*, 6 November 1975, pp. 36–43; 78–88.

90. Bernardine Dohrn, Billy Ayers, Jeff Jones, Celia Sojourn, *Prairie Fire: The Politics of Revolutionary Anti-Imperialism* (New York: Communications Co., 1974).

91. The quoted phrase comes from Thomas Waugh's review of the film, "*Underground*: Weatherpeople at Home," *Jump Cut* 12–13 (December 1976): 12.

92. De Antonio is quoted in Biskind, "Subpoena." The term has an unfortunate resonance with the criticism Dohrn and others directed at the film after its release, accusing de Antonio and some members of Weather of seeking to "'sanitize the image of the organization.'" See John Kifner, "Weather Underground Splits up Over Plan to Come Into the Open," *New York Times*, 18 January 1977.

93. By virtue of their fugitive status, the involvement of Weather in the film meant that even the most technical aspects of postproduction, including processing the camera negative and making prints, became clandestine operations, in order to evade the scrutiny of federal authorities. An attempt to force the filmmakers to testify before a grand jury was eventually abandoned, after public expressions of support from film industry notables. See Biskind, "Take One" and Hess, "Feds Harrass."

94. Hess, "Feds Harrass," p. 24.

4. DOCUMENTARY COUNTERPUBLICS

1. Nancy Fraser, "Rethinking the Public Sphere: A Contribution to the Critique of Actually Existing Democracy," in *Habermas and the Public Sphere*, ed. Craig Calhoun (Cambridge, Mass.: MIT Press, 1992), p. 123.

2. Fraser, "Rethinking the Public Sphere," p. 124. See also Michael Warner, "Publics and Counterpublics," in *Publics and Counterpublics* (New York: Zone Books, 2002).

3. Michel Foucault, *Discipline and Punish: The Birth of the Prison*, trans. Alan Sheridan (New York: Vintage, 1979), p. 216.

4. Bruce Robbins, *Secular Vocations: Intellectuals, Professionalism, Culture* (London: Verso, 1993), p. 121.

5. Tom Wicker, *A Time to Die* (New York: Quadrangle/The New York Times Book Co., 1975), pp. 3–4.

6. Robbins, *Secular Vocations*, p. 122.

7. Wicker, *A Time To Die*, p. 65.

8. Wicker, *A Time To Die*, pp. 124–25.

9. Wicker, *A Time To Die*, pp. 58–59.

10. Gayatri Chakravorty Spivak, "Can the Subaltern Speak?" in *Marxism and the Interpretation of Literature*, ed. Cary Nelson and Lawrence Grossberg (Urbana: University of Illinois Press, 1988), p. 275.

11. Michel Foucault, "Intellectuals and Power: A Conversation Between Michel Foucault and Gilles Deleuze," *Language, Counter-Memory, Practice: Selected Essays and Interviews*, ed. Donald F. Bouchard, trans. Donald F. Bouchard and Sherry Simon (Ithaca, N.Y.: Cornell University Press, 1977), p. 207.

12. Quoted in Spivak, "Can the Subaltern Speak?" p. 274.

13. Gilles Deleuze, quoted in Michel Foucault, "Intellectuals and Power," p. 206.

14. Foucault lays out his idea about a project on prison as a critique of Durkheimian functionalism in a 1972 interview with John Simon. See "Michel Foucault on Attica: An Interview," *Telos* 19 (Spring 1974): 154–61.

15. Deleuze, "Intellectuals," p. 212.

16. Spivak, "Can the Subaltern Speak?" p. 276.

17. Spivak, "Can the Subaltern Speak?" p. 275. In "The Evidence of Experience," *Critical Inquiry* 17 (Summer 1991), Joan W. Scott applies Spivak's argument to the historiography of difference that began to appear in the wake of the so-called New Social Movements of the 1970s and 1980s. These standpoint epistemologies beg the question, Scott writes, of "how subjects are constituted as different in the first place" (p. 777).

18. Fredric Jameson, "Class and Allegory in Contemporary Mass Culture: *Dog Day Afternoon* as a Political Film," in *Signatures of the Visible* (New York: Routledge, 1990), pp. 35–54.

19. Jameson, "Class and Allegory," p. 38.

20. Jameson, "Class and Allegory," p. 38.

21. Jameson, "Class and Allegory," p. 41.

22. See Nat Segaloff, *Hurricane Billy: The Stormy Life and Films of William Friedkin* (New York: William Morrow, 1990); and Thomas D. Clagett, *William Friedkin: Films of Aberration, Obsession, and Reality*, 2nd ed. (Los Angeles: Silman-James Press, 2003).

23. A. William Bluem, *Documentary in American Television: Form, Function, Method* (New York: Hastings House, 1965), p. 197.

24. "Illinois Hears Conflicting Views on Sparing Life of Murderer," *New York Times*, 30 July 1962.

25. See John Irwin, *Prisons in Turmoil* (Boston: Little, Brown, 1980); and Jessica Mitford, *Kind and Usual Punishment: The Prison Business* (New York: Knopf, 1973).

26. "Illinois Hears Conflicting Views."

27. See Irwin, *Prisons in Turmoil*, pp. 37–40.

28. Mitford, *Kind and Usual Punishment*.

29. Irwin, *Prisons in Turmoil*, pp. 41–42.

30. Jessica Mitford, "A Talk With George Jackson," *New York Times*, 13 June 1971; Tad Szulc, "George Jackson Radicalizes the Brothers in Soledad and San Quentin," *New York Times*, 1 August 1971.

31. I thank David Galbraith for bringing the song to my attention.

32. "Random Notes," *Rolling Stone* 97, 9 December 1971, p. 4.

33. Bob Dylan, "George Jackson (Acoustic Version)," Columbia Records 4-45516/ ZSS15602, 1971.

34. See Anthony Scaduto, "'Won't You Listen to the Lambs, Bob Dylan?'" *New York Times*, 28 November 1971.

35. I am grateful to Brian Horne and Betsey Brada for their musicological assistance.

36. Régis Debray, "In Settlement of All Accounts," in *Prison Writings*, trans. Rosemary Sheed (London: Allen Lane, 1973), p. 176.

37. Michel Foucault, "Of Other Spaces," trans. Jay Miskowiec, *Diacritics* 16, no. 1 (Spring 1986): p. 24.

38. In an interview about the making of *Titicut Follies*, Marshall mentions that Timothy Asch, another ethnographic filmmaker, had shot footage of the "Follies" from which the film took its name, though Asch is not credited in the film. Carolyn Anderson and Thomas W. Benson, "Put Down the Camera and Pick Up the Shovel: An Interview with John Marshall," in *The Cinema of John Marshall*, ed. Jay Ruby (Langhorne, Penn.: Harwood Academic Publishers, 1993), p. 143.

39. For a detailed account of the criminal and civil cases in which the film was involved, see Anderson and Benson, "Put Down the Camera." National press coverage of the film or the court cases it was involved in between 1967 and 1969 included reviews and articles in the *New York Times*, *Time*, *Newsweek*, the *New Yorker*, *Life*, *Playboy*, and the *New Republic*. See Carolyn Anderson and Thomas W. Benson, *Documentary Dilemmas: Frederick Wiseman's* Titicut Follies (Carbondale: Southern Illinois University Press, 1991), p. 190 n. 96.

40. Anderson and Benson, *Documentary Dilemmas*, p. 12.

41. Bill Nichols, *Ideology and the Image: Social Representation in the Cinema and Other Media* (Bloomington: Indiana University Press, 1981), p. 234.

42. Wiseman achieves this sense of the "empty" time specific to the prison despite a documentary method that requires him to compress a vast amount of footage into a relatively small space: for *Titicut Follies*, the ratio of footage to final edit was about twenty-seven to one (Anderson and Benson, *Documentary Dilemmas*,

p. 30). Barry Keith Grant, "'Ethnography in the First Person': Frederick Wiseman's *Titicut Follies*," in *Documenting the Documentary: Close Readings of Documentary Film and Video*, ed. Barry Keith Grant and Jeannette Sloniowski (Detroit: Wayne State University Press, 1998), pp. 241, 243, notes the absence in *Titicut Follies*, as throughout Wiseman's work, of devices that conventionally indicate a passage of time in the transition from one sequence to another: dissolves, wipes, and titles. Grant remarks as well on the importance of the film's symmetrical structure, with the Follies both introducing and concluding the film, for the effect of "timelessness."

43. The first title reads: "The Supreme Judicial Court of Massachusetts has ordered that 'A brief explanation shall be included in the film that changes and improvements have taken place at Massachusetts Correctional Institution Bridgewater since 1966.'" This text fades to black, and a second title appears: "Changes and improvements have taken place at Massachusetts Correctional Institution Bridgewater since 1966." The titles were one of the conditions of the court's 1969 decision to permit restricted screenings of the film for educational purposes.

44. David MacDougall, "Prospects of the Ethnographic Film," in *Movies and Methods: An Anthology*, vol. 1, ed. Bill Nichols (Berkeley: University of California Press, 1976), p. 136. Stressing the ideological value of this comparative mechanism, James Clifford argues that ethnography always treats its object as the basis of a general statement about a broader human trait. "The story of an occurrence somewhere in the Kalahari Desert cannot remain just that. It implies both local cultural meanings and a general story of birth. A difference is posited and transcended." Clifford calls this structure of transcendence *allegory*. See James Clifford, "On Ethnographic Allegory," in *Writing Culture: The Poetics and Politics of Ethnography*, ed. James Clifford and George E. Marcus (Berkeley: University of California Press, 1986), p. 96.

45. Nichols, *Ideology*, p. 209.

46. See Frederick Wiseman, "'You Start Off With a Bromide': Wiseman on Film and Civil Liberties; an interview by Alan Westin," in *Frederick Wiseman*, ed. Thomas R. Atkins (New York: Monarch Press, 1976), pp. 47–66.

47. Anderson and Benson, *Documentary Dilemmas*, p. 94.

48. Quoted in Anderson and Benson, *Documentary Dilemmas*, p. 100.

49. Anderson and Benson, *Documentary Dilemmas*, 97.

50. See Nichols, *Ideology*, p. 211.

51. This was the import of some early reviews of the film, which warned the viewing public against its "sickening" effects. See Grant, "'Ethnography in the First Person,'" p. 249.

52. MacDougall argues that Rouch's method "reveals [his subjects] to us as they would like to be, and it enables us to approach aspects of their culture of which they are unconscious" ("Prospects of the Ethnographic Film," pp. 139–40).

53. Grant, "'Ethnography in the First Person,'" pp. 241–42.

54. "He who is subjected to a field of visibility, and who knows it, assumes responsibility for the constraints of power; he makes them play spontaneously upon himself; he inscribes in himself the power relation in which he simultaneously plays both roles" (Foucault, *Discipline and Punish*, p. 202).

55. Foucault, *Discipline and Punish*, p. 216.

56. In his chapter on *Titicut Follies* in *Technologies of Truth: Cultural Citizenship and the Popular Media* (Minneapolis: University of Minnesota Press, 1998), esp. 225–31, Toby Miller parses this debate and shows how it has often devolved into the stark and unproductive opposition of (amateur) exploitation and (professional) social concern.

57. This characterization of Wiseman comes from an essay by Carolyn Anderson and Thomas Benson, the authors of one of the few full-length studies of Wiseman's films, and is quoted by Toby Miller in *Technologies of Truth*, p. 229. Anderson and Benson describe this view of Wiseman as the position taken by "some activists" on his work; their source for this evidence is an essay by Thomas Waugh, although nowhere in Waugh's essay can this sociological characterization of Wiseman be found in quite these terms. See Anderson and Benson, "Direct Cinema and the Myth of Informed Consent: The Case of *Titicut Follies*," in *Image Ethics: The Moral Rights of Subjects in Photographs, Film, and Television*, ed. Larry Gross, John Stuart Katz, and Jay Ruby (New York: Oxford University Press, 1988), p. 82; Thomas Waugh, "Lesbian and Gay Documentary: Minority Self-Imaging, Oppositional Film Practice, and the Question of Image Ethics," in *Image Ethics: The Moral Rights of Subjects in Photographs, Film, and Television*, ed. Larry Gross, John Stuart Katz, and Jay Ruby (New York: Oxford University Press, 1988), pp. 248–72.

58. On Arendt, see Michael Warner, *Publics and Counterpublics* (New York: Zone Books, 2002), p. 58; on Habermas, see Peter Uwe Hohendahl, "Recasting the Public Sphere," *October* 73 (Summer 1995): 32–33.

59. Hohendahl, "Recasting the Public Sphere," p. 32.

60. Shortly after the scandal of *Titicut Follies*, for instance, rumors of shocking abuses in Arkansas prisons began to surface. Thomas Murton, a reformer brought in to investigate and institute changes, discovered that Arkansas's underfunded prison system was set up to maximize profit, effectively perpetuating the economy of slavery. In the absence of sufficient numbers of guards and administrators, prisoners had been put in positions of authority, and they organized the prison in a vicious parody of self-government. They exploited and killed one another with the tacit approval of the state, which replaced Murton when he discovered and publicized evidence of the corruption and violence that had overrun the system, including a mass grave of prisoners. See Scott Christianson, *With Liberty For Some: 500 Years of Imprisonment in America* (Boston: Northeastern University Press, 1998), pp. 258–64; Tom Murton, "One Year of Prison Reform," *The Nation*, 12 January 1970, pp. 12–17.

61. Carlo Ginzburg, *The Cheese and the Worms: The Cosmos of a Sixteenth-Century Miller*, trans. John and Anne Tedeschi (New York: Penguin, 1982), p. xviii. Ginzburg is referring generally, and skeptically, to Michel Foucault's studies of institutions of repression.

62. Later films, such as *Being A Prisoner* . . . (Suzanne Jasper, 1975) and *Inside Women Inside* (Christine Choy and Cynthia Maurizio, 1978), pursued this pluralist vision in the analysis of women's incarceration. One cannot argue that this feminist emphasis was merely the effect of the female authorship of these films, since the two films about Attica I examine in this chapter, which are by and large unconcerned with issues of gender, are also the work of women.

63. Angela Y. Davis, "Lessons: From Attica to Soledad," *New York Times*, 8 October 1971.

64. Davis, "Lessons."

65. New York State Special Commission on Attica, *Attica: The Official Report of the New York State Special Commission on Attica* (New York: Praeger, 1972), p. 332.

66. New York State Special Commission, *Attica: The Official Report*, p. xxi.

67. Craig Calhoun, "Civil Society and the Public Sphere," *Public Culture* 5 (1993): p. 269.

68. New York State Special Commission, *Attica: The Official Report*, pp. 105–6.

69. New York State Special Commission, *Attica: The Official Report*, p. xxxvii.

70. Michael T. Kaufman, "Inquiry on Attica Scores Governor Over 1971 Revolt," *New York Times*, 13 September 1972; Alvin Krebs, "TV Film Focuses on Attica Report," *New York Times*, 14 September 1972.

71. The New York public television station took over a year to provide Firestone with copies of this video material and did so only a day before the station's tapes of the hearings were erased. Cinda Firestone, interview with author, New York City, May 2, 2007.

72. For a thorough analysis of the social effects of video in a different but related context, see Kimberlé Crenshaw and Gary Peller, "Reel Time/Real Justice," in *Reading Rodney King/Reading Urban Uprising*, ed. Robert Gooding-Williams (New York: Routledge, 1993), pp. 56–70.

73. While the immediacy of the television image carries the stigma of control and "strategy," the immediacy of the *vérité* film image connotes, on the other hand, a "tactical" application of intimacy. The story Cinda Firestone tells of how footage from inside the yard was collected captures the sense of antagonism between the two media: "there was all this footage shot in the yard by Roland Barnes. He was in a rather peculiar position regarding the footage because he was on assignment for a TV station in Buffalo to do something else. He'd said, 'I would really like to go to Attica and film,' and they said, 'No, no, it's not important,' and asked him to go to a cornerstone laying, or whatever it was. Anyway, he disobeyed the station and went off to film Attica" (Cinda Firestone, "Attica" in *The Documentary Conscience:*

A Casebook in Film Making, ed. Alan Rosenthal [Berkeley: University of California Press, 1980], p. 296).

74. The line is actually repeated again later in the film; Crowley's speech also appears in Wicker's account of the uprising in *A Time To Die*, p. 97.

75. Hannah Arendt, *Eichmann in Jerusalem: A Report on the Banality of Evil* (1963; New York: Penguin, 1987), pp. 289–90; Angela Y. Davis, "Lessons: From Attica to Soledad," *New York Times*, 8 October 1971; Bettina Aptheker, "The Social Function of the Prisons in the United States," in *If They Come in the Morning: Voices of Resistance*, ed. Angela Y. Davis et al. (New York: New American Library, 1971), p. 59; Norman Mailer, *The Armies of the Night: History as a Novel, the Novel as History* (New York: New American Library, 1968), p. 211.

76. In addition to the television broadcast of the hearings, the McKay Commission's report was published in a mass-market paperback edition in 1972 by Bantam Books.

77. "I didn't think it necessary to be fair to both sides, and in any case Rockefeller and Oswald had ample coverage to show their side" (Firestone, "Attica," p. 297).

78. In order for the contest of voices to form the argument of the film, the image must often be relegated to a kind of accessory of speech. A slight contradiction emerges between the visual and aural levels of the film's argument: at the level of the soundtrack, the film insists that the viewer must "listen to all sides," but at the visual level, the shot can become a merely transparent channel of the competing points of view. See Thomas Waugh's assessment of the role of the interview in de Antonio's films "as an integral element of his characteristic form of collage." By downplaying the "poetic" role of the camera in *cinéma vérité*, de Antonio's approach to the filmed interview constitutes "an affirmation of the vital role of speech, of dialogue, of logic in radical discourse" (Thomas Waugh, "Beyond *Vérité*: Emile De Antonio and the New Documentary of the Seventies," in *Movies and Methods: An Anthology*, vol. 2., ed. Bill Nichols [Berkeley: University of California Press, 1985], pp. 246, 247).

79. This sense of experience is, according to Miriam Hansen, an important aspect of Negt and Kluge's use of the concept in *Public Sphere and Experience*, and it puts them in the debt of previous critical theorists like Benjamin and Kracauer: "On the one hand, it refers to the capacities of having and reflecting upon experience, of seeing connections and relations, of juggling reality and fantasy, of remembering the past and imagining a different future; on the other, it entails the onslaught of industrialization, urbanization, and a modern sense of consumption. With a dialectical twist, then, experience in the emphatic sense comes to include the ability to register and negotiate the effects of historical fragmentation and loss, of rupture and change" (Miriam Hansen, foreword to *Public Sphere and Experience: Toward an Analysis of the Bourgeois and Proletarian Public Sphere*, by Oskar Negt and Alexander Kluge, trans. Peter Labanyi, Jamie Owen Daniel, and Assenka Oksiloff [Minneapolis: University of Minnesota Press, 1993], p. xvii).

80. The fatalism of the prisoners' pledges to "die like men" has a political in-flection that the film sometimes seem to subordinate to a sentimental treatment of the rebels as heroes: these expressions of the futility of the prisoners' struggle would seem also to be a kind of statement that the racist and classist imbalance of power the state protects with its monopoly on violence makes any attempt to fight injustice a suicidal endeavor. Like other revolutionary positions inflected by the Black Power movement, the idea that prisoners are "already" dead becomes some-thing of a pop commonplace. In the TV movie of *Helter Skelter* (1976) for instance, Charles Manson—whose "revolutionary" fantasy is largely a racist inversion of the Black Panthers' program—fixes the judge at his trial with his evil stare and scowls "you can't kill me, I'm already dead." And Gary Gilmore's entire struggle to force the state to execute him can be seen, at least it the account provided by Norman Mailer in *The Executioner's Song* (1979), as an elaborate Nietzschean articulation of this idea.

81. What Champden actually says is, "Okay, how are you gonna apologize to a dead man?" This sardonic remark comes at the end of a long section of the film that refutes the claims initially made by the prison officials that seven of the hos-tages died when their captors slashed their throats and that one was emasculated. Although four of the nine hostages being held at knife- or spear-point in view of the attack forces were in fact slashed, two quite seriously, all of the deaths turned out to be the effect of police bullets. Firestone shows how the rumor that the pris-oners might kill the hostages or had already killed or brutalized some of them was used to justify the aggressive use of force in the eventual raid and to prematurely shut down negotiations. The film tacitly accuses the news media of colluding in this hysterical elevation of tensions and casts doubt on the motivation of a group of reporters shown demanding an explanation from a prison spokesman. The fol-lowing shot "answers" this demonstration of principle: it records William Kustler's denunciation of the conduct of the media ("I want to especially criticize the news media, which accepted as true . . . the statements of the prison authorities and the government"). The placement of Kunstler's remarks not only calls the news media's ethics into question but also endorses Firestone's own.

82. New York State Special Commission, *Attica: Official Report*, p. xxix.

83. According to Firestone, *Attica* began as a series of photographs: "It did not start as a film at all. I intended to do a pamphlet for the Attica Defense Committee. A friend of mine had already done tapes but wanted pictures for a pamphlet, so I went up to Attica mainly to do the photography" (Firestone, "Attica," p. 294).

84. A somewhat different version of this speech appears in *Fighting Back! Attica Memorial Book, 1974* (Buffalo: Attica Now, 1974), p. 24, a collection of statements, poetry, and images collected for the Attica Brothers Legal Defense fund.

85. One is reminded of André Bazin's description of the magical "ontology of the photographic image," in particular, of the capacity of photographs to capture

"the disturbing presence of lives halted at a set moment in their duration, freed from their destiny." Bazin ends the "Ontology" essay with a dramatic reversal of the usual account of the place of the photographic arts in the history of art, calling photography a *liberator* of the arts of realism that it replaces, rather than the final nail in their coffin. Firestone rehearses this interpretation in her use of photography, throughout the film, and particularly in this sequence: the photographic images at once kill their subjects (in their reference both to the immobility of the prisoners' dead comrades and to the historical relation between photography and the art that replaces it, cinema) and release them into the liberatory movement of the masses. André Bazin, "The Ontology of the Photographic Image," in *What is Cinema?* vol. 1., ed. and trans. Hugh Gray (Berkeley: University of California Press, 1967), p. 14.

86. Guy Debord, *The Society of the Spectacle*, rev. ed. (Detroit: Black and Red, 1977).

87. A typical example is the *Attica Book* produced by the Black Emergency Cultural Coalition and Artists and Writers Protest Against the War in Vietnam a year or so after the riot. In addition to writing by convict poets and authors, the book included artwork by Romare Bearden, Camile Billops, Leon Golub, Duane Hanson, Jacob Lawrence, Robert Morris, Alice Neel, Faith Ringgold, and Nancy Spero. Benny Andrews and Rudolf Baranik, eds., *Attica Book* (South Hackensack, N.J.: Custom Communications Systems, n.d.). Images from *Attica Book* were reproduced in other publications, for instance, *Fighting Back!*

88. The end credits of the version currently distributed by Third World Newsreel describe it as a film by Third World Newsreel, although Choy dates the change of her production unit's name from Third World Collective of New York Newsreel to Third World Newsreel to 1974. Scott MacDonald, interview, "Christine Choy (and collaborators Allan Siegel, Worth Long, and Renee Tajima)," in *A Critical Cinema 3: Interviews with Independent Filmmakers*, by MacDonald (Berkeley: University of California Press, 1998), p. 202.

89. See David James's reading of the film in *Allegories of Cinema: Film in the Sixties* (Princeton, N.J.: Princeton University Press, 1989), pp. 219–20.

90. According to Choy, *Teach* did well among black student groups and churches, unions, and local political organizations, and it was purchased by Dutch television. Christine Choy, e-mail correspondence with author, July 27, 1999. Third World Newsreel's business in its first few years of operation came mainly from rentals to college groups; the group's funding came almost entirely from its distribution activities. See Bill Nichols, *Newsreel: Documentary Filmmaking on the American Left* (Ph.D. diss. UCLA, 1977) (New York: Arno, 1980), p. 132.

91. In fact, the circumstances of the production of *Teach* were something like this. Its makers, Christine Choy and Susan Robeson, had had little experience in production when they set out to make a film about the Attica uprising. According to Choy, the budget for *Teach* was between $1,000 and $2,000, which she suggests was

one-twentieth of the budget of *Attica*. Choy, e-mail correspondence with author; MacDonald, "Christine Choy," p. 202; Nichols, *Newsreel*, pp. 29–32.

92. It is difficult to say with certainty, from the videotape copy of *Teach Our Children* I consulted, what appears on this second flag. The print from which the videotape copy distributed by Third World Newsreel was made appears to have been, even at the time of the transfer, in poor condition. At the time of this writing, Pacific Film Archive held the only known 16mm print of the film and had begun steps to preserve and restore the film from this print.

93. The lines are from a speech Malcolm X made in Detroit in November 1963.

94. Jonas Mekas's ecstatic 1966 prescription for *cinéma vérité* begins: "There are so many things happening round us, from the ghettos of L.A. to the smoky outskirts of Chicago and all across the country and in Vietnam, and in our own small city—big things, and small things, ugly things, and things like the eyes eaten out by smog, falling out and rolling into the gutters; and how the GIs are dying smiling and happy and in glory like butterflies. Things like that. We see nothing in our movies! And I am not talking about our poets: Our film poets have made the most beautiful poems in the world. I am talking about newsreels and about documentaries and about real life commentaries. With all the new techniques and equipment available to us, with almost weightless and almost invisible cameras, 8 mm. and 16 mm., and with sound, we can go today into any place we want and put everything on film. Why do we neglect film journalism? Eight mm. movies should be secretly shipped from the South; 8 mm. movies taken by the ten-year-old Harlem kids armed not with guns but with 8 mm. cameras—let's flash them on our theatre screens, our home screens; 8 mm. movies smuggled out of prisons, of insane asylums, everywhere, everywhere. There should be no place on earth not covered by 8 mm. movies, no place without the buzzing of our 8 mm. cameras! Let's show everything, everything. We can do it today. We have to go through this, so that we can go to other things" (Jonas Mekas, *Movie Journal: The Rise of the New American Cinema, 1959–71* [New York: Macmillan, 1972], pp. 235–36).

95. Two decades later, the videotaped beating of black Los Angeles motorist Rodney King, and the use of this tape to corroborate opposing arguments about the apparently self-evident brutality of the police officers accused of his beating, made it necessary to establish this point again, particularly since the formalist methods of film analysis—the reading of individual frames, for instance—resulted in the acquittal of the four officers. See Crenshaw and Peller, "Reel Time/Real Justice." The so-called Rodney King case was not, of course, without precedent: see, for instance, James Baldwin's account of the hysterical local and national responses to the Atlanta child murders of the early 1980s in *The Evidence of Things Not Seen* (New York: Henry Holt, 1995).

96. This music, unidentified in the credits (and used without permission, as is the case with all of the recorded music on the soundtrack), is Donny Hathaway's

song "The Ghetto," recorded in 1970 and a soul hit of the period. I am grateful to Joann Edmond and David James for their help in identifying this and other songs on the soundtrack.

97. Irwin, *Prisons in Turmoil*, pp. 109–10.

98. Foucault, "Michel Foucault on Attica," p. 155.

99. This description of a particularly explicit example of metonymy comes from Kaja Silverman, *The Subject of Semiotics* (New York: Oxford University Press, 1983), p. 112; the example Silverman uses is the relationship between the car being used to smuggle heroin and the intelligence of the dealer who organizes the shipment in the film *The French Connection*.

100. Philip Rosen, "Document and Documentary: On the Persistence of Historical Concepts," in *Theorizing Documentary*, ed. Michael Renov (London: Routledge, 1993), p. 79.

101. Rosen, "Document," p. 81.

102. *Teach Our Children* only enacts in cinematic terms the problem of cultural criticism Barthes announces at the end of his 1957 preface to *Mythologies*, trans. Annette Lavers (New York: Hill and Wang, 1972), p.12: "What I claim is to live to the full the contradiction of my time, which may well make sarcasm the condition of truth."

5. THE VISION THING

1. This chapter's epigraph is from Cinda Firestone, "'The Real History of Our Times Is on Film': Filmmaker Emile de Antonio Talks About Nixon, the '50s, and Now," in *Emile de Antonio: A Reader*, ed. Douglas Kellner and Dan Streible (Minneapolis: University of Minnesota Press, 2000), p. 255.

2. Max Weber, "Politics as a Vocation," in *From Max Weber: Essays in Sociology*, ed. and trans. H. H. Gerth and C. Wright Mills (New York: Oxford University Press, 1946), p. 78.

3. Weber, "Politics," p. 78.

4. Weber, "Politics," p. 79.

5. Weber, "Politics," p. 79.

6. I will be focusing here on the use made in liberal and leftist documentary of humiliating images and ad hominem techniques of political criticism. But similar techniques have been used on the right as well; see, for instance, *The Clinton Chronicles: An Investigation Into the Alleged Criminal Activities of Bill Clinton and His Circle of Power* (Citizens' Video Press, 1994), a widely circulated attack on the Clintons produced by Citizens for Honest Government, a conservative nonprofit organization, and promoted and distributed on television by the Rev. Jerry Falwell.

7. Walter Lippmann, *Public Opinion* (1922; New York: The Free Press, 1965), p. 13.

8. Craig Calhoun, "Populist Politics, Communications Media, and Large Scale Societal Integration," *Sociological Theory* 6, no. 2 (Autumn 1988): 233.

9. Douglas Kellner, *Television and the Crisis of Democracy* (Boulder, Colo.: Westview, 1990), p. 158. This view is shared by political operatives: according to a staffer for one of the 2004 Democratic candidates for president, people "care whether they're going to like their Presidents. They're going to watch him on television for four years and have feelings about him every time, and they vote for someone they like and want to keep liking" (Philip Gourevitch, "The Shakeout," *New Yorker*, 9 February 2004, p. 31).

10. Calhoun, "Populist Politics," p. 233.

11. John Grierson, "Learning from Television," in *Grierson on Documentary*, ed. Forsyth Hardy (London: Faber and Faber, 1979), pp. 210–19.

12. Grierson, "Learning," p. 210.

13. Grierson, "Learning," p. 210.

14. Kellner, *Television*, p. xiii.

15. Samuel Weber, "Television: Set and Screen," in *Mass Mediauras: Form, Technics, Media*, ed. Alan Cholodenko (Stanford, Calif.: Stanford University Press, 1996), p. 116.

16. This problem is dramatized by the performances of the late Warner Wolf, the legendary sportscaster for the New York City CBS affiliate, whose signature phrase, "let's go to the videotape," introduced highlights from the day's sports news. Wolf's command was accompanied by a strange *gestus*: upon uttering his catchphrase, Wolf would point to an area off-camera and bow his head, as if it were necessary to avert one's gaze—whether from fear, respect, or shame was never clear—before the gaze of video.

17. Weber, "Television: Set and Screen," p. 110. Anna McCarthy raises similar questions, although from a quite different theoretical perspective than Weber, in *Ambient Television: Visual Culture and Public Space* (Durham, N.C.: Duke University Press, 2001).

18. This projection also works in reverse, as demonstrated by a poll that "found that 86 percent of Americans agreed that PBS provided 'an important alternative to network television.'" See James Ledbetter, *Made Possible By . . . : The Death of Public Broadcasting in the United States* (London: Verso, 1997), p. 3. Ledbetter doubts the authenticity of this statistic, but whether it can be verified or not, it makes perfect sense as a wish-fulfillment or an expression of the social dynamic Slavoj Žižek calls "interpassivity": thank God there are others watching something of value while I am wasting my time with this junk. See Slavoj Žižek, "The Supposed Subjects of Ideology," *Critical Quarterly* 39, no. 2 (Summer 1997): 39–59.

19. Stanley Cavell, "The Fact of Television," in *Video Culture: A Critical Investigation*, ed. John Hanhardt (Rochester, N.Y.: Visual Studies Workshop Press, 1986), p. 205.

20. Alexis De Tocqueville, *Democracy in America*, rev. ed., vol. 1, trans. Henry Reeve (New York: The Colonial Press, 1900), pp. 202–3.

21. *Larry King Live*, 27 December 2006, http://transcripts.cnn.com/TRANSCRIPTS/0612/27/lkl.02.html.

22. "Vice President Cheney's Statement on Death of Former President Gerald R. Ford," http://www.whitehouse.gov/news/releases/2006/12/20061226-3.html.

23. David Stout and Jeff Szeleny, "After Ford's Death, Tributes Are Set for Capital," *New York Times*, 28 December 2006.

24. Alessandra Stanley, "In Death Coverage, a Broadcast Rite of Passage Manages to Avoid Melodramatic," *New York Times*, 28 December 2006.

25. Mark Leibovich, "Chevy Chase as the Klutz in Chief, and a President Who Was in on the Joke," *New York Times*, 29 December 2006.

26. "Excerpts From Interview with Nixon About Domestic Effects of Indochina War," *New York Times*, 20 May 1977.

27. Michael Rogin, "The King's Two Bodies: Lincoln, Wilson, Nixon, and Presidential Self-Sacrifice," in *Ronald Reagan, the Movie: And Other Episodes of Political Demonology* (Berkeley: University of California Press, 1987), p. 83.

28. This is Lauren Berlant and Lisa Duggan's comment on the effect of the Clinton-Lewinsky affair. Lauren Berlant and Lisa Duggan, "Introduction," in *Our Monica, Ourselves: The Clinton Affair and the National Interest*, ed. Lauren Berlant and Lisa Duggan (New York: New York University Press, 2001), p. 2.

29. John Hartley, *Uses of Television* (London: Routledge, 1999), p. 92.

30. Hartley, *Uses of Television*, p. 97.

31. Jean Baudrillard, "The Ecstasy of Communication," trans. John Johnston, in *The Anti-Aesthetic: Essays on Postmodern Culture*, ed. Hal Foster (Seattle: Bay Press, 1983), p. 131.

32. Baudrillard, "The Ecstasy of Communication," p. 129.

33. Marshall McLuhan, *Understanding Media: The Extensions of Man* (New York: McGraw-Hill, 1964), p. 329. To critical ends quite different than mine, Stella Bruzzi discusses the documentary images of Nixon and Kennedy, and several of the films I deal with here, in a chapter of her book *New Documentary*, 2nd ed. (London: Routledge, 2006), pp. 155–84.

34. There is considerable difference of opinion, among scholars, critics, and filmmakers, about which term applies to the (North) American practice of unrehearsed documentary of 1960 and after; Jack Ellis, for instance, claims that direct cinema replaced *cinéma vérité* in American usage in order to distinguish the former from the approach associated with Jean Rouch, which Edgar Morin, Rouch's collaborator on *Chronique d'un été* (1961), gave the name *cinéma-vérité* in honor of Dziga Vertov and his method of *kino-pravda*. I find little evidence of any such rigor in academic or critical usage, but since early accounts of the American style often use the French term (and sometimes the correct French spelling), I will generally follow

convention and refer to this work as *cinéma vérité*. See Jack Ellis, *The Documentary Idea: A Critical History of English-Language Documentary Film and Video* (Englewood Cliffs, N.J.: Prentice Hall, 1989), p. 225. A question about the critical orthography of *cinéma vérité* that I posed in September 2007 on a listserv associated with the annual Visible Evidence conference generated too many responses for me to thank every respondent by name, but I am grateful to all those who shared their thoughts about the number and meaning of accents, and about the value of *cinéma vérité*, relative to cognate terms.

35. McLuhan, *Understanding Media*, p. 336.

36. Sidney Kraus, ed., *The Great Debates: Kennedy vs. Nixon, 1960* (Bloomington: Indiana University Press, 1977), is the definitive account of the technical and logistical details of these programs.

37. Michael Curtin, *Redeeming the Wasteland: Television Documentary and Cold War Politics* (New Brunswick, N.J.: Rutgers University Press, 1995), p. 238.

38. Richard Hofstadter, "The Paranoid Style in American Politics," in *The Paranoid Style in American Politics and Other Essays* (New York: Alfred A. Knopf, 1965), p. 4.

39. Hofstadter, "The Paranoid Style," p. 4.

40. Hoftstadter, "The Paranoid Style," p. 4.

41. See Michael Warner, *Publics and Counterpublics* (New York: Zone Books, 2002), pp. 78–79.

42. Laura Kipnis, "Adultery," *Critical Inquiry* 24, no. 2 (Winter 1999): 316.

43. David Antin, "Video: The Distinctive Features of the Medium," in *Video Culture: A Critical Investigation*, ed. John Hanhardt (Rochester, N.Y.: Visual Studies Workshop Press, 1986), p. 151.

44. Examples of the frantic scene in local television newsrooms can be seen in a documentary produced by Dallas PBS station KERA to mark the fortieth anniversary of the event, *JFK: Breaking the News* (2003).

45. See Robert C. Allen and Douglas Gomery, *Film History: Theory and Practice* (New York: McGraw-Hill, 1985), pp. 233–37.

46. Curtin, *Redeeming the Wasteland*, p. 31.

47. On the desirability to advertisers of the audiences of documentary television, see Allen and Gomery, *Film History*, pp. 226–29. On the role of documentary in the expansion of international markets for American television in the 1960s, see Curtin, *Redeeming the Wasteland*, pp. 60–91.

48. Curtin, *Redeeming the Wasteland*, p. 5.

49. See Rhona J. Bernstein's helpful study of early television, "Acting Live: TV Performance, Intimacy, and Immediacy (1945–55)," in *Reality Squared: Televisual Discourse on the Real*, ed. James Friedman (New Brunswick, N.J.: Rutgers University Press, 2002).

50. Quoted in Bernstein, "Acting Live," p. 27.

51. The analysis of *Primary* in this paragraph is indebted to Jeanne Hall's essay "Realism as a Style in Cinéma Vérité: A Critical Analysis of *Primary*," *Cinema Journal* 30, no. 4 (Summer 1991): 24–50.

52. See the section on "The Public and Private Realm" in Hannah Arendt, *The Human Condition* (Chicago: University of Chicago Press, 1958), pp. 22–78, where the classical political—in Arendt's terms, public—subject is possible only by sharply delineating public from private experience, in contrast to the degraded contemporary state of publicity, where individuality is promiscuous and "objective."

53. This characterization of *cinéma vérité* is from an interview with Patricia Jaffe, who edited a number of films for the Drew Associates. Quoted in Allen and Gomery, *Film History*, p. 218.

54. Richard Leacock, quoted in Gomery and Allen, *Film History*, p. 218.

55. Art Simon and David M. Lubin offer detailed accounts of the lives of this footage; Lubin's account is largely derived from Simon's and is incorrect about certain details. David M. Lubin, *Shooting Kennedy: JFK and the Culture of Images* (Berkeley: University of California Press, 2003); Art Simon, *Dangerous Knowledge: The JFK Assassination in Art and Film* (Philadelphia: Temple University Press, 1996). The Rivera quotation comes from John J. O'Connor's *Times* review of the show, "TV: Two Programs Exploit Subjects," *New York Times*, 27 March 1975.

56. See Simon's analysis of the film's many iterations and reiterations in *Dangerous Knowledge*, pp. 35–54.

57. The 1968 Nixon campaign had, in fact, hired Eugene Jones, the maker of a *cinéma vérité* documentary film about the Vietnam War, *A Face of War* (1968), to help remake Nixon's image through a series of documentary-style television advertisements. See Joe McGinniss, *The Selling of the President, 1968* (New York: Trident, 1969); on *A Face of War*, see David E. James, *Allegories of Cinema: American Film in the Sixties* (Princeton, N.J.: Princeton University Press, 1989), pp. 199–201.

58. Firestone, "'The Real History,'" p. 255.

59. Norman Mailer, *Miami and the Siege of Chicago* (1968; New York: Donald I. Fine Books, 1986), p. 42.

60. McGinniss, *Selling*, p. 187.

61. McGinniss, *Selling*, p. 187.

62. McGinniss, *Selling*, p. 189.

63. McGinniss, *Selling*, p. 31.

64. Grierson, "Learning," p. 210.

65. Michael Shamberg and Raindance Corporation, "Meta-Manual," in *Guerrilla Television* (New York: Holt, Rinehart, and Winston, 1971), p. 7.

66. Shamberg, "Meta-Manual," p. 9.

67. Shamberg, "Meta-Manual," p. 12.

68. Mailer, *Miami*, p. 156.

69. Mailer, *Miami*, p. 181.

70. Mailer, *Miami*, p. 172.

71. Deirdre Boyle, *Subject to Change: Guerrilla Television Revisited* (New York: Oxford University Press, 1997), pp. 36–38. Boyle's book provides a thorough account of TVTV and its contemporaries.

72. TVTV, quoted in Boyle, *Subject*, p. 39.

73. Jean Baudrillard, *In the Shadow of the Silent Majorities; Or, The End of the Social and Other Essays*, trans. Paul Foss, John Johnston, and Paul Patton (New York: Semiotext[e], 1983), p. 19.

74. A script that organized the events right down to the details of when speakers would pause was leaked to the press on the second day of the convention and then reported widely in the national media. See Timothy Crouse, *The Boys on the Bus* (New York: Ballantine Books, 1974), pp. 176–77.

75. Roger Mudd, who appears in *Four More Years* snidely refusing to even acknowledge Blumberg's polite questions, perhaps understood that their techniques would change his profession. He complained elsewhere that "you're always worrying about this shot or that shot and you can't quite concentrate on what the candidate is saying because you're worrying about the mechanics, and you're thinking *Oh, Christ, we ran out of film!*" (Crouse, *The Boys on the Bus*, p. 154).

76. This activism extended to lending a press pass to Ron Kovic, one of the leaders of Vietnam Veterans Against the War, so that he could stage a noisy protest of the nomination ceremony, an event captured by TVTV. See Boyle, *Subject*, pp. 60–61.

77. Nora Sayre, "The Republicans," in *Sixties Going on Seventies*, rev. ed. (New Brunswick, N.J.: Rutgers University Press, 1995), p. 299.

78. Lauren Berlant argues that presidential discourse has recently "reanimated" an "archaic logic of sacred embodiment," in part as a response to what she calls "sarco-political" forms of identity politics. These forms challenge abstract, universalizing expressions of citizenship—voting, for instance—by making visible on a massive, national scale the violence that attaches to particular bodies: those of African Americans or women, for instance, or, more recently, of people with HIV/AIDS. I am persuaded by Berlant's analysis (which complements arguments she has made elsewhere) but would suggest that the suffering presidential body she has in mind predates Clinton by many years. See Lauren Berlant, "Uncle Sam Needs a Wife: Citizenship and Denegation," in *Materializing Democracy: Towards a Revitalized Cultural Politics*, ed. Russ Castronovo and Dana Nelson (Durham, N.C.: Duke University Press, 2002), p. 148.

79. Joan Copjec, "The *Unvermögender* Other: Hysteria and Democracy in America," *New Formations* 14 (1991): 27–41.

80. Roland Barthes, "The Reality Effect," in *The Rustle of Language*, trans. Richard Howard (Berkeley: University of California Press, 1989), p. 142.

81. Joseph Lieberman, quoted in Katharine Q. Seelye, "Lawmakers Call for Explanation in Lewinsky Case," *New York Times*, 3 August 1998.

82. Jean Baudrillard, *Simulations* (New York: Semiotext[e], 1983), p. 54.

83. Slavoj Zizek suggests that it is in fact the viewers, not the performers, who are objectified in pornographic representation. See Slavoj Zizek, *Looking Awry: An Introduction to Jacques Lacan Through Popular Culture* (Cambridge, Mass.: MIT Press, 1991), pp. 107–11.

84. Jean Baudrillard, "The Ecstasy of Communication," p. 127.

85. Jürgen Habermas, "The New Obscurity: The Crisis of the Welfare State and the Exhaustion of Utopian Energies," in *The New Conservatism: Cultural Criticism and the Historians' Debate*, ed. and trans. Shierry Weber Nicholson (Cambridge, Mass.: MIT Press, 1989), p. 51.

86. Bill Readings, "Foreword: The End of the Political," in *Political Writings*, by Jean-François Lyotard, trans. Bill Readings and Kevin Paul Geiman (Minneapolis: University of Minnesota Press, 1993), p. xv.

6. TENSE TIMES

1. Raymond Williams, *Marxism and Literature* (Oxford: Oxford University Press, 1977), pp. 128, 130.

2. William Stott, *Documentary Expression and Thirties America*, pbk. ed. (1973; New York: Oxford University Press, 1976), p. 27.

3. Williams, *Marxism and Literature*, p. 130.

4. Mary Ann Doane surveys major statements on indexicality by film and art theorists in her introduction to "Indexicality: Trace and Sign," a special issue of the journal *Differences*, edited by Doane and devoted to the topic. See Mary Ann Doane, "Indexicality: Trace and Sign: Introduction," *Differences* 18, no. 1 (2007): 1–6. Like most recent work in film and media studies on indexicality, technological changes in image culture, including the development and proliferation of digital-imaging hardware and software, are cited by Doane and many of her contributors as the impetus for rethinking the concept of the index, although Doane and others make reference to the painful images circulated from historic scenes of violence (at Columbine high school, the World Trade Center, Abu Ghraib, etc.) as a sign that referential effects survive the "crisis" of the digital. For other theorists, the historical condition of trauma provides the reason to reconsider indexicality; see, for instance: W.J.T. Mitchell, "The Unspeakable and the Unimaginable: Word and Image in a Time of Terror," *ELH* 72 (2005): 291–308; Lisa Saltzman, *Making Memory Matter: Strategies of Remembrance in Contemporary Art* (Chicago: University of Chicago Press, 2006).

5. For a number of years, the sentence "Public confidence in the 'real' is everywhere in decline" appeared in the front matter of each volume in the Visible Evidence series, the only series of books on documentary published by a North American academic press.

6. Digital photography, remarks Jane M. Gaines, presents documentary scholars with "the need to redefine indexicality completely." See Jane M. Gaines, "Introduction: 'The Real' Returns," in *Collecting Visible Evidence*, ed. Jane M. Gaines and Michael Renov (Minneapolis: University of Minnesota Press, 1999), p. 16. Other discussions of indexicality in the context of documentary film theory include Bill Nichols, *Representing Reality: Issues and Concepts in Documentary* (Bloomington: Indiana University Press, 1991), 149–55 and passim; Philip Rosen, *Change Mummified: Cinema, Historicity, Theory* (Minneapolis: University of Minnesota Press, 2001), pp. 301–49 and passim. It is interesting to compare the more recent of these discussions to Nichols's use of the term in *Ideology and the Image: Social Representation in the Cinema and Other Media* (Bloomington: Indiana University Press, 1981), where it is not freighted in the same way with the specter of its technological extinction. On performance and performativity in documentary contexts, see, for example: Stella Bruzzi, *New Documentary*, 2nd ed. (London: Routledge, 2006), pp. 185–218; Carol Flinn, "Containing Fire: Performance in *Paris Is Burning*," in *Documenting the Documentary: Close Readings of Documentary Film and Video*, ed. Barry Keith Grant and Jeannette Sloniowski (Detroit: Wayne State University Press, 1998), pp. 429–45; Thomas Waugh, "Walking on Tippy Toes: Lesbian and Gay Liberation Documentary of the Post-Stonewall Period, 1969–84," in *The Fruit Machine: Twenty Years of Writing on Queer Cinema* (Durham, N.C.: Duke University Press, 2000), pp. 246–71. Amy Villarejo provides a succinct review of the liveness paradigm and its value for the study of documentary in "*Bus 174* and the Living Present," *Cinema Journal* 46, no. 1 (Fall 2006): 15–20; see also Mark Williams, "History in a Flash: Notes on the Myth of TV Liveness," in *Collecting Visible Evidence*, ed. Jane M. Gaines and Michael Renov (Minneapolis: University of Minnesota Press, 1999), pp. 292–312. Theories of interactivity in computer-based new media have thus far had relatively little uptake in documentary studies; this is perhaps partly due to the tendency of digital theorists to assert historical and phenomenological differences of kind, not degree, between the realism and interactivity of film and television and what one encounters in, say, certain kinds of video games. Some digital theorists have, by contrast, suggested the importance of certain documentary films or codes for theorizing new media effects; see, for instance, the use that Lev Manovich makes of Dziga Vertov in *The Language of New Media* (Cambridge, Mass.: MIT Press, 2001), and Alexander R. Galloway's suggestion that Bazin's conception of realism should inform gaming theory, in "Social Realism in Gaming," *Game Studies* 4, no. 1 (November 2004), available at http://www.gamestudies.org/0401/galloway. Aspects of digital visuality can be seen quite clearly in a number of the films discussed later in this chapter.

7. See, for example, Alexandra Juhasz and Jesse Lerner, eds., *F Is for Phony: Fake Documentary and Truth's Undoing* (Minneapolis: University of Minnesota Press, 2006).

8. See Rey Chow, *The Age of the World Target: Self-Referentiality in War, Theory, and Comparative Work* (Durham, N.C.: Duke University Press, 2006).

9. Baudrillard, "The Gulf War: Is It Really Taking Place?" in *The Gulf War Did Not Take Place*, trans. Paul Patton (Bloomington: Indiana University Press, 1995), p. 30.

10. The Society for Cinema Studies resolved that:

1. The verdict to acquit four white Los Angles Police Department officers contradicts powerful visual evidence—video evidence of excessive police brutality seen globally.

2. The reaction in the streets of Los Angeles and other cities is fueled by the jury's deliberate refusal to "see" this visual evidence the way that most of us—regardless of color—saw these images.

3. But how did they "see" this video? They saw it repeatedly, repeatedly—desensitized to its power and effect. They saw it in slow motion, analytically—as the defense supplied a "reading" of the appropriateness of each officer's reaction. This demonstrates how close readings can incur misreading. Our outrage is that, even with visual evidence, Blacks' experience of police brutality does not count.

4. As media educators, we must voice our outrage at this verdict and endorse all efforts to indict the LAPD officers for civil rights violations.

Quoted in Editors, "After Cosby/After the L.A. Rebellion: The Politics of Transnational Culture in the Post Cold War Era," *Jump Cut: A Review of Contemporary Media* (July 1992): 2.

11. Dade Hayes and Addie Morfoot, "'Sicko' Could Heal Doc Flock," *Variety* 407, no. 5 (18–24 June 2007): 7.

12. Pat Aufderheide, "The Changing Documentary Marketplace," *Cineaste* 30, no. 3 (Summer 2005): 25. Moore reproduces a number of newspaper and magazine articles about *Fahrenheit 9/11* and its relation to public discontent with the Bush administration and the Iraq war in *The Official Fahrenheit 9/11 Reader* (New York: Simon and Schuster, 2004). See also Lynn Smith, "Docu Derby," *Los Angeles Times*, 15 June 2004; David Sterritt, "A Perfect Storm of Issue Films," *Christian Science Monitor*, 18 June 2004, p. 13; Elaine Dutka, "Politics Plays at the Box Office," *Los Angeles Times*, 26 July 2004; Pete Hammond, "Can Lame Ducks Still Fly?" *Variety* 397, no. 1 (22–28 November 2004): 18; Paul Arthur, "Extreme Makeover: The Changing Face of Documentary," *Cineaste* 30, no. 3 (Summer 2005): 18–23. Arthur is somewhat more cautious than Aufderheide about attributing the increase in revenues from documentary to any particular social or psychological factors and hesitates to identify the then-current box-office trends as a lasting change (although he takes a different position the following year in a brief article in *Film Comment*; see "Reality Check: The Year in Documentary," *Film Comment* 42, no. 2 [March–April 2006]: 59).

13. Significant examples of the documentary turn in contemporary art include the exhibition "Reprocessing Reality," curated by Claudia Spinelli for the P.S. 1

Contemporary Art Center in New York City, and the two events curated by Mark Nash under the title "Experiments with Truth," a title derived from Mahatma Gandhi's autobiography, first as a conference during Documenta 11 in Germany in 2001 and then as an exhibition of international documentary film and video art at the Fabric Workshop and Museum in Philadelphia in 2004 and 2005; the latter included works by Isaac Julien, Amar Kanwar, Ulrike Ottinger, Yervant Gianikian and Angela Ricci Lucchi, and Igloolik Isuma Productions. See Mark Nash, *Experiments with Truth* (Philadelphia: Fabric Workshop and Museum, 2004). The turn is also addressed in Hal Foster, *The Return of the Real: The Avant-garde at the End of the Century* (Cambridge, Mass.: MIT Press, 1996), esp. p. 196, and, in particular, in the essay "The Artist as Ethnographer," although in Foster's account, the "real" that returns owes more to Jacques Lacan than to Gandhi or, indeed, any frame of reference wider than the American university system and the North Atlantic museum world. Given Foster's legitimate concern that "the deconstructive-ethnographic approach can become a gambit, an insider game that renders the institution not more open and public but more hermetic and narcissistic," this is a curiously narrow formulation of the problem of "reality" in contemporary art, one belied by the work Nash gathered for his Philadelphia exhibition.

14. See Edward Wyatt, "A Show That Trumpeted History but Led to Confusion," *New York Times*, 18 September 2006. Influential liberal webloggers like Atrios were invited to a meeting with Clinton, where they were urged to spread the word that the film was factually imprecise and biased. Personal conversation with Atrios (a.k.a. Duncan Black), September 2006.

15. Bob Herbert, "Warfare as It Really Is," *New York Times*, 1 May 2006.

16. See http://loosechange911.blogspot.com/2006/10/what-media-hid-from-you-this-past-11th.html. Accessed 27 October 2006.

17. Nancy Jo Sales, "Click Here for Conspiracy," *Vanity Fair*, August 2006; Jonathan Curiel, "The Conspiracy to Rewrite 9/11," *San Francisco Chronicle*, 3 September 2006.

18. The connection between Baldwin's cut-and-paste method and his diagnosis of a paranoid strain in American mass consciousness and politics are explored in Michael Zryd, "Found Footage Film as Discursive Metahistory: Craig Baldwin's *Tribulation 99*," *The Moving Image* 3, no. 2 (Fall 2003): 40–61. Ed Halter notes the similarity between the textual styles of 9/11 conspiracy films and the structure of thought in the online sources, including Wikipedia, from which much of their information and imagery is drawn; see Ed Halter, "Fakes on a Plane," *The Village Voice*, 9–15 August 2005, pp. 29–30.

19. Patricia R. Zimmermann, *States of Emergency: Documentaries, Wars, Democracies* (Minneapolis: University of Minnesota Press, 2000), p. xv. See also Zimmermann, "Public Domains: Engaging Iraq Through Experimental Digitalities," *Framework* 48, no. 2 (Fall 2007): 66–83, her contribution to a dossier of articles from the February

2007 Yale conference "War, Documentary, and Iraq," published in the journal *Framework*, and Pat Aufderheide's contribution to the same dossier, "Your Country, My Country: How Films About the Iraq War Construct Publics," *Framework* 48, no. 2 (Fall 2007): 56–65.

20. The phrase "topical common space" comes from Charles Taylor; see "Modernity and the Rise of the Public Sphere," http://www.tannerlectures.utah.edu/lectures/Taylor93.pdf, p. 229.

21. Fredric Jameson, "Postmodernism and Consumer Society," in *The Anti-Aesthetic: Essays on Postmodern Culture*, ed. Hal Foster (Seattle: Bay Press, 1983), p. 116; Jean-François Lyotard, "Answering the Question: What Is Postmodernism?" in *The Postmodern Condition*, trans. Régis Durand (Minneapolis: University of Minnesota Press, 1984), p. 71; Jürgen Habermas, "The New Obscurity," in *The New Conservatism: Cultural Criticism and the Historians' Debate*, ed. and trans. Shierry Weber Nicholson (Cambridge, Mass.: MIT Press, 1989), pp. 50, 51.

22. Jean Baudrillard, "The Gulf War Will Not Take Place," in *The Gulf War Did Not Take Place*, trans. Paul Patton (Bloomington: Indiana University Press, 1995), pp. 27–28.

23. See Rosen, *Change Mummified*, pp. 253–63. See also Bruzzi, *New Documentary*, p. 6.

24. Linda Williams, "Mirrors Without Memories: Truth, History, and the New Documentary," *Film Quarterly* 46, no. 3 (Spring 1993): 11.

25. Williams, "Mirrors Without Memories," p. 17.

26. Baudrillard, "The Gulf War Will Not Take Place," p. 28.

27. Jean Baudrillard, *Simulations*, trans. Paul Foss, Paul Patton and Philip Beitchman (New York: Semiotext[e], 1983).

28. Baudrillard, "The Gulf War: Is It Really Taking Place?" p. 48.

29. I am here drawing on Rey Chow's analysis of the American prosecution of total war in Asia during World War II as "a certain kind of knowledge production," one that "act[s] out . . . a moral obligation to expel an imagined dangerous alienness from the United States' self-concept as the global custodian of freedom and democracy" (Chow, *The Age of the World Target*, p. 36).

30. The distance between *Antonia* and her later work can be measured by a remark Godmilow makes to Scott MacDonald in an interview around the time that *What Farocki Taught* (1998) was released: "I was afraid that to take [Farocki's] place [in the film] might look like some kind of feminist gesture" (Scott MacDonald, interview, "Jill Godmilow [and Harun Farocki]," in *A Critical Cinema 4: Interviews with Independent Filmmakers* [Berkeley: University of California Press, 2005], p. 156.

31. John F. Burns, "After Ten Years, Hussein Is Firmly in Control," *New York Times*, 26 February 2001; Barbara Crossette, "Children's Death Rates Rising in Iraq, Unicef Reports," *New York Times*, 13 August 1999; Hadani Ditmars, "Iraqis' Suffering Worsens as Sanctions Drag On," *New York Times*, 14 December 1997.

32. Jennifer Horne and Jonathan Kahana, "A Perfect Replica: An Interview with Harun Farocki and Jill Godmilow," *Afterimage* 26, no. 3 (November/December 1998): 12.

33. Horne and Kahana, "A Perfect Replica," p. 13.

34. See Chow, *Age of the World Target*, pp. 14–15. One could say that *What Farocki Taught*'s repetition of Farocki's film makes a tactical virtue of stupidity in the manner endorsed by Baudrillard when he avers that the only thing more stupid than "to demonstrate the impossibility of war just at the moment when it takes place" would be to not take this risk (Baudrillard, "The Gulf War: Is It Really Taking Place?" p. 37). While "intelligence hides," observes Avital Ronell, "stupidity exposes" (Avital Ronell, *Stupidity* [Urbana: University of Illinois Press, 2002], p. 10).

35. The foremost theorist-practitioner of this deconstructive approach to documentary is Trinh T. Minh-ha; this approach is emblematized in the title of her essay "Documentary Is/Not a Name," published not long before Godmilow's own deconstructive turn. There, Trinh observes that the concept of documentary as a tradition, "far from undergoing crisis today, is likely to fortify itself through its very recurrence of declines and rebirths"; it is possible to read *What Farocki Taught* as an attempt to induce a crisis by stalling or retarding this cycle of tradition. See Trinh T. Minh-ha, "Documentary Is/Not a Name," *October* 52 (Spring 1990): p. 56.

36. Michael Renov, "Documentary Disavowals and the Digital," in *The Subject of Documentary* (Minneapolis: University of Minnesota Press, 2004), p. 147.

37. Bruzzi, *New Documentary*, p. 2 and passim, takes performativity as the defining characteristic of the "new." In *Blurred Boundaries: Questions of Meaning in Contemporary Culture* (Bloomington: Indiana University Press, 1994), Bill Nichols revises the taxonomies established only a few years earlier in *Representing Reality* to incorporate performativity as a new mode. Also see Bill Nichols, *Introduction to Documentary* (Bloomington: Indiana University Press, 2001), pp. 130–37.

38. Nichols, *Blurred Boundaries*, p. 94.

39. The *Tongues Untied* controversy is detailed in B.J. Bullert, *Public Television: Politics and the Battle over Documentary Film* (New Brunswick, N.J.: Rutgers University Press, 1997), pp. 91–122. Judith Butler raises concerns about the use of *Paris Is Burning* as a performative critique of sex and gender identity in an influential chapter of *Bodies That Matter: On the Discursive Limits of "Sex"* (New York: Routledge, 1993), pp. 121–40. Butler's essay is itself in part a response to bell hooks's equally influential negative review of the film in *Z Magazine*, reprinted as "Is Paris Burning?" in *Black Looks: Race and Representation* (Boston: South End, 1992), pp. 145–56. See also Philip Brian Harper, "'The Subversive Edge': *Paris Is Burning*, Social Critique, and the Limits of Discursive Agency," *diacritics* 24 (1994): 90–103, which expands upon Butler's critique of oversimplifications of performative action by some readers of the film.

40. Nichols, *Blurred Boundaries*, p. 106.

41. Roland Barthes, "Writers, Intellectuals, Teachers," in *The Rustle of Language*, trans. Richard Howard (Berkeley: University of California Press, 1989), p. 310.

42. Deleuze and Guattari, *A Thousand Plateaus*, p. 76.

43. The connection to street theater, and to its use in New Left counterculture as a mode of affective politics, was suggested to me by Annette Michelson in conversation and e-mail correspondence in July 2007.

44. The term "antiepistemology" is Peter Galison's, from "Removing Knowledge," *Critical Inquiry* 31 (Autumn 2004): 236. *Secrecy* (work-in-progress), Galison's film with Robb Moss, uses a more conventional style of documentary to describe the institutional and epistemological practices on which *It's Not My Memory of It* meditates. Tess Takahashi explores the relation between Meltzer and Thorne's work and film-theoretical conceptions of indexicality and medium-specificity; see "The Stakes of the Index: Photography in the Age of the Digital," in "Impure Film: Medium Specificity and the North American Avant-garde (1965–2005)," Ph.D. diss., Brown University, 2007.

45. See Michel Foucault, *The Archaeology of Knowledge*, trans. A. M. Sheridan Smith (New York: Pantheon, 1972). Meltzer and Thorne's reflections on documentary appear in Naeem Mohaiemen, "But Will We Live at All? Naeem Mohaiemen in Converation with The Speculative Archive/Julia Meltzer and David Thorne," *Bidoun* 11 (Summer 2007), http://www.bidoun.com/issues/issue_11/07_all.html#article. Trinh's reflexive gesture on the soundtrack of her meta-ethnographic film *Reassemblage* (1983), restating the question she was asked about that film while she was making it—"'but *what* about Senegal?'"—is an obvious point of reference for Meltzer and Thorne's approach.

46. See Cindy Patton, "How to Do Things With Sound," *Cultural Studies* 13, no. 3 (1991): p. 467 and passim.

47. Alejandro Cesarco, ed., *Between Artists: Paul Chan/Martha Rosler* (New York: Art Resources Transfer Press, 2006), p. 17.

48. Judith Butler, "Precarious Life," in *Precarious Life: The Powers of Mourning and Violence* (London: Verso, 2004), pp. 129–30.

49. Baudrillard, "The Gulf War: Is It Really Taking Place?" p. 37.

50. Butler, "Precarious Life," p. 144.

51. Walter Lippmann, *Public Opinion* (1922; New York: The Free Press, 1965), p. 239.

52. Nichols, *Blurred Boundaries*, p. 106.

53. Nichols, *Blurred Boundaries*, p. 106.

FILMOGRAPHY

This list contains the titles of all films discussed in the text, as well as the name(s) of the producer(s), country and year of production, and running time of each film. The names given are typically those of the credited director or producer; where a film is the work of an organization or collective, a group name is given. Country of origin usually refers to the geographical site of production but may also reflect the source of funding or production personnel. This information is taken from a variety of sources, including on-screen credits, reviews, library records, and databases; not all sources agree on all details. Because different copies or versions of certain titles may be (or have been) in circulation, the given running times do not always correspond to extant versions. Except where the convention in English-language criticism is to preserve the original language of a foreign title, I have used the English translation of foreign-language titles.

Africa Speaks!. Dir. Paul L. Hoefler. USA, 1930. 56 min.
American Dream. Dir. Barbara Kopple. USA, 1990. 100 min.
An American Family. Prod. Craig Gilbert. USA, 1973. 720 min.
Antonia: A Portrait of the Woman. Dir. Jill Godmilow and Judy Collins. USA, 1974. 58 min.
The Atomic Café. Dir. Jayne Loader, Kevin Rafferty, Pierce Rafferty. USA, 1982. 89 min.
Attica. Dir. Cinda Firestone. USA, 1973. 80 min.
Attica: The Official Report of the New York State Special Commission. Dir. Jon Wilkman. USA, 1972. 90 min.
Baghdad E.R. Dir. Jon Alpert and Matthew O'Neill. USA, 2006. 64 min.
Baghdad in No Particular Order. Dir. Paul Chan. USA, 2003. 51 min.
The Battle of Midway. Dir. John Ford. USA, 1942. 18 min.
Being A Prisoner . . . . Dir. Suzanne Jasper. USA, 1975. 28 min.

The Big Bird Cage. Dir. Jack Hill. USA, 1972. 87 min.

The Big Doll House. Dir. Jack Hill. USA, 1971. 94 min.

Black Legion, Frontier Films. USA, 1937. 6 min.(?).

Black Panther [a.k.a. *Off the Pig!*]. Dir. [San Francisco] Newsreel. USA, 1968. 14 min.

Bonnie and Clyde. Dir. Arthur Penn. USA, 1967. 111 min.

Bowling for Columbine. Dir. Michael Moore. Canada/USA, 2002. 120 min.

A Brief History of Time. Dir. Errol Morris. UK/USA, 1992. 83 min.

Bring 'Em Back Alive. Dir. Clyde E. Elliott. USA, 1932. 60 or 70 min.

Bush Family Fortunes: The Best Democracy Money Can Buy. Dir. Steven Grandison and Greg Palast. USA, 2004. 62 min.

Bush's Brain. Dir. Joseph Mealey and Michael Shoob. USA, 2004. 80 min.

Celsius 41.11: The Temperature at Which the Brain . . . Begins to Die. Dir. Kevin Knoblock. USA, 2004. 71 min.

The Chair. Dir. Robert Drew. USA, 1962. 58 min.

China Strikes Back, Frontier Films. USA, 1937. 24 min.

Chronicle of a Summer. Dir. Edgar Morin and Jean Rouch. France, 1961. 85 min.

Cicero March, The Film Group. USA, 1966. 7 min.

The City. Dir. Ralph Steiner and Willard Van Dyke. USA, 1939. 45 min.

The Clinton Chronicles: An Investigation Into the Alleged Criminal Activities of Bill Clinton and His Circle of Power, Citizens' Video Press. USA, 1994. 83 min.

Columbia Revolt. Dir. [New York] Newsreel. USA, 1968. 50 min.

Confronting the Evidence: A Call to Reopen the 9/11 Investigation. Dir. James Walter. USA, 2005. 160 min.

Congorilla. Dir. Martin Johnson and Osa Johnson. USA, 1932. 67 min.

Control Room. Dir. Jehane Noujaim. USA, 2004. 84 min.

The Cool World. Dir. Shirley Clarke. USA, 1963. 105 min.

Crisis: Behind a Presidential Commitment. Dir. Robert Drew. USA, 1963. 52 min.

Crossroads. Dir. Bruce Conner. USA, 1976. 37 min.

Deep Throat. Dir. Jerry Gerard [Gerard Damiano]. USA, 1972. 61 min.

Detroit Workers News Special 1932: Ford Massacre. Detroit and New York Workers Film and Photo League. USA, 1932. 7 min.

Dog Day Afternoon. Dir. Sidney Lumet. USA, 1975. 130 min.

Dont Look Back. Dir. D. A. Pennebaker. USA, 1967. 95 min.

Drifters. Dir. John Grierson. UK, 1929. 41 min.

Easy Rider. Dir. Dennis Hopper. USA, 1969. 94 min.

The Energy War. Dir. D.A. Pennebaker, Chris Hegedus, and Pat Powell. USA, 1978. 300 min.

Execution of Czolgosz, With Panorama of Auburn Prison. Thomas A. Edison, Inc. USA, 1901. 4 min.

The Exorcist. Dir. William Friedkin. USA, 1973. 122 min.

A Face of War. Dir. Eugene S. Jones. USA, 1968. 72 min.

Fahrenheit 9/11. Dir. Michael Moore. USA, 2004. 122 min.

Fahrenhype 9/11. Dir. Alan Peterson. USA, 2004. 78 min.

Far From Poland. Dir. Jill Godmilow. USA, 1984. 110 min.

Feed. Dir. Kevin Rafferty and James Ridgeway. USA, 1992. 76 min.

The Fight for Life. Dir. Pare Lorentz. USA, 1940. 70 min.

The Fog of War: Eleven Lessons from the Life of Robert S. McNamara. Dir. Errol
  Morris. USA, 2003. 107 min.

Four More Years. Dir. Top Value Television. USA, 1972. 61 min.

The French Connection. Dir. William Friedkin. USA, 1971. 104 min.

The General Line. Dir. Sergei M. Eisenstein and Grigori Aleksandrov. USSR,
  1929. 75 min.

Ghosts of Abu Ghraib. Dir. Rory Kennedy. USA, 2007. 78 min.

Gimme Shelter. Dir. Albert Maysles, David Maysles, and Charlotte Zwerin. USA,
  1970. 90 min.

Going Upriver: The Long War of John Kerry. Dir. George Butler. USA, 2004.
  88 min.

The Graduate. Dir. Mike Nichols. USA, 1967. 105 min.

Grass: A Nation's Battle For Life. Dir. Merian Cooper and Ernest B. Schoedsack.
  USA, 1925. 71 min.

The Ground Truth. Dir. Patricia Foulkrod. USA, 2006. 72 min.

Gunner Palace. Dir. Petra Epperlein and Michael Tucker. USA, 2004. 85 min.

A Happy Mother's Day. Dir. Richard Leacock and Joyce Chopra. USA, 1963.
  26 min.

Harlan County, U.S.A. Dir. Barbara Kopple. USA, 1976. 102 min.

Head. Dir. Bob Rafelson. USA, 1968. 86 min.

Heart of Spain. Dir. Leo Hurwitz and Paul Strand for Frontier Films. USA, 1937.
  33 min.

Hearts and Minds. Dir. Peter Davis. USA, 1974. 112 min.

Helter Skelter. Dir. Tom Gries. USA, 1976. 119 min.

The Hour of the Furnaces. Dir. Octavio Getino and Fernando Solanas.
  Argentina, 1968. 260 min.

Housing Problems. Dir. Edgar Anstey and Arthur Elton. UK, 1935. 15 min.

The Hunting of the President. Dir. Nickolas Perry and Harry Thomason. USA,
  2004. 90 min.

I Am a Fugitive from a Chain Gang. Dir. Mervyn LeRoy. USA, 1932. 90 min.

An Inconvenient Truth. Dir. Davis Guggenheim. USA, 2006. 100 min.

Inextinguishable Fire. Dir. Harun Farocki. West Germany, 1969. 25 min.

Inside Women Inside. Dir. Christine Choy and Cynthia Maurizio. USA, 1978.
  28 min.

Interviews with My Lai Veterans. Dir. Joseph Strick. USA, 1970. 27 min.

In the Year of the Pig. Dir. Emile de Antonio. USA, 1968. 101 min.

Iraq in Fragments. Dir. James Longley. USA, 2006. 94 min.

It's Not My Memory of It: Three Recollected Documents. Dir. The Speculative Archive [Julia Meltzer and David Thorne]. USA, 2003. 25 min.

I Want to Live!. Dir. Robert Wise. USA, 1958. 120 min.

Jane. Dir. Robert Drew. USA, 1962. 54 min.

JFK: Breaking the News. Prod. Krys Boyd Villaseñor. USA, 2003. 146 min.

Journeys with George. Dir. Alexandra Pelosi and Aaron Lubarsky. USA, 2002. 76 min.

The Land. Dir. Robert Flaherty. USA, 1941. 44 min.

Les Maîtres fous. Dir. Jean Rouch. France, 1955. 30 min.

Letter from Siberia. Dir. Chris Marker. France, 1957. 62 min.

Loose Change (second edition). Dir. Dylan Avery. USA, 2005–2006. 90 min.

Man with a Movie Camera. Dir. Dziga Vertov. USSR, 1929. 68 min.

Medium Cool. Dir. Haskell Wexler. USA, 1969. 110 min.

Mega Fix: The Dazzling Political Deceit That Led to 9/11. Dir. Jack Cashill. USA, 2004. 90 min.

Men and Dust. Dir. Sheldon Dick. USA, 1939. 17 min.

Michael and Me. Dir. Larry Elder. USA, 2004. 90 min.

Michael Moore Hates America. Dir. Michael Wilson. USA, 2004. 125 min.

Millhouse: A White Comedy. Dir. Emile de Antonio. USA, 1971. 93 min.

Moana: A Romance of the Golden Age. Dir. Robert Flaherty. USA, 1926. 76 min.

Monterey Pop. Dir. D. A. Pennebaker. USA, 1968. 98 min.

Mr. Death: The Rise and Fall of Fred A. Leuchter, Jr. Dir. Errol Morris. USA, 1999. 91 min.

My Country, My Country. Dir. Laura Poitras. USA, 2006. 90 min.

National Archive V.1. Dir. Travis Wilkerson. USA, 2001. 15 min.

Native Land. Dir. Leo Hurwitz and Paul Strand. USA, 1942. 88 min.

The Negro Soldier. Dir. Stuart Heisler. USA, 1944. 40, 42, or 46 min.

Nehru. Dir. Robert Drew. USA, 1962. 53 min.

The New Frontier. Dir. H. P. McClure. USA, 1934. 10 min.

The New Spirit. Dir. Wilfred Jackson. USA, 1942. 7 min.

No End in Sight. Dir. Charles Ferguson. USA, 2007. 102 min.

No Game. Dir. [New York] Newsreel. USA, 1968. 16 min.

Now Promise Now Threat. Dir. Paul Chan. USA, 2005. 33 min.

Occupation: Dreamland. Dir. Ian Olds and Garrett Scott. USA, 2005. 78 min.

Off to War. Dir. Brent Renaud and Craig Renaud. USA, 2005. 452 min.

Painful Deceptions. Dir. Eric Hufschmid. USA, 2003. 120 min.

Painters Painting. Dir. Emile de Antonio. USA, 1972. 116 min.

Paris Is Burning. Dir. Jennie Livingston. USA, 1991. 78 min.

The Path to 9/11. Dir. David L. Cunningham. USA, 2006. 240 or 263 min.

People of the Cumberland. Dir. Robert Stebbins [Sidney Meyers] and Eugene Hill [Jay Leyda]. USA, 1938. 22 min.

People's War. Dir. [New York] Newsreel. USA, 1969. 40 min.

The People Versus Paul Crump. Dir. William Friedkin. USA, 1962. 52 min.

Persons of Interest. Dir. Alison Maclean and Tobias Perse. USA, 2003. 63 min.

The Plow That Broke the Plains. Dir. Pare Lorentz. USA, 1936. 28 min.

Point of Order. Dir. Emile de Antonio. USA, 1963. 97 min.

Power and the Land. Dir. Joris Ivens. USA, 1940. 33 min.

The Power of Nightmares: The Rise of the Politics of Fear. Dir. Adam Curtis. UK, 2004. 180 min.

Primary. Dir. Robert Drew. USA, 1960. 53 min.

Pumping Iron. Dir. George Butler and Robert Fiore. USA, 1976. 85 min.

Reassemblage. Dir. Trinh T. Minh-ha. USA, 1982. 40 min.

Riot in Cell Block 11. Dir. Don Siegel. USA, 1954. 80 min.

The River. Dir. Pare Lorentz. USA, 1937. 31 min.

Roger & Me. Dir. Michael Moore. USA, 1989. 91 min.

Rush to Judgment. Dir. Emile de Antonio. USA, 1966. 98–122 min.

San Francisco State: On Strike. Dir. [San Francisco] Newsreel. USA, 1969. 20 min.

Secrecy. Dir. Peter Galison and Robb Moss. USA, work-in-progress. 67 min.

The Selling of the Pentagon. Dir. Peter Davis. USA, 1971. 60 min.

Sherman's March. Dir. Ross McElwee. USA, 1986. 155 min.

Shocking and Awful: A Grassroots Response to War and Occupation. Prod. Deep Dish TV. USA, 2004. 326 min.

Shut Up and Sing. Dir. Barbara Kopple and Cecilia Peck. USA, 2006. 93 min.

Sicko. Dir. Michael Moore. USA, 2007. 123 minutes.

South of Ten. Dir. Liza Johnson. USA, 2006. 10 min.

The Spanish Earth. Dir. Joris Ivens. USA, 1937. 52 min.

Speaking Directly: Some American Notes. Dir. Jon Jost. USA, 1973. 110 min.

Spin. Dir. Brian Springer. USA, 1995. 57 min.

Strange Victory. Dir. Leo Hurwitz. USA, 1948. 72–73 min.

Strike. Dir. Sergei M. Eisenstein. USSR, 1925. 94 min.

Summer '68. Dir. [New York] Newsreel. USA, 1969. 60 min.

Sunnyside. Frontier Films. USA, 1937. 6 min.(?).

Super Size Me. Dir. Morgan Spurlock. USA, 2004. 100 min.

Tabu. Dir. F. W. Murnau. USA, 1931. 82 min.

Teach Our Children. Dir. Third World Newsreel [Christine Choy and Susan Robeson]. USA, 1972. 34 min.

The Thin Blue Line. Dir. Errol Morris. USA, 1988. 103 min.

3000 Years Plus Life. Dir. Randall Conrad and Stephen Ujlaki. USA, 1974. 44 min.

Titicut Follies. Dir. Frederick Wiseman. USA, 1967. 84 min.

Tongues Untied. Dir. Marlon Riggs. USA, 1989. 55 min.

A Tour of the White House with Mrs. John F. Kennedy. Dir. Franklin J. Schaffner. USA, 1962. 60 min.

Tribulation 99: Alien Anomalies Under America. Dir. Craig Baldwin. USA, 1991. 97 min.

Turksib. Dir. Viktor Turin. USSR, 1929. 57 min.

Uncovered: The Whole Truth About the Iraq War. Dir. Robert Greenwald. USA, 2004. 56 min.

Underground. Dir. Emile de Antonio with Haskell Wexler and Mary Lampson. USA, 1976. 88 min.

Unprecedented: The Story of the 2000 Presidential Elections. Dir. Richard Ray Perez and Joan Sekler. USA, 2002. 50 min.

Untitled footage of the assassination of John F. Kennedy. Dir. Abraham Zapruder. USA, 1963. 30 sec.

Untitled interviews on Attica revolt. Dir. Portable Channel. USA, 1971–72.

Untitled Video on Lynne Stewart and Her Conviction, the Law, and Poetry. Dir. Paul Chan. USA, 2006. 17 min.

Up Against the Wall, Ms. America. Dir. [New York] Newsreel. USA, 1968. 6 min.

Valley Town. Dir. Willard Van Dyke. USA, 1940. 30 min.

The War Room. Dir. Chris Hegedus and D. A. Pennebaker. USA, 1993. 96 min.

The War Tapes. Dir. Deborah Scranton. USA, 2006. 97 min.

The Weather Underground. Dir. Sam Green and Bill Siegel. USA, 2002. 92 min.

We Will Live to See These Things, Or, Five Pictures of What May Come to Pass. Dir. The Speculative Archive [Julia Meltzer and David Thorne]. USA, 2007. 47 min.

What Farocki Taught. Dir. Jill Godmilow. USA, 1998. 30 min.

When the Levees Broke: A Requiem in Four Acts. Dir. Spike Lee. USA, 2007. 256 min.

Why We Fight. Dir. Eugene Jarecki. USA, 2005. 98 min.

Winter Soldier. Dir. Winterfilm Collective. USA, 1972. 95 min.

WMD: Weapons of Mass Deception. Dir. Danny Schecter. USA, 2004. 98 min.

Women in Cages. Dir. Gerardo de Leon. USA/Philippines, 1971. 78 min.

Woodstock. Dir. Michael Wadleigh. USA, 1970. 184 min.

The World's Largest TV Studio. Dir. Top Value Television. USA, 1972. 59 min.

Young Mr. Lincoln. Dir. John Ford. USA, 1939. 100 min.

INDEX

California State Emergency Relief Adminis-
tration, 56
"Camera I, The: Observations on Documen-
tary" (Kuhn), 365n39
Canby, Vincent, 187; on *Winter Soldier*, 194
capitalism: art replaced by, rituals of, 252;
Benjamin on, 71–72; film as weapon
against, 172; industrial, 106, 380n39;
New Deal and expansion of, 130; Nykino
and, 75; social principle of, 117; violence
of, 85
Capra, Frank, 140
Carnegie Corporation, 106
Carville, James, 312
Cavell, Stanley, 274–75
CBS (Columbia Broadcasting System), 188,
233, 234, 285, 300, 304
CBS Reports, 14
celebrity: as allegory of ordinary people, 153;
portrait, 152
*Celsius 41.11: The Temperature at Which the
Brain . . . Begins to Die*, 370n8
Chair, The, 216
Champden, Roger, 248
Chan, Paul, 352, 353
Cheney, Dick, 276, 324
Chicago Freedom Movement, 157
China Strikes Back, 75
China Syndrome, The, 156
Chion, Michel: on audiovisual illusion, 93;
on Chris Marker, 381n46
Chow, Rey, 411n29
Choy, Christine, 255, 399n91
Chronique d'un été, 403n34
Cicero March, 25, 156–64; camerawork in,
159; competing documentary sources
in, 160, 162; final image, 162; liberating
function of, 160; profanity in, 159, 160;
repackaging of, 162; sound in, 159
Cineaste, 15, 187, 377n81, 385n2, 409n12
cinéma vérité, 13, 143, 150–64, 329; de Antonio on, 388n40; crisis structure in, 158;
criticism of, 224, 295; Curtin on, 291;
debate over, 294; as exploitation, 155;
Jeanne Hall on, 405n51; inconsistencies
of, 294; Mekas on, 400n94; narration in,
156; Nixon and, 297; *Primary* as first successful American example of, 291; rhetoric of, 152; signature movement of, 291;
simulation and, 283; social situations
scrutinized in, 153; sponsors of, 283, 295;
as uncontrolled filmmaking, 296; voice-
overs, 146; Waugh on, 388n40
City, The, 89; audiovisual syntax of, 104;
funding for, 106; optimism in, 103; social
forms in, 105
civic responsibility, 123–24

civil rights: marches, 162; in prison, 237
civil rights movement, 158; discontent generated by, 309
*Claiming the Real: The Griersonian Documen-
tary and its Legitimations* (Winston), 26
Clarke, Shirley, 222
class: betrayal of, 71; bourgeois print
culture and, 21; conflict, 73; consciousness, 57–58, 211; economics and, 211;
government and, 132; interrelationships
between all, 58; middle, 56, 73, 179–80;
nation and, 61; New Deal conception of,
16; objectification of, 70; prisoners and
social, 223–24, 228, 237; radio and, 92;
reality based in, 75; seeing outside of
own, 57; struggle, 15; subaltern, 208,
265; violence, 257–58; working, 61–62,
72–73
Clifford, James: on allegory, 7, 95; on ethnography, 394n44
Clinton, Bill, 311, 312, 313
*Clinton Chronicles, The: An Investigation Into
the Alleged Criminal Activities of Bill Clinton and His Circle of Power*, 401n6
Clyde, Ethel, 76
Cohen, Sacha Baron, 32
Collingwood, Charles, 284
Collins, Judy, 341
Columbia Revolt, 172
Commonwealth v. Wiseman, 222, 235; outcome of, 227
community: bridging gap between citizen
and, 12; Dewey and, 101, 379n27; documentary as message for, 4; general public
v., 17; imaginary, 287; organic forms of,
140; political, 106–7; rock festivals and,
106–7; technological development and
primitive, 125; television and, 274
*Confronting the Evidence: A Call to Reopen the
9/11 Investigation*, 331
Congorilla, 116
Congress. *See* U.S. Congress
Congress of Racial Equality, 157
Conner, Bruce, 255, 352
Conner, Steven, 93, 377n10
connoisseurship, 71
Conroy, Jack, 72
conspiracy theories, 287; 9/11, 331
consumption, 335, 383n74, 384n80; moral,
383n73
Control Room, 328
Cool World, The, 222
Copjec, Joan, 310
Copland, Aaron, 106, 120
Council of Industrial Organizations, 86
counterhistory, 266
counterperformativity, 349

FILM AND CULTURE

A series of Columbia University Press
Edited by John Belton